MEDIA
VS
REALITY

A Guide to the New World

JAMES MCINTOSH

**MEDIA VS
REALITY**

Media Vs Reality – A Guide To The New World
© 2021 by James McIntosh

Published in the United States by Media Vs Reality

Cover Design: Premiumsolns
Illustration: Kaleb Sokowlowski
Book Design: Beth Martin

ISBN: 979-8794092448

Disclaimer

Although this publication is designed to provide accurate information in regard to the subject matter covered, the publisher and the author assume no responsibility for errors, inaccuracies, omissions, or any other inconsistencies herein. This publication is meant as a source of valuable information for the reader, however it is not meant as a replacement for direct expert assistance. If such level of assistance is required, the services of a competent professional should be sought.

Fair Use

Copyright Disclaimer under section 107 of the Copyright Act 1976, allowance is made for "fair use" for purposes such as criticism, comment, news reporting, teaching, scholarship, education and research.

Fair use is a use permitted by copyright statute that might otherwise be infringing.

**MEDIA VS
REALITY**

CONTENTS

Introduction	**1**
Chapter 1: How The Media Can Ruin Your Life	**5**
Chasing Shadows	9
The Global Village – The Impossible Comparison Game	19
How The Media Replaces Your Life	24
How The Media Misleads You About Success	31
The Media And Body Image	35
Supernormal Stimuli – The New Addiction	44
Chapter 2: The 5 Laws Of Media	**53**
Law 1: The Medium Is The Message	54
Law 2: Media Is An Evolutionary Mismatch	57
Law 3: Technology Never Moves Backwards	60
Law 4: Media Is About Profit	62
Law 5: You Are In The Media Hierarchy	64
Chapter 3: "The News"	**73**
The Bad News Filter – The World Isn't As Bad As You Think It Is	79
Why People Get Upset About The Wrong Stories	96
Mass Shootings	103
The Brutal Truth About The Mainstream Media	110
The Smear Campaign – How The Media Destroys Reputations	123
The Podcast And A Revolution Of Truth	142
Deepfakes And The Post-Truth World	150

Chapter 4: The Internet **163**

 Filter Bubbles – The Invisible Polariser 174

 Why The Comments Section Is Full Of A**Holes 187

 Why It's So Hard To Focus On The Internet 194

 Your Smartphone Isn't On Your Team 198

 Dark Patterns – How You're Manipulated Into Buying More 205

Chapter 5: Social Media **221**

 Social Media - The Human Marketplace 221

 Online Dating 227

 The Photo-Retouching Arms Race 236

Chapter 6: Pornography **239**

 Porn In The 21st Century 239

 Camgirls – The Digital Stripclub 250

 Online Findom – A New Phenomenon 258

Chapter 7: Advertising **265**

 How Advertising Really Works 265

 The Power Of Image 272

 How Animals Are Used In Marketing 287

 Why You Think Smoking Is Cool 290

 Diamonds – The Greatest Marketing Scheme Of All Time 299

Chapter 8: Gaming **307**

 Video Games 308

 How MMORPGs Turn You Into A Labrat 316

 Mobile Games – The Addictive Time Sink 326

Chapter 9: How The Media Misled You About Everything   **335**

You Know Nothing About Violence   337

You Know Nothing About Food   343

You Know Nothing About Psychopaths   353

You Know Nothing About Romance   359

Chapter 10: Bursting The Filter Bubble   **373**

Political Filter Bubbles – How Social Media Splits Societies In Half 374

The Fatlogic Filter Bubble   383

The Looksmaxxing Filter Bubble   391

Chapter 11: How To Live In The New World   **399**

Media Diet – The Key To A Fulfilled Life In The 21st Century   400

Social Media Mindfulness – A Necessity   404

Creating Your Own Subconscious Patterns   412

The Commandments Of Media Use   415

Epilogue   **419**

References   **423**

INTRODUCTION

The world has changed. Much of the advice passed down to us by our parents and grandparents is no longer applicable. As it has throughout history, technology has radically changed the landscape we live in, all within the span of a couple of decades. To put it simply, we are in unknown territory. We've been born into a world that we don't understand. The technology that surrounds us is hundreds of years of human ingenuity in the making – it's far older than us. You might imagine that some expert somewhere, with a large white beard and a pair of glasses, understands how all of this new technology is affecting human beings and has everything under control. No such person exists. We're speeding into the future at 100 miles an hour without a brake to pull and we have no idea where our technological journey will take us.

The infamous Canadian media theory scholar Marshall Mcluhan once told us that *"we look at present through a rear-view mirror. We march backwards into the future"*. Most of us continue to see the world as it was in the past. Very few of us are able to come to grips with what the world is in the present and what it shall become in the near and distant future. Much of the advice from the old world is still valid and will continue to be helpful. Many of the teachings of Jesus, Buddha, Mohammed and other religious figures are timeless and will continue to apply to human beings no matter how much our world changes. But today we have new problems that the wise beings from the past never encountered, new problems created by the advanced technological landscape we live in that would be completely foreign to Jesus, The Buddha or Mohammed. We all carry electronic rectangles inside our pockets. We use these electronic rectangles to communicate with the outside world more than our own eyes and mouths. We battle for social status through the use of images, posts and like-counts through social media. Social media and dating technologies have become a central factor in competing on the sexual marketplace and finding girlfriends, boyfriends, wives and husbands. We have more information than we can possibly handle, all of which is being introduced to us through algorithms locked in the vaults of enormous tech companies that we have no access to. Instant access to an endless tidal wave of pornography allows us to see any sexual fantasy we can possibly imagine played out on screen.

The new world has arrived. Technology and media have taken the world our ancestors, grandparents and parents lived in and wildly transformed it in a way that almost nobody could have predicted. The technology of the printing press completely changed the society our ancestors of the 15th century lived in. The television entirely transformed the society our parents lived in. These were radical changes indeed. But here in the 21st century, we have not just one or two new forms of media to deal with, *but an explosion of thousands.* In the space of a couple of decades, humanity has suddenly introduced to social media, high-speed pornography, online gaming, search engines, a huge surge in advertising, algorithmic filter bubbles, the continual breakdown of traditional news media, image retouching, online dating, synthetic audio, deepfakes, an endless stream of fake news and mis/disinformation, smartphones, the attention economy, camgirls and dark patterns. How can we possibly hope to deal with or even understand this insane technological landscape we've inherited? How can we stay on top of this tidal wave of new technologies upending our lives and our societies every few years? How can we stop ourselves from being manipulated on a daily basis by these incredibly powerful forms of media? And finally, how can we live a happy and fulfilled life in our new world? The modern individual needs to charter this unknown territory without a map or a compass. Our parents and grandparents have no advice to give us on navigating this new world – they're even more befuddled than we are. More than ever, people find themselves outraged, distracted, confused, angry and helpless about technology-filled world they find themselves in.

This book is your map to the new world.

This book will describe the new world you're living in. It will explain how it functions, many of the life-ruining pitfalls you need to avoid and strategies for living in alongside technology in a harmonious manner. The generations who came before us simply can't relate to what it's like to grow up in a world filled to the brim with addictive technologies. That's why you need someone like me. I was part of the first generation to grow up alongside high-speed internet porn, online gaming and social media. As I matured, so did the internet. Older generations can only provide us vague, generalised advice based on the old world. Having lived it personally, directly and first-hand, I can give you advice based on real experience.

This book is for the confused young guy in his early 20's who finds themselves completely hooked on pornography and video games. This book is for the young woman who finds herself in a vicious digital competition to make her life look better than her friends on social media. This book is also for the man in their 30's or 40's who wants to understand the strange, electronic media landscape they find themselves in. And this book is for the mother, father, uncle, aunt or grandparent who wants to understand what this new world of technology is and help their sons, daughters, nephews, nieces and grandchildren to live in a healthy relationship with technology. Much of this book will be based around helping you to understand the media landscape you find yourself in, including many of the dangerous rabbit holes found within it. At the same time, this book isn't supposed to simply leave you feeling bitter and negative. This book is about changing your habits around media use so that you can live the most fulfilled and successful life you possibly can – as such, a large part of this book focuses on how you can change, personally, in your attitude and actions towards technology in order to better your life. By the time you finish this book, you will understand much of the truth about our new technological world.

You live in a new world. It's about time you understand It.

chapter 1

HOW THE MEDIA CAN RUIN YOUR LIFE

The Spirit Of Seeing – A Story About The Internet

"He'll do great things that boy.."

That's what the village people said about him. Strong, co-ordinated, talented, smart and charming. The young man felt as though he could become anything he wanted. He stood tall with his shoulders back and his blue eyes spoke of a steady self-confidence held deep within him. His body was strong, built through hours of intensive sword training.

After endless hours of sword practice, he began to stroll through the village back to his home. A number of girls waved to him as he walked by and he politely waved back. Upon arriving home, he began sharpening his swords ready for training the next day.

Suddenly, a spirit appeared behind him, calling his name. The young man spun around ready to attack, only to find an incredibly plain looking spirit floating harmlessly in the centre of his room.

Neither male nor female, the spirit held an entirely blank expression. Neither happy nor sad, as though there were no emotion inside it whatsoever. The spirit spoke, "Jean of Furthershore, I am the Spirit of Seeing".

The young man stood facing the spirit confrontationally. "What do you want?" he said drawing his sword. The spirit remained completely unafraid.

"Only to show you my powers. I can show you anything you can possibly imagine. For I am the Spirit of Seeing", the spirit replied plainly.

The young man observed the spirit carefully. It continued to float passively in the air and seemed to pose no threat. "You can show me anything huh..? Show me..the stables of Furthershore" the young man said curiously.

The spirit blew a puff of smoke, and inside the smoke the stables could be seen clearly. The image of the stables hung in the air for several moments before disappearing. The young man smiled. How interesting, he thought to himself. Another idea immediately came into his mind, "Show me the most beautiful girl in the world" he suggested with a smirk on his face.

Without a word, the spirit blew another puff of smoke, and in it appeared the most beautiful girl the young man had ever seen. Her long, dark hair lay delicately over her pretty head. She had big, piercing brown eyes, a delicate nose and plump lips. One hand lay perfectly on the hips of her gorgeous hourglass figure.

The young man's pupils dilated as he stared at the girl in wonder for a full five minutes.

Remembering where he was, he cleared his throat and composed himself once again. While he felt slightly embarrassed, the spirit maintained and empty gaze seemingly unaffected by the young man's embarrassing display.

Another idea entered the young man"s mind. "Show me a great warrior" he commanded. As usual, the spirit blew yet another puff of smoke with an image of exactly what the young man had asked for. The perfect warrior stood looking into the distance, his body toned and muscular, with a stern expression on his face.

The young man marvelled at this great warrior, pledging to himself that he too would one day be a great warrior just like this man.

The young man had had enough. "You may leave now spirit. I have seen enough", he said dismissively as he went back to sharpening his swords. The spirit of seeing spoke without emotion: " I shall remain here in the corner of your room, ready to show you my powers on your command".

The young man shrugged his shoulders in acceptance. The spirit didn't seem to mean him any harm.

As the weeks went by, the young man became accustom to the spirit in his room. He used it to see the weather of the day, to see what his friends were doing and he even started looking at beautiful girls with their clothing removed — after all, the spirit of seeing would show him anything he wanted.

The weeks turned into months.

He started leaving his sword training an hour early. And then two hours early. And then three. For the spirit of seeing was far more stimulating than dull, repetitive sword training.

The girls in the village waved, but the young man stopped waving back. They were plain, he said to himself. One day he would find a girl as beautiful as the ones he watched through the spirit, he thought.

He began using the spirit to watch great battles. He cheered aloud as his favourite hero turned the tide of the skirmish at the very last minute. Watching with eagerness, thinking that one day soon he would lead his own army into battle.

He thought of these battles while he practised his sword-work. He even began reciting lines he had heard his favourite hero speak as he swung. And he would leave training after just a few hours to rush home and watch another great battle (not before seeing more beautiful naked girls, of course).

A year passed.

And the girls in the village had stopped waving. Some had wedded a husband. Most could be heard screaming the name of another boy in the village from the archery range each evening. Apparently he was skilled with a bow. The young man cursed and muttered under his breath – something about real warriors not attacking from afar.

He now often trained only for a few short hours and some days he would skip training altogether. He would walk at a quick pace through the village to get home, uninterested in exchanging pleasantries with the village folk.

He had begun using the spirit to watch as a number beautiful naked women perform sexual acts upon one another. It seemed now that a single naked woman was no longer interesting.

His admiration for his favourite hero had turned into jealousy. He would watch the hero defeat enemy after enemy, the gap between himself and the hero seeming to loom ever larger.

He could no longer run much of a distance. His shield felt heavy. His sword skills no longer matched other warriors of his own age.

Several more years passed.

The young man had given up on becoming a hero, although he would still re-watch his favourite battles through the spirit from time to time. Still unmarried he had become deeply frustrated and sad. His sword lay quietly in the corner of the room collecting dust.

On the night of his 30th birthday, the man, nearing the end of his youth sat alone in his room feeling worse than he had ever felt.

The clock struck 12.

Suddenly, the spirit of seeing began to laugh. The man was startled, the spirit had never laughed before. In fact, it had never shown any emotion whatsoever. He looked up at the spirit who caught his gaze. Slowly, the spirit of seeing grew a wide smile.

For the first time in 10 years, the spirit spoke. "My work here is done" it said in a deep voice.

"What are you talking about spirit?" the man spoke fearfully.

The spirit laughed again. "I shall reveal what I have kept secret for the past 10 years. I am the ultimate concentration of evil. I am root of all the darkness in the world. I am the devil himself", the spirit spoke pridefully.

The man became terrified. His mouth wide open and speechless.

"A demon will attack this village tonight. A prophesy foretold that you were the one destined to defeat it. But it is I that has defeated you. And now the souls of this village are mine", the spirit spoke with a tone of utter glee.

"Why wait ten long years?", the man spoke with a shaky voice, "why not fight me face to face the first time we met?".

The spirit let out another laugh."If I had fought you face-to-face, you would have conquered me. But I am cunning, and the slow drip of poison given to you through the means of endless fantasy has rendered you too weak to fight. And now this village is mine..."

The man could do nothing other than slowly sit down onto the bed. A deep, dark pain settled inside his stomach. One that he knew would never go away. Only the devil himself could inflict the deep, tormenting inner anguish he felt pulsing through his mind.

The torture in his mind was too much to bare. He needed something to quell the pain.

"Can I see those beautiful girls just one more time?"

A wide grin grew across the devil's face. "Always".

chasing shadows

YOU STRETCH YOUR ARM AS HIGH AS IT CAN GO.
GRASPING AT THE SUCCESS IN FRONT OF YOU.
IT'S IN REACH! FINALLY, ALL OF YOUR DREAMS ARE ABOUT TO
COME TRUE! YOU CLENCH YOUR FIST. YOUR FINGERS PASS
THROUGH THE OBJECT. ANOTHER SHADOW.
YOU REMEMBER WHERE YOU ARE. YOU CLOSE YOUR LAPTOP.

Through modern media you can experience anything. A dramatic story. The superpowers of a superhero. Sex with the most attractive person possible in any situation you can imagine. Commanding a medieval army. Meeting the perfect man and having the perfect wedding. You're exposed to all of the possible incredible experiences that a human being can have. The media shows us that we could be doing countless things. You *could* be doing this. You *could* be doing that. But what *are* you doing? Perhaps you imagine yourself as a pimp in a rap video. Making it rain. Surrounded by beautiful girls. *But this reality will never come to pass.* Maybe imagine yourself becoming an NBA star like Lebron James. The crowd going wild as you make that shot in the last second of the game. *But this reality will never come to pass.* Or perhaps you imagine yourself as Ironman. Full of slick one-liners as he flies around destroying enemies. *But this reality will never come to pass. Endless streams of men – of all ages – messaging "Hey how are you?" to the most attractive women on OkCupid. Imagining themselves dating these 10/10 women and often passing over the more realistic options available to them. But of course, this reality too will never come to pass.* Imagining yourself doing this. Imagining yourself doing that. But *doing* nothing. **Chasing Shadows.**

Every single day, people around the world spend their time chasing the shadows cast in front of them by their screens. *Chasing one shadow after the next after the next* and grasping nothing but air. Never being able to put together a satisfying life for themselves. Imagining themselves as everything yet becoming nothing. Living as a legend in their own mind while their reality stagnates. Many will chase shadows all the way to their deathbeds, spending all of their free time watching others live their lives on an electronic screen. Honestly, *what a tragic life this is.* A tragic life no doubt, but in the modern world this is the kind of life many people lead. How did so many of us (both young and old) become this way? And how can we grab onto something solid and build a life for ourselves instead of continuing to grab nothing but air.

THE UNENDING CLIMAX

The typical commercial goes as follows:

> *00:00: MAN IS WORKING AT HIS COMPUTER AT HIS OFFICE 9-5 JOB*
>
> *00:01: WORK ENDS. HE LEAVES THE OFFICE*
>
> *00:02: CUT TO MAN IN THE BAR WITH HIS BUDDIES. ALL OF THEM LAUGHING HYSTERICALLY*
>
> *00:03: HOT BLONDE CHICK NUDGES HIM FLIRTATIOUSLY AND HANDS HIM A BUDWEISER*
>
> *00:05: BLONDE CHICK RUBS GUYS ARM WHILE ALL HIS BUDDIES CONTINUE TO LAUGH AT HIS JOKE.*

What happened to the 8 hours spent at work? What about the journey from the office in rush hour traffic? How long did it take for these guys to become such good friends? How did he impress the blonde girl? All of these inconveniences are left behind.

When you see a Volkswagon driving stylishly down a mountain road, you're watching a climactic moment. If you wanted to drive across a mountain road yourself, you would have to make preparations; perhaps you'd need to get someone to take care of the kids. Maybe, if you don't live near the mountains, you'd have to make a 6 hour journey to get there. None of these realities are ever presented in the commercials we watch on a daily basis.

It's climax after climax. The work is already done. The game is won. Beautiful young people jump up and down in ecstasy before reaching for

NOT INCLUDED: HOW LONG DID IT TAKE HIM TO SAVE UP FOR THIS CAR? HOW LONG DID IT TAKE HIM TO GET TO THE MOUNTAINS?

cans of Diet Cola. A man sprays a can of Axe Body Spray on himself and thousands of beautiful women come running over the hilltop. There are no mundane moments. No downtime. No lengthy hours practising your craft. Just win after win. The same unending climax pattern can be found on social media. On social media, everybody's lives are excellent. All the time. Exciting moments. Happy faces. Interesting events. Weddings. Newborn Babies. Parties. Holidays. New apartments. Career successes. Mundane moments? Brushing your teeth in the morning? Pre-makeup faces? Waiting in traffic? Going food shopping? Paying bills? Career failures? Awkward moments? Fashion blunders? Running late to work? Sleepless nights? *Forget it.* Everybody is always winning and nobody admits to any shortcomings. On social media, everyone is successful; even the biggest failures among us can put on a relatively convincing front of success and happiness when they can use digital tools to filter our perceptions of them.

The main problem with all this is the message it sends about to the audience about the rhythm of life. It's climactic moment after climactic moment after climactic moment. There is no in between time. There is no work. There is no process. *Only shot after shot of pure happiness.*

Most media is an alternate reality that we can never be a part of. It's the beginning of the emergence of a perfect second world. In this second world, everybody is happy, successful, attractive and dressed perfectly for the occasion. This second world will grow even larger after the rise of virtual reality puts this second world into a 3D space. And some day in the future, we will be able to interact with this perfect second world as if it were our own. (**Law 3: Technology Never Moves Backwards**). It will be a world in which you always have everything you want already. But of course, this emerging second reality isn't like our primary reality. Our primary reality consists of mostly of mundane moments strung together and routines repeating themselves day after day. Success in our reality

A SEARCH FOR "MAN" ON STOCK
IMAGE WEBSITE PEXELS.COM
(NOTICE IT'S NOT "HAPPY MAN"
OR "SUCCESSFUL MAN" THAT'S
BEING SEARCHED FOR). WHEN
IT COMES TO MOST MEDIA –
PERFECT IS THE DEFAULT

takes endless hours of dedicated practise, self-doubt, disappointment and doesn't necessarily mean being dressed perfectly for every occasion.

We have two different patterns that represent the world entering our subconscious. The pattern of slow, steady improvement signalled by the real world, and the pattern of endless climax signalled by the second, perfect world we view on our screens. Which pattern will claim dominance over our mind? That depends how much time we spend viewing our world through screens. Spend too much time viewing the second, perfect world we see in advertising and social media and we begin to feel as though we *should have everything we want already.* The fact that we aren't yet successful becomes unacceptable, and we begin to look for quick-fixes. **We start chasing shadows.**

These are just a handful of ways people **chase shadows** in the modern day:

☞ *Instead of building a genuine career for themselves they attempt to become yet another "Influencer" on social media (Not that there aren't successful influencers, just that for many it's used as a means of avoiding real work)*

☞ *Instead of putting time into dating others in the real world, they spend their time sending hundreds of messages to the most beautiful people on online dating websites/apps and fantasising.*

☞ *Instead of truly trying to change anything about society, they post a few political messages on social media, feel good about themselves, and move on.*

☞   *Instead of gradually adapting to healthy eating habits, they try another fad diet. Or take a diet pill. Or convince themselves that being fat isn't unhealthy and that they're beautiful the way they are under the guise of the fat acceptance community. (See chapter 10)*

☞   *Instead of taking the time to build a real business from the ground up, they put their trust in a pyramid scheme or a get-rich-quick scam.*

This is what chasing shadows is — pursing endeavours that supposedly produce fast results but have a 0.001% chance of producing any success. *Wasting your life reaching for one shadow after the next.* Never understanding the difference between a shadow and something real you can hold onto. Consume enough media and the pattern of endless climax will be imprinted onto your subconscious mind. This subconscious pattern will manifest itself in your outward behaviours. And you will start looking for the quick-successes (shadows) instead of pursuing long-term successes that involve hard-work and consistency.

"Our dedication to the illusion of endless climaxes puts us on a collision course with the human psyche" — George Leonard in *Mastery*

ACCESS TO EVERYTHING

"Welcome to the internet, have a look around. Anything that brain of yours can think of can be found" - Bo Burnham

Technology makes us feel as though we hold the world in our hands. We can navigate the entire world in Google Maps. We can see pictures of Earth from space. We can watch documentaries about cultures from around the world. The internet is the great equaliser. We can be anything we want. You could be a musician. You could be an entrepreneur. You could be a writer. You could invent the next Facebook. You could become a Youtube sensation. You could become Insta-famous. You could become a life coach. You could become a politician. An endless number of options are available to us. There is so much potential. *But potential is nothing.* You *could* be anything. But what *are* you? Despite the endless amount of potential success displayed to you through media you might find that your reality is lying around your bedroom gawping at a screen in your boxer shorts.

Media causes many people to spend large chunks of their time living vicariously through others. Daydreaming about the various successes you could be having but taking no real action towards achieving those goals. In fact, the very act of consuming media displaying the success you want is often counter-productive to achieving the success being displayed. The time you spent watching a Vlog of a successful entrepreneur take a trip on a private jet could have been spent taking real action towards your own entrepreneurial ventures. Sure – media can be used as a means for getting inspiration towards your goals. But there is a line between getting inspiration and living vicariously. That line is probably drawn at about

TIME SPENT CONSUMING MEDIA SHOWING

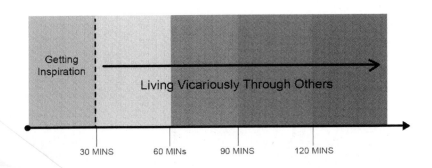

Getting Inspiration

Living Vicariously Through Others

30 MINS   60 MINs   90 MINS   120 MINS

the 30 minute mark of media consumption.

Before the media, people had a better idea of who they were because the options were incredibly limited. They were a baker, a blacksmith, a knight, a doctor, a nurse or a cook. The roles were so necessary and so obvious that there was little time to question *what should I do with my life, does this career really suit me* or *am I missing out?* It was likely that nobody you knew was much better off than yourself. For each individual, the purpose of their life was relatively clear. But with the invention of media came **access to everything.** For the first time in history we were able to see countless different potential lifestyles, which was then amplified even further by social media. We can see clearly that others are enjoying life (or appear to be) far more than ourselves. There is a seemingly endless number of careers and lifestyle options for a young person to choose. This gives many of us decision paralysis when trying to create a life for ourselves, because dedicating ourselves to a life path means sacrificing everything else we *could* be. But at some stage in life you have to accept that your endless fantasies aren't actually going to become true. The countless fantasy scenarios you've witnessed through media will never come to pass in your real life. *You must sacrifice the potential of being everything for the reality of becoming something.* Eventually you have to choose a lane. While the patterns you see through media may suggest that you can have everything and be everything, the truth is your lifespan is limited. You are limited. *You can be something but you can't be everything.* If you decide not to choose a frame, then you sacrifice the possibility of being successful in anything. And you become the 40 year old child - forever chasing shadows. You get to choose your sacrifice. But don't you get to choose not to make one.

**"There's a sacrificial element to maturation.
You have to sacrifice the potentiality of
childhood, for the actuality of a frame".
- Jordan Peterson**

A SHALLOW UNDERSTANDING OF EVERYTHING

If you want to be successful, it goes without saying that you must be using the internet. The internet is an incredible and essential tool that is 100% necessary to achieve success. Right? Carl Jung - one of the most influential thinkers of the 20th century – didn't seem to require the internet to become a world famous success. Jung built a tower made of stone in the small village of Bollingen where he would spend a full 2 months of every single year from 1922 - 1961.

CARL JUNG'S BOLLINGEN TOWER RETREAT

There was no electricity in the tower. He locked the door and kept the key on him at all times. Yet it was here he developed his world famous theory of the collective unconscious. A theory that people are still attempting to fully understand today. "In my retiring room I am by myself," Jung said of the space. "I keep the key with me all the time; no one else is allowed in there except with my permission." This is what the author Cal Newport describes as *Deep Work: Professional activities performed in a state of distraction-free concentration that push your cognitive capabilities to their limit. These efforts create new value, improve your skill, and are hard to replicate.*

While Carl Jung's Bollingen Tower was the perfect place for deep work the internet is almost the exact opposite. Most of the internet is filled with Top 10 listicles, clickbait, viral videos and hit pieces. Most blog posts and Youtube videos are under 10 minutes long. *Deep content is not incentivised on the internet.* Shallow content draws in clicks and a 15 minute read is too long for the average user. A Youtube video longer than 10 minutes has a high chance of being closed. On the internet - shallow content is king. It's true that the internet allows access to an endless amount of information. But it also allows access to an endless number of distractions. Each blog post is filled with hyperlinks encouraging you to switch your focus to another page. Every Youtube video has a "recommended for you" sidebar that uses sophisticated algorithms to present you with the videos you're most likely to click on. The electronic rectangle in your pocket presents tempting notifications encouraging you to switch your focus throughout your entire day. This is the internet environment: Quick pieces of information and a focus that is constantly moving from one thing to another. What's worse - overtime your brain gradually adapts to this environment. So much so that today many people find themselves completely unable to sit down and read a book for 1 hour. Because their brain is expecting to move on to the next stimulus like it does on the internet.

Browsing the internet often means *getting a shallow understanding of everything and a deep understanding of nothing:*

☞   *Reading blogs titled "New study shows that eating beef gives you diabetes". Not taking enough time to notice that the study is bogus and the author just wants clicks.*

☞   *Watching political content that agrees entirely with your existing beliefs and only describes opposing arguments as strawmen.*

☞   *Forming your opinion on particular issues by scrolling Twitter and reading various 240-character limited opinions on the subject.*

Feeling informed. Yet doing nothing but chasing shadows. And never really developing a deep understanding about anything. After all gaining a deep understanding about something requires deep work and real-world experience, not typing terms into Google and clicking the first listicle you come across. Most of the content creators - those who create shadows on the internet - are also chasing shadows themselves. They do themselves a disservice by continuing to create shallow content instead of producing their best work. Writers create shallow content that bends towards the will of the algorithms instead of writing what they truly want to write about. Youtube creators make short videos that satisfy the algorithms instead of making the 2-hour-long documentary they're capable of creating. In an effort to get clicks - content creators sacrifice their potential of being an incredible world-changing creative capable of creating deep, lasting content. Instead they opt for the short-term of win of creating shallow content with a clickbait title that feeds the algorithms.

So perhaps you may find the following advice helpful: Leave the distracted masses and join the focused few. Stop imagining yourself as 1000 things you will never become. Sacrifice the endless fantasies and choose a real path. Surrender to deep work and produce a real result. Stay on the narrow road and pursue reality. *Stop chasing the shadows cast by your screens and start pursuing fulfilment in the real world.*

the global village – the impossible comparison game

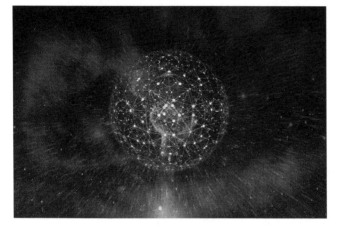

You probably take the following things as normal:

☞ *You hear news about people you've never met in a place you've never been.*

☞ *You watch documentaries about situations you've never experienced.*

☞ *You can see your friend or family member on the other side of the planet on a Zoom call.*

☞ *You have large amounts of knowledge about celebrities who don't even know of your existence.*

To a large extent, we have erased time and space. Information can be transferred to the other side of the planet instantaneously. You can sit in an apartment in London, England and send a Facebook message to your friend in Sydney, Australia with almost no delay. A man in India can make a funny video of himself and upload it to Youtube, this video can then be watched by a married couple sitting on their sofa in Argentina. A sexy Instagram influencer can post photos of themselves and receive praise, not only from people in their own country, but of people from around the entire planet. A baby is born to the royal family in the United Kingdom and the entire world hears about it. An earthquake happens in Haiti and everybody immediately becomes aware. A Hollywood star is charged for sexual assault – the world knows.

This is the global village. The Global Village is an electronic nervous system that connects all human beings together. As Marshall Mcluhan put it back in the 1960's: *"The global village is as big as a planet and as small as the village post office"*. The world is the same size it ever was, only it now feels much smaller because of our technology. You might assume that a world of human beings that are electronically connected together is a good thing. Certainly, the global village has all kinds of advantages, yet for many of us, this global village is having quite an impact on our feelings of self worth. Think you're a good guitar player? You're no Jimmy Hendrix. Want to become a writer? You're no Ernest Hemingway. The is internet crammed full of bloggers and there are 3.4 million ebooks on Amazon. Thinking of learning a new language? Check out Bill's Youtube videos. He's bilingual in 8 languages. Thinking of getting into shape? Check out Stacy's Instagram. She has a gorgeous body and has 2.7 million followers. *Our hierarchies of accomplishment are now dizzyingly vertical.* At every single turn someone is better. No matter how good you are at something, there is someone out there who makes you look incompetent. And not only do you have access to best individuals in the world of every single hierarchy, but these individuals are actively pushed into your consciousness.

Former US Preident Theodore Roosevelt once said that "Comparison is the thief of joy". If comparison was the thief of joy in the 20th century, then comparison is the thief of sanity in the 21st century. Humans have always evaluated their personal attributes against those of their neighbours . *What's different now is that the pool of people we compare ourselves to is infinitely bigger. We've gone from comparing ourselves to other members of our 150 person (maximum) tribe, to the entire 4.5 billion+ of the human race connected to the internet.*

While studying primates, Robin Dunbar discovered a correlation between the size of neo- cortex and the size of the average social group. When applying this theory to humans, he arrived at a cognitive limit for the number of social relationships we can have. **150**. Try to have more than 150 friends and you start to forget names and relationships inevitably break down. The number 150 seems to be a number that roughly applies to all groups of humans:

☞   *Average Christmas card network: 153*

☞   *Average number of wedding guests: 148*

☞   *Most military companies top out at around 150*

☞   *The average village size in 11th century England was 150*

☞   *In the 18th century, the average English village had around 160 residents*

☞   *A 2011 study of 1.7 million twitter users showed that people maintain a stable relationship with 100-200 users.*

☞   *The average number of Facebook friends is 150-200 (Numbers higher than this are not genuine relationships).*

We don't live in villages or tribes anymore. In the global village, we have the potential to have thousands of friends. Tens of thousands even. But our brain can't understand more than 150 relationships (**Rule 2: Technology Is An Evolutionary Mismatch**). One of the biggest reasons for life dissatisfaction today is that people feel as though they can't find their place in the tribe because they feel like every position is already taken by someone better.

It was easier for to be good at something when we lived in small rural communities. There was one chef. Two mechanics. One writer. One guitar player. One basketball star. And before then, in our tribes. David was the best spear thrower. Lucy was the best chef. Mark was the best at skinning animals. Sophie was the best at finding berries. In these small communities, each person was a local hero who got to experience the serotonin-fuelled confidence of being the best. Of being truly useful.

"Humans don't mind hardship, in fact they thrive on it; what they mind is not feeling necessary. Modern society has perfected the art of making people not feel necessary" Sebastian Junger in *Tribe*.

The effects of the global village have been hanging over your head and you didn't even notice. Dashing your spirits every time you decide to develop yourself. Encouraging you to quit before you even start. Our ancestors never dealt with this sense of inadequacy. Life may have been tough, but they had a firm identity within the tribe. They were truly valuable to the group. In the global village, many of us are robbed of that pure sense of identity.

Leon Festinger developed his social comparison theory in 1954. Social comparison theory states that individuals determine their own social and personal worth based on how they stack up against others. As humans, we're constantly evaluating ourselves across multiple domains: attractiveness, wealth, intelligence and success. And this makes perfect sense. When you're in a tribe of 150 people, how else are you supposed to determine your worth? Are you going to compare yourself to trees? Or clouds? Of course you compare yourself to others. You need markers to determine who you are. and these markers are otther people. This mechanism worked flawlessly for the 150 person tribes our brain is evolved for. We have a perfect comparison mechanism provided to us by nature, but this is completely distorted by our connected media environment. If a stone age girl wasn't the prettiest in her tribe the difference wasn't likely to have been dramatic. Everybody had opportunities to to see others look at their worst. They saw each other tired, hungry and sick on a regular basis. But in the global village, society searches through millions of young women to select the best faces and bodies, perfects them in Adobe Photoshop and displays them to us constantly in advertising, music videos, movies and through social media. How is the average teenage girl supposed to compete with the super-enhanced images of female beauty they're exposed to on a daily basis? The advice for the old world would be "don't compare yourself to others", and that's all very well and good. But this advice simply isn't good enough for a teenage girl in the new world. Comparison is a perfectly natural mechanism for teenage girls, and simply telling them not to compare themselves with others isn't going to stop them from doing it. Teenage girls should be comparing themselves to other members of their tribe, but instead they're comparing themselves with enhanced images of the entire global village. They'll make this comparison either consciously or subconsciously whether they like it or not. It's no surprise at all that depressive episodes have increased since the advent of social media. (More on this later). And it isn't just attractiveness that's measured against the global village. It's wealth, talent, intelligence. When you expose yourself to media, very single attribute you have is weighed up against the absolute best of the entire connected planet. We have a natural mechanism in our brains that constantly compares ourselves to others. But because our entire planet is connected, these comparisons are completely unrealistic. Because the pool of people for comparison is so incredibly huge, almost everyone feels like a loser in the global village.

The global village may encourage a sense of inadequacy to rise up in your gut. You're progressing slower than you should be. You weren't born with the right talents. You're too old to achieve anything. You're flawed in this way. And in that way. And it's hopeless. It's a waste of time. It's too late. What do you do when your little goals seem pathetic and worthless in the face of the amazing things others have achieved? You can start by recognising the insanity of trying to compare yourself to the absolute best in the population of 4 billion+ people connected to the global village. The media is tricking you. You are not competing against the people you see on media. There is plenty of room for everyone to be be successful in their own right. You think: *What's the point. There will always be people better than me.* But this kind of thinking, while seemingly logical on the surface, doesn't hold up to scrutiny. In the first place, the very act of perusing your goals will make you happy. Which will in turn make your friends and family happy. Which will proceed to make the people in their lives happy. For that reason alone, pursuing your endeavours is truly important. But further than that, because of the nature of our connected global village, we are not isolated individuals with no means to effect anything. Every single one of us is a node in a network. You'll probably know 1,000 people in the course of your life, and they will also know 1,000 people. This puts you just one person away from a million and two people away from a billion. And that's without taking into account the use of social media and the internet. The actions you take have ripple effects across our global network that you can't possibly comprehend. So while the global village may make your ideas, goals and actions seem insignificant and pointless, this is actually an illusion. The global village means that your actions are more important and more significant than they've ever been.

how the media replaces your life

It's that moment. When you realise you haven't been living your life properly for the last 10 years. When you realise your entire experience on this planet has been dampened by media. Instead of fulfilling your natural human urges you short-circuited them by consuming media. Instead of having a satisfying love life, you binged on romcoms. Instead of having an incredible sex life, you watched 1000 hours of porn. Instead of living an exciting life, you consumed countless shows on Netflix Instead of enjoying the company of close friends, you collected hundreds of followers on Instagram. Instead of playing sports, you lived vicariously through younger, fitter men. When we're not working almost all of us decide to spend the rest of our time consuming media. You've been living in a fantasy world. Think that's an exaggeration? Just how many hours have you spend consuming media? Really, how many of those precious hours have you carelessly whittled away? How much time have you spent focused on something that isn't even real? For many of you reading, this is the ultimate reason why your life sucks. You've been searching high and low for why. Why do I feel incomplete? Why aren't I fulfilling my potential? Why do I feel like I'm constantly pushing the accelerator with the breaks on? It's been staring you in the face for years. Why? It's simple. You've been replacing your life with media. You've been pointing your face at screens instead of reality. Because instead of following your natural human urges to the very end, you take the path of least resistance and satisfy these urges with an incomplete stimulus instead.

ALL MEDIA THAT YOU CONSUME IS AN INCOMPLETE VERSION OF WHAT YOU CAN ALREADY EXPERIENCE IN THE REAL WORLD.

Social Media Vs Human Interaction: When you connect with others in the real world, you take in their facial expressions, their vocal intonation, their body language and that particular look in their eyes. When you speak with someone in the real world, you get to communicate their entire being.

'en you use social media, you communicate with a still image, a few lines of text and a few emojis. *This is an incomplete stimulus of social interaction.* Perhaps you're even talking with a video image of the other person. It's still an incomplete stimulus. You can't touch them. You can't smell them. And you can't feel their true presence.

Romantic Movies Vs Real Relationships: You experience real relationships through a first-person point of view. It's happening to you, personally. You lock eyes with your partner. They see you and you see them. Maybe they even understand you. You experience the same full range of brain chemicals that have been drawing couples together for millions of years.

In contrast, you see romantic comedies from a 3rd person perspective. You live vicariously through the characters in the movie. It's not happening to you. There's no eye contact. No physical contact. The full range of brain chemicals that fire off when you meet an amazing partner do not fire off while watching a Romcom (Eg. Oxytocin). *Romantic movies are incomplete stimulus compared to reality.*

Porn Vs Sex: With porn, there's no physical contact, no eye contact and no feeling of respect and acceptance from another human being. Watching from a 3rd person perspective (Unless you're watching VR porn). No sense of accomplishment. Experienced with the full knowledge that it's not happening to you, personally. Despite the sheer amount of variety of porn available, it will never include the chemicals that fire in your brain when you're in the physical presence of a partner. Therefore, *porn is an incomplete stimulus of real sex.* And no matter how advanced sex technology gets, it always will be.

With real sex there are real physical sensations. There's closeness, intimacy, eye contact, respect and acceptance from another human being. A sense of accomplishment. Occasional unforgettable experiences. Experiencing the intense pleasure that human beings have been experiencing for millions of years.

When media replaces your life, it leaves you with nothing.

Every human being has within them natural guides to a happy life. We have urges that push us in particular directions. The urge to find a romantic partner. The urge for excitement. The urge to have sex. The urge to connect with others. This thirst for natural stimuli is dampened by the artificial and incomplete stimuli provided by media. While you might have otherwise taken actions in the real world to quench this thirst, you no longer do so, because the thirst is has been semi-quenched by media. You could have asked out that cute girl at the train station, but your consumption of pornography earlier that day dampened your natural urges and now you can't summon the willpower necessary to take the risk. You could have used your intelligence to study something new, but instead you watched an episode of *Sherlock* and lived vicariously through the character of Sherlock Holmes as he displayed his genius in solving crime. You could have used your natural urge for a more exciting life to join a new club in your local town, but instead you opted to watch younger, fitter men play sport on television. You could have organised a meet-up with your mates on boring Sunday afternoon, but you instead fulfilled your natural urges to be social by sending GIF's back and forth with a couple of friends on Facebook. *Media takes your natural productive desires, consumes them and gives you nothing in return.* You watched. You sat. You consumed. You clicked. You tapped. You scrolled. You typed. But you didn't really *do* anything. Why do most of us consistently choose the incomplete stimulus of media over the complete stimulus of real life? Why do we continually make choices that make our life less complete and less fulfilled than it should be? Because the incomplete stimulus of media is the path of least resistance.

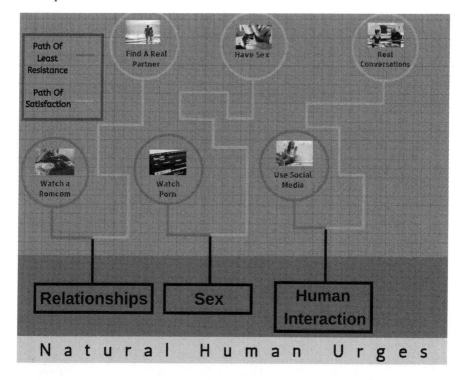

All human beings have a natural instinct to minimise time and effort. For our ancestors, this laziness was an effective survival strategy. Laziness meant not wasting precious energy. After all, they never knew when food would be in short supply. And laziness meant being less likely to hurt yourself doing something physically active. Like a bolt lightning or water running downhill, human beings naturally take the path of least resistance. Our capitalist economy means that for every single one of your natural urges, a path of least resistance is available for you. Businesses position their product on the path of least resistance and make a fortune as the masses give in to their desire to be lazy. Mcdonalds serves us food that appeals directly to our evolved taste buds that give us instant gratification, rather than the long-term nutrition our bodies require. Pornography gives us the experience of sex without going through all the difficulties of finding a partner. Rather than needing to go on a date, go to a bar, or socialise in order to meet someone of the opposite sex, we can have a sexual experience with the click of a few buttons. We can watch a scene of a perfect wedding, the whole family crying as the beautiful woman in her wedding gown walks down the aisle towards her handsome smiling husband, simply by sitting in the comfort of our own bedrooms and pressing play on Netflix. Of course, a real relationship would take years of effort and commitment, as well as plenty of setbacks along the way. Instead of gradually improving ourselves in the real world, we can progress inside a video game – where you improve your character's levels with a clear sense of progression.

This is why all modern societies have reclusive adolescents and adults who have withdrawn from society and decided to stay in their bedrooms 24/7. Because all of their natural human urges can be met with these incomplete stimuli. Of course these people are never satisfied, but it's enough for them to stay relatively sane. Hikikomoris, which are a growing problem in Japan, are a clear example of what happens when human beings entirely replace their natural human urges with the artificial stimuli on their screens. Would Hikikmoris and shut-in adults exist un such high numbers without screens? Unlikely. Their natural human urges would eventually push them out into the real-world, it's the fact that they can artificially semi-fulfil these urges with screens that keeps them inside.

Our screens also cause us to spend a large amount of time living vicariously through others. We watch as the hero saves the day. We watch as our team wins 2-0. We watch as beautiful people have sex with each other. We watch as reality stars relax in their million dollar homes. We watch as James Bond takes down yet another villain. We watch. We watch. We watch. We watch. And what do we do? We sit still. Motionless. Our eyes wide open and our bodies still.

Each of us has mirror neurons in our brain that help us to feel empathetic towards others. We cringe as others get into embarrassing situations. We pump our fists and cheer along with the football player as he scores a goal. We cry with others when we see them in pain. These mirror neurons may be a useful tool for human beings, but they also give us the tendency to spend a lot of our time living vicariously through other people. If we're not careful, we can spend half of our lives imagining we're someone other than ourselves. Pretending to be other people while our real self is neglected. If any of this is feels familiar to you, then I have a simple message to give you: You are not batman. You are not playing in the world cup. You are not fucking a gorgeous woman. You are not getting married to the man of your dreams. You are not solving crimes. You are not in a car chase. You are not the influencer you follow on Instagram. You are sat starting at a screen. *And the people you're watching don't even know you exist.*

What happens if humanity continues to collectively take the path of least resistance and we collectively continue to fulfil our urges with artificial stimuli provided to us through screens rather than fulfilling those urges in the real world? In the dystopian world of *Wall-E (2008)*, all of humanity is obese, lazy and yet perfectly content. They have their needs

WALL-E (2008)

met at all times by the AI running the spaceship they're living in. You might consider this fantasy scenario to be completely impossible. And to that I say, why? The technology of virtual reality is fast improving, and it's inevitable that eventually we'll be able to create a perfect second world. A world in which we can have anything we could ever want. With virtual reality, we will have the ability to meet up with our friends without ever leaving the house I, we will have the ability to have sex with anybody we like (through the use of deepfake technology) and we will be able to have incredible adventures through VR video games. All of this will available to us on the path of least resistance, all of this will be sold to us frantically by businesses and they will all include the same addictive mechanisms that already hook people onto MMORPG's, mobile games and other video games today.

When it comes down to it, would you choose the imperfect primary world filled with challenges or the secondary virtual world where you could have everything you ever dreamed of? Would you be able to resist the temptation to live in the virtual world? Are we going to live our lives taking the path of least resistance, living half-lives consisting mostly of incomplete stimuli provided to us by technology? Or are we going to commit to the challenges of the real world? What will we choose when an entire virtual world is available to us? A virtual world in which all of the experiences, pleasures and luxuries we can possibly imagine are available to us. *A time will come when each of us has to make a choice: technology or reality.*

Every single day, two paths are available to you. You can take the path of least resistance. You can spend 6 hours a day consuming media. Watching from afar as characters on-screen have incredible adventures. Imagining yourself having sex with impossibly gorgeous women. Daydreaming about falling in love with the perfect man in the most romantic situations. You can continually take this path for your entire life. Forever safe inside your house. Forever chasing shadows. And yet because all of these things are incomplete stimulus' you will be forever unsatisfied. Continually reaching for the next incomplete stimulus within arms reach to satisfy those natural human urges within you. Sure, you can take this path. Just know that every single time you do, you are moving further and further away from what you actually want. Because media isn't only a distraction from life. **Media replaces life.** Alternatively, you could choose the hard path. The path full of struggles, disappointments and the complete stimuli of the real world that you were you were born to experience. You could choose the path of satisfaction. You could choose

reality. And you could make a commitment to choosing reality every single day.

Now this isn't easy. The natural human tendency towards the path of least resistance is never going away and million-dollar businesses are hell-bent in addicting you to their media for their own profit. You live inside your own box. You may live away from your family. You may

WALL-E (2008)

not even have many close friends. The support of the community that our ancestors enjoyed is no longer available to us. Against the multitude of billion-dollar industries on the other side of your screens, you stand alone. But if you do decide to step away from your screens, if you do make a commitment to choose reality over the incomplete, artificial stimuli of media, you may find that it changes the trajectory of your entire life in a more positive direction. When you understand that **media replaces life,** and that your time in this life is limited, you may begin to find that you have very little time for media at all. You may find that you begin to

develop a craving for reality that never goes away.

"Reality is my drug. The more I have of it, the more power I get and the higher I feel" - Curtis Jackson "50 Cent"

how the media misleads you about success

The dominant medium of the time will decide what the mainstream idea of success is. (**Law 1: The Medium Is The Message**). During the television era, success for men was a big house, a nice car, a yacht and a sexy wife. For women it was having the perfect body, having perfect children and a perfect husband. The existence of the television helped create these materialistic goals for our culture. For many decades, it was all about the accumulation of expensive things. The more expensive things you owned, the more successful you were. But we are no longer in the television era, we have moved into the the social media era. This new era has created an entirely new mainstream model for success. Today, success is not about buying expensive material objects, it's about having experiences and living a particular lifestyle. It's about having the perfect Instagram page and accumulating large amounts of followers and likes and it's about having a vibrant social life. It's no longer about *having things*, it's about *doing things*. How many countries have you travelled to? Are you invited to exclusive parties? How many Twitter followers do you have? Do you have a blue check-mark? Are you Insta-famous? How many subscribers do you have on Youtube? These are the success indicators of the new world. *You own a red Ferarri?* You're probably compensating for your small dick. *You have an giant mansion?* Cool, I guess. But what's the point in a giant mansion if you don't have a social media network of cool friends to host an epic house party? *You're a doctor? A lawyer?* Meh, but you only have 400 Instagram followers, so who even are you really?

The current, social media success model doesn't accept people who are quietly and diligently working on their own success. It leaves no room for the introverted artist writing poetry alone in her room, or the scientist studying the nuances in chemistry in the lab. Anybody who is doing real work (and not constantly showcasing it on social media) does not fit in with the current model of success. In our current mainstream idea of success, a pretty 21-year old girl taking selfies in the club is more successful than a talented scientist making exceptional progress in biology. This model of success suits extroverted socialites, while many more introverted types try to force themselves into following suit – going to the club, taking their own selfies and trying to fit themselves into the model. Oftentimes for these introverts, it's like trying to fit a square peg into a round hole.

All of this, of course, assumes that you actually buy in. After all, instead of trying to a fit a success model that mainstream society gives you, it's possible to create your own definitions for success. What does success mean to you? Is it creating incredible works of art? Is it raising a family? Maybe it's living off the grid in a motorhome and growing your own food. Perhaps it's simply taking your dog for a walk around the park. The point is, *you don't have to buy in to what the media tells you success is.* Don't allow your life goals to be given to you by the culture. In the television era, endless numbers of people spent years of their life trying to get that big house and that expensive car, only to find themselves feeling empty when they finally acquired these things. Choose for yourself how you want to live your life, and don't spend your limited years chasing something that, deep down, you never even wanted in the first place.

While we're at it, we may as well tackle two other false ideas about success given to us by the media. The first I like to call *The Talent Scout.* You've seen the following scene a hundred times:

YOU SIT UNDER THE TREE, ACOUSTIC GUITAR IN HAND. YOU'VE BEEN THROUGH A ROUGH BREAKUP AND YOU NEED TO LET THE EMOTIONS OUT. YOU PLAY.

EVERY NOTE AMPLIFIES THE EMOTIONS YOU'RE FEELING INSIDE.

JUST NEARBY, UNNOTICED BY YOU, IS THE MANAGER OF A HIGH PROFILE RECORD LABEL RELAXING ON THE GRASS. BY CHANCE, HE OVERHEARS YOUR MUSIC AND WATCHES YOU WITH WONDER.

THIS IS IT, HE THINKS, THIS IS EXACTLY THE KIND OF TALENT I'VE BEEN LOOKING FOR.

HE APPROACHES YOU UNEXPECTEDLY AND INTRODUCES HIMSELF. HE INVITES YOU TO RECORD A DEMO IN HIS STUDIO.

IT BECOMES A HIT. 4 WEEKS LATER YOUR SONG IS BEING PLAYED ALL OVER THE RADIO WORLDWIDE.

YOU BECOME A HOUSEHOLD NAME AND SPEND THE REST OF YOUR LIFE PLAYING TO YOUR ADORING FANS AND SIGNING YOUR NAME ON BODY PARTS.

Still waiting for that talent scout? Yeah, so is everybody else. This is the premise of countless movies. Movies you may have watched as a child in the early stages of brain development. The idea is that if you're truly talented, somebody will discover you someday. It's destiny, after all. In the film Good Will Hunting (1997) the university janitor (Matt Damon) is spotted solving complex mathematics equations in the school at night. His therapist (Robin Williams) realises his potential and sets him up on the path to greatness.

But this trope isn't only something found in movies. Talent contest shows like XFactor and America's Got Talent base their whole show

WILL THE JANITOR SOLVES ADVANCED MATHEMATICAL EQUATIONS IN SECRET BEFORE HE'S SPOTTED BY A PROFESSOR (THE TALENT SCOUT). HIS TALENT IS FINALLY RECOGNISED BY THE WORLD AND HE RISES TO GREATNESS.

around this concept. Millions of people line up outside for days for their chance to be "discovered". And these are some of the most viewed shows in existence. The dream of *The Talent Scout* is nothing more than a pie in the sky fantasy. The truth is, nobody is going to "discover" you. Nobody is going to put you on. If you want an audience for your talents, you need to learn how to market yourself.

The second false idea about success you may have picked up through the media is that it's possible to become successful both quickly and easily. This is quick-fix culture. The fad diet. The lottery. The abs machine that contracts your abs while you sit on your computer chair. The before photo shows a fat slob, the after photo shows a sexy hunk with ripped abs. You've seen it all before. Maybe you laugh at these kinds of adverts, but these quick-fix products often sell incredibly well.

This is how a "Quick fix" product appears on the market. Take anything in life that requires a long-term process of hard work and consistent effort. Losing weight, building a business, learning a skill, making money or living a healthy lifestyle. The only way to achieve any of these things is with consistent effort over a long period of time and with any long-term process like this there is always a demand from the public for this goal to be solved quickly. *When there is a demand in the market businesses will always fill this demand with the solution, even if the solution is impossible.*

Take the diet pill as an example. Businesses that sell diet pills don't particularly care whether the product actually helps the customer lose weight, the only thing they care about is selling as many diet pills as they possibly can. They will produce a pill that technically makes a person lose weight through meaningless methods such as suppressing appetite or shedding water weight but offers no real long term solution to weight loss. The truth is, some things in life simply don't have a quick solution and probably never will.

the media and body image

Women today live in two worlds. The first is a perfect world. In this perfect world, every woman is flawless. They have beautiful bodies, perfect facial bone structures, a healthy complexion, whitened teeth, bright eyes, an hour glass figure and a juicy booty. The second world is an imperfect world. Women in this world come in much greater varieties. Some have acne, some have bags under their eyes, some have double chins, some have chubby cheeks and some have stained teeth. Women in this world come in a various kinds of body shapes and facial bone structures. The first world is the one we can find on our screens. The second world is the one we were born into. Teenage girls spend an equal amount of time in both of these worlds and adult women spend spend roughly a third of their time in the perfect world. Most women live their lives with one foot in each of these worlds. Hopping between them constantly. Taking information from both worlds and using both sets of information to inform themselves about the other. One world is real. One world is a lie. But the subconscious brain can't understand the difference between the

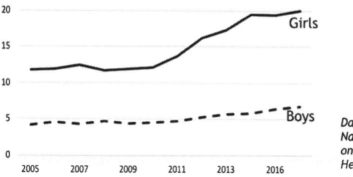

Persons Aged 12-17 Who Had At Least One Major Depressive Episode in the Past Year (%, By Gender)

Girls

Boys

Data from National Survey on Drug Use and Health

NOTICE HOW THE INCREASE IN MAJOR DEPRESSIVE EPISODES BEGINS IN 2009. EXACTLY WHEN SOCIAL MEDIA BEGAN TO BECOME PREVALENT. AND WHY THE DIFFERENCE IN BOYS AND GIRLS? BECAUSE SOCIAL MEDIA AFFECTS GIRLS FAR MORE THAN BOYS. (BOYS TEND TO HAVE MORE PROBLEMS WITH VIDEO GAMES AND PORN).

two.

Jonathon Haidt noticed the clear correlation between the surge in popularity of social media and smartphones with an increase in depressive episodes amongst teenagers, particularly teenage girls. The reason for this is obvious. Women today find themselves competing against, not only their friends, but the entire global village. The hierarchy of female attractiveness is dizzyingly steep for the average woman as she compares her own body and appearance to that which she sees on social media as well as traditional media sources like television and magazines. As usual, almost everyone feels like a loser when they compare themselves with the very best of the entire internet connected world.

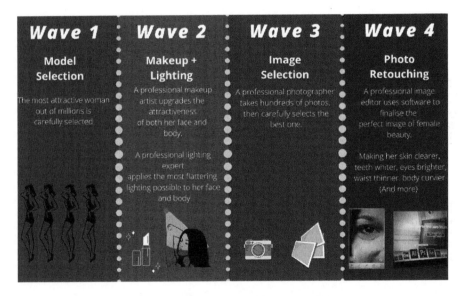

Wave 1	Wave 2	Wave 3	Wave 4
Model Selection	**Makeup + Lighting**	**Image Selection**	**Photo Retouching**
The most attractive woman out of millions is carefully selected	A professional makeup artist upgrades the attractiveness of both her face and body.	A professional photographer takes hundreds of photos, then carefully selects the best one.	A professional image editor uses software to finalise the perfect image of female beauty.
	A professional lighting expert applies the most flattering lighting possible to her face and body		Making her skin clearer, teeth whiter, eyes brighter, waist thinner, body curvier (And more)

Every single image of female beauty you see in traditional media is the result of a team of experts using makeup and lighting to *increase her attractiveness as much as possible* and finally using photo retouching software to transform her into the *perfect image of female beauty. Even the images of your friends on social media may be the result of photo-retouching apps like Facetune or Perfect 365 to improve their own appearance.* Teeth are whitened. Eyes are brightened. Noses are reshaped. Foreheads are adjusted. Necks are slimmed down. Curves are added. And waists are narrowed. Many images of female beauty in traditional media even use things like "Leg doubles". That's right, if a model's legs aren't attractive enough - they will replace them with another models legs. This practice is known as "frankenstein editing". *The image of female beauty on that advertising billboard you always see on the way to work might be might be the result of multiple women digitally sewn together.* And it's not only images - videos can also be retouched simply by using the "beautycam" function that comes with many modern smartphones. In images and videos, a woman's beauty is now routinely artificially enhanced. It's now incredibly easy for the average person to edit images of themselves. With a few taps on the app, faces can be perfected (down to the smallest detail) and bodies can be reshaped. Worse yet, images can be retouched incredibly subtly. *If your friend is editing her images on social media you probably wouldn't have any idea.* Social media has created a second world. A world where everybody looks substantially better and happier than they do in reality. When using dating apps like Tinder, many men have now gone through the strange experience of meeting a girl for a date in the real world and being surprised to find that the girl they meet in person looks almost unrecognisable from the images he previously saw on Tinder.

It's like an open secret. *Everyone does it but nobody talks about it.* In the modern day, I don't think it's too far-fetched to say that most women habitually retouch their own images. This has been quietly accepted by the culture without anybody raising the question: *Is this really ok?* What is this constant barrage of images of enhanced female beauty doing to the psychology of women? What's it doing to teenage girls? And should we really just lay back and accept this insane world that technology has thrust upon us?

How does the subconscious brain deal with images of enhanced female beauty? Using evolutionary theory, we can make a good guess.

(Law 2: Technology Is An Evolutionary Mismatch) The oldest part of our brain, the lizard brain, didn't evolve to understand screens. Our lizard brain is prepared to live a tribal lifestyle, with a maximum of around 150 tribe members (Dunbar's law). For the tribal woman, it was important to always have an understanding of where she stood in the tribe. Was she high-status? Or low status?. The brain is constantly *pinging* off of others to understand what position that particular individual has within the tribe. Female attractiveness was important for the survival of women's genes. The more attractive the woman, the better partner she would be likely to attract. So for women, comparing their appearance to other women is *hardwired.* This was a useful psychological mechanism for women within the tribal environment. But then, over the past 200 years, the advancement of technology skyrocketed. And the older part of the brain hasn't evolved with the times. This causes all kinds of

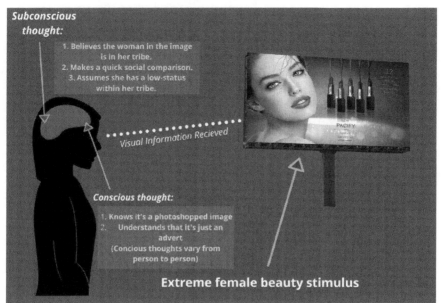

Subconscious thought:

1. Believes the woman in the image is in her tribe.
2. Makes a quick social comparison.
3. Assumes she has a low-status within her tribe.

Visual Information Recieved

Conscious thought:

1. Knows it's a photoshopped image
2. Understands that it's just an advert
(Concious thoughts vary from person to person)

Extreme female beauty stimulus

evolutionary mismatches. In essence, *the lizard brain doesn't understand that a still image of somebody isn't a real human being.* The subconscious, or lizard brain simply receives stimulus from the environment and absorbs it. If your subconscious receives a visual stimuli of a beautiful woman (even it's just a photograph), it will react to it as if it's a real woman. (After all, men get aroused by looking at still images of beautiful women that they can't possibly have sex with. Because the subconscious receives the visual stimulus of the beautiful woman and assumes she must be there in the room with him). Women see images of impossibly beautiful women all the time. Day in, day out. On billboards. In advertising. In music videos. On the Instagram news feed.

Woman are continually bombarded with visual stimuli that tells their subconscious brain that they're uglier than the other members in their "tribe". It's this continual bombardment that is likely causing a skyrocket in major depressive episodes amongst teenage girls. When it comes to unrealistic images of female beauty in the media, according to evolutionary theory, *exposure alone may be enough to have a negative effect on a woman.* With all of these images surrounding us on a daily basis, it's not much of a surprise that psychological disorders like body dysmorphia and anorexia seem to have become more prevalent. *Images are powerful and they have an effect.* Of course there are plenty of environmental factors involved for each woman too. Women who are lonely and socially isolated are more likely to be hit harder by these negative media effects. Not every woman will become psychologically ill because they're exposed to these images, but a minority will. And we should take this minority seriously, because our media landscape has contributed significantly to making them mentally ill.

All of this raises the question – why are there so many images of female beauty everywhere? Pay attention to the world and you'll realise just how prevalent images of female beauty are in our society. As you walk around the shopping malls, as you stare at your smartphone screen, as you watch TV, as you watch music videos – female beauty is plastered everywhere. (Images of male beauty are also incredibly prevalent. These also negatively effect male body image. But images of female beauty are probably at least four-times as common, so for the sake of convenience, I'm focusing on these). Some will argue that it's because we live in a male dominated patriarchy. They say that we see so many images of women being sexualised because of the "male gaze". Perhaps there's an element of truth in this idea, but it's far from the root of the problem. The real reason we're constantly bombarded by these images of female beauty is because **female beauty sells.**

FEMALE BEAUTY SELLS

Take the magazine rack as an example. Magazines go through a process of natural selection. They evolve in the same way any living species does. Over the years, thousands of attempts have been made at creating a successful magazine. The magazines with the most effective front covers sell successfully, while those with ineffective front covers die out. At the end of this process, the only magazines left on the shelf are those with the most effective front covers. One look at the picture above and it's quite clear that the most effective front

cover for a women's magazine is a perfect, wrinkle-free, gorgeous, photo-shopped woman. Any women's magazine that chose not to use this type of image on their front cover was gradually beaten by the competition. And what other possible image would be as attention grabbing as a beautiful woman? A building? A tree? A sunset? As human beings, we're drawn to beauty. And that's why it's a great way to sell products. This effect of natural selection exists not only on the magazine rack, but on all kinds of other products. Music videos, movies, TV shows, Instagram pages, cosmetics commercials and fashion commercials. Female beauty is even used to advertise: Jobs, real-estate, fast food, holidays, cars and the list continues. After several years of experimentation, all of these industries realised that using female beauty is the most successful method of marketing their product.

So how exactly does female beauty sell products? For women, female

DON'T YOU WANT TO BE A CUTE CALL CENTRE AGENT LIKE HER? CONSCIOUSLY OR SUBCONSCIOUSLY, SEEING THIS IMAGE OF FEMALE BEAUTY MEANS YOU'RE NOW MORE INTERESTED IN APPLYING FOR THIS JOB.

DON'T YOU WANT TO BE A BEAUTIFUL WOMAN IN A SWIMSUIT RIDING A BOAT? CONSCIOUSLY OR SUBCONSCIOUSLY, YOU'RE NOW MORE LIKELY TO PURCHASE THIS PACKAGED HOLIDAY.

Call Centre Agents
(Wellawatte Head Office)

Walk the streets of Jerusalem and experience 3,000 years of history in a day. Live like a local in Tel Aviv and hit the beach, enjoy the restaurants, fashion and nightlife until dawn! Israel, come enjoy the journey of a lifetime!

ISRAEL
VACATION BEYOND BELIEF

www.israel.travel

beauty is used by associating a product with an aspirational image that they would like to aim for. If you're going to advertise a brand of lipstick - you need to associate it with an image of incredible female beauty. Any lipstick brand that decides to use an image of a more average woman in their advertising likely sells less lipstick than their competitors. *Female beauty can be associated with anything.*

Job advertisements need to use an image of female beauty in order to encourage women to apply for the job.

Take any product that women buy and you can associate it with female beauty in order to increase sales. Female beauty is used to sell products to men in a slightly different way. There is nothing more attention grabbing for (heterosexual) men than female beauty. The (heterosexual) male brain is hard-wired to pay attention to female beauty. Female beauty is like a cheat code into the male brain, it will always get male attention. The male brain has evolved through millions of years of evolution to take notice of signs of female sexual initiation. Upon seeing an image of a woman showing sexual signals, the synapses in the male brain will begin firing – after all, the lizard brain doesn't understand that a real woman isn't actually present. No matter how intelligent you may be, if you're a straight male, female beauty will get the attention of your lizard brain. Your pre-frontal cortex, the most recent part of the brain,

TREY SONGZ – ANIMAL. CURRENTLY STANDS AT 86 MILLION VIEWS AS OF 2020.

doesn't stand a chance of ignoring images like these. One of the biggest problems marketers face is getting the attention of their audience in the highly saturated modern marketplace. And now here you have a method that more or less forces every male that sees the advert to pay attention. The advert doesn't have to be clever, creative or unqiue. The female sex signalling displayed in the advert will grab male audience attention no matter what. And the more attention an advert receives, the more the products are likely to get sold.

Just take just take music videos for example. The amount of female nudity in music videos has increased more and more throughout the

SIMPLY MY PLACING AN IMAGE OF FEMALE BEAUTY IN THE AD, IT'S GUARANTEED TO GET MALE ATTENTION.

decades. Why? Because we live in a male-dominated patriarchy and men want to exploit the female body? Not really. Female nudity has become more and more prevalent because music video producers have realised it's an incredibly effective way to get attention from a male audience. Especially on a platform like Youtube, an area filled with teenage boys between the ages of 13-18, using female beauty/nudity is a guaranteed way to bring in a high-view count. Is the music good? It doesn't matter. Is the artist talented? Who cares. Feature beautiful women shaking their ass at the camera, and the music video is guaranteed views. The most successful products in the world are always the ones that line up perfectly with our evolutionary desires.

It's not sexism. It's the free market at work. Female beauty is an incredibly useful tool for marketing and there are currently very few regulations against it. So of course there are images of female beauty everywhere you look. The fact that we're surrounded by images of unrealistic female beauty is simply the result of millions of businesses trying to turn a profit. The executives at marketing companies aren't setting out to intentionally make women feel bad. It's just that they don't care if they do or not. They care about profit and profit alone. Men too are up against the image of image of the broad shouldered, scowling man with a chiseled six-pack. Like women, men's bodies come in all shapes and sizes. Some have narrow shoulders. some lose their hair in their early 20's, some only stand at 165cm, others naturally hold on to a lot of fat around their bellies. Plenty of men will also be affected by the constant barrage of perfect male bodies being pushed into their consciousness.

Unrealistic beauty is everywhere. It's harmful to teenage girls. It's harmful to adult women. It's harmful to men. The truth is, this problem isn't ever going away. No matter how many times feminists may complain and protest about unrealistic female beauty in media, nothing will change. Female beauty will always sell products. Now that photo retouching technology is available for everyone, people won't stop editing their photos. And people won't stop portraying a perfect version of themselves on social media. The technology will continue to improve. And people will have more and more ability to make themselves look perfect in the virtual world. (**Law 3: Technology Never Moves Backwards**)

But there are realistic actions that could be taken to mitigate against the effects of unrealistic beauty standards in media on the body image:

1. *Label Digitally Retouched Photos: All images used in advertising that have been digitally retouched must have a warning label on them": *This image has been digitally altered*. A simple reminder like this can go a long way in breaking the illusion these images have.*

2. *Photo Retouching Apps Should Have an 18+ Age limit: All apps that easily allow users to edit images of themselves should have an age limit of at least 18. And this wouldn't mean checking a box saying "I am over 18 years old". It would mean that apps like Facetune require new users to take a photo of their Passport or Drivers Licence to prove their age,*

3. *Educate Students About Unrealistic Beauty In Media: Learning about the media and becoming media literate should be mandatory education. Nobody should leave school without understanding that the images they see around them aren't real.*

These kinds of realistic solutions could actually make a difference in solving this problem. And perhaps even reduce the anxiety, depression and body dismorphia among teenagers as well as adults. Otherwise, we continue the path we're on—living in a world surrounded by images of perfect humans, while the real humans suffer.

supernormal stimuli – the new addiction

(**Law 2: Technology is an evolutionary mismatch**) We live in a world of addicts. Just look around. Almost everybody is hooked on something. Smartphones. Sugar. Cigarettes. Video Games. Television. Social Media. Shopping. Drugs. Porn. Gambling. Internet. Mobile Games. Alcohol. Which one are you hooked on? It's a rare individual who doesn't at least have a partial addiction to one of these things. We're all addicted. And we're all suckers for the companies that sell our addiction to us. What the hell happened to us? Each of us has only one life to lead. One precious life with a finite amount of time. If that's the case, then why do we spend so many hours on social media even when we don't want to? Why are so many men watching porn instead of having sex? Why do we spend so much time sat still staring at a glass box of wires? Why do we choose to progress inside video games instead of in the real world? Why do some of us eat junk food all the way to our deathbeds? What the hell is wrong with human beings? Are we all insane? Our actions don't make any sense. But there is logic to our actions. It's just that the logic we use is based on the environment we lived in 20,000 years ago. If you want to thrive in the modern world, there is something you need to understand: *The modern environment is a minefield of supernormal stimuli.*

WHAT IS A SUPERNORMAL STIMULI?

Earlier chapters discussed the incomplete stimuli that we often choose instead of the natural stimuli found in the real world. But in a kind of strange paradox, many of these incomplete stimuli are also far stronger than natural stimuli. They're incomplete, yet supernormal stimuli and often highly addictive. Niko Tinbergan was the first to discover supernormal stimuli. Early on in his career he spent some time studying the stickleback – the most common freshwater fish in Holland. The male stickleback has a red underbelly and will viciously attack any other male stickleback that enters its territory. Tinbergan had a theory that he needed to test, so he and his students created dummy sticklebacks, colouring the underbelly of the "fish" in red. Tinbergan was shocked to find that the male sticklebacks would attack the dummy fish, perceiving it to be a male competitor. They concluded that that it was the colour red that triggered the instincts of the male stickleback to attack. They then designed and tested all kinds of other very non fish-like shapes, but as long as the underbelly was coloured red, the male stickleback would perceive it as a threat. Even if the intruder looked nothing like a fish, if it had a red colour on it's underbelly area, the male stickleback would attack it. Some male sticklebacks in the aquarium even tried to attack a *red postal van* that drove by during the experiments. But this was not the major discovery of the experiment. The real breakthrough occurred when Tinbergan discovered that the stimuli of a dummy stickleback not only fooled the stickleback with a dummy fish, but that he could design fish that attracted the male sticklebacks instincts *more than a real fish*. He released into the stickleback's territory both a dummy fish with an underbelly coloured in a bright red colour, and a real competing male fish. The male stickleback attacked the dummy fish instead of the real competing fish. This dummy fish triggered its attack instincts more than the real fish. To the male stickleback, this dummy fish was a *supernormal stimuli*.

In another experiment while studying geese, Tinbergan managed to create artificial eggs that a goose would prefer to its own real eggs. He exaggerated the colour, size and markings on these artificial eggs and left it near the goose's nest. The goose proceeded to ignore its own eggs and instead roll these artificial eggs back to its nest. At one stage, one goose made a valiant attempt to roll a *volleyball* back to it's nest. The goose acted this way because it's evolved is evolved to look for certain markers on the egg (the size for example) and prioritise these eggs over the others. To this goose, the volleyball (that has similar features to a giant goose egg) was a *supernormal stimuli*. It saw what appeared to be a huge goose egg and all of its instincts told it to roll it back into the nest as quickly as possible.

In a similar fashion, female barn swallows are evolved to choose their mate based on the intensity of the colour brown on a male's chest. The colour brown is an indicator of reproductive fitness for the female swallows. Take a previously rejected male swallow, colour his chest a darker shade of brown with a felt-tip marker and suddenly the females line up to mate with him.

You might chuckle at these cute, stupid animals being so easily fooled. But it only takes a moments consideration to realise that humans too are easily susceptible to supernormal stimuli. *In fact, businesses sell us supernormal stimuli every single day.* Businesses create artificial superstimuli that we actually prefer to natural stimuli and our primative brains are not evolved to deal with them. Capitalism has created extreme versions of stimuli that we as humans find almost impossible to ignore. For example, sugar was scarce in the environment we're adapted for and we're hard-wired to consume as much of it as we can. However, sugar is no longer scarce in our environment. In fact, its everywhere. It's a cheap ingredient that makes food tastes great, so it's perfect for food manufactures who want to improve their profit margins. And not only is it everywhere, it's refined. They have become experts at refining sugar at the chemical level. So the sugar in our food is far sweeter than the sugar found in the sugarcane. Sugar is extremely addictive (which is another reason food manufacturers love it so much). Have one piece of candy and you immediately want another. The insane state of the obesity crises and the extreme rates of diabetes are testament to the damage that a legal supernormal stimuli can do.

Social media is also a supernormal stimuli (**Law 2: Technology is an evolutionary mismatch**). We are deeply social creatures and we are evolved to live in tribes of roughly 150 people. In our tribes it was beneficial for us to know what other members of our tribe were up to. It was necessary to know who was sleeping with who, who was angry with who and who was friends with who in order to maintain social harmony within the tribe. After all, not being in sync with the social harmony of the tribe could have resulted in abandonment, and abandonment from your tribe meant almost certain death. Therefore, we have a strong natural instinct to want to know what other people are doing, and this is especially true for women. In our tribes, we would have spoken to each other at various times throughout the day to find out the latest of what was happening in the tribe. On social media, we're in contact with others on a 24/7 basis - we can see what everyone is doing all the time. Our instinct for social cohesion is switched into 6th gear as we scroll our newsfeeds checking what our friends are doing every single day. Social media is a superstimuli our brains are not evolved for, so when we have constant access to our friends, many of us can't help but get hooked on it.

And let's not forget about television. Humans have a basic instinct to pay attention when we notice any novel stimulus in our environment such as movement or sound. Russian neurologist Ivan Pavlov called this reflex the "orienting response". The orienting response evolved to help us spot predators and prey. When the orienting response is activated we turn our eyes and ears in the direction of the stimulus and freeze. This is a response we share with animals. You've probably seen animals act this way before.

Television is full of pans, cuts and zooms. New characters are introduced. There are sudden noises. Dramatic events occur. Characters

THIS RABBIT IS DEMONSTRATING THE "ORIENTING RESPONSE" AS IT SPOTS A NOVEL STIMULUS IN THE ENVIROMENT

shout. Characters laugh. All of these stimuli activate our orienting response, which means we often can't help but face the television and pay attention to it. Have you ever had a conversation with somebody while the television is playing in the same room? It's almost impossible not to periodically glance at the TV screen, even if it's a programme you're not remotely interested in. By the age of 6 months, even babies begin having the orienting response to television screens. Following this bombardment of stimulus the viewer displays a strange mix of high and low attention. The body is still, the eyes are focused on the TV but levels of learning and memory drop. After the TV is turned off many people feel as though the TV has somehow sucked out all of their energy and they are often in a worse mood than they were before they started watching.

For years many of us have been watching various sports on television screens. Millions of football fans spend their weekends cheering on our team and getting angry if the referee makes a decision they're not happy with. Of course, the players they're shouting at can't hear their cheers of encouragement and the referee can't hear their rage. Think of it – millions of people around the world shouting and screaming at an electric box of wires and glass. Is this really so unlike stickleback fish attacking the dummy fish with the red underbelly?

Hundreds of millions of men (and women) around the entire world, get sexually aroused by the pornography on their screens. Some of them even get more aroused by pornography than they do by real sex. Think about it, when a man gets aroused by pornography, there is no female present in the room, just wires, metal, plastic and various other materials. And yet these men become intensely aroused. Usually, the women in pornography have their sexual features far more enhanced compared with a real woman. Big tits, big asses, heavy makeup, perfect lighting and exaggerated moans of pleasure (uh! Ah! Yes! Yes!). Each of these exagegerated displays of female beauty are supernormal stimuli for the human male. Are we really so different from the female barn swallows that get sexually aroused when scientists darken the brown pigment on a male swallow's chest?

But it's not only men, women have their own supernormal stimuli that cater to their own sexual desires. Romance novels are almost as big of a market as porn – over 2000 English language romance novels were published in 2000, generating over $1.2 billion in sales. In an analysis of over 45 best-selling romance novels, anthropologist April Gorry made a number of interesting findings: the heroes in these novels are an average of seven years older than the heroine. Heroes are usually tall with "over six-feet" being a popular generalisation. Adjectives to describe Mr Right were, in order of frequency: muscular, handsome, strong, large, tanned, masculine, and energetic. Common personality descriptors were: bold, calm, confident, and intelligent. Often times, the hero would want the women more than anybody else, find her sexually attractive, want to protect her and consider her unique.

Aside from romance novels, women often fall in love with characters they see on their screens all the time. Just take the modern phenomena of the boy band. Westlife, One Direction, NSYNC all pulled enormous crowds filled with screaming girls and young women. Teenage girls around the world have posters of their favourite boyband member pinned onto their bedroom walls. Do they know these boys in real life? No. Does this boyband member even know of their existence? No. These boybands have teams of marketing experts making sure they put forward exactly the kind of image that teenage girls will fall in love with. The boys are always charming, funny, talented singers, dressed perfectly and have handsome, symmetrical faces with an attractive bone structure. Each of the boys have a slightly different "personality", one might be "the bad boy" of the group, another might be "the creative one". These varying "personalities" are created to appeal to as much of their young female audience as they possibly can. The enormous size of the crowds these boy bands pull in are testament to the power of a supernormal stimuli that falls perfectly in-line with female sexual desire. The crowds themselves are also part of the effect of the stimuli, after all, social proof and status are important markers for sexual attractiveness in men. While having schoolgirl crushes on celebrities seems to us a normal part of growing up, this is actually a brand new phenomena. A few generations ago, having a crush on someone you had never met and lived thousands of miles away was completely unheard of. More than that, it wasn't even possible; no media existed that was capable of providing this to us.

Look at any product that seems to sell obscenely well, and you'll probably find that it's a supernormal stimuli. The most successful products in the world take our tribal instincts and stimulate them to an unnatural degree. We're all hooked on supernormal stimuli, and we're all being played by the companies who sell our addictions to us.

Junk food. Porn. Television. Social Media. Video games. These things are all normal. *And yet when you take a step back and look at them closely, they're not normal at all.* Human beings have been around for millions of years, while these supernormal stimuli are all less than 100 years old. You might be reading this article now and realising that these supernormal stimuli are actually quite strange. But after you put down this book and head back into the world, they will begin to feel normal again. And you will forget once again how strange they are. The psychological effect of normalisation has its effect on you every single time you see somebody else using one of these supernormal stimuli. The modern world has entirely normalised the sale, purchase and use of supernormal stimuli. Every corner store has piles of junk food at the checkout. Porn is all over the internet. Every household has a TV in the living room. Everybody is on social media. Most men under 30 years old have a games console. If you walk down the street drinking a can of Coke people won't think anything of it. But if you walk down the street eating a cucumber people will think you're an oddball. We see other people using them all the time, and when we see other people doing something, we assume it must be normal. But you have to wonder: Is it normal that one third of Americans are clinically obese? Is it normal that a huge number of men masturbate to digital images of sex more than having real sex? Is it normal that people in developed nations around the world are spending an average of five hours a day sat still staring at the glass box in the corner of the room? You can be the judge.

The world is a minefield of supernormal stimuli trying to steal your time and money - stimuli that your biological instincts are fatally attracted to. It may even be the case that these supernormal stimuli are the main obstacles preventing you from living a happy and fulfilled life. At times, it can seem impossible to avoid these supernormal stimuli, after all, if all of your evolved instincts are telling you to eat another slice of chocolate cake, then how can you possibly hope to resist it? Well, if you were a dog, you wouldn't stand a chance of resisting. But luckily, we're human. And us humans have a secret weapon: Giant brains. We have the ability to go against our reflexive instincts.

So how do we use our giant brains to combat these supernormal stimuli that surround us? Don't allow the supernormal stimuli that surround you to be normalised in your mind. Once they're normalised they blend into the background and you lose the ability to avoid them. The hardest part is remembering that supernormal stimuli are not normal when everybody else is using them without any issue. Plenty of people around you are drinking Coca-Cola and stuffing their faces with junk food without a second thought. You may begin once again to think this is normal. But having a sugar addiction is not ok. The reason so many people seem to have no problem with eating sugar filled junk food is because they're barely aware that there is any problem with doing so. Sure, people "know" they shouldn't eat junk food. But their actions suggest that they don't really "know". They only "know" on a surface level. So you need to identify the supernormal stimuli that surround you on a daily basis. The video games. The porn. The junk food. The social media newsfeeds. Become truly aware of these irresistible stimuli.

Now that you've identified them, it's time to actively avoid them. 100% avoidance isn't realistic (unless you want to go and live in the mountains), so you will have to make compromises with some of them. But if you are going to engage with these superstimuli, be aware of their incredible capacity to suck you in. Understand that when you're using super stimuli, you're playing with fire. Am I exaggerating? Just think of it. Hundreds of millions of people are compulsively eating sugar every day of their lives. This leads them to gain weight, age faster, develop type 2 diabetes, increase their risk of cancer as well as countless other potential health issues. Many people waste almost all of their free time watching television (that includes Netflix). People habitually watch porn at the expense of their real dating lives. You think you can just eat one chocolate? You're just going to watch one porn video? You're just going watch one more episode on Netflix? You're just going to check Facebook for 2 minutes? Please. Don't underestimate supernormal stimuli. Respect their power and keep your distance.

Our pleasure mechanism is surprisingly flexible and will respond to what it's told to respond to. It all depends on your habits. People get pleasure from what they're used to getting pleasure from. Either you get pleasure from eating a slice of chocolate cake or you get pleasure from eating healthy and nutritious foods. Either you get pleasure spending by 4 hours watching television or by spending an hour in the gym. Either you get pleasure from stalking your friends on social media or by finishing a book.

Don't let the modern world ruin your life.

chapter 2

THE 5 LAWS OF MEDIA

American historian Melvin Kranzberg created what he called "The laws of technology". Law 1: Technology is neither bad nor good; nor is it neutral. Law 2: Invention is the mother of necessity. Law 3: Technology comes in packages, big and small. Law 4: Although technology might be a prime element in many public issues, nontechnical factors take precedence in technology-policy decisions. Law 5: All history is relevant, but the history of technology is the most relevant. Law 6: Technology is a very human activity – and so is the history of technology.

In this book, I want to create my own 5 laws of media. I believe that these 5 laws are essential in understanding the media and technology that surrounds us today. Almost all media follows these 5 basic laws, and once you know them, you will have a deep understanding of media. So, without further ado, here are the 5 laws of media.

law 1:
the medium is the
message

**"Only those who know nothing of the
history of technology, believe that a
technology is entirely neutral or adaptable"
- Neil Postman.**

When speaking about technology, people often conclude the following:
The technology isn't the problem, it's *us* that are the problem. Or in other
words, *technology is neutral.*

TECHNOLOGY IS NOT NEUTRAL.

Every piece of technology and every medium has characteristics built
within it that will naturally emerge overtime and humans interact with
each individual technology in very specific ways. Each technology
changes the way think, the way we feel and the way we communicate. The
deepest parts of the human brain have been left unchanged for around
200,000 years, as such, these older parts of the brain will always react to
technology in a very particular way. For example, both Chinese people
and American people both act in similar ways in the comments section
despite having grown up in entirely different cultures with different values.
In Vietnam, people endlessly scroll through their Instagram newsfeed in
exactly the same way as they do in the United Kingdom. Men with access
to a smartphone watch pornography in Africa, just as they do in Brazil.
Much of the relationship between human psychology and technology
is about nature, not nurture. No matter the cultural differences, human
beings have similar reactions to the technology they encounter.

"There is a huge technology involved in TV which surrounds you physically. And the effect of that huge service environment on you personally is vast. The effect of the programme is incidental"

This was Marshall Mcluhan speaking on the effects of television in 1977. At a time when many were discussing things like: *What should we allow on TV? Should we allow this programme? Or that programme.* Mcluhan turned the argument upside-down by suggesting something else entirely; that the most important message coming from television was *the very existence of the medium itself.*

The existence of television changed the entire landscape that we lived in. It even changed the very way in which we think. Just look at how the television transformed politics. Before the television, political debates were held on the radio, a medium in which it's the content of that's spoken which takes centre stage. The audience listens carefully to the radio, focusing on each individual word the speaker says, with no visual media to look at. These debates were often long, and candidates spoke in great detail about the policies they wanted to implement. Then the television arrived, and for the first time the audience was able to see what the politician looked like as they spoke. From the moment the television arrived, a politician's image became an extremely important factor in winning elections. Any politician who was too short, too ugly, too awkward or too unfashionable was discriminated against by the visual medium of television. To be the leader of the country, you now had to *"look presidential"*, or voters wouldn't feel confident your leadership. Political debates generally became more and more shallow, with actual policies taking a back-seat to a politicians image. On television, image is more important than content or character. Today, all the candidates stand lined up on our screens and have a team of people ensuring that their appearance looks just right. Each candidate is given only 2-3 minutes to speak at the most. (Apparently, presidential candidates are supposed to discuss complex issues like foreign policy or healthcare reform in the space of 3 minutes). To put it simply, the medium of television transformed politics. It wasn't about *what* was on TV, it was the very existence of television that transformed the relationship between politicians and the public. The medium is the message.

Twitter is also a medium. Today billions of people across the the world communicate directly through Twitter. Is the content of individual tweets important? Or is it the effects of the medium itself we should be concerned about? What kind of medium is Twitter? It's a medium that limits your messages to a maximum of 280 characters. It's also a text-based medium – people do not communicate with voice or video on twitter, only text. Can we say that Twitter is a neutral platform? Can we say that it's not the technology that matters, it's just how we use it? The 280 character limit incentivises quick, emotional "zingers" and deincentives nuanced discussion. Text-based mediums remove eye-contact, facial expressions and body language – this reduces empathy between people and encourages them to say things they would never dare say in the real world. People think that Twitter is neutral, and because they think it's neutral, they don't notice the effect it's having on the way they communicate with others. They don't notice that they've become meaner, less forgiving, less empathetic and more sarcastic than they are in real world conversations.

Every medium affects human psychology in very particular ways. Whatever medium you're using to communicate, consider the effects it's having on yours and others psychology. Technology is not neutral. The medium is the message.

law 2:
media is an evolutionary mismatch

Our brains are evolved to live a hunter-gather lifestyle in tribes of roughly 150 people, around 200,000 years ago on the savannahs of Africa. The brain evolved through a process of evolution over millions of years. The parts of the brain that evolved earlier (those we have in common with other mammals) are responsible for our basic instincts: eating, drinking, sex and escaping from danger. Overtime, our brain evolved layer by layer, until we finally developed the pre-frontal cortex – the newest part of the brain. The pre-frontal cortex is responsible for logical reasoning, problem-solving, self-control and acting with long-term thinking in mind. Generally speaking, our emotions and feelings come from our more primitive brain, while our logical reasoning comes from our pre-frontal cortex.

Our present world is incompatible with these instincts because of the radical increases in population densities, pollution and, of course, technology. Evolution hasn't been able to keep pace with such radical change. An evolutionary mismatch occurs when the instincts we're born with are disadvantageous in the current environment. For example, over millions of years natural selection adapted the human body to eat a diet of fruits, vegetables, wild game, seeds, nuts and other foods that are rich in fibre but low in sugar. Then the modern food industry was born and brought us foods absolutely loaded with sugar and depleted of fibre. The body isn't adapted to this kind of diet, hence the spread of type 2 diabetes and a host of other chronic illnesses. Sugar was very scarce in our hunter-gatherer environment thousands of years ago, so we're naturally hardwired to seek it out. In the past, we would have probably gotten our sugar from fruit, but now sugar is available everywhere – in highly concentrated forms. Because of this evolutionary mismatch, human beings find sugar incredibly addictive, which leads to addictive behaviour around junk food which is one of the main reasons we have such an obesity epidemic today.

One of the simplest forms of evolutionary mismatch is caused by migration. White people living in Australia and New Zealand have the highest rate of skin cancer in the world. White skin evolved in colder, northern climates and is adapted to absorb more UV radiation as this helps the body create the Vitamin D it needs to stay healthy. For all of human history, white people lived in the northern climates, and over millions of years the skin adapted to the environment by decreasing the amount of melanin it contained (which is what gives it it's white colour). Then, on January 26 1788, Captain Arthur Phillips guided a fleet of ships to drop off a group of convicts onto the land of Australia. White people have only been living in Australia for around 250 years, and their skin does not contain the high levels of melanin necessary to protect it from the sun's UV radiation, which leads to higher levels of skin cancer. As you can see, this an evolutionary mismatch; the body is maladapted to the environment it lives in. In exactly the same way, black people living in the colder climates of Europe and North America suffer from a lack of Vitamin D absorption. Black skin evolved over millions of years in the far hotter climate of Africa, and adapted to the environment by producing more melanin in the skin. This, however, means that the skin also absorbs Vitamin D more slowly and leads them to being Vitamin D deficient when living in colder climates.

A mismatch generally occurs when a common stimulus either increases or decreases beyond levels for which the body is adapted. Mismatches are caused by stimuli that are too much, too little or too new. Other diseases that may be caused by a mismatch include: asthma, ADHD, anxiety, acne, depression, cavities, osteoporosis, some cancers, sleep apnea, coronary heart disease, lower back pain, insomnia, myopia, high blood pressure and the list goes on and on.

Media is also an evolutionary mismatch.

All media that we consume today was created *after* our brain evolved. Our brain is evolved to live in the old, tribal environment, not the modern technological environment we find ourselves in. While our pre-frontal cortex understands that the horror movie we're watching isn't real, the older, primative part of our brain can't tell the difference between a horror movie and reality. That's why we get scared of horror movies despite the fact there are no physical dangers present. Logically, we know it's only images on a screen, but emotionally we believe it to be real. That's why we're aroused by pornography, envious of people rtising and excited by progression inside video games. What then, when the artificial stimuli on our screens are stronger than the natural stimuli in our environment? We get hooked. The older part of our brain isn't prepared to understand that the images on our screens aren't happening in reality. *Our primitive brain can't tell the difference between screens and reality.* Those who understand the link between media and our evolutionary routes are able to use this power to their advantage. Advertisers and political actors create media that manipulates us at the most primal level without our knowing and understanding. Advertisers link their products to our primal desires – intimacy, sex, social approval, while political actors manipulate our tribal minds to attack their political opponents. Once you understand that *media is about our primal desires*, then you understand 50% of what's happening on the media you consume.

law 3: technology never moves backwards

If you were hoping that someday soon things would "go back to normal", then I have some bad news for you. When technology changes our society, things never return to the way they were before. Technology changes societies (and the minds of the people within them) completely. The only possible circumstances in which technology would stop moving forward would be some kind of extraordinary catastrophe; a nuclear war, an asteroid impact or a super-volcano eruption. Aside from a world-ending event, technology will continually move forward.

All technology has unintended consequences and not even the inventors of technology can control or predict what their inventions will be used for. The mechanical clock was originally invented by Benedictine monks who needed a way of timing their rituals of worship to god. They didn't realise that they had also invented a mechanism for synchronizing and controlling the actions of men. How would the Benedictine monks feel if they knew that their invention was being used by businesses to profit themselves and to run a system of capitalism based on the accumulation of money? One African tribe was completely transformed by the introduction of matches into their society. Members of this community believed it was necessary to light a new fire after each act of sexual intercourse. Consequently, sex was a rather public event; as anytime intercourse happened someone had to go to a neighbouring hut to grab a fresh stick to start a new fire. This meant that adultery within this tribe was rare – which is probably why the tradition started in the first place. With the introduction of matches, it became possible to light a new fire without going to a neighbour's hut. In a flash, a long-standing tradition was eradicated and adultery in secret became possible, completely transforming the sexual habits of this tribe. The invention of online dating apps like Tinder or OKCupid are likely transforming the sexual habits of our societies around the world in a similar way. Many people moan and gripe about how dating technology has changed the ʼing scene in a negative way, but remember, technology never moves backwards. Now that dating technology is here, it's here to stay, and things will never go back to the way they were before, no matter how much you may detest the act of choosing a partner swiping left or right on a photograph. You either adapt to the new environment, or get left behind.

Many people also detest the use of photo-retouching and filters to improves one's appearance. Photo-retouching allows people to reshape their own face and body, from very subtle modifications to dramatic ones. If you had asked the public in 2008: *do you think it would be a good idea if teenage girls were able to easily photoshop images of themselves?* The public's answer would have been an overwhelming: NO. And yet the technology was invented, the public got hold of it, and individuals wanted to use it to give themselves an advantage in their social lives and on the dating market. Within the space of a few years, photo-retouching has become commonplace. Today, teenage girls all over the planet (this technology is global, remember) are editing images of themselves on their smartphones. Are there negative psychological effects of this? Probably. Did we ever really have any power to stop this technology? Not really. The forward march of technology is unstoppable.

In the same way, weapons of war have become more and more advanced – to the point of being so destructive that they have the ability to destroy the entirety of humanity. The nuclear weapons used on Hiroshima and Nagasaki in 1945 pail in comparison to the size of the damage that can be caused by the hydrogen bombs available in 2020. Do we want these weapons to exist? No. Do they exist? Yes. Technology marches forward whether we like it or not, bringing with it both the good and the bad.

law 4:
media is about profit

For almost all media, the central goal of the creators is to make money. That's not to say there aren't movies, video games, pieces of music and other forms of media that are made purely for creative expression. It's to say that in a capitalist society such as ours, most media is business. In some way or another, most media wants to create money for itself. That could be in the form of a direct transaction from your bank account to theirs. It may be through selling your attention to advertisers, or perhaps through selling your data to them. As has now been made famous by the documentary *The Social Dilemma (2020): If you don't pay for the media, you are the product.* With some media, the transaction is simple. You pay a sum of money up-front for the movie, video game or other piece of media that you want to consume. Then you enjoy the media. Simple. Things get more complex, however, when the media is offered to you for "free".

Facebook is a "free" piece of media. You can simply create an account and begin using Facebook, without ever having to enter your credit card details. But remember, when the media is free, you are the product. Facebook sells your attention (as well as your data), to advertisers. Other companies can then buy Facebook Ads to put their advertisement in front of your eyeballs. The more attention you give to Facebook, the more money they make from it. What does this mean? It means that Facebook will do everything in its power (and within the law) to keep your attention for as long as they possibly can. If that includes purposefully trying to addict you to their platform, then so be it. They've become incredibly effective at keeping the attention of users, using all kinds of psychological tricks (which will later be discussed in this book) to manipulate their users into keeping their eyeballs on Facebook. Facebook may be "free", but the true price you pay is that your limited time and attention gets stolen by the psychological manipulators working for Facebook. As another example, the dating app Tinder may be free to download from the app store, but the entire platform is designed to encourage you to eventually pay for their premium services: Tinder Gold and Tinder+, or buying extra "boosts" and "superlikes". Upon joining Tinder, the algorithms on the app purposefully show your profile to a large number of potential dates. Within the first week, most users find they get a large number of matches. This gives them a good first impression of the app, and also hooks them onto the platform. After the first week, most users experience a disappointing drop off in matches. This isn't a coincidence, the algorithm purposefully reduces the number of people this user's profile is exposed to. The "boost" option then begins to seem particularly attractive, because it allows their profile to be seen by more users. In exchange for the "free" Tinder app, you get your romantic life and self-esteem manipulated by algorithms. (This is the same algorithmic pattern that can be found across all dating apps).

Netflix autoplays the next episode of the TV show you're addicted to because it wants to increase the overall watch-time on the platform and charge more for movie creators to have their movie placed on Netflix (on children's accounts, the autoplay feature cannot be switched off. Why do you think this might be?). News media selects particular kinds of news from the news marketplace in order to get as much attention as possible and sell their audience's eyeballs to advertisers. World events are frequently sensationalised, exaggerated and blown out of proportion in order to attract more viewers, often scaring the living daylights out of much of the audience. You watch the news for "free", yet in the process of watching most news networks, your world-view is distorted and the world is showcased in fashion far more negative than reality (bad news sells, good news doesn't). In order to receive the news for "free", you put your mental health at risk (psychiatrists frequently suggest that their patients with depression stop watching the news). Mobile games that are "free" base their entire game around the goal of getting players to make in-app purchases or micro-transactions to pay for virtual in-game items. The gameplay of most mobile games in 2020 goes something like this 1. The early game experience is fun, exciting and enticing. 2. After a short while, the player falls in love with the game. 3. As the game begins to get harder, it becomes impossible to progress further without spending money on virtual items within the game. The central aim of game isn't to entertain you, it's to take your money.

Media isn't made for you. It's made for the creators of the media. And the aim of most media is to create profit. Don't be a sucker. Recognise how each piece of media is trying to take from you.

law 5: you are in the media hierarchy

Everyone has a place in the media hierarchy, whether they're aware of it or not (Except perhaps **The Outcast**, a rare fellow). With every piece of media that you consume, you fall somewhere on the hierarchy. Where you're positioned on the hierarchy is determined not only by whether you're inside or outside media institutions, but also on your mindset and level of education in media literacy. You will also switch between positions on the hierarchy based on your mindset at any given time. I've given this hierarchy 7 categories: The Addict, The Unconscious Masses, The Conscious Consumer, The Outcast, The Conspiracy Theorist, The Employee and The Manipulator.

THE ADDICT

This character is in big trouble. A particular type of media has managed to creep itself deep inside their brain and ruin their life. They wake up every single day feeling an uncontrollable thirst for this particular type of media. It could be video games, pornography, social media or mobile games. This character is having the unfortunate experience of being on the wrong end of a behavioural addiction. This *behavioural addiction, of course, is knowingly sold to them and encouraged by the creators of the media.* The media producers are milking this individual for every dollar they have. They've hooked them on their platform and they're draining the life out of them; turning it into profit. The addict is most likely between the ages of 12-20 as the teenage brain is the most susceptible to behavioral addiction, although older addicts are still common. Social media addicts are more likely to be female and video game/pornography addicts are more likely to be male. Media producers are taking advantage of our current time period, when incorporating behavioural addictions into your media is *still legal.* The law hasn't kept up with advancing technology, therefore there are no laws against using manipulative and addictive techniques in video games and there are no barriers between pornography and young teenagers.

If you find yourself in this category, good luck. Behavioural addiction is hard enough for fully grown adults to overcome, let alone teenagers. If you are in this age group, chances are high that you don't even recognise your addiction yet. Because education hasn't kept up with technology, you may consider addiction as something associated only with drug addicts or cigarette smokers. Nobody told you that playing an online MMORPG can be like playing with drugs. Some in this category are aware of their addiction, others are in denial. But they all realise the reality of their addiction eventually. On the plus side, those that manage to become aware of and overcome their addiction have learnt an important lesson about media that our next group, the unconscious masses, have never learned.

THE UNCONSCIOUS MASSES

70% of the herd fall into this category. Here you will find the basic bitch and the basic bro. Those in this category have a number of limitations on their mind that they're not even aware of. They receive all of their news through mainstream sources, so much of their world-view is created for them by somebody else. *The only news they talk about is the news they're supposed to talk about.* They feel as though they're being intellectual as they discuss the talking points being spouted on mainstream news programs, not ever considering that the very framework for discussion has been set out for them ahead of time. Never noticing that *certain conversations* never seem to appear on their screens or in their newspapers. If they live in the west, they support western foreign policy. The wars on the other side of the planet are justified and unquestionably right. If they live in China, there is nothing negative about the Chinese Communist Party (CCP). If they live in North Korea, then King Jong-Un is a glorious leader. *It doesn't matter where in the world they live, those in the unconscious masses will always believe that the actions of their own country are morally right.*

For those in this category, the news is trustworthy They can rely on the news to give them an accurate portrayal of the world around them. They don't need to spend time reading books or seeking out alternative viewpoints, because the mainstream news has a good handle on that for them. Their idea of success is given to them. If they're a young man, success is living inside a rap video. Making it rain. Surrounded by hot girls, money and expensive cars. If they're a young woman, success is being chased by handsome men, taken away on a private jet and be proposed to in an exotic location. Or perhaps it's having the perfect Instagram page and being envied by girls and ogled by men. They're kept inside their online filter bubble, in fact, they have no idea what a filter bubble is. They don't notice that all of the content they read online seems to agree with their own views. They've never really tried to seek out alternative points of view and can't understand how the opposite side of the political spectrum can possibly have views so different to their own. They watch TV and sit through the commercial break without thinking about hitting the mute button. They're confident that advertising doesn't work on them, yet in the real world they often act out the advertiser's messages perfectly.

They have an underlying belief that their happiness will be achieved after they hit their next financial milestone. They keep up with the Jones's. Image is very important to them. They spend money they don't have on things they don't need. They live paycheck to paycheck or they're in debt. They buy brand new cars. They take out 30-year mortgages. They accumulate credit card debt. They eat junk food filled with high levels of sugar and a long list of chemicals. They start their day by immediately checking their smartphone. They're big fans of Instagram and Facebook. They get excited with each new notification and they carefully design their social media pages, they stalk the pages of their friends and make comparisons. They swipe the newsfeed for at least an hour every single day. Sometimes, they stumble upon a article or video that makes their blood boil, so they hop onto the comments section and get into arguments with others (an argument in which neither side is actually listened to). They may even get so angry, that they share the article with their friends. Never do they consider, that the subject of the article was never the point. *That the point was user engagement through outrage.*

They can't read between the lines because they don't understand how the media works. And they don't consider any motivations of media other than the ⁀arently self-evident primary motivation: *News articles just tell the news.*

Social media is just to keep up with friends. TV adverts are just, well, part of life. They feel in control, while never considering that they're being pulled around all day by agendas that are not their own through media outlets.

THE CONSCIOUS CONSUMER

This character likes to read. They see books are the most accurate way to get information. They notice the effects of media in the people around them and in themselves. They have an interest in understanding the ways in which their subconscious mind runs them. They understand that most of their actions are driven by biological urges and social conditioning. They understand that their mind has weaknesses that can be exploited and that advertising works on them. When it comes to politics, they don't bother with TV news or newspapers, other than to get the essential facts. They ignore TV debates, scandals and promises made by politicians. They read manifestos and then find out the chances of these policies actually being implemented, then they find out whether the opinions of a candidate are dictated by money from corporate interests, or whether the candidate truly believes in what they say (a rare thing). They will consider not only the debate itself, but also *the framework in which the debate is held.* And they will consider questions that are outside of the debate framework provided to them by mainstream media; *Are both political parties essentially the same? Is my government good or evil? Is my culture good or evil?* Is there some important factor not being discussed in this debate? They notice when the apps on their smartphone skilfully take their attention against their will. They notice product placement. They notice that they hear the same 30 songs everywhere they go. They take note of their mental state when using social media. *They see the dark side of the artificial happiness and the light in the overwhelming darkness shown to them by media.* They instinctively start reading between the lines, every time a piece of media comes their way.

And they ask questions: *What is the aim of this media? How does this media make money? Can this media be trusted?* They doubt themselves. They consider the possibility that everything they think they know could be utterly false. They consider how even the fiction they enjoy may have shaped their world-view and their personality. They notice small details - how the news anchor stumbles while reading the auto-cue behind the camera, or when businesses use dark patterns to try and steal more of their money. They look at conspiracy theories with an open mind, while understanding that unseen manipulators include both elaborate plans by people and other non human forces like market forces and coincidences. And finally, they live in the real world, not the fantasy one.

THE OUTCAST

This is a rare character, especially in the west. This rare fellow has never been exposed to media. They live outside society. They don't watch TV and they don't use the internet. They have a world-view closer to that of our ancestors. They're more in-tune with nature. They've never heard of Donald Trump. They don't have a Wifi password. Their interests are simple. Family, friends, sex and food. They live in the present moment. Their attention is focused and undistracted. They don't know what's happening in the world outside their family or tribe (and they don't care). The only people they compare themselves to are their immediate family and friends. They wake up at sunrise and sleep after dark. Their sense of time is dictated entirely by the sun. They've never heard of diabetes, obesity, or McDonalds. They eat a limited selection of food grown or hunted from whichever land they reside in. Life is a day-to-day struggle, but they meet each day with enthusiasm and a laser focus. They're not depressed. They may die early, through disease, accident, or a hungry predator. Or, like those on the Ryukuyu islands south of Japan, they might live a healthy and active lifestyle all the way into their 90s.

THE CONSPIRACY THEORIST

This character doesn't trust the media. At all. The media is a lie. The system is a lie. The only truth is to be found in conspiracy videos on Youtube and in online blogs in the depths of the internet. They accept anti-mainstream theories instantly. The moon landings are fake. 9/11 was a hoax. HAARP is changing our weather. The Illuminati is depopulating the earth. The earth is flat (please note, these theories are not equal in credibility). All of the world's problems come down to a few elites at the top of society manipulating everybody else. *There are no coincidences* and the government is out to get you. They know the truth and they are outside the system. So they couldn't possibly have biases of their own. They couldn't possibly be living inside an own echo chamber of their own creation, filled with other conspiracy theorists with the same world-view. They enjoy their conspiratorial view of the world because its a fun hobby and because it's something to *distract them their own shortcomings in the real world.* If they're unsuccessful in life, they don't feel so bad about it, because the blame is being placed elsewhere. On the government, the 1% or the illuminati. In some cases, they're acting out the psychological defence mechanism of displacement. Others subconsciously feel more comfort in the fact that there is a small group of people controlling the human race than the probable reality that nobody is control, nobody is leading the way and nobody knows what's going to happen.

THE EMPLOYEE

This individual knows the workings of a specific kind of media all too well. If they work in advertising, they know all of the tricks found in every piece of advertising. They speak in a different language. They talk about sales funnels. Exposure. Demographics. Pychographics. Target markets. If they work in app development, they know every little trick that apps use. While they are well versed in their particular area of media, they may well be completely blind to other areas. They may be an expert in advertising techniques but watch mainstream news without question. They may know everything there is to know about app development but may spend their spare time viewing endless hours of pornography. As they work inside media institutions, they may find it more difficult to see things clearly than The Conscious Consumer as they're often too close to the action to be able to see the bigger picture. Groupthink inside these media institutions means these individuals may not have an accurate understanding of the world outside the institution.

THE MANIPULATOR

The advertiser. The business owner. The world leader. The influencer. These individuals and groups are at the top of the media hierarchy. They send their agenda down through the media hierarchy and influence every character their message meets along the way. (Except for The Outcast)

The advertiser sees members of the public as walking dollar signs. Everybody is a mark. They're either a dumb mark (somebody who is unconsciously manipulated into buying their product) or a smart mark (somebody who understands what the advertisement is trying to do, but buys the product anyway, either through genuine need for the product or through rationalisation). To the advertising manipulator, it doesn't matter why they buy, as long as they buy. Ethics don't factor into the equation. Either they believe that their manipulation is justified, or they want power for their own selfish reasons themselves. The effects their mass advertising may be having on the mental health of the public is not important, instead what's truly important is that people buy as much of their product as possible. A small number of people in Silicon Valley working for companies like Facebook, Instagram and Youtube, use their algorithms to manipulate the behaviour of millions of people around the world. They have the power to influence public opinion and elections. Third parties can use these social media tools to cause civil unrest or "subvert" other countries if they so wish. Russian elites may use Facebook to influence the opinions of the American public, and perhaps vice-versa.

The influencers, the ones who own the news sources and those inside the government, use the news to control discussion. They are not the all knowing, all wise entity that the conspiracy theorists like to paint them as, but the mass media gives them an incredibly useful tool for controlling their own populations. They have major influence over the mainstream media, and they can often control the narrative that comes out of it. These people live in a different world. In this world, the stakes are much higher and the numbers are much bigger. Some may be driven by power. Some may be trying to do what's best for the humanity. We have no real access to these people, so understanding the extent of their control over the media and the public is difficult to know. But it's safe to say that those under their influence are often completely unaware that they're being manipulated.

Where do you stand in the hierarchy? Media is often about power. As the consumer, you're at the bottom of the food chain. Businesses manipulate their customers through advertising and dark patterns. Political powers manipulate the public's opinion through news media. When you watch media, consider where you stand on the media hierarchy. You should consider the motives of the creators of media and how you may be being manipulated by them.

chapter 3

"THE NEWS"

Joseph strolled through his town one quiet Sunday morning. The weather was cold but the sky was blue, with a pleasant amount of sunshine warming one side of his face. Horses trotted past being led by their carers, local people chatted happily together in the town square and children ran between them giggling and shouting. Joseph thought of his wife and children back home, all of whom were no doubt still sleeping peacefully in bed. 'It's a good morning', Joseph thought to himself.

Joseph was a tall man with a large frame, and he intimidated many of those he came across. But his close friends knew he was more of a friendly giant than a dangerous beast, and wasn't all that impressive in the intelligence department. He was here in the town square to buy something extra delicious for his children's breakfast – they always got a treat on Sundays. He browsed the various stalls in the marketplace selling fruit, vegetables, bread, meat and a few exotic spices from distant lands beyond the stone walls of the town. He picked up an apple from one of the fruit stalls to check it's firmness. "I'll take six of these ones" he called over to the stall owner.

"Right ya are" shouted back the plump woman behind the stall. He began placing the apples into this basket, when one fell to the floor and rolled into an alley nearby. Joseph tutted to himself and followed the apple down the narrow alleyway. Turning the corner, he noticed another stall. This one occupied by a strange looking figure wearing a black hood over his face – low enough as to only leave his nose and mouth visible. Curiously, Joseph approached the stall; it was lined with rows of strange black orbs that appeared to be made of glass – the likes of which Joseph had never seen before. Something about them seemed otherworldly to him.

"'Scuse me sir" Joseph asked politely, "What might these be?".

The hooded man spoke quietly and mysteriously, "These are orbs of truth. They tell you about the world outside your limited gaze".

"Are they...magic?" Joseph asked apprehensively.

"We know not of the methods used to create the orbs of truth. Only that they never lie", the hooded figure spoke confidently.

"So 'ow does it work then? You shake it or 'summin?" Joseph asked.

"You need only speak the words: 'tell me the truth', into the orb, and it shall do as you ask. Go ahead and try for yourself".

"Uh..ok", Joseph held the orb of truth up to his mouth and spoke "Mornin' Mr Orb of truth. Would ya mind if ya could tell me the truth?"

The orb glew red and began to whisper faintly back to Joseph in response: '4 men were murdered in the city yesterday'.

Joseph was a little startled. He had heard of a recent murder from the baker Mr Thompson, but according to the orb there were 4 yesterday. Sounds true enough, Joseph thought to himself.

"I'll take one"

"As you wish", replied the mysterious orb salesman. "There is one more thing I must tell you. The orb contains 30 charges. Once you've used the orb 30 times, come here and get it recharged for a fee of three shillings".

"A deals a deal" Joseph replied cheerfully.

Joseph, while initially apprehensive about the orb, quickly became rather fond of it. Everyday, right after waking up, he would ask the orb for the truth of the day. The messages he had received so far were: 'Councillor MacDonald was caught having an affair with a village girl', 'protests over teachers payments rage on' and 'prisoner escapes jail and injures a local man'. Joseph liked the orb, it made him feel as though he knew more than the average townsman about the goings on around the city.

"Dad. What's that?" His young daughter interrupted him as he held the orb up to his mouth to ask it for the truth once again.

"Oh this? It's a truth orb. It tells the truth ya see", Joseph answered happily.

"Can you ask it where mummy is?" his daughter asked inquisitively with a wide-eyed expression.

Joseph chuckled "No darling the orb only tells me about important things. Big things going on in the world."

"Can you ask it why daddy has such a big nose?" his daughter asked with a mischievous grin on her face. In a flash, Joseph grabbed her and wrestled her to the floor as she broke into fits of hysterical giggling.

Several weeks passed. And Joseph had now used a total of 60 charges on his truth orb. He had used the previous 30 charges in just 10 days, and now he was on his way back to pay three shillings to get his orb charged once again. He had taken the time to lock his door carefully, remembering that the orb had told him that theft was on the rise. As he strolled through the town square like usual, he noticed his friend Mr Samson sitting on the steps by the town hall and approached him.

"'Ows the 'ol armory business comin' along?" Joseph asked patting him on the back in a chum-like manner..

"Oh ya know. The usual humdrum.." replied Mr Samson boringly.

"Well. I'd keep an eye-out if I were you. The bakers over on Elderberry street were burgled last week"

"Really? I never heard about that.."

"Can't be to careful these days. Best be off! Cheerio matey!" Joseph said with a smirk and a wink, before continuing across the square.

As he was walking home, he pulled the orb out of his pocket and asked it for the third time that day, "Orb, tell me the truth". The orb responded immediately: A woman was raped in Bishops District last night. Joseph shook his head and continued home.

* * *

After several more months, Joseph had used a total of 672 charges on his truth orb, using an average of 2 charges every single day. He felt uneasy. The orb had told him that a councillor had predicted the harvest to be poor this year, and that this may lead to a food shortage in the near-future.

His wife interrupted his thoughts, "Darling...why is our basement filled with bread" she asked in curious disbelief.

Joseph shook his head at his wife's ignorance. "These are tough times. Gotta be prepared".

"Prepared for what darling?", his wife asked puzzled

"Mind ya damn business darlin', and close the door would ya?"

His wife rolled her eyes and left him be, closing the door behind her. Joseph took the orb from his pocket and spoke into it as had now become habit, 'A new plague has been discovered on the outskirts of the city. 4 killed so far'. Joseph was alarmed. He began shaking his head and spoke to himself "what is the world coming to, honestly..".

* * *

Another month passed. Joseph had been going out less; only leaving home when completely necessary. His wife had noticed that Joseph's previously positive and charming temperament had dulled somewhat of late. She noticed that he would often sigh, shake his head and mutter to himself. He now frequently made comments under his breath: "We live in tough times", "things ain't getting better," and of course, his favourite, "What is the world coming to?" She began to feel that she didn't enjoy being around him any more and, truthfully, she wished he would leave the house more often.

Finally she had to speak up, "Joseph, what's the matter with you these days? You always have a frown on your face and you're always in the most dreadful mood", his wife said trying to keep her voice free from frustration. Joseph wanted to avoid the conversation, but his wife had that look in her eyes. The one that said : you're going to tell me everything right now.

Joseph quickly gave in and sighed. "I don't know Sophie, things just seem so hopeless at the moment. We have so many problems and our council are too selfish and corrupt to change anything. Everyone's just out for themselves, people ain't there for 'ya like they used to be" Joseph spoke staring at the floor. "So many thieves, murderers, rapists, everywhere 'ya look. And now this new plague going about.."

"What plague?" his wife interrupted in a frustrated tone. "I haven't heard of any plague".

"I heard it through the orb.." Joseph replied.

"The orb? What are you talking about?"

"I got one of them truth-telling orb thingamajigs from the market." He pulled out the small black orb from his pocket and held it in his hand.

His wife held a befuddled expression on her face, "How does it work?"

"Dunno, some kind of magic I suppose"

"And how do you know it's telling the truth?"

"Well the man told me that.."

"Oh! The man told you did he? Well, if the man who sold you the orb told you that it magically tells the truth, he couldn't possibly be lying about that could he! Christ almighty..." Joseph's wife stormed out the room, slamming the door behind her.

Joseph opened his mouth to shout after her. But something stopped him - the thought that she might be right. Was the orb telling him entirely made up stories? What if the orb wasn't telling the truth at all? Now that he thought of it, he was yet to see any of the orbs truths with first-hand. The plague, the food shortage, the thieves; he had never seen any of them with his own eyes.

"Damnit, maybe she's right" he said aloud to himself. Perhaps that orb seller was a con-man and he'd played him for a fool. He had blindly believed that if it was magic, it had to be telling the truth. He thought of the piles of bread in the basement and felt a wave of embarrassment. Very quickly, the embarrassment transformed into anger.

"Orb of truth my arse.." he said aloud.

He decided he was going back to the orb salesman to give him a piece of his mind, and perhaps a piece of his fist too.

* * *

Joseph marched through the town square, passing all the happy townsfolk milling around. These people don't seem to know of any plague, he thought to himself. He turned the corner of the alley to find the orb salesman standing there as always with his black hood covering half his face. He grew angry at the very sight of him. Joseph marched right up to him without saying a word, grabbed him by the scruff of his neck and slammed him up against the wall.

"You're a bloody liar!" Joseph shouted into his face, "This thing tells nothing but lies and made up nonsense!".

The orb salesman's hood fell back to reveal the face of a podgy, ordinary looking man, with a wide-eyed look on his face. "Please sir..put me down. I can explain.."

"Well ya'd better! And fast!" Joseph released his grip on the man but kept him pinned up against the wall.

"Look...The magic instilled into the orb is perfect. The orb will always tell the truth no matter what."

"Codswallop! It said there was a plague goin' round. There ain't no plague!"

The orb salesman was terrified in the presence of Joseph's large, intimidating presence. He stuttered his words as he spoke, "I.f...if the orb said there is a plague.. then th..there must be a plague. But look! There are 300,000 people in this city. It's not unusual for a plague to infect a few people in a city of this size.."

"What about the crime?! The theft?! The murder?! I ain't seen none of that happenin'!"

"Well..come now sir..there's always going to be some of that going on. That's just how people are. In a city of this size there'll always be crimes for the orb to inform you about.."

"But this bloody orb's got me thinkin' all this bad stuff is happening when it ain't!"

"That may be so sir..but the orb never lies"

Joseph's anger flared up once again. "What's your game you filthy little rat!?"

The orb salesmen grew even more desperate, "Please sir! I just sell the orbs. That's it I swear! Look..ok I'll explain. The orbs are designed to encourage the customer..that's you.. to use and buy as many charges as possible."

"What're ya' goin on about now?" Joseph muttered angrily

"The magician who created these orbs just wants to make money. He realised that customers would buy more charges if the orbs told negative truths more often instead of positive ones. That's why it told you about the plague, the crime and so on.."

Joseph calmed down a little and allowed the orb salesman some more room. He was still somewhat confused by the salesman's explanation. "So...is there a plague or ain't there?"

The orb salesman breathed a sigh of relief, "I'm sure there is a plague sir, but perhaps it's the proportions you're confused about. If a few people get sick our city of 300,000 people it's probably not much of a problem.

"So...the city is safe..?" Joseph replied apprehensively.

"Oh yes sir. The city is doing better than ever. We have more food than ever, these are the best times we've had in decades in fact. The salesmen sensed that Joseph had calmed down and decided to take advantage of the opportunity. "So.. would you like me to charge it back up sir? 3 shillings?"

Joseph stood still, thought about it briefly, before throwing the orb against the stone wall, smashing it into tiny pieces and walking away.

the bad news filter – the world isn't as bad as you think it is

The world is fucked.

Climate change. War. Poverty. Deadly pandemics. Corruption. Evil. Rampant crime. Racism. Sexism. Inequality. Overpopulation. Biodiversity collapse. Everything is broken. And humanity is doomed. What's the point in having children if they're going to grow up in a hellish environment? Why should children bother studying at school when climate change is going to destroy their lives? Humanity stands on the brink of collapse and our future will be filled with chaos, pain and terror. Right?

If you agree with everything written above, I'm here to tell you that you're completely wrong. I'm here to tell you that the image you have of the world is distorted, disfigured and wildly inaccurate. Even the smartest people you listen to may be completely wrong about the state of the world.

In a survey by Ourworldindata.com, the following question was asked to citizens from multiple countries: "All things considered, do you think the world is getting better or worse?"

The percent of people who answered "better":
United States - 6%
United Kingdom - 4%
Australia - 4%
China - 41% (take note of this)

The first reason people are pessimistic about the future is because they're uneducated about a number of important statistics about the world that I will show shortly. The second reason is that people (even the smartest among us) don't understand how the news environment is distorting their entire world view - causing them to view the world as far more negative than it actually is. The world is a complicated place. Nobody knows everything and nobody can predict the future. But I'm about to explain why your view of the world may be far more negative than the reality.

THE BEST NEWS IN THE WORLD
(THAT YOU NEVER HEARD ABOUT)

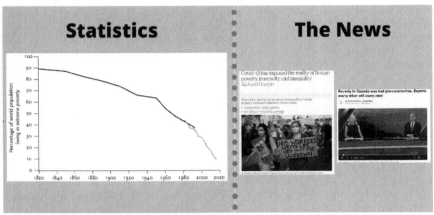

EXTREME POVERTY HAS PLUMMETED, ESPECIALLY IN THE LAST 40 YEARS.
OURWORLDINDATA.COM, ROSER & ORTIZ-OSPINA 2017, BASED ON DATA
FROM BOURGUIGNON & MORRISON 2002 (1820-1992) - FROM STEVEN
PINKERS: ENLIGHTENMENT NOW

"If you had to choose a moment in history
to be born, and you did not know ahead
of time who you would be—you didn't know
whether you were going to be born into
a wealthy family or a poor family, what
country you'd be born in, whether you
were going to be a man or a woman—if you
had to choose blindly what moment you'd
want to be born, you'd choose now".

—Barack Obama, 2016

While all of the worst news you can imagine had been fed to you on a
consistent basis, the best news in the world happened quietly, completely
⌐noticed by you. In almost every possible measure, living in the world

has drastically improved. Less war. Less crime. Less poverty. Less premature deaths. Less disease. Less car crashes, Less plane crashes. Less death from natural disasters. Less racism. Less sexism. Less homophobia. The question is - did you even know this was the case? You form your picture of the world through the news, not through statistics. Most of the information you receive about the world outside of your immediate surroundings must pass through the filter of the news. What is this filter? One in which bad news sells and good news doesn't. It doesn't matter how many different news sources you receive your information from. All news passes through the bad news filter before it reaches you. News is about things that happen, not things that don't happen. You never hear a news reporter say: "I'm here reporting from a country that has been at peace for the last 40 years", or a headline that says: "Local school is not involved in a mass shooting". Bad news often happens quickly, while good news appears gradually. Sudden events get clicks, slow change doesn't.

Now, the idea that "the world is getting better", is certainly up for debate. Some would accuse me of having a "modernist" world-view, while others would point out that the overall number of people in poverty has increased, as the world population itself has increased. Yet, even if the picture painted here is a little too rose-tinted, it's still a more accurate version of reality than the hellish landscape you often see on your screens.

This news environment is so omni-present that you actually think you came to your conclusions about the state of the world by yourself.

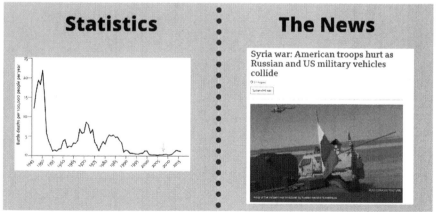

OURWORLDINDATA.COM, ROSER & ORTIZ-OSPINA 2017, BASED ON DATA FROM BOURGUIGNON & MORRISON 2002 (1820–1992) - FROM STEVEN PINKER'S: ENLIGHTENMENT NOW

What you forget is that almost everything you know about the world was not experienced first-hand. Almost all of your information about the world passed through the bad news filter. So you probably think the world is far worse than it actually is. And you might be completely oblivious to the incredibly good news humanity has had over the last 70 years.

For most of human history, war was the natural pastime of governments and peace was a mere respite between wars. Right now, we live in the most peaceful time of human history. Consume enough news, however, and your brain will be filled with stories of constant war around the world. You may even begin to get the impression that war is increasing dramatically, when the exact opposite is true. Wars take place today and wars took place in the past, so people conclude that "nothing has changed"—failing to acknowledge the difference between an era with a handful of wars that collectively kill in the thousands and an era with dozens of wars that collectively killed in the millions.

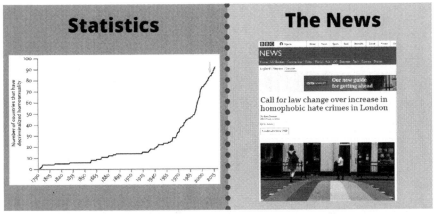

OTTOSSON 2006, 2009. DATES FOR AN ADDITIONAL SIXTEEN COUNTRIES WERE OBTAINED FROM "LGBT RIGHTS BY COUNTRY OR TERRITORY," FROM STEVEN PINKER'S: ENLIGHTENMENT NOW. OURWORLDINDATA.COM

In the past, homosexuals had to live a life of secrecy; they had to hide their sexual identities their entire lives or risk being rejected by their social circles and families. Today the world is more accepting of the LGBT community than any other time in human history. All around the world (with some exceptions), homosexuality is becoming decriminalised; from Africa to Asia, LGBT rights are becoming more and more accepted. This is great news, right? Well, if you consumed enough news, you'd think that the LGBT community was being discriminated against more than before. Consistent news articles about homophobic attacks leave you

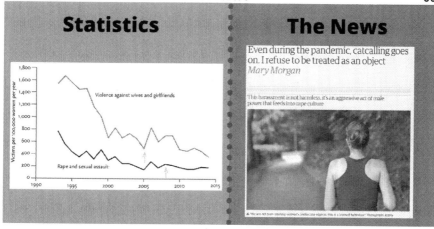

PHYSICAL ABUSE AND SEXUAL ABUSE (MAINLY BY CAREGIVERS):
NATIONAL CHILD ABUSE AND NEGLECT DATA SYSTEM,
HTTP://WWW.NDACAN.CORNELL.EDU/, ANALYZED BY FINKELHOR 2014;
FINKELHOR ET AL. 2014. FROM STEVEN PINKER'S: ENLIGHTENMENT
NOW. OURWORLDINDATA.COM

with the impression that we live in a deeply homophobic society, despite the incredible positive statistics. Once again, all-round positive news passes through the bad news filter and comes out negative.

While violence towards women was relatively common in the past, today it's much rarer. Most modern cultures have unanimously decided that violence towards women is completely unacceptable. Rapists are shamed and jailed (when enough evidence is available to convict them). While rape was incredibly common throughout history, today we have less rape than ever before. Entire villages would be attacked, raped and pillaged on a regular basis. With every war throughout history, rape was rampant. Husbands would be brutally murdered and women would be raped and kept as slaves. There is less violence towards women today than any other time in human history. But once again, watching or reading the news doesn't give this impression at all. The current narrative on this topic is that we live in a "rape culture", women are constantly harassed and that toxic masculinity needs to be eradicated to fix the problem. Why is there no celebration whatsoever for the incredible progress made in this area? Because almost every single person in our society receives their information through the bad news filter. People have built up an impression of this topic overtime through reading news headlines, instead of looking at statistics. The outline of the discussion around domestic violence and rape is set by the news. Everybody else then has their discussions within this outline. None of this is to say that we shouldn't try to continually improve in this area, it's to say that while we keep trying to lower the number of sexual assaults, that we also appreciate the progress that's already been made.

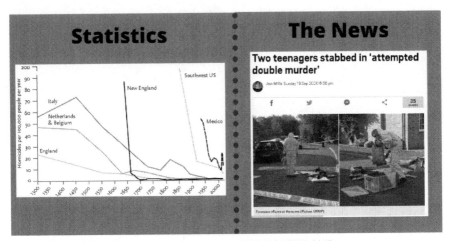

FROM STEVEN PINKER'S: ENLIGHTENMENT NOW AND OURWORLDINDATA.COM.

Sources: England, Netherlands & Belgium, Italy, 1300-1994: Eisner 2003, plotted in fig. 3-3 of Pinker 2011. England, 2000-2014: UK Office for National Statistics. Italy and Netherlands, 2010-2012: United Nations Office on Drugs and Crime 2014. New England (New England, whites only, 1636-1790, and Vermont and New Hampshire, 1780-1890): Roth 2009, plotted in fig. 3-13 of Pinker 2011; 2006 and 2014 from FBI Uniform Crime Reports. Southwest US (Arizona, Nevada, and New Mexico), 1850 and 1914: Roth 2009, plotted in fig. 3-16 of Pinker 2011; 2006 and 2014 from FBI Uniform Crime Reports. Mexico: Carlos Vilalta, personal communication, originally from Instituto Nacional de Estadística y Geografía 2016 and Botello 2016, averaged over decades until 2010.

In the past, with no CCTV cameras, no forensics and a less present police force, murders were easier to get away with. As you can see by the graph, homicides have plummeted. You are safer walking the streets today than ever before (on average, depending on where you live). But this piece of good news has not been reported to the general public. Many people believe that their country is rife with crime. If they live in America, they may believe they need a gun to protect themselves because there are so many criminals around them, even if their neighbourhood is extremely safe.

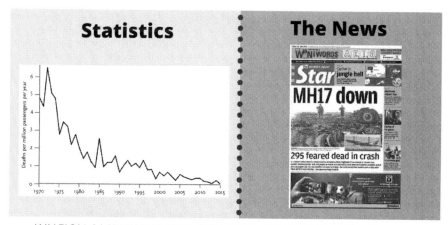

AVIATION SAFETY NETWORK 2017. DATA ON THE NUMBER OF PASSENGERS ARE FROM WORLD BANK 2016B. FROM STEVEN PINKER'S: ENLIGHTENMENT NOW

Flying has become the safest form of transport available. We can now fly all around the world, at a relatively cheap price and with near perfect safety. The chance of being killed in a plane crash has been reduced to around 1 in 11 million. What an incredible time to be alive! What other generations of human beings had the opportunity to see the world like we do? What a success story. And what great news! If you told generations of the past this news they would be overjoyed. But not us. Somehow, our system of "news" takes this incredibly positive story and still manages to pull out the small amount of bad news available. The only time the news talks about the aviation industry is when there's a crash or some other sort of problem. The incredible success story of this part of our lives is never mentioned by the news, and thus, is never appreciated by most of the public.

Think the world is a dark, scary place? All you have to do is head onto Youtube, watch some travel Vlogs and you'll soon find out the idea you had about various parts of the world was completely wrong. Because the news not only passes through the bad news filter, but also comes through a cultural filter. If you live in America, you consume mostly American news. If you live in Australia, you consume mostly Australian news. If you live in the west, you probably have a western perspective on the world.

Because of the western perspective that your media feeds you, you may still believe that the world consists of "The west and the rest". In the past

Child Mortality

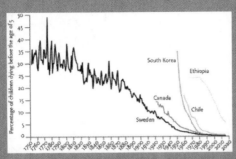

Life Expectancy

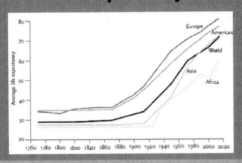

Education

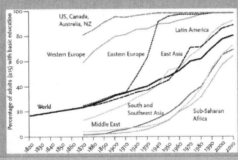

Vehicle Safety

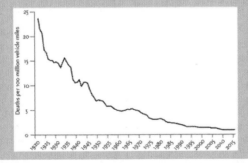

OPPOSITE: HONESTLY, WHAT BETTER NEWS COULD YOU POSSIBLY ASK FOR? WHAT ELSE COULD POSSIBLY BE CALLED "GOOD NEWS". (ALL GRAPHS AND SOURCES CAN BE FOUND IN STEVEN PINKER'S: ENLIGHTENMENT NOW OR ON OURWORLDINDATA.COM

there was an enormous gap of wealth between the west and the rest of the world. But the world has changed. We no longer have a giant wealth gap between the developed world and the third world. What we have now is a gradual slope. Asia is now richer than Europe, South-East Asia is generating wealth rapidly—even Africa has seen a massive increase in wealth over the last 20 years.

China and Korea have transformed from impoverished countries into world leaders. Thailand, Vietnam, Cambodia, Indonesia and the Philippines (all of which were previously dirt-poor countries) are quickly following their example. Just ask yourself: When you think of Vietnam, what image comes to mind? The Vietnam War? It ended 45 years ago. Vietnam now contains shopping malls, skyscrapers, a thriving tourism industry, high-quality education and fast internet connections.

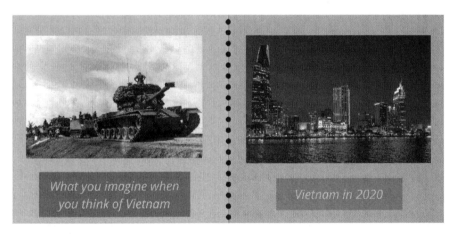

What you imagine when you think of Vietnam

Vietnam in 2020

The developing world has been rapidly lifted out of poverty over the last 50 years and nobody seems to have noticed. What news could possibly be better than a massive reduction in world poverty? Seriously, I challenge you to try and imagine a piece of news more positive than this. Yet the media barely reported it and almost nobody talks about it.

Iran

Q: "If somebody was thinking about coming to Iran, but they were maybe scared of the thought that they were going to get into trouble or a terrorist attack, what would you say to them?"

A: "I should say..don't listen to other people that say such stuff. Because it's a really, really nice country. It's a very safe country".

Somaliland

Q: If you had one thing to say to the world about Somalialand what would it be?

A: "Hey man, it's a great vacation. Come!. You see the ocean, great people here. There's not bad people. It's safe over here, it's not violent. People not going to kill you. Nothing like you see on TV."

"The amount of wealth that I've seen here is so unexpected. Range Rovers, Chevolets, Mercedes, you can't believe it"

Indigo Traveller Travelling Through IRAQ

NOT THAT SOMALIALAND OR IRAN DON'T HAVE MAJOR PROBLEMS, BUT THAT THERE ARE MILLIONS OF PEOPLE WHO EXIST WITHIN THESE COUNTRIES WHO HAVE A PERFECTLY SATISFYING LIFESTYLE (NOT WHAT YOU IMAGINE WHEN WATCHING NEWS COVERAGE OF THESE COUNTRIES). TO GET A MORE REALISTIC UNDERSTANDING OF WHAT OTHER COUNTRIES ARE ACTUALLY LIKE, WATCH TRAVEL VLOGS LIKE "INDIGO TRAVELLER" ON YOUTUBE (PICTURED ABOVE).

South Korea 1950's **South Korea Today**

Even Africa, which The Economist once called "The Hopeless Continent" in the year 2000, now shows promising economic growth. Overall, the proportion of people in Africa living in monetary poverty has clearly declined, from 54% in 1990 to 41% in 2015. If the current trends continue, Africa's absolute poverty rate will fall to 24% by 2030. What incredible news! Do you remember hearing about it on the news? Me neither.

In the west, many of us still imagine the world as it was 50 years ago.

We fail to notice just how much has changed in the developing world—they have skyscrapers, good education, fast internet access, luxury cars and the ability to travel around the world. None of this isn't to say the developing world doesn't still have huge problems to deal with, but that, in general (debatably), the news overwhelmingly good.

THE NEWS IS MAKING YOU UNREASONABLY PESSIMISTIC

Despite these facts, many people believe that humanity is doomed. The system is broken, the apocalypse is drawing near and some even believe that *humanity is a cancer on the planet that needs to be eradicated.* Perhaps you also feel this way to some extent. But you have to ask yourself: What information did you base these conclusions on? And where did you receive this information from? Did you look at actual data? Or did you just watch a lot of news media and gradually form a picture of the world in your head? It doesn't matter how smart you may be, if your information sources are flawed then you're misinformed. And if you got your information from news media, then your information sources *are* flawed.

The news is not an accurate reflection of reality. It is a very specific part of reality that is plucked out of the entirety of world's events. It doesn't matter if you get your news from multiple sources because almost all news media works in a very specific fashion in order to appeal to human beings. The news isn't an omniscient god that reports the reality of the world exactly as it is, instead the news consists of groups of human beings trying to report stories that other humans are likely to be interested in. Slow change isn't news. Fast change is. Good things tend to happen slowly. Bad news often happens fast. Therefore, bad news will always outweigh the good in news media. On top of that, almost all news media is a business. Their goal is not to accurately report facts about the world, their primary goal is to sell stories and make profit. Bad news sells. Good news doesn't. The truth is often boring and nuanced, the truth usually doesn't make good headlines or gripping news articles and the truth doesn't follow any particular narrative. Human beings love stories, and we like to build up a story of the world inside our head, even if that story is a tragedy. Data that comes along that doesn't fit with that story is confusing, doesn't follow the narrative inside our heads and is thus ignored. (The world is getting better? Impossible!)

People will adamantly tell you that the world absolutely is getting worse. Because of this problem, and that problem, and this problem. But never do they consider that all of their information about the world passed through the bad news filter that's inherent in all news organisations. The world is enormous. And there are more than 7 billion human beings on the planet, so there will always be cases of bad news. If crime is decreasing, there will still always be enough crime to fill the newspapers. Even if the crime had dropped to 5 crimes per day in each country, that would still be more than enough to fill the newspapers full of crime stories on a daily basis. In the same vein, even if the news is overwhelmingly good, there will always still be enough bad events to fill newspapers, because the world is simply so complex and huge. People also mistake their discovery of bad events in the world with the birth of those bad events. The truth is, these bad events existed before you found out about them, all that changed is that you heard about them for the first time through a news outlet. You've been exposed to more information, discovered more of the world's bad news and then falsely concluded that the number of these bad events are increasing. But the only thing that's really increased is your access to information. The world has always been full of darkness, only it's now (arguably) less full of darkness than it's ever has been.

For many, the news environment has such a grip on them that they can't possibly imagine the world in any way other than what's been presented to them on their screens. But what's the reality of the world really? When you watch the news, you make a quiet assumption that it's at least somewhat representative of the real world. But instead think of this: What are your neighbours doing? What are strangers in your town doing? What are random people in Belgium doing? What are people doing in Sydney? That's the world. The truth is, the majority of the world is made up of people simply going about their everyday business: people going to work, people eating, people talking with their friends, people sleeping. Normal human things. This is 99% of the story of humanity. But none of this will ever appear on the news.

WHAT'S THE REALITY OF THE WORLD? THE CHAOS ON YOUR SCREEN OR THE QUIET PEACE IN THE ROOM THAT SURROUNDS IT?

OBSESSION WITH THINGS OUTSIDE YOUR CONTROL

Because of media, you have access to all of the world's biggest problems. You can find out all about global warming, war, wealth inequality, poverty, politics and Donald Trump's tweets. *Exposure to all of the world's problems with no ability whatsoever to solve them.* These problems will continue to appear on your screens and you'll continue having no power to have any affect over them. It's like an itch you can never scratch. Constant messages of potential future danger (global warming) will make you anxious over and over again. With no way of eliminating the source of the anxiety. Constant messages of outrage will make you angry over and over again. With no way of eliminating the source of anger. Messages of injustices and evil deeds will continually encourage you to lose faith in humanity.

If you're worried about a job interview you address the anxiety by going and practising interview questions with a friend. If you're worried about an exam, you can go and study. If you're worried about money, you can get a second job or work overtime. The anxiety caused by these problems can be addressed because they're within your personal control. But what happens when you're worried about global warming? Or worried about the potential for nuclear war? Or about the latest pandemic? What actions can you possibly take to address your anxiety of these huge insurmountable problems? The anxiety caused by these problems cannot be addressed because they're outside your personal control. These unaddressed anxieties will continue to cause you stress as they continue to appear on your screens. Media may make you feel as though you have a birds-eye view of the whole planet, but you're not god. You're one individual among 7 billion. You are limited. These problems are entirely beyond your control, yet the media will continue to remind you of their existence. This is a source of anxiety you otherwise wouldn't experience if it weren't for the phone in your hand. During the COVID19 pandemic, many people had the experience of a "death spiral" while scrolling through their social media news feeds and browsing the rest of the internet. 20,000 cases here, 100,000 cases there. Millions of people around the world were quarantined inside their homes hiding from a dangerous virus, but far worse than that, they were stuck with the internet. During the pandemic, the internet made the toll on people's mental health far worse than it would have done were it not for our constant access to bad news.

If you want to have a positive effect on the world—choose a problem and then take direct action towards solving that particular problem. Sitting around and reminiscing about a problem you have no control over does nothing other than spike your anxiety levels. Stop obsessing over things outside of your control because your screens keep feeding you anxiety inducing stimuli. Ask yourself "What actions can I take to solve this problem". If the answer is "nothing", then you have to let it go. Not burying your head in the sand and pretending the world is perfect, but setting boundaries as to which problems you'll concern yourself with.

"No amount of anxiety makes any difference to anything that is going to happen" - Alan Watts

THE NEWS MAKES YOU SCARED OF THE WRONG THINGS

The news chooses stories based on the principles of the news marketplace, they want exciting or interesting stories that will draw in large audiences. How does this affect your perception of danger and risk? Well, it often means that *the more common or likely a danger is, the less it will be reported in the news.* Car crashes in America kill approximately 37,000 people per year, yet people still feel perfectly safe as they text and drive at the same time. The very same person replying to a Facebook message while driving may be genuinely afraid or concerned about a terrorist attack, a plane crash or a potential paedophile in their child's school. All of these events are, of course, incredibly unlikely. *People aren't afraid of what they should be afraid of.* People are more scared of ghosts than they are of the Mcdonalds Hamburger they're eating and large coca-cola they're drinking. One is probably a figment of our imagination (although you never know), and the other can cause heart disease, which kills 600,000 Americans every single year.

Why are we so awful at estimating risk? Well, partly it's human nature. Flying in a metal tube in the sky, at high speeds, unable to get off when you want to, relying on a pilot you don't know and have never met before is a recipe that's far more likely to make us anxious than driving in a car down a street near your own home. But the other side of the sto involves the news scare cycle. The news knows that if it produces fearful stories, it will draw in larger audiences. As the saying goes: *If it bleeds it leads.* So over the years, news organisations have learned which stories sell and which don't. Through trial and error, they've discovered which things human beings tend to be afraid of; unlikely, sudden, dramatic negative events get eyeballs. Anyone who frequently watches the news is exposed to weeks of coverage on the latest terrorist attack, with all of the details of the incident being reported in great detail. At the same time, the latest statistics on car crashes appear just briefly in news crawls at the bottom of the screen. Coverage of the terrorist attack includes multiple interviews of victims of the incident describing their experience of the horrific incident in great detail. The news will lay out the story step by step, almost as though it was a movie. *It was a quiet, beautiful morning in Paris. Just like any other day. Who could have known that 50 innocent people would soon be brutally murdered.* The viewer gets a visceral image of the attack in their mind. They get to imagine how it would feel to be caught up in such an attack themselves and how they might act in such a situation. *Would I run? Would I hide behind the door and jump on the terrorist when they walked in? Would I escape through the window and climb down the pipes?* Car crashes, on the other hand, are generally reported as statistics. *40,000 people died in automobile accidents this year in America.* This is forgettable. It doesn't form any particular image in your mind and is therefore not remembered. The subconscious brain of the viewer takes this information and comes to the conclusion that terrorist attacks are a major danger to watch out for. On the other hand, your subconscious brain has very little exposure to car crashes and therefore decides they can't be as much of a threat. We have one particular cognitive mechanism that scientists call the availability heuristic, which is essentially a mental shortcut that relies on immediate examples that come to a person's mind when thinking about a particular topic. There are 2 main rules to the availability heuristic: 1. If it can be recalled, it must be important 2. More recent information is more strongly recalled than older information.

200,000 years ago, if we often saw members of our tribe die from a bear attack, we would rightly become afraid of bears and learn to stay away from them. Our lizard brains don't understand the difference between a dangerous stimulus seen on a screen and a real danger, so if we often see visceral images of terrorist attacks, our lizard brain may believe that this a legitimate danger that we need to watch out for in our daily lives (**Law 2: Technology Is An Evolutionary Mismatch**). When the latest statistics for heart disease appear on our screens, we may think logically: *well, that's bad isn't it.* But emotionally we just don't *feel* it. Seeing the latest statistics on heart disease probably isn't going to do much to change an obese person's eating habits. If that very same individual sees their obese friend across the street die of a heart attack, that's an incident that's far more likely to impact their behaviour.

Governments around the world have begun to understand all of this and use it in their anti-smoking campaigns. Multiple countries around the world now have graphic images on their cigarette packages showing rotting teeth, lungs covered in black tar and all kinds of disgusting, visceral images. Simply writing *"smoking is harmful to your health"*, doesn't appeal to our lizard brain at all. Our lizard brain needs to see something to believe it, and it's our lizard brain that controls our emotional responses. Smoking rates are declining around the developed world and the WHO agrees that graphic images on cigarette packages are part of the success story.

why people get upset about the wrong stories

"One death is a tragedy. A million deaths is a statistic"- Commonly attributed to Stalin

Let's look at two stories.

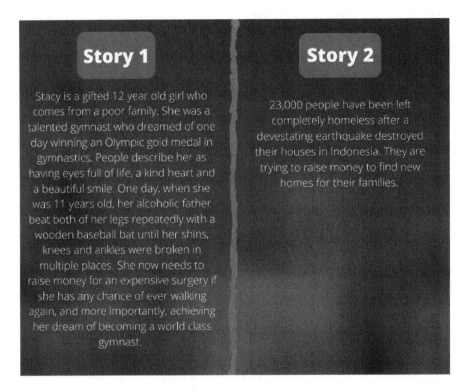

Story 1

Stacy is a gifted 12 year old girl who comes from a poor family. She was a talented gymnast who dreamed of one day winning an Olympic gold medal in gymnastics. People describe her as having eyes full of life, a kind heart and a beautiful smile. One day, when she was 11 years old, her alcoholic father beat both of her legs repeatedly with a wooden baseball bat until her shins, knees and ankles were broken in multiple places. She now needs to raise money for an expensive surgery if she has any chance of ever walking again, and more importantly, achieving her dream of becoming a world class gymnast.

Story 2

23,000 people have been left completely homeless after a devestating earthquake destroyed their houses in Indonesia. They are trying to raise money to find new homes for their families.

After reading each of these stories, which one makes you feel the most sad? Which cause would you be more likely to donate money to? Do you value the lives of those in one story more than the other? A rational thinker might conclude that the 23,000 homeless in Indonesia is a much sadder situation than the single 12 year old girl. Then again, human beings aren't rational. In a rational world, our sadness would increase linearly based on the number of victims. If 1 person died, we would be sad. If 1,000 people died, we would be 1000 times sadder. But human beings aren't machines, and our psychology isn't rational. Americans were collectively devastated by the 2,977 deaths on 9/11, yet the 600,000 (and counting) deaths from COVID19 don't seem to have caused too much of an emotional response. British people were enraged by the murder of soldier Lee Rigby on British soil by a Muslim extremest, but there was far less anger about the 3977 civilian causalities in March 2003 during the first month of the Iraq war in which the British military took part in. The public consistently gets upset about the wrong stories.

"Harm to a particular person invokes anxiety and sentiment, guilt and awe, responsibility and religion (but)... most of this awesomeness disappears when we deal with statistical death" - American Economist Thomas Schelling

Human beings are evolved to live in tribes of around 150 people. The entire structure of our brain developed in a world where we lived in small tribes; as such we can't fully comprehend the enormous societies, filled with hundreds of millions of people, we now find ourselves in. We can logically and rationally understand that 10,000 have died in a tragedy, but we cannot emotionally understand a tragedy of this scale (**Law 4: Media Is An Evolutionary Mismatch**). If a single person dies, we might cry and mourn. If 100,000 people die all we can do is shrug and say *"wow"*. Our brains simply don't have the capacity to understand these kinds of numbers. The more people who suffer from a tragedy, the less we care about them. When people are affected by a disaster, a kind of psychological numbing occurs. Though people are capable of feeling deeply for a single victim and their plight, "compassion fade" can set in when a tragedy involves large numbers of victims.

The identifiable victim effect shows us that people are more likely to help a single person about whom they have personal information than unidentified or statistical people. Kogut and Ritov (2005) found that donation appeal letters that ask for donations for a lifesaving cure are more effective when they show a single ill child than when they show 8 children with the same illness. They are even more effective when the child is identified by their name, age and picture. Charities

NATIONAL SOCIETY FOR THE PREVENTION OF CRUELTY TO CHILDREN.

Incorporated by Royal Charter.

Patron - - • -   THE QUEEN.

Director and Secretary, Rev. Benjamin Waugh.

THE SOCIETY'S PAST WORK OVER ENGLAND, WALES, AND IRELAND.

It is not possible to give any adequate sense of the meaning of the following figures :—

403,168 sufferers from neglect and starvation.

69,597 sufferers from violence.

27,344 little things exposed to draw charity.

12,079 small victims of immorality.

8,441 children in improper and hurtful employment.

Whilst ranging from 14 and 16 years downwards, a pitiable proportion of the children have been under five years old ; literally thousands of them were small babies.

By discovering, warning, supervising, and, where necessary, prosecuting, these evils have been stopped, the children delivered, and often, to an astonishing degree, the parents themselves reformed.

Estimated deficit at close of year, £13,460. Cheques should be crossed, " Bank of England, Law Courts Branch," and made payable to Hugh Colin Smith, Esq. (Treasurer), 7, Harpur-street, London, W.C.

EVEN THE EARLIEST CHARITY ADS WERE AWARE OF HOW LITTLE STATISTICS EMOTIONALLY AFFECTED PEOPLE.

have known for quite some time that it's better to focus on individuals rather than numbers, which is why charity ads tend to use images of a single suffering child rather than focusing on statistics.

Media is primal. In our tribal environment, statistics didn't exist. On the other hand, the suffering of children in our tribe did exist. That's why big images of suffering children can make us emotional, while text saying "80,000 children are homeless in the UK" doesn't. The attention we pay to different tragedies around us, is not based on their objective level of horror, but is instead based on the way in which they invoke emotions in us. People's emotional reaction to a tragedy is not based on the scale of the horror, rather it's based on the fashion in which the tragedy occurred and the media coverage of the trajety. Obesity

kills an estimated 300,000 per year in the United States. Much of this is due to a food industry that purposefully creates addictive foods in order to make profit. Yet this is a slow moving, boring tragedy that is only witnessed first hand by doctors in hospitals, so Americans don't spend much time crying over this enormous problem despite the huge amount of suffering it's caused for American citizens. On the other hand, the terrorist attacks of 9/11 that killed 2977 people (less than 1% of yearly obesity deaths), caused Americans to tear up, sing the national anthem and wage war in revenge. It was the dramatic, public fashion of the tragedy that caused people to react this way. The buildings collapsing to the ground, people jumping to their deaths, firefighters being buried underneath the rubble—this is why people reacted emotionally in the way they did. According to the data (which is up for debate), COVID19 killed 425,000 Americans in the space of a single year, yet despite the enormous number of deaths, many people seem quite disinterested in this tragedy. People responded with remarks like *"Thousands die from the flu every year"*, *"Calm down, people die every day"* or *"Death is a normal part of life"*. Ask yourself, would Americans have ever made statements like this about 9/11 (2977 deaths) or hurricane Katrina (1833 deaths)? People are able to make justifications and dismissals like this because they're emotionally unaffected by COVID death statistics. Many aren't emotionally affected by the COVID19 deaths for various reasons. First, the numbers are simply too big for our lizard brains to understand. Second, many of those who died were elderly or had comorbidities, so one might rationalise that *"they deserved it"* or perhaps *"they were going to die anyway"*. Third, most of the deaths happened behind the closed doors of hospitals away from our eyes and our cameras.

CIVILIAN DEATHS DURING THE IRAQ WAR - 2003 - 2010.

	Jan	Feb	Mar	Apr	May	Jun	Jul	Aug	Sep	Oct	Nov	Dec	Yearly totals
⬍	⬍	⬍	⬍	⬍	⬍	⬍	⬍	⬍	⬍	⬍	⬍	⬍	⬍
2003	3	2	3977	3438	545	597	646	833	566	515	487	524	12,133
2004	610	663	1004	1303	655	910	834	878	1042	1033	1676	1129	11,737
2005	1222	1297	905	1145	1396	1347	1536	2352	1444	1311	1487	1141	16,583
2006	1546	1579	1957	1805	2279	2594	3298	2865	2567	3041	3095	2900	29,526
2007	3035	2680	2728	2573	2854	2219	2702	2483	1391	1326	1124	997	26,112
2008	861	1093	1669	1317	915	755	640	704	612	594	540	586	10,286
2009	372	409	438	590	428	564	431	653	352	441	226	478	5,382
2010	267	305	336	385	387	385	488	520	254	315	307	218	4,167

In the first two months of the Iraq war, over 7000 innocent people were killed. Estimates for the total number of dead civilians during the entire war range from 100,000 to over 1 million. As usual, we're unable to emotionally react to these statistics—because: 1. The numbers are too big for us to understand. 2. The deaths were from the "enemy" and therefore justified in our minds. 3. We didn't see much footage of these deaths as the western media downplayed the atrocities, instead only focusing on American and British military deaths. As we didn't see Iraqi civilian deaths with our own eyes, our lizard brain doesn't believe they actually occurred. 4. Our main exposure to the Iraq war came through movies like *American Sniper (2014)* and *The Hurt Locker (2008)*, movies that generally avoided dealing with the topic of Iraqi civilian deaths.

The public frequently get outraged about things that don't matter, and fail to get outraged about the things that do. Governments and media manipulators know which stories make the public upset and which don't and use this to their advantage.

In 1990, teenage girl Nayirah gave her testimony describing Iraqi soldiers taking babies out of incubators and leaving them to die on the floor. This point was then repeated over and over again by news outlets as well as President George H.W. Bush. This had a dramatic impact on American public opinion towards the gulf war in Iraq, and two months

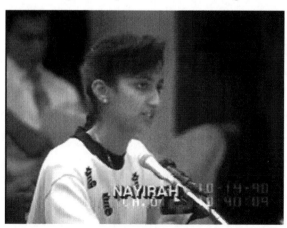

"I SAW THE IRAQI SOLDIERS COME INTO THE HOSPITAL WITH GUNS. THEY TOOK THE BABIES OUT OF THE INCUBATORS, TOOK THE INCUBATORS AND LEFT THE CHILDREN TO DIE ON THE COLD FLOOR. IT WAS HORRIFYING."

afterwards, the gulf war began. As it turns out, Nayirah's testimony was completely false. She was actually the daughter of Saud Al-Sabah the Kuwaiti ambassador to the United States, and her speech was created by American public relations firm Hill & Knowlton. This PR firm crafted a story that was perfectly designed to outrage the public. They conjured an image in the minds of the American public of innocent babies being thrown onto the floor and left to die. This story hijacked the public's natural instincts to protect children and used them to gather support for the war. The most telling line of her speech is when she says "left them to die on the cold floor". Would a normal person add the word "cold" in this sentence? Only a speech writer for a PR firm would add the word "cold" for dramatic effect like this. Which stories the public gets upset about is entirely predictable. Media manipulators know this, and use it to their advantage. (**Law 5: You Are In The Media Hierarchy**)

In 2020, a video of police officer Derek Chauvin kneeling on the neck of a man called George Floyd went viral. George Floyd died from this incident, and it sparked nationwide "Black Lives Matter" protests that continued for months. Statistics about racism towards blacks would never have inspired that much emotion in people. *No protest has ever started because of a newly released statistic.* Instead, what it takes to spark anger is the right video in the right situation. Certainly, you might say that the video simply sparked a large amount of anger that had been building amongst the black community for a long time. But that's the point. It took a video pushing particular buttons to go viral before this anger transformed into protests. When we see a man being choked to death while pleading for his life with our own eyes, we get angry. When we hear statistics about the numbers of incidents (many of which just as horrifying as the George Floyd incident), we don't get emotional about it. We get emotional about the same things we would have dealt with in our tribal environments. Seeing someone being choked to death pushes our evolutionary buttons while reading statistics does not.

"BATKID"
MILES SCOTT
POSES WITH
BATMAN

Miles Scott was diagnosed with lymphoblastic leukemia (a form of leukemia) at 18 months old. The Make-A-Wish Foundation, helped by a social media marketing agency, sent out an email asking for supporters.

The project was a wild success, and by the time the event came around, the Batkid had over 12,000 supporters. They staged an entire roleplay around the city of San Francisco, with actors, props and even a fake media broadcast asking the Batkid for help saving the city. There were multiple scenes, one with a damsel in distress and one with a villain called "The Riddler" stealing money from a bank vault. It was an enormous event, with countless resources dedicated to it, all in the name of a single child. The social media campaign was so effective because it focused it's efforts around a single child and thousands of people were touched by Miles's story and offered to help. If the campaign had asked for help in treating the illness of 10,000 children with cancer, it wouldn't have been nearly as effective.

The problem with all of this is that public policy decisions often reflect what the public cares about. And if the public continually gets upset about the wrong things, then our governments will continually put their efforts and resources towards the wrong problems. Next time you see a statistic saying 12,000 people have died, don't shrug your shoulders and say "*wow*". Remember that each and every one of those people was an individual with their own hopes and dreams, and had family who loved them just as much as you love your own family. Instead of seeing the statistics simply as numbers, imagine a stadium filled with people. If 80,000 people have died in a tragedy, then look at the image below and understand what 80,000 looks like. And try to rethink which stories you get upset about, and which you don't.

THIS IS WHAT 80,000 PEOPLE LOOKS LIKE (STADE DE FRANCE, PARIS, FRANCE)

mass shootings

"Violence is our quest for identity"
- Marshall Mcluhan

A 29-year-old man walks directly into Pulse nightclub in Orlando carrying an assault rifle and a handgun. He opens fire into an unsuspecting crowd full of unaware 18-40 year olds.

After brutally murdering countless innocent victims, he retreats into the bathroom. He pulls out his phone and checks Facebook, he wants to see if he's made it on the news.

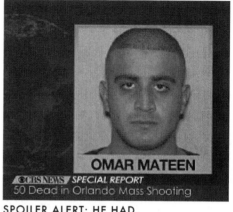

OMAR MATEEN

CBS NEWS SPECIAL REPORT
50 Dead in Orlando Mass Shooting

SPOILER ALERT: HE HAD.

What makes a mass murderer? That's not an easy question. It can be a crazy person, hearing voices and experiencing delusions. It can be a psychopath, killing without any empathy for their victims. It can be an act of revenge on a particular group of people, or simply the world itself. It can be a suicidal individual who figures they may as well take others to the grave with them. It can be for ideological or religious reasons. But for many, they commit mass murder because they want notoriety. They want to be remembered. Now these people are not special. And they're not clever. They've been around for a long long time.

HEROSTRATIC FAME

These kinds of people can be found as far back as 356 BC. Demonstrated through the legendary tale of Herostratus. One night, on 13th October, 356 BC, Herostratus crept into The Temple of Artemis and burnt it down from the inside. The people of Ephesus watched in horror as their pride and glory burnt before their eyes. Herostratus ran out to happily greet them. He made no attempt to hide what he had done. Instead, he boasted about his crime to everybody watching. He proudly told everyone his reason for committing the crime: *To be famous.*

Herostratus was a nobody. he had no riches, No achievements. And he wanted his name to live through the ages. He was executed immediately. The Ephesians wanted to ensure his plan of becoming famous was never achieved, so they hereby made the act of mentioning the name "Herostatus" illegal. But in later centuries, after the fall of the Ephesian civilisation, historians started to use his name once again. Herostratus had achieved his goal. His name is still remembered to this day and is has outlived even the judges who sentenced him to death. Named after him, a term was coined. **Herostratic Fame:** *Fame deliberately acquired by destructive means.* A kind of fame desired by many of the mass shooters today.

KILL PEOPLE, GET FAMOUS

"His face splashed across every screen, his name across the lips of every person on the planet, all in the course of one day. Seems like the more people you kill, the more you're in the limelight" - Oregon 2015 shooter - killer of 9 teenagers.

"When you see me on the news you'll know who I am. You're all going to die. Pew! Pew! Pew!" Parkland 2018 Shooter - Killer of 17 students

"Infamy is better than total obscurity. I never knew how to gain positive attention, only negative" - Isla Visa shooter - Killer of 6 people

"Everyone knows that mass murderers are the cool kids." Sandy hook shooter - Killer of 20 children.

"I know we're going to have followers because we're so fucking godlike." - One of two Columbine Shooters in 1999 - Killers of 13 people

"I'll see you on National T.V.!" 2011 Tuscon shooter - Killer of 6 people (Who then later appeared on national TV).

Is what they said wrong? When you think of the most famous mass shootings of the past, what do you remember about them? The victims? The victim's parents? The school teachers who sacrificed their lives to protect the children? Or do you instead remember the names and faces of the shooter themselves? You may remember the following names (especially if you're American): Adam Lanza, Eric Harris, Dylan Klebold, Omar Mateen, Nikolas Cruz. You may also find that a face springs to mind, or that you recognise their face when shown. Isn't something about this sickeningly backwards? That the mass shooters get exactly what they wanted (herostratic fame), while the heroes and victims are completely forgotten by the public. For a time, the mass shooter becomes one of the most famous people in their country and oftentimes, the whole world. For weeks, their face is plastered across TV news stations. internet news and newspapers. Over and over again. Their lives are talked about extensively. We hear from their friends and family. We see footage of his house, his school, where he routinely went for lunch. His motivations are discussed. *Was he bullied? Was he crazy? What kind of person was he? Intelligent? Did he get good grades at school?* In essence, the news media gives the shooter exactly what he was hoping for. If the goal was fame, then clearly they've achieved it.

Many of these shooters even wrote entire manifestos, knowing that the news media would pick it up and showcase them to the world, giving these manifestos an audience of thousands of readers and even admirers. The 21-year old Charleston shooter, who killed 9 people inside a church, left a manifesto describing his hatred for black people. The 39 year old shooter, who killed 69 people on an island in Norway, left a 1500 word manifesto stating his anti-multiculturalism agenda. The Isla Vista shooter who killed 6 people left a lengthy manifesto explaining how unfair treatment women had given him through his life justified his shooting. With each manifesto, the media will discuss its contents in seriousness, showing the manifesto to millions of viewers and debating it. Not only is the shooter remembered, but all of his ideas and beliefs are showcased to the world, as if it's an important document written by an influential thinker. These manifestos often go on to inspire others to create mass murder stories of their own.

Extensive media coverage of mass shooters also creates copycat shooters. The Sandyhook shooter was inspired by the Columbine shooters. The Oregon shooter was, in turn, inspired by the Sandyhook shooter. Each of these mass murderers express admiration for the mass murderers that came before them. Like a sick tradition being passed down the generations. Psychologists talk about a "contagion effect" in which the idea of mass murder can pass from person to person. Mass shootings seem to come in bursts; after a major mass shooting, other smaller shootings or threats of shootings all occur in a cluster. We already know that the contagion effect applies to suicides, self-harm, eating disorders, happiness and sadness, so is it really such a stretch to assume that the same could be true for mass murder? At the very least, it puts the idea in people's heads that mass murder is even a possibility in the first place.

In the past, if somebody decided to kill a handful of people in their tribe, only those close to the event would even be aware that anything happened. But today, if you decide to kill a handful of people, *the world knows*. It's not just a few people in your small tribe that knows your name, it's millions of people. And you have to ask yourself: What does this do to a person? To know that this level of fame and noterity that could be available them. To get the idea in their head, that their name could be in the history books through the decades with one simple act.

How does the news media decide to report on these tragedies? Well, let's take an ABC News report of the Sandyhook massacre:

"Tonight, nobody yet seems to be able to answer the question. Why 20 year old Adam Lanza attacked Newtown elementary school..."Adam Lanaza was the child of an affluent Connecticut town. And the child of divorce. His deadly rampage

began at the family home. Where police say this morning, he first killed his mother Nancy...."After killing his mother, the young man authorities say went to Sandy Hook elementary school. Wearing a bullet proof vest. Authorities say he was armed with a semi-automatic assault rifle and two high-powered pistols."

They sensationalise and dramatise (at least, as much as they can get away with) every aspect of the shooting to pull in as many viewers as possible. It's not the obvious kind of sensationalism you might find in an action movie, instead it's a unique brand of more *subtle sensationalism*. They sensationalise the story while keeping their "respectable news outlet" tone intact throughout.

Let's look at the coverage of mass shooter Elliot Rodgers along with images:

"IS THIS THE LATEST FACE OF EVIL IN AMERICA? AN ANGRY AND PSYCHOLOGICALLY TWISTED YOUNG MAN WHO'S PUBLIC RANTINGS EXPLODED INTO SHEAR TERROR IN A QUIET CALIFORNIA COMMUNITY TAKING 6 YOUNG LIVES AND INJURING 13..."A VIRGIN VOWING REVENGE, IN A TWISTED VIDEO HE POSTED ON FRIDAY. ADDRESSED AT HIS PERCEIVED ENEMIES: YOUNG WOMEN WHO HE SAYS REJECTED HIM. DEEP DELUSIONS, THAT WOULD TURN DEADLY"

Why is language like "the latest face of evil" and "a "a virgin vowing revenge" necessary in a news broadcast? Why is the story told in such an enticing, dramatic manner? Why do we need to see the shooter's face? The news could just as easily be told as follows: *6 are dead and 13 are injured after a shooting in California today* (in the same way you might report the latest car crash incident). And then of course, without a moments hesitation this same news media organisation decides to publish the existence of his manifesto to millions of viewers.

A few years later, this manifesto has become the bedrock to an online Incel (Involuntarily Celibate) community. A toxic community that churned out a 17-year-old high school shooter who went on to kill 10 innocent people.

At this point we have to ask: Why does the shooter get more attention than the victims? Why do they show the shooters name and face? Why do they show the weapons of choice for the murder? Why do they sensationalise and dramatise the event as if the shooter is some kind of action hero? A journalist might tell you that it's their "duty" to report all the facts to their audience. That they're just giving their audience what it wants. But it's obvious to anyone paying attention that the fundamental reason why the news media treats mass shootings the way it does is because *the primary function of the news is to make money for their advertisers* (**Law 4: Media Is About Profit**). An increase of 1-2% in a TV channels Gross Rating Point (A measure of exposure frequency of advertising) means profits of millions of dollars and each news station is competing for eyeballs on the story. *As soon as a shooting happens, the game begins.* Each news channel tries to get the latest scoop, trying to subtly inject an extra dose of drama into the story. If one TV news channel names the shooter, another one has to name the shooter too, else they lose viewers to competing news sources. If one news source is only stating vague facts about the incident and the other is going into detail about the shooters motivations, then people will switch over to the latter news source. After the San Bernadino shooting in 2015, reporters swarmed into the shooter's home after the landlord forced in the door with a crowbar. Reporters from news stations across America fumbled around the shooter's bedroom live on air, desperately trying to find something newsworthy to engage the audience. One viral tweet even shows a reporter rearranging a child's bed to place a teddy bear in view of the cameras, presumably to tug on the audience's heart strings as much as they could.

Now let's make something clear. Most of the individuals working for the news media don't see it this way. For them, they believe in what they do. They go through a lot of discomfort to report the news of mass murders to us. They actually believe they're doing a service to the world for reporting "the facts" to their audience. No, it's not the individuals. It's the fact that the very structure of the news will always be based around advertising. It's a sum of all the parts of the news machine, that will always bend towards feeding the advertisers. It's nobody's fault and it's everybody's fault.

"You show me the incentive, and I'll show you the outcome" - Charlie Munger

Why is it necessary to broadcast the shooter's name and face to the world? Ask yourself, in what way does the public benefit from learning this information? One project from Texas State University (dontnamethem. org) has one simple request for the news media: don't name the shooter, don't show the shooter's face. This very simple tweak would achieve two things: 1. It would deprive the shooters of the herostratic fame that they seek. 2. It would reduce the number of copycat killers that we have to deal with. Instead of their names going down in the history books, their names, faces and their very existence would disappear into the abyss of time – which is exactly what they deserve. You might be thinking to yourself: *You can't censor the press!* And yet we already do. Naked streakers in sports games have their face (And their private parts) censored because it helps stop copycat streakers doing the same thing. The identities of suicide victims are kept secret to prevent the suicide contagion effect. Censoring the names and faces of the shooters is a something any logical and rational news organisation would do. This of course, is quite unlikely to happen. Why? Because all news organisations are financially incentivised not to do this. News is not a public service, it's a business. And businesses will never voluntarily decrease profits. *They will continue to openly publish the names and faces of shooters to make money, despite knowing the risks of causing future shootings.*

"He sought many things from his act of terror, but one was noterity. And that is why you will never hear me mention his name. He is a terrorist. He is a criminal. He is an extremist. But he will, when I speak, be nameless. And to others I implore you: speak the names of those who are lost, rather than the name of the man who took them. He may have sought noterity, but we in New Zealand will give him nothing. Not even his name" - Jacinda Arden, New Zealand Priminister, a rare example of someone treating a mass shooter story in the correct manner.

the brutal truth about the mainstream media

It's been there since the day you were born. The mainstream media. The authority that tells you about the world outside your personal bubble. Your entire nation—millions of people—are informed by it. There it sits. On our TV screens. On our laptop screens. On our smartphone screens. Beaming information through into our consciousness. But what exactly is the mainstream media? Everybody will tell you not to trust the media. Everybody will tell you that the media lies. Some will call it The Liberal Media. Others say that it brainwashes the population. But very few people can actually tell you: How? That's what I'm here to tell you.

"The general population doesn't know what's happening and it doesn't even know that it doesn't know" - Noam Chomsky

Too many people passively accept the messages given to them without ever noticing the strangeness of what they're looking at. Too many people are so completely confused by the mainstream media that they can't tell which way is up and which way is down. Too many people have wildly inaccurate perceptions of the world around them. People continually vote against their own interests. People continually let their behaviour and their speech be controlled by the powerful. And people continue to be completely oblivious of the reality of the world around them. Nobody trusts the media, and yet everyone continually falls for it's tricks. Because they underestimate how deep the rabbit hole goes.

  It's my hope that by the end of this chapter you will have a framework for how the media actually works. And it's my hope that you can use this framework to understand the media for the rest of your life. This is the brutal truth about the mainstream media.

THE NEWS MARKETPLACE

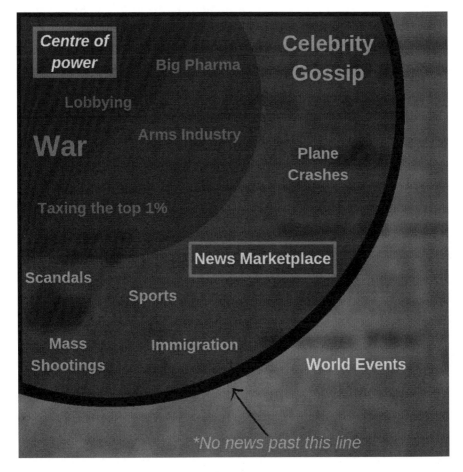

The news is a product to be sold. It's not a reflection of reality. That's the first thing you need to know about media. (**Law 4: Media Is About Profit**) In the world there exists an endless number of possible stories to be chosen as news. There was a car crash in London today. Poverty in Indonesia is down by 4%. Britney Spears shaved her head. The president tweeted something. David drank a coffee in Starbucks today. The war in Yemen is escalating. Liverpool won 2-0 against Manchester City. But out of all the possible stories in the world, only particular stories are chosen. Some stories are discussed relentlessly while others appear as crawls at the bottom of the screen. So how do journalists decide which stories to focus on? You would hope they would choose based on which stories are the most relevant and helpful to the general population. This isn't the case. *Stories are chosen based on what brings in the largest audience.* (This in the outer ring: "News Marketplace" but not necessarily true when the story is inside the inner ring: "Centre Of Power".) Mainstream news costs more than consumers could ever hope to pay. You watch the news for free. So how do they afford to keep producing news day in day out? How do they afford to pay the thousands of staff members? How do they pay for the studio, cameras and other technology? By selling their audience to advertisers. In other words: by selling you to advertisers.

"It is the consumer who is consumed. You are delivered to the advertiser who is the customer. He consumes you"
- Richard Serra

Fox news pulls in around 2,434,000 views during prime time. That's a lot of eyeballs. Advertisers will pay a lot of money to have their product showcased to 2.4 million people. So Fox News earns millions of dollars by selling their audience to advertisers (and catering to their political views to encourage them to keep watching). A good story is worth millions of dollars. That's why mass shootings get such extensive coverage. Because a dramatic story like a mass shooting pulls in large audiences, and large audiences mean large profits. That's why celebrity gossip and scandals get more coverage than the looming superbug crisis. That's why sports get more coverage than rising obesity rates. Because the news selects stories that will bring in the largest audience and make the most profit.

So most stories are chosen based on profit. This leaves the viewer with an incredibly distorted sense of reality. Most news is left in the hands of the news marketplace. But there are certain stories where different rules apply.

WHO OWNS THE NEWS?

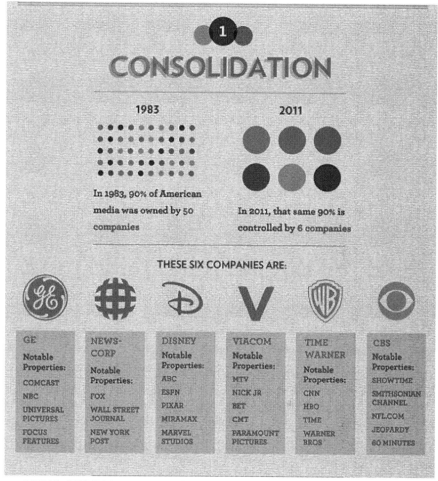

MEDIA OWNERSHIP IS A CONSTANTLY CHANGING LANDSCAPE. AS SUCH THIS IMAGE MAY NOW BE OUTDATED.

(While this section will focus primarily on America, every country has its own unique power dynamics when it comes to mainstream media.

You may think there are plenty of news sources available to you, but in fact all of the mainstream media in America is owned by only 6 companies. A small number of elites have the power to control the narrative of entire nations. (**Law 5: You Are In The Media Hierarchy**) In capitalism, monopolies are inevitable. In all areas, eventually power consolidates into the hands of a small number of people. Media is no exception. That's why the 50 companies that used to control the media in 1983 gradually merged together to become 6. Absolute power corrupts absolutely. And monopolies are dangerous. When monopolies are formed, it's generally the role of the government to break them up and stop them from getting out of control. Unfortunately, the American government itself is influenced by the big 6 media companies through general lobbying and corruption. This creates a group of elites consisting of people in powerful positions in government, CEOs and other people with incredible wealth. A group of elites who have a substantial amount of control over the mainstream media and the narrative that comes out of it. *No matter which country you live in, whenever a story comes close to the centre of power it will be controlled by the elites of that country.* That's simply how power works. While they're perfectly content to let the majority of news be left to The News Marketplace (The outer ring), when a story comes close to the The Centre Of Power (The inner ring) the narrative will be controlled carefully. War, Big Pharma, Lobbying, The Arms Industry. If these issues are discussed freely, the population may begin to realise the evil and injustices that occur in these areas.

You may think all this talk of "elites" and "controlling the narrative" sounds like an insane conspiracy theory. But just take a second to consider exactly what's at stake. We're talking about having influence over the minds of millions of people. Entire nations. The military force to destroy entire countries. And ultimately, control over the human race. Every human society throughout history has been ruled by elites. In the past, we were ruled by kings and emperors. All human societies that have ever existed have had a pyramid-like power structure; with a small number of elites controlling the rest of the population. You think about the peasants of past ages who were controlled by their kings and imagine that situation to have been left in the past. But that situation isn't left in the past. It's our present. Our quality of life has dramatically improved thanks to technology. *But we still have rulers.* These rulers have an incredible tool they never used to have: Mass media. An ability to send messages to millions of people that was never possible in the days of kings and emperors. They use this tool to control thought about any issues that are close to the centre of power (the inner ring). When Julian Assange reveals government war crimes, the elites take control of the narrative and brand him as rapist and a criminal. When Edward Snowden reveals that the NSA is spying on all of us, the elites take control of the narrative and paint him as a traitor and a criminal. When it comes to war, the elites control the narrative of the war through mass media (just as they did throughout the Iraq war). The elites will control the narrative only when it comes to the really important issues close to The Centre Of Power. The rest of the news, that doesn't have any effect on The Centre Of Power is left to The News Marketplace.

THE FRAMEWORK FOR DISCUSSION

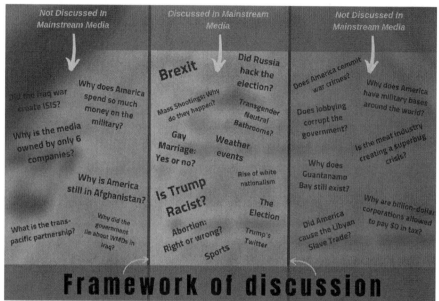

THE FRAMEWORK OF DISCUSSION IS AN EVER CHANGING LANDSCAPE. THESE EXAMPLES WERE CHOSEN AS OF 2019 AND BASED ON AMERICAN MAINSTREAM MEDIA. HOWEVER, NO MATTER THE TIME PERIOD, YOU WILL FIND THAT SOME TOPICS ARE DISCUSSED RELENTLESSLY IN NEWS MEDIA, WHILE OTHERS ARE COMPLETELY IGNORED.

> "The media may not be successful much of the time in telling people what to think, but it is stunningly successful in telling its readers what to think about"
> - Bernard Cohen in 1963.

The media doesn't tell you what to think, it tells you what to think *about*.
Gay marriage. Abortion. Presidential debates. Transgender neutral bathrooms. These issues will be talked to death on mainstream media.

This then becomes part of the cultural conversation. Everyone starts talking about these things. People will argue about the details of each of these issues. And everybody thinks they're an informed citizen. Never realising the far more important questions they're not talking about and never even considered thinking about. Why is the entire mainstream media owned by only 6 companies? This question will never be asked on mainstream. You probably never even considered who owns the media you're consuming because the subject is outside of The Framework Of Discussion. Were you aware that the US has military bases all over the world? If you weren't it's probably because this topic is outside The Framework Of Discussion.

One clear example of The Framework Of Discussion in action was during the COVID19 pandemic, when any talk of the "lab leak theory" was completely absent from mainstream news throughout 2020. Then, in early 2021, when president Biden legitimised the lab leak theory of the pandemic, the mainstream media suddenly began to discuss it.

The media sets The Framework Of Discussion. An invisible set of boundaries that can only be seen by the few who know what to look for. The mainstream media truly is a mind control tool. The media has the ability to control where our attention goes and therefore it controls what we think and talk about. But more importantly, it controls what we *don't* think and talk about. The elites at the top of society have the ability to control what the mainstream media focuses on and what it doesn't focus on. Therefore, these elites have the ability to largely control the minds of their populations. If a news item is covered frequently and prominently the audience will regard it as important. If a subject is not covered the audience will assume it's not important and not worth thinking about. During presidential television debates, the framework for discussion is also controlled. TV networks are able to control which questions are asked and which are not. In presidential TV debates, some questions are never asked: *What percentage of your money came from Wall Street? What would you do about tax avoidance from the top 1%? Do you think the Iraq war was a war crime?* The moderators in these debates only ask questions that are within The Framework Of Discussion. The people listen to the candidate's answers and make their voting choices based on what they hear. After the debates, all of the news outlets discuss the answers each presidential candidate gave. And at no stage has any topic outside of The Framework Of Discussion been mentioned. But it's not only on the

THESE ARE ALL POPULAR TALK SHOWS IN AMERICA. IF YOU LIVE OUTSIDE AMERICA, YOUR OWN COUNTRY PROBABLY HAS SIMILAR TALK SHOWS.

news where The Framework Of Dis is controlled.

Talk shows also stay inside The Framework Of Discussion. All mainstream talk shows are owned by one of the big 6 media conglomerates. The Tonight Show with Jimmy Fallon is owned by Comcast. The Late Show With Stephen Colbert and the Ellen Degeneres Show are owned by National Amusements. The View is owned by Walt Disney Company. Every talk show you see on mainstream television is confined to The Framework Of Discussion because they're owned by the very same media conglomerates the news is. Talk shows will never discuss American war crimes, Tax avoidance by the richest 0.01% or any other topic that could harm the elites. And it goes further than that. Films, TV shows or documentaries that discuss topics that threaten the elites will not be shown either. Every single thing you see on a mainstream network is inside the The Framework For Discussion. *If you watch the mainstream media, what you think about and what you **don't** think about is being controlled.*

THE JOURNALISTS

"Corporate media doesn't want to rock the boat. Corporate media IS the boat" - Phil Donahue

The 6 big media conglomerates are controlling the narrative. But what about the individual journalists themselves? If our media was being

elites, wouldn't there be plenty of journalists ready to
...ods? Absolutely not. Because of the following reasons.

...l Selection

...s you see on mainstream media are not the most talented,
they are si... ply those who hold the correct views. Every journalist on
mainstream media goes through a kind of darwinian process. By the end
of the process the only journalists who are left on your screens are those
who hold viewpoints that please the elites.

Any journalist who has views that the elites don't agree with will
never be hired to mainstream news organisations in the first place.
There are talented journalists who do real independent research, report
honestly on war and have a commitment to finding the truth. These
people aren't allowed on mainstream media. The journalists you see on
mainstream media are the sub-par journalists who have beliefs that the
elites approve of.

2. Access

Iraq War Coverage Comparison

ALJAZEERA

CNN's news coverage on the Iraq War
emphasised stories about the battle and
the US strategy in the war, but paid little
attention to fatalities and civilian
casualties. Furthermore, the news outlet
avoided broadcasting pictures of bloody or
dead civilians and soldiers in its reports. In
general, the American news-outlet painted
a picture of the war that was free from
blood and stood in contradiction to the real
scenes of the war

Unlike CNN, Al-Jazeera showed a picture
of the war full of human suffering. Pictures
of bloody and dead civilians were aired
regularly on Al-Jazeera, painting a more
violent picture of the war than most other
news outlets in the United States

Journalism cannot be a check on power. Because the very system
encourages complicity. Those in power and those who report on power
are on the same team. If you want access to the most important sources,
you need to tell the story how the elites want you to. Access is the holy

grail for journalists. Access means having prestige. Access is the mark of a successful journalist. Access means you get invited to the private parties. If you don't have access, you don't get the prestige and you're not invited to the parties. The journalists with access think they're the best of the best. When in fact they're simply the most obedient. The prestige of a journalist is based on how obedient he is to the elites.

3. Self-Censorship

LEFT: ANDREW MARR - BBC JOURNALIST RIGHT: NOAM CHOMSKY
MARR: "HOW CAN YOU KNOW I'M SELF-CENSORING?"
CHOMSKY: "I'M NOT SAYING YOU'RE SELF-CENSORING. I'M SURE
YOU BELIEVE EVERYTHING YOU SAY. BUT WHAT I'M SAYING IS IF YOU
BELIEVED SOMETHING DIFFERENT YOU WOULDN'T BE SITTING WHERE
YOU'RE SITTING."

The most insidious kind of censorship is self-censorship. Journalists know that there are certain issues they aren't supposed to cover. There are unwritten rules about covering topics the elites don't want talked about. Consciously and unconsciously, journalists will only talk about the things they're supposed to talk about. In totalitarian societies, journalists will self-censor in fear of being killed for broadcasting a message their government doesn't like. These societies exist in our world today, throughout the world. But journalists in democratic societies self-censor in fear of other things. They self-censor in fear of losing their access, being subject to a smear campaign or in the recent case of Julian Assange - being put in jail for revealing the truth about their government.

4. Censorship

American media personality Phil Donahue had a show on MSNBC in 2002 just prior to the Iraq war. He was getting great ratings. In fact, he had the most popular talk show on MSNBC. So he was bringing in lots of cash for the network. He was a strong anti-war voice, insisting that there was no proof of WMD's in Iraq and that starting a war would be an injustice. One month before the Iraq war, his show was cancelled and he was fired. Even though he was making millions of dollars for the network, he was fired because he had an opinions that the elites didn't like.

"The decision to release me (from MSNBC) came from far above" - Phil Donahue

When journalists refuse to self-censor and keep exposing truths that the elites don't like, the mainstream media will actively censor them. But what do they do when a voice emerges from someone who doesn't work for the mainstream media?

5. *The Smear Campaign*

The goal of a smear campaign is to create an association in our subconscious mind between a negative emotion and a particular person. The smear campaign appeals to our caveman brain. Instead of attacking the issue at hand, it attacks the person themselves. It makes us question the victim's character. It makes us see the victim in a negative light. And most importantly, it makes us feel as though the victim is different from us. Julian Assange published leaks from US government exposing the evil deeds that they had committed. One leaked video showed an air-strike in Baghdad of the American military murdering innocent children. At one stage, one of the American pilots said: *"Well it's their fault for bringing their kids into a battle"*. This made the elites furious. Julian Assange isn't part of the mainstream media so he can't be censored. His website, (Wikileaks.com) has a large audience, so he can't be simply ignored. So what else can they do? They can smear his reputation.

The elites have full control over the mainstream media. So very quickly, the mainstream media became filled with negative coverage of Julian Assange. Not just on the news, but on talk shows too. Rather than talk about the content of the leaks, the media instead focused on a different story: that Julian Assange had apparently smeared shit on the walls of the Ecuadorian Embassy (a story that insiders say is completely false). Whether Assange rubbed shit onto the walls or not is entirely unimportant. The viewer certainly doesn't benefit in any way from learning this information. So why

JUST A HANDFUL OF THE ACCUSATIONS AIMED AT JULLIAN ASSANGE.

NOT A REAL JOURNALIST

RUSSIAN AGENT

SHIT SMEARER

TRAITOR

ATTENTION SEEKER

SEX OFFENDER

CRIMINAL

HACKER

did the mainstream media focus on this insignificant detail to such an extent? Because they want the audience to build an association in their subconscious mind between Julian Assange and a feeling of disgust. Smear campaigns appeal to our emotional, subconscious brain. You might agree with the actions of Julian Assange, but after being exposed to the smear campaign of him on mainstream media you might just feel that you don't like him very much. Rationally you might agree with his actions, but emotionally you're not on his team. *It's cool that he exposed the war crimes of the government and all but he **did** smear shit on the embassy walls. So I guess he's a bit of a werido...*Now your thought patterns have changed. Now you're less motivated to support him. And the smear campaign is a success.

Whenever anybody with a large audience challenges the elites, they will be smeared. In the run up to the election any candidate who the elites don't approve of will be smeared. Tulsi Gabbard, an American war veteran running for president was smeared as being unpatriotic. Rationally speaking, this accusation is completely absurd. But it doesn't matter. The smear campaign doesn't have to make any rational sense. It only needs to make you *feel* differently about the victim. Smear campaigns are incredibly common in mainstream media. They can be easily identified; just look for stories that focus on attacking the individual's character rather than the issue itself.

So this the brutal truth about the mainstream media. Behind its friendly and comfortable appearance is a world of lies, manipulation, war crimes, money and psychopathy. The solution to this? It's very simple. Don't watch it. *If your goal is to be informed about the reality of the world, the mainstream media will lead you in exactly the wrong direction.* Consume the mainstream media and you become more confused than ever. Your world-view will be based on the sensationalism of the news marketplace and the manipulation of the elites.

You knew the mainstream media couldn't be trusted. Now you know exactly why.

the smear campaign – how the media destroys reputations

You've witnessed countless smear campaigns throughout your life, but you didn't notice. You've had your opinion about particular individuals shaped for you without your consent on multiple occasions (**Law 5: You Are In The Media Hierarchy**). Think of a politician or celebrity that you dislike. Did you form that negative opinion of them by yourselves, or have you been manipulated? What do you think about Julian Assange? What do you think about Jordan Peterson? What do you think about Russell Brand? Or perhaps there's a politician or public figure in your own country that you dislike. Why do you dislike them? If you believe that you've personally formed all of your opinions about all the famous people you know, then you're severely underestimating the power of the media, and the power of the smear campaign. If you want to have an understanding of what's happening when you consume media, you need to understand the smear campaign. Without understanding what the smear campaign is and how it works, you'll be manipulated just like the rest of the public. Haven't you ever wondered why the media is constantly attacking particular people? Haven't you ever wondered why there are so many claims about anti-semitism, racism and sexism about people in newspapers? Haven't you ever wondered why every single month there's a new buzzword or narrative in the media about politicians?

The following is a comprehensive guide on how a smear campaign works, which I have split into 6 sections:

1.   *Labelling*

2.   *Find a weak spot and attack it relentlessly*

3.   *Remove context*

4.   *Guilty by association*

5.   *Use the right images*

6.   *Don't make it obvious.*

The goal of a smear campaign is character assassination. They're a highly effective technique powerful people utilise through the media in order to attack individuals they don't like. The public are absolute suckers for smear campaigns. It's my hope that after reading this chapter you'll be able to identify smear campaigns when you see them in the media and become less easily manipulated by them. And it's my hope that you'll stop being such a sucker for smear campaigns, and go on to teach others what you've learned.

This is how the media destroys reputations.

1. LABELLING

"If you tell a lie big enough and keep repeating it, people will eventually come to believe it" - Joseph Goebells - Nazi Minister of propaganda

If Julian Assange exposes war crimes and secrets of the American government, they can retaliate with a media smear campaign. They can repeat the same labels again and again on TV news, online news and in newspapers: Criminal, Russian Agent, Traitor, Not a real Journalist, Sex offender. Use the same labels, over and over again, and eventually much of the public will come to assume that these labels have a certain amount of truth to them. After all, there's no way that lies could be told so loudly, so blatantly and repeated so often, is there? The labels will be repeated again and again, often with a straight face and an authoritative tone of voice on TV News (people are easily fooled by non-verbal cues such as these). These labels don't have to be clever, sophisticated or even accurate—they just need to change the way the audience of the smear campaign feels towards the victim. The goal of a smear campaign is to create a link in our subconscious mind between a negative emotion and a particular person. Of course, none of this is new, people have been attacking each other with labelling for centuries. During the American presidential campaign of 1800, Thomas Jefferson was called "an uncivilized atheist, anti-American, a tool for the godless French." The only difference now is that the mass media is able to spread these labels to millions of people simultaneously.

In print media, you can find these labels placed throughout the article in hit pieces. On TV media, you will notice the same terms being said again and again on multiple channels. You might find yourself wondering what this latest buzzword means. You assume this buzzword arose organically, when in fact the buzzword you keep hearing is part of a planned smear campaign that's trying to stick a particular label on somebody.

QUESTION
Will you condemn "Bernie Bro" behavior?
CNN PRESIDENTIAL TOWN HALL WITH SEN. BERNIE SANDERS #CNNTOWNHALL

THE QUESTION IS ASKED WITH THE UNDERLYING ASSUMPTION THAT "BERNIE BRO'S" ARE REAL IN THE FIRST PLACE. THEY AREN'T. IT WAS A NARRATIVE ENTIRELY FABRICATED BY THE MEDIA IN ORDER APPLY A NEGATIVE LABEL TO BERNIE SAUNDERS. BERNIE CAN ATTEMPT TO DEFEND HIMSELF FROM THE QUESTION, BUT WHATEVER HE SAYS, THE LABEL WILL STICK.

For example, during the 2020 US election Bernie Saunders was suddenly stuck with the "Bernie Bro" label. Apparently, Bernie's supporters had been acting abusive online (as are a minority of supporters of all political candidates). Quickly, TV news channel pundits on multiple platforms began sitting around discussing Bernie Saunders's "Bernie Bro" problem as if it was a legitimate problem. Of course, the "Bernie Bro" narrative was entirely fabricated by the media in an attempt to smear Bernie Saunders's reputation.

Let's take a look at another example of the labeling technique at work:

A ☰ Q   Popular   Latest   *The Atlantic*

PETER NICHOLS / REUTERS

Updated at 12:22 a.m. ET on April 15, 2019.   1

2   In the end, the man who reportedly smeared feces on the walls of his lodgings,
     mistreated his kitten, and variously blamed the ills of the world on feminists and   3
4   bespectacled Jewish writers was pulled from the Ecuadorian embassy looking every inch
     like a powdered-sugar Saddam Hussein plucked straight from his spider hole.

FOUR LABELS ARE QUICKLY APPLIED TO JULLIAN ASSANGE:
1. THE SHIT SMEARER
2. ANIMAL ABUSER
3. FEMINIST HATER
4. ANTI-SEMITE.
ALL WITHIN THE OPENING PARAGRAPH.

Notice how the subject of American war crimes is not the focus of the article, instead it focuses on the personal characteristics of Julian Assange. Smear campaigns are character assassinations. They do not attack the issue at hand, they attack the person. We have emotional and tribal minds, so attacking a person's character is often an effective method of changing our opinion about somebody (**Law 2: Media Is An Evolutionary Mismatch**). In particular, the idea that Julian Assange smeared faeces on the wall of the embassy he was trapped inside was repeated again, and again, and again throughout the media. (Of course, this story was unproven). Why did they tell us again and again that Julian Assange smeared faeces on the walls of the embassy? Because it links Julian Assange with a feeling of disgust in our subconscious mind. Those who may have been more vocal about supporting him begin to feel less motivated to do so. Labelling attacks our subconscious and manipulates how we feel, emotionally, towards a particular person.

Let's look at labelling once again in the following hit-piece on now world-famous academic and psychologist, Jordan Peterson:

Psychology   1

How dangerous is Jordan B Peterson, the rightwing professor who 'hit a hornets' nest'? 2

3
Since his confrontation with Cathy Newman, the Canadian academic's book has become a bestseller. But his arguments are riddled with 'pseudo-facts' and conspiracy theories   4

Dorian Lynskey
Wed 7 Feb 2018 15.20 GMT

f y ✉ 3,099 | 2,119

FOUR LABELS IN THE TITLE AND SUBHEADING ALONE: 1. HE'S DANGEROUS 2. HE'S RIGHT-WING (IS HE A NAZI?) 3. HE'S A LIAR, OR STUPID 4. HE A CONSPIRACY THEORIST.

Of course, Jordan Peterson isn't an extreme right-winger. He doesn't present "pseudo-facts", in fact he has over 10,000 citations in academic journals. And he certainly isn't a conspiracy theorist. The accuracy of the labels isn't important, only that they change the opinion of large chunks of the audience against the victim of the smear campaign. Many who read this hit-piece on Peterson will make their mind up about him immediately. From then on, every time they're exposed to Peterson, they will view him through the negative filter given to them by the hit-piece. Those taken in by the hit-piece they've read previously will no longer be able to accurately evaluate the content of the ideas of the smeared individual. Their opinion about this individual has effectively been created for them.

Let's look at another example of labelling being used to target British politician Jeremy Corbyn:

These labels are of course, either outright lies or enormous exaggerations. But, as discussed earlier, the accuracy of the labels are

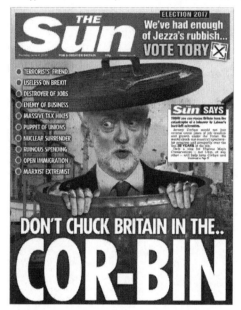

THE SUN TAKES THE LABELLING TECHNIQUE TO THE EXTREME, LISTING THE LABELS RIGHT ON THE FRONT PAGE OF THEIR NEWSPAPER.

unimportant, only that they influence the opinion of the audience. You might wonder if a front cover as ridiculously biased as this could fool any audience. Unfortunately, it can and does. These labels will enter the subconscious mind of much of the audience and influence how they feel about Corbyn.

Labelling is the first obvious sign that you're looking at a smear campaign. If you see a piece of media that focuses on labelling an individual's character rather than the content of their arguments, you're consuming a smear campaign, and should be immediately disregarded as manipulative and untrustworthy.

"It is not propaganda's task to be intelligent, its task is to lead to success"
- Joseph Goebbels
- Nazi Minister of propaganda

2. FIND A WEAK-SPOT AND ATTACK IT RELENTLESSLY

If your opponent has an injured knee, you kick and punch his knee again and again until they forfeit. This is exactly what smear campaigns do. Only in this case the attacks aren't on the victim's body, instead they attack the victim's reputation. Everyone has a weak spot. If you look hard enough you can find it. And if you can't find one, you can create one. Despite Bernie Saunders's net worth being just under $2 million dollars, which is far poorer than most other members of congress, the news media

BERNIE SANDERS BUYS HIS THIRD HOUSE

THE NEWS MEDIA FINDS BERNIE SAUNDERS'S WEAK SPOT.

The perpetually aggrieved Vermont senator helps himself to a modest lakefront property.

 BY TINA NGUYEN
AUGUST 9, 2016

continually used the "Bernie three houses Saunders" label to smear him while he tried to run for the democratic nominee. This was an effective smear. Bernie Saunders often talks about millionaires and billionaires being a major problem with America, yet he is technically a millionaire himself. This is a perfect weak spot. People don't like hypocrites, and this was the perfect opportunity to paint Bernie Saunders as a hypocrite. His opponent in 2016 Hilary Clinton, who has a net worth of $120 million dollars, received no such criticisms of her wealth. This is because she was the favoured candidate of the corporations who control the media.

Politicians and celebrities often have professional media handlers who make sure that they're never caught in any photographs that can be used to smear them and ruin their reputation. Jordan Peterson has no such media handlers. People who are in the public eye are often

"I'VE PROBABLY HAD MY PHOTO TAKEN FIVE OR SIX THOUSAND TIMES IN THE PAST YEAR (...) THERE WERE A LOT OF PEOPLE LINED UP, THEY WERE DOING A LOT OF THINGS, THIS WAS ONE OF THINGS, IT TOOK ABOUT 30 SECONDS" - JORDAN PETERSON

THE "HYPOCRITE" LABEL IS AN EFFECTIVE WEAK SPOT AGAINST ANYBODY WHO ATTACKS MILLIONAIRES AND BILLIONAIRES.

photographed thousands of times every single month and it only takes a single photograph in the wrong situation to smear someone's reputation. This particular photograph was held up by a presenter on CBC news while she asked "Is this you..?" to a frustrated Jordan Peterson during an interview. The photo was used again and again in hit-pieces on Peterson throughout online media.

Russell Brand begins to see increasing popularity for his Youtube videos critising large corporations and big business. So begins the smear campaign. The news media quickly targeted Russell Brand's most obvious weak spot—the fact that he's a wealthy celebrity. Everyone has a weak-spot. And those conducting a smear campaign will always find it, no matter how small it may be.

3. REMOVE CONTEXT

While discussing Incels ("involuntarily celebate" men who are unable to find a romantic partner), Jordan Peterson proposed that a solution to the problem of Incels might be "enforced monogamy". Media outlets used this to smear his reputation, making it appear as if he was proposing that women should be forced to partner up with unattractive men in order to keep them happy.

> "The implication that that part of the New York Times article was that I wanted to take young women at the point of a gun and deliver them to useless men. It's like: no one has ever believed that" - Jordan Peterson

As anyone who listened to Jordan Peterson in context would know, "enforced monogamy" simply means having a society that encourages people to be monogamous, rather than polygamous (which is hardly a controversial statement). But by removing context the news was able to make Jordan Peterson look both crazy and sexist at the same time.

JEREMY CORBYN HAD HIS REPUTATION REPEATEDLY SMEARED BY THE MEDIA OVER HIS RELATIONSHIP WITH THE IRA (IRISH REPUBLICAN ARMY, A GROUP RESPONSIBLE FOR A NUMBER OF BOMBINGS IN THE UK).

When asked to condemn the bombings, he was reported saying the following:

Corbyn: *Look, bombing is wrong, all bombing is wrong. Of course I condemn it."*

Interviewer: *"But you're condemning all bombing, can you condemn the IRA without equating it to …"*

Corbyn: *"No."*

Of course, this interview has had it's full context removed in order to smear Corbyn. What the news media failed to report was what he said just afterwards:

Corbyn: *"No, I think what you have to say is all bombing has to be condemned and you have to bring about a peace process. Listen, in the 1980s, Britain was looking for a military solution in Ireland – it clearly was never going to work. Ask anyone in the British army at the time … I condemn all the bombing by both the loyalists and the IRA."*

You may have noticed that politicians have a certain strange way of answering questions; it often seems as though they're unable to give a simple answer to a simple question. This is because they have to be incredibly careful at all times not to say anything that could be taken of out context by the news media. *Politicans can't speak like normal human beings, because if they do they news media will take them out of context and smear their reputation.*

When you see somebody quoted in an article, ask yourself: am I seeing the full context? If possible, go to the source material on Youtube or wherever you can find it, and watch the full interview. Stop being manipulated by news media who quote people out of context.

vilification. Depending on where you stood, he'd either swept away a lot of woolly thinking or produced a guidebook for the kind of embittered men who formed Donald Trump's praetorian guard of Proud Boys.   1

We should hope for more revolts like the one against Peterson, and the one that occurred when Simon & Schuster dropped racist provocateur Milo   2 Yiannopoulos. Of course, there are strategic calculations, because a huge

of secular prophet ... in an era of lobotomised conformism". He is also adored by figures on the so-called alt-light (basically the "alt-right" without the sieg heils and the white ethnostate), including Mike Cernovich, Gavin McInnes and Paul Joseph Watson. His earnings from crowdfunding drives on Patreon
         5   3   4
Cathy Newman was wrong to call Peterson a "provocateur", as if he were just Milo Yiannopoulos with a PhD. He is a true believer. Peterson is old enough
         6
irritation, the better Peterson came across. The whole performance, which has since been viewed more than 6m times on YouTube and was described by excitable Fox News host Tucker Carlson as "one of the great interviews of
                                         7
experienced floods of hatemail, including physical threats. Newman received so much abuse that Peterson asked his fans to "back off", albeit while suggesting the scale had been exaggerated. "His fans are relentless," says Southey. "They have contacted me, repeatedly, on just about every platform possible."   8

JORDAN PETERSON BEING SMEARED USING THE "GUILTY BY ASSOCIATION" TECHNIQUE:

1. "Proud Boys" - A group of right-wing white nationalists.
2 + 6. "Milo Yiannopoulos" - Right-wing political commentator.
3. "Mike Cernovich" - Right-wing social media personality.
4. "Gavin McInnes" - Right-wing social media personality.
5. "Paul Joseph Watson" - Right-wing social media personality.
7. "Tucker Carlson" - Fox News Host.
8. "His fans" - Jordan Peterson's fans.

4. GUILTY BY ASSOCIATION

When a smear campaign tries to place a negative label on a particular person, there's no easier way to do so than simply associating them with others who carry that label. Jordan Peterson isn't particularly politically right-wing (In fact, he's performed long-form lectures explaining the horrors of Nazi Germany). However, associating Peterson with other right-wing figures persuades the audience that he too must somehow be right-wing. The truth is, Jordan Peterson has more or less no connection with any of people named in the article. But the simple act of mentioning the name of a right-wing individual in an article about Jordan Peterson leads the reader to assume that there must at least be some connection between them.

The Association Fallacy is a known psychological fallacy. It's like saying: Adolf Hitler was a vegetarian, therefore all vegetarians must be evil. Or: Some charities have been fraudulent, therefore all charities must be fraudulent. With the example of Jordan Peterson the logic is: Some famous extreme right-wing individuals have supported Jordan Peterson, therefore Jordan Peterson must be extreme right-wing. Smear campaigns reach deep into our psyche to try and manipulate how we feel about a particular person. The guilty by association technique can trick our subconscious mind into associating people we don't like with the smeared individual. Of course, like all techniques used by the smear campaign, the guilty by association technique is an ad-hominem attack that focuses on an individual's character rather than the content of their ideas. Nobody has the power to control who associates with them. Nobody can control who shares or supports their work, so the smeared individual is more or less powerless to defend themselves.

The guilty by association technique can be done in a rather subtle manner. The smear campaign doesn't have to state outright that Bad Person A supports Person B. It can simply name-drop Bad Person A while discussing Person B. The mere name-dropping of Bad person A leads the audience to assume that they must have some connection with person B, even if that so-called connection isn't made clear. Another common use of this technique is to associate an individual's fans or followers with the individual themselves. A common smear of US politician Bernie Saunders was that his "Bernie Bro" followers were harassing his political opponents online on their behalf. By focusing on the behaviour of a few fanatics leaving abusive messages online, the media can associate these badly behaved fans with the individual themselves. All popular figures have fans acting poorly online, which means this particular smear can be applied to anyone at anytime. Criticising someone because of how their fans behave is meaningless, yet most of the public will fall for this smear tactic over and over again.

5. USE THE RIGHT IMAGES

If you have your photo taken enough times, eventually you'll end up looking stupid, ugly, insane or power mad in at least one of them. The human face ends up in all kinds of odd, distorted positions if you freeze it in motion. Smear campaigns often use images where the target looks a

ANYONE CAN BE MADE TO LOOK STUPID OR INSANE IF YOU CHOOSE THE RIGHT IMAGE.

particular way. The smear campaign rarely uses images where the target is stood pridefully, confidently, with their shoulders back and looking heroically into the distance. Instead, they use images that carry negative connotations. Some newspapers go to great lengths to portray the victim of their smear campaign in the most unfavourable way they possibly can.

You might think that such an obvious smear campaign like the one above wouldn't be effective. Think again. Human beings are tribal creatures. Our older, lizard brain is evolved to live in tribes of 150 people. In the environment our lizard brain is adapted to, photographs didn't exist. At a base level, we react to still images as if they're real human beings, after all, still photographs are completely foreign to our lizard brain. When you see a still image of someone looking insane, this can effect the way you emotionally feel about the individual in the image

THE GOAL OF THIS IMAGE IS TO PLACE A SUBCONSCIOUS ASSOCIATION IN THE MIND OF THE AUDIENCE BETWEEN JEREMY CORBYN AND A FEELING OF RIDICULOUSNESS, IDIOCY AND CLOWN-LIKE CHARACTERISTICS.

(**Law 2: Media Is An Evolutionary Mismatch**). You may have your feelings towards that individual changed on the subconscious level. In the case of the "Court Jezter" image above, you may begin to view Jeremy Corbyn as someone who's not to be taken seriously.

"Do you know what your rating is on Trustpilot? 84% 1-star for the BBC, 59% 1-star for ITV, and 72% 1 star for channel 4. I don't care what you say, you're just smear merchants. Not one of you can tell me what I believe. Not one of you knows, but all of the public know, because they can go to my Youtube channel, Sargon Of Akkad, and just watch for themselves. I've been doing this for 5 years, I have over a million subscribers just go and have a look. I'm not answering your questions, I'm not apologising for anything you dirty, dirty smear merchants" - **Carl Benjamin** *speaks directly to the news media.*

Smear campaigns are about manipulating your deepest tribal emotions. In our tribal environment, a man holding up his hand towards us would be a defensive gesture. The exact same body language is captured and displayed here to make you feel as though Carl Benjamin is being defensive or being dishonest. This image was not chosen randomly, it was selected carefully by editors in order to smear the reputation

THIS IMAGE SHOWS UKIP MEMBER CARL BENJAMIN HOLDING HIS HAND UP TOWARDS THE CAMERA. THIS BODY LANGUAGE COMMUNICATES DEFENSIVENESS, THE IMPLICATION BEING THAT HE'S DESPERATELY TRYING TO DENY THE CLAIM IN THE HEADLINE ABOVE HIS HEAD.

I might rape MP Jess Phillips, says Ukip candidate Carl Benjamin

of Carl Benjamin. When you see an image of Carl Benjamin holding defensive body language at the top of the article, you will then read the rest of the article through the emotional filter created by the image. Using the right images is an important component of an effective smear campaign.

6. DON'T MAKE IT OBVIOUS

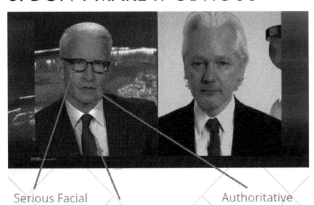

WHEN THE MEDIA SMEARS SOMEONE'S REPUTATION BY MISREPRESENTING THEM, THEY NEED TO CARRY A VEER OF PROFESSIONALLISM TO GET AWAY WITH IT.

Serious Facial Expression

Respectable and professional appearance

Authoritative vocal tonality

While purposefully ruining somebody's reputation, media outlets need to keep an aura of seriousness and respectability; non-verbal cues are a powerful of upholding this image. For many people, if someone on the news wearing a suit and tie tells them something with authoritative tone of voice, they will unquestionably believe them. At the very least, most people assume what the person (who appears to carry authority) is saying must have at least *some* credibility to it. In reality, there are many cases where a professionally dressed man on CNN spews utter lies and misrepresentations.

Hit-pieces must at least give the impression that the author has made some effort to be fair-minded and unbiased, even if the overall purpose of the piece is to smear somebody's reputation. If a smear campaign goes too far, it becomes too obvious to the audience that the media just wants to attack the individual rather than give them a fair hearing. The more sophisticated smear campaigns will keep up the appearance of an unbiased news outlet, all the while framing the issue in a totally biased manner.

WHO CONDUCTS SMEAR CAMPAIGNS AND WHY?

Ecuador says Julian Assange smeared poop on embassy walls

By Ebony Bowden   April 11, 2019 | 5:44pm | Updated

A LITERAL "SMEAR" CAMPAIGN.

When an individual threatens a power structure, the power structure will do everything they possibly can to destroy that individual. In some countries, if a journalist goes against the government (the centre of power), the government will simply assassinate or imprison them. In more developed countries, assassination isn't an option, so they need to rely on more covert means. *The smear campaign is a weapon.* If you can't attack the person directly with physical force, you can instead destroy their reputation and encourage the public to turn against them.

Julian Assange was smeared because he exposed the war crimes of the United States government. They responded by using their immense power to shape a negative narrative around Julian Assange throughout multiple countries. Bernie Saunders was smeared because he wanted to give free healthcare to all Americans, which would destroy billions of dollars in profit for the pharmaceutical industry. He also wanted to impose a tax on Wall Street. The news media in America is controlled by big business, so in order to protect their wealth, they launched a smear campaign against Saunders. Jeremy Corbyn was smeared because he wanted to increase taxes on big business. Russell Brand was smeared because he began to become an influential force in challenging big business and the existing power structures. Remember, the mainstream media is not an independent entity, it is controlled by powerful people and powerful organisations.

If you challenge a centre of power, you will be smeared by the media. There are many centres of power around the world, mostly consisting of governments and giant corporations. Whether you challenge the Chinese government, Wall Street, the Australian government or the government of Saudi Arabia, your reputation will be smeared and large chunks of the public will be manipulated into turning against you. Of course, smear campaigns can often be shocking and interesting. Therefore they bring in plenty of clicks and plenty of revenue. News media can often act as "smear merchants" who sell their ability to smear the reputation of others to powerful people and organisations. The news media loves to smear people because it generates controversy, clicks, revenue and pleases powerful people.

THE SMEAR CAMPAIGN - A TOOL OF THE PSYCHOPATH

Do you feel it? That toxic vibe? That toxic feeling? That sick feeling in your stomach? If you're a more sensitive type, the topic of smear campaigns will be hard to think about. How can people be so manipulative? How can the media purposefully destroy the careers of perfectly innocent people. How can they manage to turn millions of people against a single individual with lies and misrepresentations? Can you sense that toxicity? It's because the smear campaign is a tool of the psychopath.

Psychopaths are people without a conscience. They feel no empathy for people who are suffering, and as such, they live their lives like a giant chess game, using people as mere pawns to "win" their own personal games. They target vulnerable people in order to use them and achieve their own selfish goals. It is estimated that psychopaths make up roughly 1% of the population (there are certainty plenty of psychopaths working in the media). If you step on the toes of your psychopathic work colleague, they will spread rumours about you, make covert "suggestions" about you, convince others at your workplace that you're crazy and untrustworthy and conduct a character assassination on you. It's not uncommon for a pathologically envious sociopathic co-worker to feed misinformation about someone to their colleagues and bosses in order to remove them as a "threat" in order to climb the corporate ladder.

> **"Covert predators like these will spread falsehoods to slander your reputation or smear your credibility to others. This is a form of gaslighting intended to manage your image in the public eye to ensure that no one would believe you were being abused" - Psychcentral.com**

The media is psychopathic. It's run by both actual psychopaths and sociopaths, as well as normal people who feel self-justified to act in a psychopathic manner - they feel justified as they smear the reputation of an innocent person. When you're able to see through smear campaigns, when you just how manipulative the media can be, it can make you sick to your stomach. That's because you're sensing the vibes of psychopathic behaviour. Yet there are effective ways of dealing with a smear campaign:

If you are being met with any kind of smear campaign, stick to the facts. As difficult as it may be, try not to become emotionally responsive in public – narcissists will use your emotional reactions against you to further depict you as the "crazy" one" - Psychcentral.com

The best way to reduce the effectiveness of smear campaigns is to call them out and educate people on what they are and how they're used. We can help to reduce the impact of these manipulative, psychopathic techniques by educating others on how they work so that they can recognise a smear campaign in action themselves.

Let's eradicate the smear campaign from the face of the earth by educating as many people about their existence as possible. Once you know what a smear campaign is, and are able to identify them, you can no longer be easily manipulated by them.

the podcast and a
revolution of truth

For decades, most of our information came through the television, newspapers and the radio. News organisations presented everything we knew about the outside world to us and we accepted what they told us. Hugely complicated issues were condensed into 5 minute segments squished between commercial breaks. The brutal truth about the mainstream media is that a small number of corporations controlled all of the information we were able to see; they were the bottleneck through which all of the information about the world came to us. These corporations chose which news stories were highlighted and which were kept in the dark. They chose what we focused on and what we didn't focus on. They chose which political candidates were able to have their voices heard. They chose how stories were framed. They chose how the public thought about particular people. For decades, they had an overwhelming influence over the minds of the public in most developed countries. In the old informational environment, the average person was clueless and helpless. When talking about the world outside their personal sphere, they might have started their sentence with *"I heard something about that on the news"*, or made statements like: *"I like that political candidate X, he seems like a good guy"*. The average person had absolutely no idea just how little they knew about the complexities of the world. Only the minority who put in the effort to read books on particular subjects would have had any idea about the truth of any particular issue. But the information landscape has changed, and we have a shining light of hope that has the ability to lead to a wiser, more enlightened human race: The Podcast.

Bernie Saunders ran to be the Democratic nominee in both 2016 and 2020. He advocated for free, universal healthcare for all Americans. This would mean an enormous drop in profits for the pharmaceutical industry in America. So, of course, the mainstream media, (which is controlled by big business) produced a smear campaign against Bernie. He became Bernie "three houses" Saunders. "He became "Radical Bernie"". He became "Sexist Bernie". He became "Racist Bernie". He even became "Narcissist Bernie" And his supporters became "Bernie Bros". Whenever you find an individual repeatedly being given negative labels by the media, you know a smear campaign is underway. The public fell for the smear

DEMOCRATIC CANDIDATE
BERNIE SAUNDERS APPEARS
ON THE JOE ROGAN PODCAST

campaign of Bernie (as they usually do), and millions of people had their opinions of Bernie Saunders decided for them. But while the elites may control all of the mainstream media, they don't control The Joe Rogan Podcast. And all it took was a single hour long podcast (with an unbiased interviewer without an agenda) to change the minds of thousands across the internet. Bernie Saunders appeared on the Joe Rogan Podcast for 1 hour and 7 minutes, and spoke about his ideas in detail.

Most of the comments underneath the video carried a similar sentiment. One comment reads: *"I had Bernie Saunders completely wrong, I fell into the assumption that he was too radical. All he did was be an American, he stood up for what was right. Poor guy."* Another Youtuber writes *"He's not mad at all like the media makes him out to be."*

The mainstream media has the ability to create a false impression about any individual they choose. And because most people are media illiterate, they're not able to see a smear campaign in action. All it took was a single hour of uninterrupted speech in a podcast for many people to entirely change their minds about Bernie Saunders. Aside from commenters realising they had gotten the wrong impression about Bernie Saunders, many of them began to compare the podcast with mainstream media coverage. One commenter writes, *"There was more policy in the first 10 minutes of this interview than the entire second debate, both of them. CNN should be embarrassed. They're the ESPN of politics".* Another user received 47,000 likes on his comment:, *"This feels like a watershed moment for alternative media. Random MMA guy has a far better interview with a presidential candidate than any mainstream media".* And along a similar vein, another user writes, *"So this is what it feels like to hear an ACTUAL conversation about policy and politics. THANK YOU JOE ROGAN!!!!. Better than any cable news show".*

These comments show that people are finally beginning to realise just how much mainstream media has been manipulating public opinion for the last few decades. When we hear political candidates speak in TV debates, they're given 1-2 minutes to try and explain incredibly complex issues like healthcare or economic policy, which is of course completely impossible. When politics is discussed in sound-bites, it becomes a media game. A game to sound good in a short space of time. A game to make the other person look stupid. A game to say the right thing that will sound best when put as a 30 second clip on the evening news. In the mainstream media, no real political policy is discussed, and the audience is left with nothing more than a few "zingers" they can gleefully repeat to their friends. Of course, it's this way by design. When politicians are only given 1-2 minutes to talk, what they say can be more easily controlled. The choice of questions asked to politicians are also controlled by the media corporations, which ensures that no alternative ideas are ever discussed. The mainstream media is able to choose where our attention goes and where it doesn't go by controlling the framework of the debate.

But now we have the podcast and long-form content, and these allow far greater and deeper understanding into topics. You are able to hear real nuance in an issue rather than only basic points and "zingers". You are able to hear people thinking out loud, rather than only hearing the end of their thinking process. You able to understand the depth and minute details of the issue, and crucially, you are able to hear the opposing side of the argument in-detail rather than a strawman argument. Some issues desperately need long-form content. America can't ever hope to have a debate about gun ownership when the discussion format is two people shouting over each other on Fox News for 5 minutes before being interrupted by a commercial break. We can't hope to have any real understanding of what the military is doing in other countries when all discussions of the topic happen through a mainstream news channel that wants you to think a certain way about it.

Posers, sociopaths and manipulators thrive on short-form content and sound bites because it allows them to hide their true character. People who tell the truth, genuine people who truly believe in what they're saying thrive on long-form content because it allows their true character to naturally unfold. What would Hilary Clinton sound like in 2 hour podcast? How would Joe Biden answer unconventional questions asked by a host that had no agenda? How would Donald Trump come across when asked to describe his political policies in detail? We've never seen these important political figures sit down and talk for 2 hours. Not once. And as such, we have no idea who they actually are or what they believe. We can only guess and speculate on whether they're telling the truth, pretending or making calculated responses based on upholding their personal image. On the other hand, we know who Bernie Saunders, Andrew Yang and Tulsie Gabbard are because they've all appeared on The Joe Rogan Podcast and spoken at length on their policies and ideas. When you see someone sit down and speak for a lengthy period of time, it becomes impossible for them to hide who they are. When people sit down and talk for a long period of time, it gradually becomes clear who they are and what they stand for. Human beings can understand each other when they sit down, face to face, and talk for long periods of time. We can see the truth in their eyes, their body language and their tone of voice. This is how we communicated in our tribal environment for hundreds of thousands of years. *It's the synthetic filters of media that allow lies to be spread amongst populations.*

Would America have gone to war in Iraq if the population had been able to listen to George W Bush explaining his reasoning on a 2 hour podcast? Would homosexuals have been discriminated against throughout the 20th century if the public had had access to long-form podcasts of homosexuals telling us about their suffering? Could entire societies have been racist for hundreds of years if they'd had access to lengthy podcasts from those of other races speaking their truth? Would the German population have turned against the Jews in Nazi Germany if they'd had access to long-form podcasts of real Jews explaining themselves? The truth keeps evil at bay. *While the mainstream media is the perfect medium for evil-doers, liars and psychopaths to manipulate the public and carefully craft their image, the podcast is the perfect medium for truth-tellers and people of good-will.* The podcast and long-form content have the ability to spread truth and change the world for the better.

"It is deceit that produces the terrible suffering of mankind: the death camps of the Nazis; the torture chambers and genocides of Stalin and that even greater monster, Mao. It was deceit that killed hundreds of millions of people in the twentieth century. It was deceit that almost doomed civilization itself. It is deceit that still threatens us, most profoundly, today" - Jordan Peterson

There are University lectures, debates and podcasts on serious issues throughout Youtube, many of which have view-counts into the tens of millions. Why are people watching these long-form educational videos?

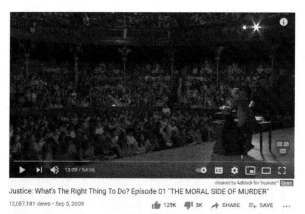

THIS HOUR-LONG HARVARD LECTURE ABOUT MORALITY HAS OVER 13 MILLION VIEWS.

Justice: What's The Right Thing To Do? Episode 01 "THE MORAL SIDE OF MURDER"
13,067,181 views • Sep 5, 2009   129K   3K   SHARE   SAVE   ...

Wasn't the general public supposed to be stupid and uneducated? Nobody knew that the market for long-form educational content existed, yet it was there all along. Traditional media organisations would often justify their low quality, sound-bite, shallow content by saying something along the lines of "we're giving the public what they want". What they didn't realise was that instead of giving the public the type of content they wanted, they were actually shaping audience tastes. To a large extent, the public watched shallow mainstream content simply because that's what was provided to them.

If you ask a mainstream media watcher a question about why they voted for Hilary Clinton in the 2016 election, they would probably tell you something along the lines of *"Because Donald Trump is a scumbag"*, or perhaps, *"Because I think we should put a woman in the white house"*. Basic answers, with no real understanding of politics behind them. On the other hand, if you ask a podcast listener the same question, they would likely have a far more sophisticated answer. Something like: *"Hilary Clinton has plenty of flaws. She was for the Iraq war in 2003, and often supports military interventions in other countries. But I also believe that Donald Trump could be a threat to American democracy and stability due to his blatant disregard for facts and truth, so I decided that Hilary was the lesser of two evils"*. Whether you agree or disagree with the opinion given here, there's no denying that it's far more nuanced and demonstrates a much greater depth of understanding of politics. This is the difference between someone who consumes long-form content and someone who consumes mainstream media. To put it simply, for decades the mainstream media has been keeping people dumb. But the podcast and long-form content has the ability to create a smarter, wiser and more enlightened population.

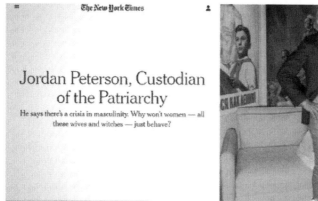

Jordan Peterson the right-wing nut. Jordan Peterson the sexist. Jordan Peterson the grifter. Jordan Peterson the transphobe. Jordan Peterson the fraud. Endless numbers of hit-pieces have been written about Jordan Peterson. Certainly, these hit-pieces have an effect on his reputation, after all, search "Jordan Peterson" into Google and the first result is likely to be a hit-piece portraying him in a negative light. However, we live

in a world with podcasts and long-form content. Jordan Peterson has endless hours of lectures on Youtube, and appears on hundreds of podcasts. He speaks in great detail about what he believes and what he does not. If somebody wants to find out who Jordan Peterson is, they don't need to listen to a journalist tell them what to think about him, they can simply go and find the original source material online. Journalists who write hit-pieces seem ridiculous when the lies and misrepresentations they write can be immediately be fact-checked by watching a couple of Youtube videos. For decades, the mainstream media has had the power to destroy the reputation of anybody they like. This power has been weakened greatly by podcasts and long-form content.

For most of human history, we communicated with the spoken word. We sat together around campfires and told our stories to each other. Even in a ancient Greece, the famous philosopher Socrates would refuse to write anything down as he believed the spoken word was superior. The truth is, a lot of people don't like to read. A large number of people find reading boring, tiresome and difficult to stick at for longer than 20 minutes. On the other hand, people are much more able listen for long periods of time. Podcasts and long-form content are a media revolution. The spoken word now has the same reach as the written word, and the spoken word, in it's digital form, now lasts forever just as any digital text does. This is unprecedented in human history. The spoken word has advantages that the written word doesn't. We can hear the emotion in the speaker's vocal tonality. We are able to really feel the message a speaker is trying to put out in a way that isn't possible with the written word. Also, listening is far less work for our brain, and we can consume podcasts while we do other things: washing the dishes, driving the car etc.

Podcasts and long-form content mean that a huge number of people who don't read now have access to highly intellectual and nuanced information. People are getting smarter. And smarter is exactly what humanity needs to become if it's going to survive. (At least, those who listen to podcasts and long-form content are getting smarter, while those who continue to only consume mainstream news will be left behind). Intellectuals are already becoming more popular. Sam Harris and Jordan Peterson have already held live events drawing crowds of thousands of people. These intellectuals are treated almost like rock-stars; people want their autograph, people scream and applaued as they walk on stage and people line up to speak with them after the show. This is all because of podcasts and long-form content. In our information rich environment, it's important and necessary that humanity gets collectively smarter. And the podcast and long-form content are the ideal tool to achieve this goal.

Podcasts and long-form content are changing the world.

DEEPFAKES AND THE POST-TRUTH WORLD

What do you know about the world? No really, what do you actually know? What one thing do you know to be 100% true? *The earth spins around the sun.* Really? Have you been into space? Did you see it for yourself? Or did somebody else tell you about this "fact"? *Hitler killed millions of Jews during the holocaust.* Did you personally see it happen? Were you there? Or did you hear it from your history teacher? Where did your history teacher get this information from? A history book? What if this history book was written by the government who lied in order to spread propaganda against the Nazis? Can you say with 100% certainty that this isn't a possibility? *I am a man called David.* How do you know you're a man? Maybe you're a woman plugged into a digital simulation. You can't disprove this possibility. And is your name really David? Or did two people claiming to be your parents just tell you your name is David? Are you sure they're your parents? Did you conduct a DNA test on them? Or did you just believe what they told you?

Almost all of the information you have about the world was given to you by another human being and human beings may not always be reliable sources of information. You didn't study history first-hand. You've never been into space. You probably have no idea how the internet works. You don't know what your government is doing. You don't even know where your food comes from (You may know what you've been told about where your food comes from, but you didn't personally witness it's journey from the environment to the supermarket).You know almost nothing first-hand. Which means you need to trust experts, journalists and various other people to tell you the truth. But what is *truth?*

We used to have gatekeepers. A select number of media outlets who would tell us about the state of the world. Newspapers. TV news. Radio news. Books written by experts. The times have changed. The internet has arrived. Technology has advanced. And we're about to enter (or have already entered) an era of post-truth. In the digital world, trivial information is accumulating every second, digital information that never deteriorates. Rumours. Opinions. Misinformation. Disinformation. Fake news. All this junk data is preserved in an unfiltered state and is growing constantly. Organisations create their own truths for financial gain. Others create truths that prove their political ideologies correct. And algorithms separate society into their own filter bubbles, each with their own truths. Nobody is invalidated. But nobody is right. The world is being drowned in "truth". In 2020, we're already in a situation where people are finding it increasingly difficult to decide on facts. How will we continue to keep a grasp on *truth* when the advent of new technologies allows us to create any reality we can imagine.

DEEPFAKES

So far, we've dealt with the manipulation of text in the form of fake news and the manipulation of images with photo-retouching. These have already caused huge problems. Now we have the manipulation of video and audio on the horizon in the form of deepfakes. And it's on the verge of changing everything. It is now possible to take somebody's face, put it onto the body of someone else and make it look realistic. It works by giving the AI a large number of sample images of an individual's face to study (these images are easily found on Google images or social media). The AI can then effectively make it appear as though their lips are saying specific words. Not only that, but you can literally put words into somebody's mouth. Programs like Adobe Voco allow you to take anybody's voice and make it sound like they're saying anything you want them to. The AI analyses a sample of an individual's voice and can then digitally recreate new words in the exact same voice. *Audio and video can now be convincingly faked.* At least, it almost can. At this moment, it's still possible to tell the difference between a manipulated video and a real one. But it's not easy. And experts say that within just a few years the fake will be indistinguishable from reality. In the near future, anybody with a laptop will be able to create realistic, fake videos.

Video can no longer be trusted and the deepfake arms race has begun. Already organisations have been formed in an attempt to keep ahead of the new technology. As of right now, there are still methods of differentiating a deepfake from a real video. One method is checking for unusual blinking patterns. Another is looking for the subtle change in skin colour during a person's heartbeat. But if there's one thing we know about regulators, it's that they're always forced to play a cat and mouse game. Athletes who use blood doping and performance enhancing drugs are always one step ahead of the regulators; the same situation will occur with deepfakes. Every time the regulators find a method of detecting a deepfake, the deepfake creators will find a new method of getting past the regulators. It will be an endless cat and mouse game with the creators of deepfakes always being one step ahead. Imagine a convincing fake video of the President of the United States announcing a nuclear strike on North Korea being released. Within 3 minutes North Korea may have responded with a real nuke of their own before discovering that the video is fake. Imagine a fake video being released of an Iranian celebrity burning an image of the Prophet Mohammed. The celebrity would quickly have a mob of blood-thirsty Muslim extremists at their door. And deepfakes don't only work on faces, they work on all of reality. One image that previously showed anti-gun activist Emma Gonzalez ripping up a shooting target was replaced by her ripping up the US constitution. Eventually people will learn to stop trusting videos. Overtime, the world become accustom to deepfakes.

Yet the problem is far more insidious than any of that. The real question is: What will the world be like after people stop trusting video? Video is essentially a recording of reality; there is no other medium that captures the world as fully and completely as video. In fact, much of our current society is based around the video. What happens when the legitimacy of every single video you see is brought into question? If you can't trust a recording of reality, what can you trust? Video is the final frontier. After video there's nothing left. You can't trust text. You can't trust images. What happens when you can't trust video and audio either? It's certainly possible that we will enter into a world where the truth doesn't exist. The truth will be created by those with the most power and those with the most advanced technology. Anything outside your own personal experiences will be suspect. And the truth will be decided by who states their own version of truth the most effectively. If a politician is caught on video doing or saying something scandalous, that video will be meaningless. This politician can simply claim "deepfake" and have a legitimate case. In a world of deepfakes, a video of Donald Trump being caught saying he would *"grab 'em by the pussy"* could simply be denied as a deepfake. Who could possibly know if a video like that was genuine or fabricated? During presidential campaigns political parties will be able to create fake videos showing their opponent engaging in some kind of disgusting act. Sure, the public will suspect a fake video, but the subconscious connection between the presidential candidate and this disgusting act will be made in the minds of the public. TV debates will be reduced to arguing over whether video footage is real or not. It's certainly possible that deepfakes could lead to the breakdown of democracy. And what about the law? How can CCTV footage be admissible as evidence after trust in video is gone? A videotape of a murder may become useless in a courtroom. Body cameras on police will also be suspect. Sure, there will be laws against manipulating the footage from police body cameras, but that doesn't mean that the public won't be suspicious of this footage. If a police body camera shows an officer shooting an unarmed black man, then perhaps it was faked by the government who wants to push an anti-white agenda. Why not? Any conspiracy is admissible when you can't trust the reality of video.

With the invention of deepfakes, it is now possible to take any face you like and put them into a pornographic scene. As you can see from the above image, celebrity deepfake porn is already freely accessible online. On a website called "MrDeepfakes.com", you can watch videos of celebrities in sexual scenarios. Currently, some videos are poorly made; the face isn't well attatched to the body and occasionally glitches. But other videos appear strangely realistic, and this technology will only continue to improve the realism of the videos. Further than that, with the technology of VR you will be able to have a first-person VR sexual experience with anybody you like. How?

1. *Feed multiple images of the desired person's face to the AI. (Considering almost all of us have pictures of ourselves all over social media, these will be easy to find)*

2. *Take a similar body shape to the person you want to have sex and put their face onto this body.*

3. *"Have sex" with this person from a first-person perspective while making eye-contact with them in a VR simulation (And with the future incorporation of sex robotics, you'll have something physical to have sex with).*

Relatively soon, it will be more or less impossible to stop total strangers getting off by having simulated sex with you. In fact, it's likely that in the future it will become accepted into the culture that people are having VR sex with you without your consent. So much so, that it will probably become the subject of wink wink, nudge nudge jokes around the office. This is not a theory of some fictional sci-fi thriller. *This technology is going to become available and it will become possible to have VR sex with anybody you like.* **(Law 3: Technology Never Moves Backwards)**

With the invention of realistic deepfakes, we may also enter a period of "post history". Picture this scenario: It's the year 2050, and a video of Osama Bin Laden shaking hands with George W Bush has been created, along a realistic conversation created between them explaining how the 9/11 attack on the World Trade Centre was an orchestrated plan using voice technology. The video has gone viral throughout social media. Plenty of fact-checkers are explaining that the video is a fake and the scene never took place, but the fact-checkers themselves aren't trusted by the general public. The creators of the video claim that the video is genuine and that the fact-checkers are hiding the truth. How would you know who to believe? And what happens when thousands of videos attacking the truth of history are created? It's simple, we will enter a period of post-history – where history can no longer be created or trusted. History will instead become a story created by those with the most power.

But it's not only deepfakes that are causing the very nature of *truth* to be under threat. To a large extent we are already living in a post-truth era. Do you feel a little confused about the world lately? It seems like every time you manage to get a grasp on the truth on a particular subject new contradictory evidence appears to muddy the waters. Often it seems as though the more you research a subject, the more confused you become. In the modern world of nutrition we have the perfect example. Let's start with a simple question: *Is Milk Healthy?*

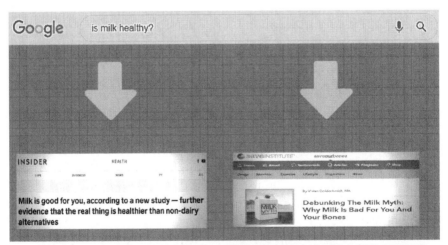

LEFT: THISISINSIDER.COM RIGHT: SAVEOURBONES.COM. BOTH RESULTS FOUND ON THE FIRST PAGE OF A GOOGLE SEARCH QUERY FOR : "IS MILK HEALTHY?"

We were told for decades that milk was good for your bones and teeth because it contains calcium. But now it seems possible that the exact opposite is true: that milk makes your bones and teeth *weaker* by depleting calcium from your body. We were told for decades that eggs were bad for you because they're high in cholesterol. But now it seems possible that eggs are actually an incredibly healthy super-food. Should we be on the paleo diet? Or a vegan diet? Is fat good or bad? Is milk healthy or unhealthy? Are eggs healthy or unhealthy? Go to the internet and you can find 1000 different answers from every direction and walk away more confused than when you started.

Then there's the world of healthcare. Picture this scenario. You're unexpectedly diagnosed with cancer and the doctor tells you You have 6 months to live. The doctor suggests immediate chemotherapy as the only option for a chance of survival.

Then you go on Youtube and see this:

Chemotherapy is a Waste of Money
iHealthTube.com ✪ 808K views • 7 years ago

http://www.ihealthtube.com Dr. Peter Glidden talks about the incredibly low success rate for chemotherapy as a cancer treatment.

Chemo and Radiation Usually Don't Work-Find Out Why 1 Minute into This Video!
iHealthTube.com ✪ 96K views • 4 years ago

http://www.ihealthtube.com Dr. Tony Jimenez explains why traditional cancer treatments like chemotherapy and radiation ...

Doctor Gets Cancer - Refuses Chemo Therapy
TheWatchmanReport • 775K views • 5 years ago

Chemotherapy Treatment Kills - Why You Should Never Do It
Cancer Wisdom TV • 26K views • 1 year ago

In this video you learn why chemotherapy treatment is a deadly method to treat cancer and something you need to avoid.

Followed by this:

Can we eat to starve cancer? - William Li
TED-Ed ✓   876K views · 4 years ago
View full lesson: http://ed.ted.com/lessons/can-we-eat-to-starve-cancer-william-li William Li presents a new way to think about ...

God's Cure for Cancer - PERFECT DIET
John Caleb Warren · 491K views · 6 years ago
This is a segment out of the video # 2 from Kent Hovind called "The Garden of Eden". Interesting facts on Vitamin B17 that is found ...

Every Cancer Can be Cured in Weeks explains Dr. Leonard Coldwell
iHealthTube.com ✓   7.4M views · 7 years ago
Help support iHealthTube so we can continue to make free videos: https://www.patreon.com/ihealthtube Dr. Leonard Coldwell ...

Heal All Cancer With This Diet
The Raw Life Health Show · 952K views · 5 years ago
Tom Fisher had stage 4 cancer and was given a 40% chance to live more than 5 years. He learned about the raw food diet and 13 ...

Woman Cures Cancer without Medicines
Satvic Movement · 95K views · 1 year ago
I had the opportunity of interviewing Gigi Jones, who healed herself from colon cancer, without any medicines. She gave up all ...

I SURVIVED CANCER WITH A PLANT BASED DIET 🌱
High Carb Hannah ✓   78K views · 10 months ago
Subscribe to Candice! - https://bit.ly/2KxewMl ☆ RECIPE BOOKS & WEIGHT LOSS GUIDE ...

So what do you do? Do you trust the qualified doctor who is insisting on chemotherapy? Or do you trust the mass of contradictory evidence found on the internet? Which *truth* do you believe when your life hangs in the balance?

CONFIRMATION BIAS

The world is infinitely complex. From the galaxies in the solar system to the atoms in your living room carpet; your brain can't possibly hope to understand it all. So your brain takes shortcuts. We see what we want to see. And we believe what we want to believe. The human brain is not logical, in fact, it's predominantly emotional. We make up our mind based on emotional considerations and then seek to justify them with rationality. This is confirmation bias. Confirmation bias is big business **(Law 4: Media Is About Profit).** Fox news was created to cater to the confirmation bias of those on the right-wing. The entire business is based on taking an non-objective, right-wing viewpoint on everything in an effort to build a loyal audience that they can sell to advertisers. But it's not just Fox news. There are websites, blogs and Youtube channels all over the internet throughout every niche that are making money by spouting the same ideology on permanent repeat. Left-wing, Right-wing, Feminism, MGTOW. These are digital markets based on appealing to the confirmation bias of the audience. Likes and shares are guaranteed when you tell people what they want to hear. Nuanced content containing opinions that don't align with the target audience do not bring in clicks. The internet financially incentives content that caters to confirmation bias and people believe what they want to believe because it's easier. Confirmation bias is a *subtle* brain mechanism and is incredibly difficult to spot in yourself; you may be convinced that you're seeing things from an entirely rational perspective, but confirmation bias can easily sneak up on you and influence your thought patterns without you realising.

STATISTICS

APPLE CEO STANDING IN FRONT OF AN IMPRESSIVE LOOKING YET MEANINGLESS GRAPH OF CUMULATIVE IPHONE SALES. THE GRAPH SIMPLY SHOWS THE TOTAL NUMBER OF IPHONE SOLD BY APPLE, EVER.

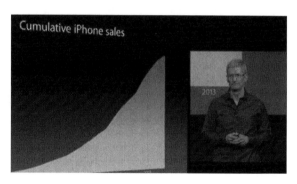

Statistics never lie. Right? There's something about numbers and graphs that just seem so concrete. It's data. It's facts. It's *truth*. But just like anything else, humans can manipulate and misrepresent data. Statistics and graphs are not to be trusted either. When the founder of Apple Tim Cook conducted this presentation, the quarterly sales of iPhones had actually decreased. A decrease in sales would lower confidence in Apple's brand. So what did they do? They misrepresented statistics. They simply put up a graph of cumulative sales (A meaningless number showing the total number of iPhones ever sold) that gives the impression that iPhone sales are doing fantastic.

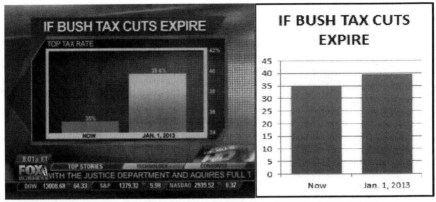

LEFT: FOX NEWS REPRESENTATION OF DATA. RIGHT: ACCURATE
REPRESENTATION OF DATA

Here we have two charts, both displaying the exact same data.
Graphs are a visual medium. The content of the data isn't important to
most viewers, instead it's how the data *looks* that counts. When people see
two rectangles that are vastly different in size, they immediately make
a conclusion. And because it's a graph there's no arguing with it! It's
just data after all. Yet when you take a look at the Y-Axis of the graph
displayed by fox news, you'll notice it only ranges from 34-42%. The real
representation of the data (with the Y-axis starting at 0) would look like
the graph on the right. Now the situation seems far less dramatic.

Hilary Clinton, a presidential candidate, proves that post-truth is
already here with her tweet *"20 years ago, women made 72 cents on the dollar to
men. Today it's still just 77 cents. More work to do. #EqualPay #NoCeilings"*. True,
the statistic she states here is completely correct, but the problem is that the
statistic carries an implication. The implication is this: The gender wage
gap is caused solely by gender discrimination. This implication is wrong.
There are endless possible reasons why the pay gap exists. Job choices.
Lifestyle choices Biological differences in personality between genders.
And yes, gender discrimination too. But is gender discrimination fully
responsible for this statistic? Of course not. How could it be? We don't
know what percentage of the wage gap is due to gender discrimination,
but it certainly isn't 100%. Hilary Clinton is fully aware that the statistic
is misleading. But she's also fully aware that her fan-base doesn't care.
Confirmation bias insures that her fan-base will read the statistic how
they *want* to read it.

9 out of 10 dentists who tried Colgate would recommend it. This
is not untrue. The survey asked dentists to list all of the toothpastes
they would recommend. They were not asked to pick their favourite.

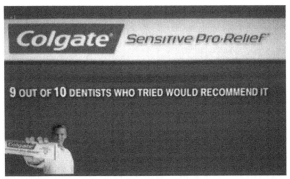

The truth is, different brands of toothpaste are more or less exactly the same and contain the same essential ingredients. This statistic is meaningless as dentists would recommend almost all brands of toothpastes. Advertising campaigns use misleading statistics constantly because they know the audience won't look into them. When it comes to advertising, the truth isn't important, it's what the audience *feels* that counts.

LIES OF THE ESTABLISHMENT

Unfortunately, lies are not only found on the internet and in advertising campaigns. There are real lies being told to us by the government itself. If you want truth, you can't turn to the establishment media. CNN. MSNBC. BBC News. Sky News. These are all giant corporations with their own agenda and their own truths. (BBC news is not a for-profit corporation but is still largely controlled by the establishment).43% of Americans believed that Sadam Hussain was personally involved in 9/11 in 2006. He wasn't. Sadam Hussain had nothing to do with 9/11. But it was this lie sold to the public by establishment media that drove the country to war. The WMD's that Sadam supposedly had were never found. Another lie. Operation Northwoods was a plan by the US government to kill US civilians and blame it on Cuba, in an effort to rally the public in a war against Cuba. This is not a conspiracy. This is a real plan by the government that was almost implemented. The Gulf of Tonkin incident, where the USA exaggerated an attack on US destroyer Maddox in an attempt to increase support for their involvement in the Vietnam war. During the COVID19 pandemic, the mainstream media assured the public that the theory that virus escaped from a lab in Wuhan was nothing more than a conspiracy. Yet a year later, the theory has been revealed as a legitimate theory. While establishment news media positions itself as "neutral" and "reasonable", they have their own agenda and they're largely influenced by some of the most powerful forces in the world. The establishment media will always place serving the needs of the powerful over the search for truth.

MERCHANTS OF DOUBT

The cigarette industry spent millions of dollars on their PR campaign with ads like the one here (with the full knowledge that cigarettes were deadly), in an attempt to induce doubt among the general public about the new information being discovered that cigarettes were harmful.

Doubt is a business. Doubt can be bought and sold. Some people make a living from selling doubt to the public. Smoking. Sugar. Climate Change. When there's a multi-billion dollar industry behind something, they have the ability to shape public opinion of their industry. If their product is causing harm to the public, they can cause confusion and doubt about this truth.

If smoking is causing cancer, they can manufacture a scientific study to say that smoking doesn't cause cancer. Then they can then use their immense financial resources to spread this study throughout the media. If sugar is causing a health crisis, then they can manufacture scientific studies that put the blame major health problems on fat instead. If fossil fuels are destroying the environment, they can manufacture scientific studies that conclude that humans are having no affect on the climate of the planet. Sure 97% of the world's climate scientists share a consensus that CO2 emissions are causing climate change. But as long as there's doubt, fossil fuel companies can continue selling their coal and oil a little longer. As pathetic as it is, there are people out there who feel no guilt in selling doubt to the public, no matter the consequences to the world.

THE PUBLIC

At the very centre of the post-truth era will be a public that isn't interested at all in seeking truth.

People on the street. People on the subway. People in their cars. The crowd at a U2 concert. Selfies on your social media newsfeed. Commenters under Youtube videos. The 107 million followers of Katy Perry on Twitter. The 50 million subscribers of Pewdiepie. This is the public. Full of irrationality. Voting with their emotions. Repeating what they heard from others without thinking. Believing what they want to believe. Believing what feels good. Believing what's convenient. Or believing wild conspiracy theories. Having arguments in comments sections on the internet. Repeating statistics they heard somewhere. This is the public. Who buy diet pills. Who buy penis pills. Who believe the earth is flat. Who watch WWE wrestling. Who stare at TV commercials. Who believe fake news they find on Facebook. Who vote for the same political party no matter what. This is the public. Apathetic. Eating Mcdonalds. Drinking Coca-Cola. Addicted to drugs. Addicted to porn. Addicted to their smartphones. Scrolling the Facebook newsfeed. Smoking. Gambling at the slot machines. Buying brand new cars. Buying things they don't need with money they don't have. These people don't care about truth. *They only want to feel good.* Easily manipulated. Easily controlled. Media illiterate. But fully confident in their world-view. These are the people who will allow the post-truth era to unfold.

An era of post-truth may well be dawning on us. As technology continues to advance (**Law 3: Technology Never Moves Backwards**) picking apart the truth from the false will only become more and more difficult. Fake media will become increasingly convincing, until it reaches the point where it's indistinguishable from reality. After this point is reached, the truth will be stated by whoever holds the most powerful and whoever states their version of the truth the loudest and most convincingly.

THE REAL BECOMES THE FAKE BECOMES THE REAL.

chapter 4

THE INTERNET

A Town Of Two Bubbles – A Story About The Internet

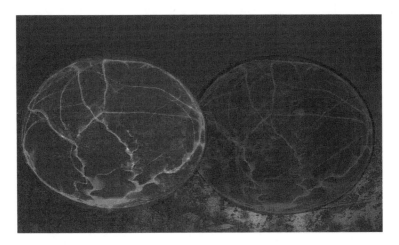

PART 1

A peaceful town lay between the hills for hundreds of years. This town was made up of two tribes who lived in harmony with one another; the Mezakis and the Jasims.

The Mezakis believed in caring for the sick and elderly and having an equal and fair society. While the Jasims believed in creating wealth, individual freedom and advancing the village into greater lands.

The two tribes had weekly meetings in the main hall, where they discussed important decisions about the future of their beloved town. These meetings were filled with disagreements, debates and passionate argumentation.

In this state, the town steadily moved forward. The townspeople lived better, more fulfilled lives with more opportunity than their grandparents ever had. Plentiful crops were grown every harvest, leaving everybody with plenty of food to fill their bellies.

That is, until one fateful night would change this peaceful town forever.

* * *

The witch hovered silently over the town upon her broomstick in the dead of night. This would be where she would cast her experiment.

She pointed her magic wand down towards the east side of the town and muttered the words of enchantment under her breath. Out of the wand came a stream of red electric energy firing towards the ground – quickly expanding into an enormous red sphere that covered half of the town.

She peered downwards. The night remained quiet and still. It seemed as though the townspeople hadn't been alerted to her presence. With this, she pointed her magic wand down towards the west side of the town and began murmuring the second enchantment. This time it was a blue electric energy that shot out of her wand – expanding into a huge blue sphere that surrounded the other side of the town.

She looked downwards upon her magicwork; two giant electric spheres, one red, one blue, both covering each half of the town.

The spells were a success.

"I'll be back in exactly one year to see the results", she thought to herself. And with that, the witch disappeared quietly into the night.

PART 2

People across the town emerged from their wooden homes and gazed up at the sky in bemusement. Two enormous spheres of electric light covered their town – the Mezaki side of town was covered by a giant red sphere, while a blue sphere covered the Jasim side.

Two Mezaki worksmen stood side by side gazing up at the sky. They both wore simple brown robes with sandals.

"What's all this then?" One said to the other.

"More witch magic probably", the other muttered irritably.

"What do you think it does?"

"Only god knows"

"You two!" A voice shouted at them from behind "A meeting has been called!"

The two men hurriedly followed the crowd into the meeting hall.

The hall filled quickly. Every Mezaki in town had been gathered together for the announcement. Men, women, children; all Mezakis stood gazing up at the wooden stage at the front of the hall.

Finally, their leader climbed up onto the stage. He was an overweight gentleman with balding grey hair wearing simple beige robes, yet the lines on his face spoke of wisdom and experience.

"Mezakis!" the leader's voice boomed from the stage. "As you're all aware, some witchcraft has fallen upon our great village! Now, we have tested the red barrier that surrounds us and it appears to be entirely impenetrable."

Some concerned and nervous chatter spread throughout the crowd.

"But fear not friends! The barrier extends way into our farmlands and beyond the outer gate. In essence, we can continue our lives as normal! The children shall even have ample space to play!"

Sighs of relief and relaxed conversation filled the meeting hall. Rarely did Mezakis or Jasims venture beyond the outer gate into the dangerous lands anyway.

"Whatever this witchcraft is, it seems as though the caster is merciful. We shall simply continue life as we've always done – with compassion for each other and to a long peaceful life!"

The crowd cheered and quickly dispersed out of the hall, heading back to their normal daily tasks. The two Mezaki worksman walked out together.

"What do you think the Jasims are talking about right now?"

"Probably thinking of how to use this to profit themselves as much as possible."

The first Mezaki worksman chuckled. "Probably."

PART 3

"Quiet please!" A stern voiced shouted from upon the stage of the Jasim main hall. The Jasims gathered inside the hall quickly and hushed each other into silence to hear their leader speak.

Upon the stage stood their leader, a well dressed man wearing a pair of round-framed glasses. He held a kind, yet serious expression on his face.

"You've all witnessed the strange blue energy that surrounds our side of the village. First and foremost: Do not panic! The barrier extends far outside our village walls and beyond the farmlands. As such, we can continue our usual harvest without any issues whatsoever."

The crowd breathed a collective sigh of relief. Conversational murmuring spread through the crowd. The leader raised his hand and the crowd hushed each other to silence once again.

"It seems as though we're entirely cut off from our good friends the Mezakis for the near future.."

"Maybe now we can get some real work done!" a boisterous voice yelled from somewhere amongst the crowd, followed by the laughter of a handful of people towards the back of the room.

The leader smiled, amused at the interruption.

"Now, now. We've lived and prospered alongside the Mezaki's for almost 100 years. Let's give them the credit and respect that they deserve."

A much larger part of the crowd jeered in agreement with the sentiment their leader.

"Ladies! Gentlemen! There is nothing more to be said. Everyone – back to your duties. Let us continue to live free and prosperous lives!".

The crowd cheered and pumped their fists into the air, before dispersing out of the meeting hall and back to their daily tasks. Two Jasim men spoke to each other as they left the hall.

"What do you expect the Mezakis are talking about right now?" said one.

"Probably the same as us. Only with more crying and hugging" said the other.

The two Jasims put their arms around each other and laughed together.

PART 4

As the weeks passed, both the Mezakis and the Jasims grew accustomed to the witchcraft that separated them. It didn't take long before the enormous spheres of light surrounding them were barely spoken of at all. After all, there was nothing to say. Witchcraft had always been strange and impossible to understand.

The two tribes continued their lives more or less as normal, only without any communication between each other.

While meetings between the two tribes in the past had been full of heated debates, arguments and the occasional spat of violence; meetings now seemed like pleasant occasions for both tribes.

The Mezakis could discuss ideas with other Mezakis. And the Jasims could discuss ideas with other Jasims.

The Jasims drew plans for expansion of the town's territory into the coal mines that lay just a mile north of the barrier. This would allow the village to become rich and be more competitive with other nearby towns.

Meanwhile, the Mezakis made plans to feed more of the town's poor and under privileged, as well as discussing steps towards equality for the blue-eyed minority who has long been discriminated against. There was some belief amongst some of the townspeople that the blue-eyed were a product of witchcraft, and for decades they had been denied the right to hold any positions of power.

Both tribes found that they were able to make fast progress without the constant pushback from the other.

The Jasims found they were able to push forward business plans rapidly, without the Mezakis constantly raising questions of fair wages and inclusivity. While the Mezakis were able to focus on making the town a more enjoyable and peaceful place to live, without having to deal with attempts of the Jasim seniors to siphon off profits for their own families at every occasion.

Two months passed.

And three Jasim men sat around the dinner table having just finished a long day's work.

"How's business Stephan?" said one.

"Excellent thanks Marcus" the oldest of the three replied respectfully. "Profits are up. And we've just bought some land in the coal mining program that will be ours as soon as it's up and running."

The youngest of the three chimed in "But the coal mine is a mile beyond the barrier. Why buy land out there?"

"All witchcraft fades eventually Jacob, you know that. The coal mine will be up and running soon enough."

"I suppose. As long as the Mewackys don't try to get in the way" The youngest of them spoke teasingly.

The oldest began stroking beard as he replied "I'm sure the Mezakis will see reason. And if they don't, well..."

The three Jasim men exchanged knowing looks.

* * *

Three Mezaki women sat around a campfire, each holding newborns to their chest. All three of them wore simple robes and sandals to cover their feet.

"How's your eldest coming along Bessie?" asked the oldest Mezaki woman with a caring, considerate look.

"Almost 14 now. She'll be joining the workforce soon. Wants to be a doctor." Answered the second Mezaki woman.

"Really? Is that going to be ok? She is..a blue-eyed after all. You know some of the elders refuse to listen to anyone of her kind..."

"I don't care about that Jasim nonsense", the second Mezaki woman spat. "Besides, the inclusivity law should be passed soon."

"Haha, true. As long as those Jasim imbeciles don't try to block it" spouted the youngest mother.

"Cynthia. That's offensive. Imbecility is a real condition you know. You need to learn to be more inclusive to all people. Think before you speak." the oldest woman responded sternly.

The youngest of the mothers became quiet and sheepish, not daring to say another word.

PART 5

Six more months passed.

And it was time for the two tribes to elect their new leaders. While previous elections had been quite dull affairs, this time emotions were running high and the air was filled with tension.

The Mezakis crowded into the village hall to listen to the two candidates. A lot had changed in the past 6 months and the atmosphere in the room was electric. It was going to be a close election and everyone knew it. The crowd gradually quietened down as the current leader took to the stage.

The leader stood calmly waiting for the crowd to simmer down. His balding grey hair and withered face shimmered in the light of the fires from the torches around the room.

"Mezakis! Friends! It's an honor to be stood before you once again in an attempt to win your hearts for reelection. Over the past 4 years we have a achieved so much, though not without our setbacks. We have marched steadily forward, improving our quality of life year after year, alongside our Jasim friends.."

Hissing, muttering and cursing erupted throughout the hall at the mention of the Jasims. The current leader raised his hand in an order of silence, his wise eyes peering down at the crowd.

"Our food is more plentiful, we have had successful harvests year on year. Our children's education is improving, almost all younglings in the village can read and write. And our government and businesses are more accepting and inclusive than ever before in Mezaki history.."

At this remark, a group to the right of the stage burst into a loud forced laughter – in an attempt to demonstrate their disagreement with the statement.

The leader raised his hand once again.

"Now now, let's just-"

"Equality now! Justice now! Equality now! Justice now! Equality now! Jus.." The chants from the small group to the right side of the stage continued on for several minutes, ignoring the current leader's calls for silence. Eventually, the chanting died down.

"As I was saying. We are no longer in the dark days of the past, where our ancestors struggled for food every single harvest. Where our ancestors battled the diseases and plagues every single year. Mezakis! I would be overjoyed to continue our steady forward march into the future! I know you'll make the right choice. Thankyou."

The audience applauded as the current leader stepped towards the back of the stage, his face filled with pride.

As the applause died down, the opposing candidate confidently strided onto the stage. A woman, with short, neat, dark hair and big wide eyes stared over the top of the audience. Every Mezaki knew her as Sashim, and she had become suprisingly popular over the previous 6 months.

Sashim cleared her throat loudly. "Mezakis. Comrades. It's time for change!. No longer can we accept the Jasim's selfish money hoarding. They sit in their enormous houses in front of their cozy fireplaces, while we live in wooden shacks. And what did they do to deserve such privilege? They stole from the rest of us!"

"Equality now!" screamed one enthusiastic member of the audience.

"Mezakis have always been about caring for one another. But where is the care for the elderly who die sick and alone? Where is the care for the Mezaki women among us who've been held back from the livelihoods they dream of? Where is the care for the blue-eyed among us who've been oppressed for hundreds of years?! Equality now! Justice now!"

Sashim screamed into the crowd, followed by more chanting from the crowd: "Equality now! Justice now! Equality now! Justice now!..".

"My opponent is not a woman. Nor is he a blue-eyed man. What does he know about oppression and hardship? Nothing! He's just as privileged as the Jasim elders! Let's move this town into the future. And shame on those who would stand in the way. Under my leadership, our great Mezaki tribe will become free of injustice and inequality forever! Equality now! Justice now!"

As the fierce short haired woman finished speaking the crowd erupted into applause and aggressive chanting. The current leader stood with a nervous smile on his face, sweat glistening on his forehead.

PART 6

The Jasim hall filled up quickly. Both candidates stood on the stage together. On the left—the current leader, wearing his signature round-framed glasses stood patiently. The opposing candidate, named Furlock, stood to the right — a man with a shaved head, wild eyes and a stern look upon his face. He was built big, his t-shirt was ripped at the sleeves revealing his bulging biceps.

As soon as the crowd quietened down, the current leader took a step forward to speak.

"Friends! It's that time again! Time for you to choose the future of our great town! We have prospered for decades. We live better, more comfortable and richer lives than ever before—and for that we must be grateful. With me as your leader, this trend shall continue as it has done the past 10 years. Us, together with the Mezakis, shall accomplish.."

"Mewacky lover!" a loud voice interrupted rudely from the crowd, followed by laughter and jeering from a group towards the back of the room. The current leader laughed nervously, trying to stay on good terms with the crowd.

Attempting to regain some authority, the current leader raised his hand, "Ok, ok. Let's just.."

"Blue-eyed lover!" another voice interrupted from the crowd. Laughter spread across the back of the room once again.

The current leader began to get somewhat angry.

"Jasims! Let us not stoop so low as to.."

"Furlock! Furlock! Furlock!", the chant started from the back of the room and gradually spread throughout the crowd. Furlock, the shaved headed opponent, pumped his fist towards the sky and much of the crowd roared with pride.

Furlock began to speak with a deep booming voice, ignoring the protests of the current leader.

"Brothers! The time has come! For too long we have squandered our in-born Jasim potential. For too long we have allowed the weak to lead us nowhere. The Jasims are the greatest tribe the world has ever seen! And yet..that's not what the world thinks of us brothers.."

Furlock carried such charismatic energy that the crowd was completely enthralled with his speech.

"Do you know what the neighbouring towns say about us? They say we're weak!. The leader of the city of Dowlin actually called us "insignificant". Insignificant.. can you believe that brothers?"

Angry boos and jeers echoed through the crowd as Furlock paused.

"The question is, brothers, why do they think this? Well, the truth is..we are weak!" The crowd turned completely silent.

"Or rather, we've been weakened, poisoned, by the Mewacky fools at our side!" Much of the crowd cheered in agreement, while others shuffled uncomfortably.

"For years, we reasoned, argued and debated the Mewacky fools over building the coal mine to the north. To increase our wealth and become the great tribe we truly are! But no. They would rather cozy up to the blue-eyed outsiders and remain weak. They even want to allow blue-eyeds to become doctors, teachers and even priests! The Mewacky fools are too weak to create their own wealth, so they want to steal ours. They talk of "equality", but what they truly are is weak! So brothers! Let me lead you! Let us pure-blooded Jasims become the great tribe we always were! Let the world know of our greatness!"

Much of the crowd roared with pride, others clapped politely, some clapped nervously. The current leader had already slipped out the back entrance.

PART 7

It was the dead of night and the witch hovered above the town once again. She floated silently upon her broomstick and gazed down upon the town she had visited precisely one year before. The blue and red barriers still remained perfectly intact.

"Right" the witch muttered under her breath.

She raised her wand down towards the ground and quietly murmured a reverse enchantment. The spell activated and quickly the red barrier began to be sucked back into her wand. After several seconds, the red barrier was completely absorbed.

The witch then pointed her wand down towards the other side of town and cast the same reverse enchantment, sucking all of the blue energy that made up the barrier back into her wand.

The witch took a breath and spoke to herself, "Well then, let's see what happens."

PART 8

I am reporting exactly 6 months after the completion of experiment #137.

The results were...fascinating.

Upon removal of the barriers, both the Mezakis and the Jasims immediately began working on their own projects with extreme enthusiasm.

While the Jasim leader, Furlock, seemed to have some dangerous ideas, he only had a small amount of support and so could not act upon his wishes.

It was the Mezaki leader, Sashim, who managed to cause the most havoc. It seemed as though her message of inclusivity and equality was received well by most Mezakis, and as such she became incredibly popular.

She began by allowing women and so called "blue eyes" to occupy positions of power. Gradually, her and her fanatic followers started publicly shaming those who made any disagreement with their plans – accusing them of holding prejudice toward the blue-eyed's.

After only two months, it seemed as though most Mezakis were too afraid to question anything Sashim or her follows said or did. So when she started having both Mezakis and Jasims removed from their jobs for making "anti blue-eyed" comments, there was little resistance.

And there was even less resistance as she began imprisoning those she personally deemed "anti-equality". Within three months, she was even imprisoning members of her own supporters for speaking out of line.

The Mezaki tribe which, on the surface, appeared to be a caring a loving people, seemed to have been drastically affected by the year inside the barrier. Without push-back from the Jasims, extreme ideas seemed to have circulated and grown quickly.

Sashim then announced that she would take all the coal from the coal mine. She decided that all coal would be placed into the hands of the Mezaki leadership to be "distributed equally" amongst the town.

That was when the Jasims turned.

Anti-Mezaki feelings had been growing for quite some time amongst the Jasims. Because of Sashim's poor leadership, the harvest had been poor that year and many had gone hungry. Many Jasims had lost their esteemed jobs as teachers, priests and business owners for "anti-equality" speech.

Furlock quietly gathered a large group of young Jasim men and invaded the Mezaki side of town in the dead of night.

It is said that 72 Mezakis were murdered on that first night alone.

The Jasims, who had always had greater weaponry, completely overwhelmed the Mezakis. Within 2 weeks, all 721 blue-eyed townspeople had been hunted down and slaughtered ruthlessly, along with those Mezakis who tried to hide them.

After only 1 month, 15% of the Mezakis had been killed – a total of 3281 deaths.

The Mezaki end of town was set in flames, Sashim was burned to death at the stake, and in the end the Mezakis had no choice but to accept Furlock's overwhelming power.

At the time of this report, Furlock has complete power over the town. He rules both the Jasims and the Mezakis under an iron-fist, and controls the people under the threat of violence. At the present moment it seems as though he's arming the townspeople for war against the nearby city of Dowlin. The population has been militarized, and all men must wield a sword and join the fight.

And so concludes my report of experiment #137. What does all this mean? I couldn't say. I'm not interested in such matters. I only came to see out the experiment's success.

Perhaps you, who hears this report, can draw your own conclusions about my work and use it to shape the future in a positive manner.

Good luck to you.

filter bubbles – the invisible polariser

In December 2009, Google made the decision to begin using fifty-seven different signals - signals such as your location, which browser you're using, what you've searched for in the past and other signals – to make guesses about what kind of sites you might like. Very quietly, Google had become personalised to the individual. More or less nobody noticed this change, but from this moment onwards each of us has been inside our own personal filter bubble (term coined by Eli Pariser in his 2011 book *The Filter Bubble*). And ever since this moment, not coincidentally, societies around the entire planet have become more and more polarised. In the first decade of the new millennium, there was a sense across the world that the internet would be an incredible tool that could connect people all over the world. No longer would people have narrow points of view. Everybody would understand each other as information travelled between societies and groups freely. Many even looked ahead into the future and hypothesised that the internet would mean the end of war. One world consciousness, so connected together that war would be impossible. Any active internet user will have fond memories of a kind of digital wild west, with very few restrictions and an endless source of interesting new information and points of view. But since 2009, a major shift has occurred online. The internet has become personalised. *There is no standard Google any more.* Every single person has Google results that are tailored specifically to them. If two people search for "America" into Google, their results will be completely different from each other (besides a Wikipedia page and some basic information on the sidebar). A patriotic individual would likely see content with headlines like "Why America is STILL the greatest country in the world", while a less patriotic individual might see "Do Americans need to adapt to an America in decline". With shockingly few exceptions, the content you find on Google will only confirm your existing beliefs. And it's not only Google that uses algorithms to personalise their content; Facebook, Youtube and just about every social media network does the exact same thing. Rather than a standard, static internet where everybody gets the same search results, we now each get search results tailored personally for us. And the bubble is incredibly difficult to see. How would you know if your search results were different from somebody else's? Each and every individual is inside their own invisible filter bubble and only very few are really conscious of it's existence.

This isn't the wild west any more. Instead of users being able to roam freely around the open landscape of the internet on horseback, they're jailed in by their own personal filter bubble As these algorithms have developed overtime, more recently we've begun to see all of the personal filter bubbles merge into much larger, collective filter bubbles. These larger filter bubbles contain millions of users that share the same ideology. Feminism. MGTOW. Flat earthers. Left-Wing politics, Right-Wing politics. The list is endless.

But let's slow down for a second. Why did Google, Youtube, Facebook and others decide to personalise their websites rather than leaving them as the open sources of information they were pre-2009? Simple, it's good business **(Law 4: Media Is About Profit).** The Youtube recommendation sidebar is the perfect example of just how effective personalisation is for increasing user engagement. The vast majority of video views on Youtube come from the side bar personally recommending other videos to the audience. The algorithm takes into account what you've watched previously, then cross-references your watch history with millions of other users with similar watch histories to choose the *perfect* selection of videos that you, personally, are most likely to click on. The power of this algorithm should not be understated. If Youtube decided to recommend you a random selection of videos, or perhaps just other random videos inside the category you're currently watching, the amount of time spent on their website would probably decrease by at least 40-50%. Personalisation keeps people on the website, increases their overall watch time and allows Youtube to sell their advertising at a higher price (because they have more eyeballs on their videos). And it's not only about the sheer amount of time spent on a platform. The more personally relevant the data they collect on you is, the more ads they can sell, and the more likely you are to buy they products they're selling. The more they learn about your watch habits, the more money they make.

The following is an example of how personalisation on the internet traps people inside a filter bubble and changes their views:

You're an 18 year old girl still in college and your boyfriend cheats on you right in front of you. After days spent crying in despair you wipe away your tears and head to Google for answers. In your misery you search "Why are men so stupid". You receive the following top 3 results.

Research Confirms That Men Are, In Fact, Idiots | Psychology Today
https://www.psychologytoday.com/us/blog/.../research-confirms-men-are-in-fact-idiot... ▾

10 Dumb Things Indian Men Need To Stop Assuming About Women ...
https://www.huffingtonpost.in/2016/06/16/women-tinder_n_10500404.html ▾

Men Are Alarmingly Dumb, Science Says - Jezebel
https://jezebel.com/men-are-alarmingly-dumb-science-says-1670265289 ▾

All 3 top results confirm your suspicions that men are in fact stupid. You click the first link and Google's algorithms record the click.

You never took much interest in feminism before but the article mentions it a few times and you're in pain and open to new ideas. You spend the rest of the evening clicking the links of feminist articles learning about the social movement. Google records all of your clicks.

The following day after another hour spent crying into your pillow you clear away the tears again and hop back onto Youtube for some cute kitten videos to help ease the pain. But before you can click on any kitten videos another video catches your attention.

SERIOUS QUESTION: ARE MEN DUMB?!😬
✔ 54K views • 5 days ago

Here's my newest Vlog: https://youtu.be/zC7k4OqFkrA Ladies, comment below on the

New   CC

Unaware to you, Google used the information from the previous day's searches to ensure other content that you are likely to be interested in appears to you. Youtube, after all, is owned by Google.

Still hurting from your cheating boyfriend, this thumbnail speaks to you. You click it and watch the pretty Vlogger explain 10 reasons why men are dumb. After the video ends another thumbnail to the right hand side of the video speaks out to you.

WHY I'M A...FEMINIST *gasp*

✓ 4.2M views • 3 years ago

this isn't even a quarter of my list O__O ❤ join my patreon community! -
http://www.patreon.com/lacigreen facebook friend me! http://

CC

You remember now that you spent last night reading all about feminism.
You click this video and watch as you find yourself relating to the young
girl in the video and agreeing with many points that she makes. At the end
of the video she politely asks for you to like her Facebook page "Feminism
for young women". You kindly oblige and you go ahead and "Like" her
Facebook page.

Facebook records the click.

The following day you open up Facebook to stalk your ex-boyfriend and
shout angrily at a digital image of his face. But before you can, an article
appears on your newsfeed that catches your interest.

 9 February · ●

"Lloyd oversees detained unaccompanied minors, yet has no experience in
refugee resettlement and has a long history of promoting anti-woman
rhetoric."

Meet the Man Trying to Force Undocumented Women to Reverse Their Abortions

After months of doing everything in its power to prevent several undocumented
women from accessing abortion, news has broken that Trump's Office of Refugee...

After many months of daily internet browsing you miraculously find yourself
becoming a devout feminist, and now have strong opinions on all kinds

of subjects: Abortion, gender equality in STEM fields, immigration, rape, the #METOO movement, workplace sexual misconduct, female gentile mutilation, safe spaces, domestic violence and the wage gap.

The world begins to feel incredibly unfair. It just seems as though men have it so much better. It's like everywhere you look there is injustice against women. And that's because it is.

It is everywhere you look. The Youtube front page. The Facebook news feed. Your Twitter news feed. Your Google searches.

You are inside the filter bubble.

While the girl in this scenario believes she just happened to become interested in feminism, actually this was an interest created, not necessarily by her own doing, but by algorithms. This isn't to say that an interest in feminism is a good or bad thing, only that this exact same pattern pulls individuals into all kinds of different filter bubbles across the internet. Men's rights activists, Incel/Black Pill Ideology, Left-wing politics, Right-wing politics, conspiracy theorist communities (Qannon for example),

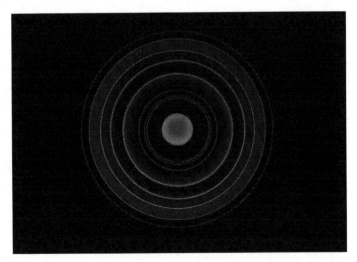

baby boomers, millennials and countless other bubbles.

Every single one of these filter bubbles has a gravitational pull towards the exact centre of the ideology inside of it. The closer to the centre you're pulled, the more extreme your views become.

You can start by searching "Girls are annoying" and be pulled into the MGTOW filter bubble until you're reading posts like "Why feminists are so fat and ugly" and "Women only want you for your wallet" Without a conscious resistance against it, you're pulled into extreme points of view. Content creators are desperate for clicks and are encouraged to write more and more extreme content. Because inside each filter bubble is a market of competing content that wants your attention. Balanced nuanced content doesn't draw in many clicks. It's the sensationalised, provocative Youtube video that draws in an audience, so content creators are incentivised to create content stating extreme opinions, usually accompanied by clickbait headlines. EG. *"Why are millennials such snowflakes"* or *"How the baby boomers ruined the world"*. This is where the gravitational pull comes from; you're more likely to click the more the sensationalised headlines and be exposed to more extreme content. The more time you spend consuming the same online ideology, the harder it is to understand any opposing points of view. And the walls of your filter bubble get stronger as Google and Facebook's algorithms feed you more and more of the same content.

It's not only that the content changes to suit you, it's also that *you change to suit the content.* Bit by bit, with each piece of content your consume, your views about the world will gradually change to fit the bubble the algorithms have sorted you into. For someone who spends a considerable amount of time online, their views can change quite drastically over the course of a single year. You may have started the year as a person who feels a slight sense of distrust towards the mainstream media, and then end the year as a devoted follower of the Qannon conspiracy that believes that there's a paedophile ring inside Hollywood. You may start the year as a compassionate person who dislikes racism against black people and end the year saying things like "Fuck all white people" and "All white people are racists". Without reasonable pushback from ideas outside the filter bubble, people's views become more and more extreme as they continue to draw their conclusions about the world based only on the content they've consumed from inside their filter bubble. An echo-chamber is created in which everyone inside it generally has the same world-view. Sure, individuals inside the filter bubble may argue about the specifics of their ideas, but the general world-view or ideology inside the filter bubble is the same. Then, on the rare occasions where they encounter view-points from outside the filter bubble, they find it unfathomable that somebody could have a world-view so different from their own.

Inside the filter bubble, the other side is constantly strawmaned. The arguments of the opposing bubble are turned into 2D caricatures of the actual argument. Inside the feminist bubble, men's rights activists (MRAs) are just a bunch of women hating crybabies. Inside the MRA bubble, feminists are just a bunch of blue haired, shrieking, fat lesbians. Inside the right-wing bubble, "lefties" are a bunch of irrational extremeists, who always want handouts from the government and are too lazy to seek success themselves. Inside the left-wing bubble, right-wingers are greedy, selfish, stupid, white, privileged and evil. Each filter bubble is filled with propaganda about those that oppose the bubble.

On the scale of the society, this means polarised elections and more and more extremist political groups. Between the years of 2009 (when filter bubbles began) and 2020, extremism has risen throughout the entire world and polarisation has occurred in different countries around the globe. Trump in America, Brexit in United Kingdom, Bolsanaro in Brazil and a rise in Nazi ideology in Germany. How else can you explain such extremism and polarisation at the exact same time across the entire planet? Personally, I am of the opinion that filter bubbles are the *primary reason* for the polarisation and extremeism we've seen over the last decade (More on this in chapter 10). In our personal lives, filter bubbles mean that men and women are being ideologically torn further and further apart from each other. Men and women tend to have different interests and are therefore often pulled into different filter bubbles online. Many of these filter bubbles have toxic views towards those of the opposite sex. Large parts of the feminist filter bubble have incredibly negative views towards men (even if they claim not to) and many of those in the Red Pill filter bubble have toxic views towards women. Yet these bubbles are not only dark pits of negativity, within them are also positive and helpful messages. The Red Pill community helps men to achieve their goals and stop drifting through life, while the feminist community helps women to empower themselves be confident with who they are. Both of these communities have great messages embedded within them, but they also tend to cause people to resent or distrust the opposite sex. These filter bubbles create both positive and negative effects in people.

Once you're inside the filter bubble, the gravitational pull makes it incredibly difficult to leave and seek real alternative perspectives. *What you've clicked on in the past determines what you'll see next*, a cycle that you're doomed to repeat over and over again. You get stuck in and endless loop of watching the same type of content over and over again, and without self-awareness, you become more and more unabashedly sure that your world-view is correct. Those who don't share your world-view must be stupid, evil or liars. And those in the filter bubbles you're not a part of think exactly the same thing about you. Echo chambers have always been a problem, especially in politics. But it seems as though right now the internet is not only encouraging echo chambers to exist but also dragging unsuspecting users into them and then building digital walls to make sure they don't escape.

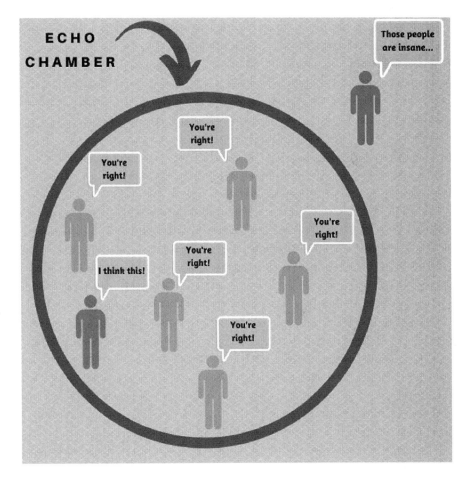

HOW FILTER BUBBLES ARE CHANGING YOUR PERCEPTION OF REALITY.

LEFT: HOW PEOPLE WITH ASTIGMATISM SEE THE WORLD. RIGHT: HOW A NORMAL PERSON SEES THE WORLD

The above image was tweeted in April 2019. It shows the difference between the way those with astigmatism see the world vs those who don't. It went viral, and thousands of people were in disbelief that they could be seeing the world so differently from those around them (astigmatism is an imperfection in the curvature of your eye's cornea or lens that can cause blurry vision). One user tweeted *"...my life and seeing is a lie, I thought everyone saw the lines"*. Another user wrote *"I always thought this was normal wtf"*.

We think those around us see the world the same way we do and yet there are others who view the very structure of light differently from ourselves. If this is the case, just how different are the perceptions of those around you to your own? People walking past you in the street. People sitting opposite you in the coffee place. People in their cars. What's going through their heads? How do they see the world? Do they have similar perceptions to yours? Or are they living in an entirely different reality to your own?

The main factor in how somebody perceives the world is what they pay attention to. But before I explain how the algorithms are changing your perception of reality, you need to understand the Reticular Activating System (RAS).

And you need to understand the Invisible Gorilla.

In this now world famous experiment, a video of 6 students passing basketballs to each other was shown to volunteers. One team wearing white shirts, the other wearing black shirts. Volunteers were asked to count the number of passes between the students in white shirts while ignoring any passes from those in the black shirts. Many volunteers guessed the correct number of passes, 34. What many of them didn't

DAVID SIMONS (1999).

see however was the student *wearing a full-body gorilla suit* that walked right into the centre of the frame, looked at the camera, pounded their chest and then slowly walked off camera.

Volunteers were then asked some follow up questions:

> **Q: Did you see anything unusual while watching the video?**
>
> A: No
>
> **Q: Did you notice anything other than the players?**
>
> A: Well, there were some elevators and some S's painted on the wall. I don't know what the S's were there for.
>
> **Q: Did you notice anyone other than the players?**
>
> A: No.
>
> **Q: Did you notice a Gorilla?**
>
> A: A what?!

Unbelievably, around 50% of the volunteers failed to see the Gorilla right in the middle of the screen pounding it's chest. This experiment has been replicated over and over again, in multiple countries under varying conditions. Yet the results are always the same; roughly half of the participants fail to see the gorilla. One of the most interesting things about this experiment was the reaction of the participants. They were completely shocked. Some spontaneously shouted "No way!" or "I missed that?!". Others accused the experimenters of lying or switching the tapes for the 2nd viewing. How could people fail to see something right in front of their eyes? Because their RAS (Reticular Activating System) was focused on the task of counting passes and wasn't looking for a gorilla.

The RAS is a bundle of nerves near the bottom of our brainstem that acts as a filter for information. It decides what information gets in and what doesn't. It takes what you decide to focus on and creates a filter for it. Of course, it's an entirely subconscious mechanism. You've experienced the RAS in action before. When you're in a crowded room full of people talking and you hear someone mention your name from across the room. Out of the hundreds of things being said in the room, your RAS filters

through the information and feeds you that which is relevant to you. Or perhaps you decide to buy yourself a new car. A Toyota, for example. Suddenly you may start noticing other Toyotas everywhere you go. Where did all these Toyotas come from suddenly? Did this brand suddenly get incredibly popular? No.The Toyotas

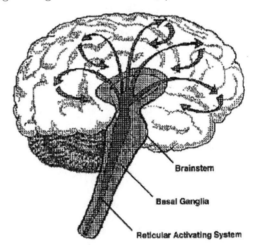

were there all along. You just never noticed them before. The Toyota is the invisible gorilla you couldn't see before because you weren't focused on it. Your RAS simply started to focus on them because this information became relevant to you.

What determines which information your RAS lets in? Your past experiences. Your goals. And your world-view. This means that everybody around you is focusing on different things than what you're focusing on. Their RAS is filtering through different information. *The people around you aren't seeing the world the same way as you because their attention is focused on different things.* Your RAS filters information through to you that you expect to see based on your world-view. If you believe the world is a dark and cruel place, you'll notice all of the negative things around you. The beggars on the street. The rats in the gutter. The miserable expressions of the people on the crowded train. If you believe the world is a happy and cheerful place, you'll notice all of the positive things around you. The children playing. The people laughing happily in the bar. The sun on your face. *Your world-view determines what you see.*

The human eye has a singular focus. It works just like a camera lens (The camera lens, of course, was modelled after the human eye). Hold your thumb out in front of your face and focus specifically on your thumbnail. Now, while continuing to stare at your thumbnail, try to notice everything behind it. Don't look around the room. Keep staring at your thumb. But notice everything that lies behind it. You'll see that everything behind your thumb is blurry and out of focus. You think you see the world as it is but actually your focus is extremely narrow. The question is: What are you focusing on? And what is fading into the background unnoticed? What are your invisible gorillas? Are you the feminist who notices the "man-spreading" on the train but fails to notice the four homeless men they saw on the way to the train station? Are you the businessman who loves our capitalistic society but fails to notice the ills contained within it? Are you the guy who believes that America are the "good guys" while failing to notice unnecessary wars created around the world by America? Your world-view determines which aspects of the world are in-focus and which are left out of focused in the background. So your world-view determines what you see.

But what shapes your world-view? Where do you get most of your information about the world? The media. *The media you consume influences what you focus on.* Without the media, we would all be focused on the things that are immediately around us. Focused on your goals. Your friends. Your family. Your town or village. Everyone you know would have a similar perspective of the world to yourself. This is how our ancestors lived. But we live in the information age and because of the media (the internet in particular) people are beginning to have wildly different perspectives of the world around them. More importantly, each of us live inside digital filter bubbles created by algorithms. Because Google and Facebook personalises what we see using algorithms (In an effort to maximise engagement with their platform), the information you see online is generally information you agree with. *The algorithms are shaping the information you see and therefore are shaping what you notice in the world.* The information in your digital filter bubbles shapes your world-view. Then you go out into the world and your RAS pays attention to things that confirm the world-view that was created largely by consuming content inside your digital filter bubble.

It goes like this: An individual with right-wing political beliefs spends a year on the internet. Searching for various terms on Google and following different Facebook groups that they're interested in. The algorithms on Google, Facebook and Youtube (Youtube is owned by Google) feed them content they're the most likely to click—which is content that confirms their right-ring political beliefs to be accurate. They consume countless hours of content discussing the negative aspects of mass immigration. Then they head out into the world and their RAS focuses on any occasion they see someone from another country conducting any sort of negative behaviour (fighting, being rude, littering, spiting) because this confirms their current world view (Again, this world-view was largely created by the digital filter bubble they're in). Their RAS will also tend to filter out any occasions when they come across an immigrant who is indulging in a positive behaviour as this does not confirm their world view. Now they're only paying attention to things that confirm the world view that was created by the algorithms of Google and Facebook. *Therefore, algorithms are changing their perception of reality.*

The exact same effect is present on those with left-wing political beliefs. Or any other kind of beliefs. In fact, the same effect will likely occur in anyone who spends a large amount of time on the internet. The more time you spend on the internet, the more this effect will impact your psychology. As you walk through the world, what do pay attention to? Which information from the world is in focus and which is left unnoticed by your RAS? What are your invisible gorillas? And how much of what you're seeing in the world around you is being determined by the filter bubbles you're trapped in?

"Every man takes the limits of his own field of vision for the limits of the world"
- Arthur Schopenhauer

why the comments section is full of a**holes

"I've gotta take a leak" you tell your friend. He nods and continues to stare down at his pint of beer. You pass by a table of drunk teenagers laughing loudly and make your way to the bathroom.

The toilet is full of cracked tiles and stains on the walls. The urinal is blocked, so you use the cubicle instead. As you're doing your business, you notice the wall is covered in writing. One message written with a black marker stands out more than the others. It reads:

WHOEVER USES THIS TOILET IS A VIRGIN

The message is followed with an arrow pointing down into toilet you're currently pissing into.

You raise your eyebrow at the childish message. But then you notice that the black marker pen has been left on the floor. "Fuck it" you say to yourself. You pick up the marker and write your reply:

WHOEVER WROTE THIS MESSAGE IS A FUCKING IDIOT

The next week you come back to the same bar. "I've gotta take a leak" you say to your friend. He nods silently while looking down at his pint of beer like always.

You're about to unzip your pants when you notice that a new message has been added to the wall.

BE QUIET LIBTARD

This makes you angry for two reasons. One: The level of stupidity. Two: Why the hell is this guy assuming that I'm politically liberal? The black marker pen has been left on the floor again, so you pick it up and write your response:

NOT THE SHARPEST TOOL IN THE SHED ARE YOU MORON

Every week you and your friend visit the same bar and every week this idiot has left a new message. This guy is obviously a complete imbecile, but you find it kind of entertaining. So you continue replying to this idiot's messages and the conversation continues:

WHOEVER USES THIS TOILET IS A VIRGIN
WHOEVER WROTE THIS MESSAGE IS A F**KING IDIOT
BE QUIET LIBTARD
NOT THE SHARPEST TOOL IN THE SHED ARE YOU MORON
I HOPE YOU DIE TODAY
GO TAKE A WALK INTO TRAFFIC
DO THE WORLD A FAVOUR AND KILL YOURSELF
PLEASE. DON'T HAVE KIDS. YOUR GENES ARE TOXIC

This goes on for several weeks.

One day, you're hanging out with your friend at the bar like usual. Talking nonsense. Making jokes.

As he picks up his pint of beer and starts to drink you notice something.

Black ink on his fingertips.

Each technology interacts in its own unique way with human psychology and people communicate differently through technology than they do in the real world (**Law 1: The Medium Is The Message**). Considering that text based communication is the main way that we communicate with each other - wouldn't it be a good idea to actually understand the effects this has on our psychology? After reading this chapter you will be able to browse the internet in peace. You will no longer get frustrated, angry or depressed by the way others act on the internet. You will understand why the comments section is full of assholes. And you won't hold it against them quite so much.

There are 6 main factors that encourage people to act far more negatively on the internet than they do in the real world:

1.   *The Empathy Deficit*

2.   *Asynchronous Communication*

3.   *Lack of Authority*

4.   *Solipsistic Introjection*

5.   *Audience Size*

6.   *Likes, Comments, Follows, Shares*

(1-4 are based on the online disinhibition effect coined by Suler,J in 2004)

1.THE EMPATHY DEFICIT

In a real conversation you make eye-contact. You see facial expressions. You hear vocal tonality. You see body language. You see that look in their eyes. You can tell when they're upset, when they're frustrated and when they're being sarcastic (most of the time). When you're staring face to face with someone your mirror neurons fire up. These are the same mirror neurons that allowed us to learn from our parents when we were younger. The same mirror neurons that allowed our ancestors to teach their children how to build a fire. When you see someone get punched in the nose, you wince because the mirror neurons in your brain make you feel a piece of that pain yourself. *We've evolved to have face-to-face conversations, not communicate by text.* (**Law 2: Technology Is An Evolutionary Mismatch**). Communication by text results in an unnatural empathy deficit. We don't see facial expressions. We don't hear vocal tonality. And we don't see that look in their eyes. Therefore empathy breaks down. That's why many people have no problem telling others to kill themselves in the comment section. That's why many people have no problem leaving death threats in other's inboxes. That's why tens of thousands of people can attack a single person on Twitter and feel no guilt whatsoever. Imagine that instead of communicating in the Youtube comments section, a crowd of people spoke together face to face to exchange their thoughts on the video they'd just watched? How would their communication change? Would tens of thousands of people mob a single person walking down the street like they do on Twitter? Shouting horrific insults and death threats right to their face? I don't think so.

2.ASYNCHRONOUS COMMUNICATION

In the comments section (and in messenger apps) people don't deal with real-time reactions from others, just like leaving messages on a toilet wall. You can leave a comment and then immediately disappear. Often you won't get a response for hours, days or weeks. Not having to deal with someone's immediate reaction disinhibits people. People are braver than they are in the real world because they don't have to deal with feedback. On the other hand, face to face communication is a continuous feedback loop between two people. For every single thing that you say, there will be immediate feedback from the other person. This feedback loop encourages civil behaviour that conforms to social norms. When there are long delays in this feedback loop, civil behaviour often breaks down and people feel free to type any toxic message that they want.

3. LACK OF AUTHORITY

In the comments section everyone is equal. Everyone has exactly the same status. There is no way of knowing who is an expert on the subject at hand and who has absolutely no idea what they're talking about. In the real world we have experts with experience and qualifications on particular topics. We have authority figures. Authority figures express their status and power with their dress, facial expressions, body language, qualifications and social reputation. Human beings intuitively pick up cues of authority. We know when someone is sure of themselves and when they're not. Our brains are evolved to live in tribes. If our ancestors spoke loudly and obnoxiously to an authority figure in their tribe, they could have been killed. So we have a natural instinct to respect authority.

But in the comments section where figures of authority are minimised, people are much more likely to speak out and misbehave. Those with no authority on a subject feel like they can can voice their opinions loudly and confidently. They feel as though have an equal status to everybody else present. This results in a comments section full of loud and confident people who feel free to state their uninformed opinion as loudly as they like. On Reddit there are moderators who have the ability to ban particular users from a group. This is one reason why people are generally more respectful to each other on Reddit than in the Youtube comments section, where the only authority figure is the creator of the video (who has no real incentive to moderate the comments).

4. SOLIPSISTIC INTROJECTION

When people read text, they create images in their mind. When you read a fictional novel, you create an image in your mind of the characters being described in the book. In exactly the same way, you create an image of the user you're talking to. Not only that, you might even recreate their voice. You may even imagine their whole identity. You don't know who this person is, what they look like or what they sound like. So your mind may create its own image of them. This image will be based on your own perception of the world. For example, if you're a men's rights activist and you read a pro-feminist comment, you may create an image in your head of the commenter. A man-hating, blue haired, shreaking, overweight, ugly woman. An image that is probably not accurate to reality. On the other hand, if you're a feminist and you read an anti-feminist comment you may also create a particular image in your head. An angry, misogynist, uneducated, ugly and frustrated man. You may have already created the perfect negative stereotype of the commenter in your mind before replying to them. *In the comments section, you argue with figments of your own imagination.* Our brains don't fully understand that we're talking with another human being. After all, there are no other human beings present, only words on a computer screen. To our lizard brain it doesn't feel as though we're communicating with another human being. So we argue with our own imagination instead.

5. AUDIENCE SIZE

It only takes a few toxic people to ruin a comments section. Negative energy spreads from person to person. If you want proof of this go to any Youtube comments section (on more or less any video) and see how one toxic comment turns into 10 toxic comments. One user will leave a toxic comment on the video "The guy in this video looks like Jabba The Hut". Then someone else will reply to him in a toxic manner "Shut up douche you're probably as fat as he is". Following this exchange 5 other users will join the conversation and post toxic comments of their own. This is how negative energy flows from person to person. One toxic user turns into 10 turns into 50. And pretty soon the entire comments section is filled with personal insults, radical generalisations and other toxic behaviours. The bigger the audience, the more toxic users are commenting. And it only takes a small number of toxic users to infect everyone else. That's why the worst comments sections are usually on Youtube, Facebook and Twitter. Smaller websites are capable of having civilised comments sections because the audience is small enough that there aren't too many toxic users. *The bigger the audience, the more toxic the comments section.*

6. LIKES, COMMENTS, FOLLOWS, SHARES

The comments section is an environment where you have a very short time to impress your reader. Most people don't read comments more than a few sentences long. A well-balanced point takes at least a few paragraphs to make (especially as the internet shortens our attention spans). Anger is incentivised. Outrage is incentivised. Snarky one liners are incentivised. These are the comments that get likes. The well-balanced, thoughtful comments? These fade into obscurity. People love to be validated by others. The "like" you receive on your comment makes you feel good. People crave likes. And they'll adapt their behaviour in order to get them. In an effort to chase "likes", each user will try to post an even snappier "zinger" than the person before them. It doesn't matter if the zinger is negative or harmful, as long as it pleases the crowd and makes them click "like". But it's not only "likes". It's "follows" too. A well-placed snarky comment that gets 1000 likes can also get followers. And followers give you influence. On Twitter, which essentially a giant comment section— enough followers can turn you from nobody into somebody. So the incentive to make a comment full of outrage, anger or snark is extremely high. The internet is full of people desperately saying whatever it takes to get the likes and follows they desire.

THE WORST POSSIBLE COMMUNICATION MEDIUM

The entire planet is communicating predominantly via text based communication. Sure there's video. There's voice. But most of the internet is text based. And most communication is done through messages. Friends, family and lovers communicate with text. Tweets are mainstream news. Most political discourse happens online via text. Considering all the flaws of text based communication (The Empathy Deficit, Asynchronous communication, Lack of authority, Solipsistic Introjection) is it really the best idea to have most of our conversations through this medium? For most people, the internet is their main chance to see the people outside their own personal social circle. Spend an afternoon on Twitter and you may begin to feel as though the world is full of cruel, stupid and negative people. And yet when you step away from your computer and actually go outside into the real world everything is completely different. People are generally civil. People are chatting happily with each other. People are focused on their jobs. Why is there such a huge difference between Twitter and the real world? Because in the real world we're communicating the way we're evolved to communicate. Face to face.

Many people assume that the internet reveals the truth about how people really are. They believe that due to the anonymity, people take off their masks and show us all their true colours. This is false. As we've discovered here, the internet changes how people act. It doesn't *reveal* how people really are. It *changes* how people are. The internet isn't a clear lens into the rest of the world. It's a distorted lens. Because technology isn't neutral. Text based communication may actually be the worst possible communication medium. And yet this is our main global communication medium. What is text based communication doing to our political dialogue? Our relationships? Our mental health?

My advice for you is this: Don't get upset by the toxic behaviour on the internet. Know that if everyone was standing in a room talking face to face they would act completely differently. And not because they're hiding their true feelings, but because they're not communicating through the distorted filter of text based communication.

why it's so hard to focus on the internet

Ok. Time to start my essay.

Click Google Chrome. "American Civil War Facts" search into Google. Click Wikipedia Page. Read opening paragraph. Skim through hyperlinks to find relevant information. American Civil War started in 1865.

BING! Stacy tagged you in a photo on Facebook. Click on photo. Read comments. Click on Stacy's profile. Browse through 7 photos. Clark has sent you a message. Check message. A funny GIF. Find the correct GIF to reply with. Onto Facebook Newsfeed. Scroll. Scroll. Scroll. Hilarious Youtube video. Click.

Finish video. Another funny video in the recommended section on Youtube. Click. Read through comments on video.

Ok back to the essay. Google search "Why did the American Civil War start?" Click first article. Read first two paragraphs and take notes. Article goes off topic. Back to search results. Next article. This article is boring.

BING! @SarahisAwesome Mentioned you on Twitter. Check Sarah's tweet. Tweet back to Sarah. Scroll through Sarah's old tweets.

Alright. Back to the essay. Google Search. "How long did the American Civil war last for?". Open wikipedia page. Skim, skim skim skim. Ah! The American Civil War lasted for 4 years. Time to write the opening para..

BING! Clark has replied to your message. Clark says "What you up to? :D" You reply to Clark: "Working hard on my essay, you?"

You might believe that you choose for yourself how to use the internet, but does it actually feel that way? Doesn't it feel more like your attention is being pulled against its will to places you don't want it to go? Just ask anybody who's been through a University course in the last 5 years. You head to the library to start your 10000 word dissertation and wake up an hour later realising you spent the entire time stalking your friends on Facebook, scrolling through Twitter and getting lost down a Youtube rabbit hole. Is that how you *wanted* to spend the last hour? No it's not. You desperately want to write a kickass dissertation and get yourself a solid degree. But you couldn't do it. Now you can say that any student that can't hold their attention for a single hour had no hope in the first place.

It's about self-discipline, you might say. Maybe, if you're from the older generation, you might consider how the younger generation is so terribly lazy, afraid of hard work and want everything handed to them. What very few people mention, however, is that the internet actually changes the neurological structure of your brain.

For a long time we thought that the structure of the brain was fixed from around age 20 onwards. We now know this to be false. Throughout your entire life your brain is constantly adapting itself to become better and better at what you expose it to. If you play guitar for 2 hours a day for 5 years, your brain will create strong synaptic pathways that make you more and more competent at playing the guitar. This is neuroplasticity, the ability for your brain to constantly change throughout your entire life. In 2018, the average adult (in America) spent 24 hours on the internet every single week. With such a high volume of exposure, the synaptic pathways the brain builds for using the internet become strong. Now you have to ask, what kind of synaptic pathways are these? What kind of behaviour does the internet encourage? Quick pieces of information and a focus that's contantly moving from one thing to another. This is the environment your brain is adapting to when you use the internet. So even when you're not using the internet, your brain still wants to collect information the same way it does when online. Sit down to read a book and you might find yourself already looking for distractions after 2 pages. Switch your phone off for an hour to focus on something and you may find yourself straining not to turn it back on after 10 minutes. Your brain is expecting to use the same synaptic pathways as it does while using the internet.

Even with its incredible access to an infinite amount of information, the internet still isn't the best way to learn new information. Instead, the book is still the best way to learn. When we read a book there is no multi-tasking. You are focused on a single subject for an extended period of time, and your mind more able to relax and absorb the information. Not only that, but a book will give you a full understanding of a subject rather than a superficial one. Because only when your mind has explored the subject in detail and had a chance to reflect on the information can you genuinely have an understanding of something. The internet makes this kind of deep learning difficult. For most people, research on the internet generally leaves you with knowledge of a few important facts and a few concepts. But nothing more. And that's if you can resist the strong pull coming from the distractions of social media and online video. Read through one article and included will be hyperlinks to several other articles; articles and blog posts benefit financially from you hopping around from one page to the next rather than staying on a single page for an extended period of time. Each click on a new article means a new set of advertisements are shown to the user user, which in turn creates more profit for the website owner. Books don't have this problem. In fact, books don't even have advertisements.

The biggest problem with all this is that the information you see on the internet is rarely ever transferred to long-term memory. When you browse online the information generally enters the short-term memory and leaves again within a matter of minutes. To put it simple, almost all of the time you spend on the internet is completely forgotten. Think back to yesterday. What do you remember about the time you spent on the internet. Exactly. What's more everything is done on the same device. Your work, your social media, your schedule, online videos. Everything is only a click away at all times. You can't hide from the internet. The internet is necessary for your work life, your social life, your education, your news, your finances. It's interwoven into every aspect of your life. To avoid the internet would be to avoid society. Essentially you would need to live off the grid in the mountains somewhere.

FUCK YOU
INTERNET

While your laptop contains an infinite amount of information to learn from, it also contains an infinite number of ways to waste your time. The Facebook newsfeed, clickbait articles, videos of dogs doing funny things, Twitter debates, pointless Google searches, memes, celebrity slideshows, and pornography. All of these things provide a nice dose of the addictive brain chemical dopamine and all of these things can be accessed in less than a second with the simple click of a mouse. The distractions are simply too accessible. Almost everybody finds themselves distracted against their will by the internet at one time or another: students, teachers, office workers, writers, music producers, graphic designers, video editors. Everybody.

We learn from the previous generations. We listen to the regrets and truths uttered by those of the generation that came before us. *"I wish I had travelled more"*, I wish I had told _____ that I love him/her", *"I wish I had pursued my dream career in _____"*

Here's a statement you may find coming from those who lived their youth between the years 1970-2000: *"I wasted my life watching television"*. You've heard about the life wasted working a 9-5 job in an office, coming home then spending the rest of the evening sat in front of the TV eating junk food. Monday to Friday. Day in day out. Until suddenly you wake up with your gut hanging over your belt buckle at 50 years old wondering what happened to your life. The main danger of the television is that it encourages passivity. You sit and watch. This encourages the synaptic pathways in your brain to adapt to a lifestyle of passivity. Essentially, it dumbs you down on the neurological level. When your parents told you "That TV will rot your brain!", they had a point. If there's one thing the baby boomer generation learned it's that you will deeply regret spending so much time in front of the TV. This collective wisdom has been passed on. As a generation, many of us millennials have it burned into our brain that spending 6 hours a night watching TV is not a good idea.

We've learnt this through advice from our parents and teachers. But more than that, we've learnt it from the regrets of the previous generation. Yet technology changes fast and we have a new beast to battle with now. In respect to wasting your life on media, the internet is the new television. As millenials and Gen Z begins to reach their 30s and 40s, you can be sure that you'll soon begin to hear the following statement: *"I wasted my life on the internet"*. You might find yourself warning your children *"That internet will rot your brain"*. And you'd have a point. When you think of the people throughout history who really achieved something: Albert Einstein, Nelson Mandela, Plato, Leonardo Da Vinci, William Shakespeare, you'll notice they all had one thing in common: The ability to focus on one particular thing for an extended period of time. If you want to avoid reaching 60 years and finding yourself saying "I wasted my life on the internet", then it's time to begin seriously changing your relationship with the internet. Are you going to be one of the millions of regretful, or are you going to take control of your relationship with technology?

your smartphone isn't on your team

That little electronic rectangle. Lying on your bed. Hugging your thigh inside your pocket. Kept safe from harm in your handbag. Or cradled in your hand.

You love spending time with it. You go everywhere together. You stroke it. You play with it. You hold it gently. You tell it everything about yourself. You miss it frantically when it's gone. And you cry when it dies.

You stare into it. And it stares back.

It's there when you're happy. When you're angry. When you're frustrated. When you cry. It spends more time with you than anyone else. More than your friends. More than your family. More than your wife. More than your children. More than yourself.

It's your most loyal friend. The one who wakes you up in the morning. The one who tells you where to go. The one who teaches you about the world. The one who captures your memories. The one you can count on in an emergency. The only friend you can truly trust.

For all the trust you've built over the years you've been together, perhaps there's one thought that you never allowed to cross your mind.

That perhaps your smartphone has an agenda of it's own.

What if all those secrets you've been telling it over the years weren't kept secret? What if it's been talking about you behind your back? What if it's manipulating your behaviour against your will? What if, while pretending to be your most loyal friend, it's actually your greatest enemy?

We live in attention economy. The more eyeballs that media has, the more it's worth. It's a very simple equation: Attention = Money. Facebook, Youtube, Netflix, Instagram, Twitter, Reddit and every other app on your smartphone are all desperate for your attention. While your smartphone might seem to be an innocent little object ready to serve you, on the other side of that black screen are 1000's of the world's best tech engineers trying to steal as much of your attention as they possibly can. Look at your smartphone home screen, every single one of those apps is competing with each other to get you to spend time on it. Any app that decides not to do everything in its power to grab your attention will lose you to other apps (**Law 5: You Are In The Media Hierarchy**). And they're not only in competition with each other. They're also in competition with *your life*. They're in competition with speaking to your friends, going to the gym, walking your dog and even your sleep.

Attention is a scarce resource. Every human being only has so much attention they can give during any given day and most people have a life that they need to pay attention to. Most people want a fulfilling work life. A comfortable family life. A passionate love life. Hobbies they enjoy. Interests they pursue. Projects they complete. Goals they achieve. And a good night's sleep. This is your agenda. This is what you want. *But your smartphone has an agenda that doesn't match up with your own.* Your smartphone has only one agenda. It wants you to use it. As much as possible.

And you have to ask yourself, who's agenda is winning? It steals your attention from your family around the dinner table. It interrupts you while you try to focus on a project. It distracts you from your goals. And it certainly keeps you up at night while you should be sleeping. Just ask the CEO of Netflix:

"You get a show or a movie you're really dying to watch, and you end up staying up late at night, so we actually compete with sleep, and we're winning!" - Reed Hastings, CEO of Netflix

If you want the benefits of using a smartphone, you need to wrestle with it each and every day to make sure you're following your own agenda and not the agenda of your phone. It's no accident that you check a notification and wake up later wondering why you spent the last 20 minutes on Facebook. What's the best way to keep somebodies attention? Addiction. That's why tech companies hire attention engineers to try to addict you to their apps. It's a fight between some of the most advanced attention engineers in the world and you every time you pick up your phone. It's no wonder you get sucked in all the time. You blame yourself for getting distracted by your phone so easily, when in fact you never really stood a chance in the first place.

Your smartphone is a slot machine. When your pocket buzzes there are many things you might find. Maybe it's a useless notification. Maybe it's spam email. Maybe it's suggesting that you add some stranger on Instagram. But maybe it's an email for a job offer. Maybe someone messaged you on Facebook. Maybe someone liked your Instagram photo. Or maybe you got a new match on Tinder. Each time you check your phone it's like unwrapping a gift at Christmas. *You don't know what you'll get until you check it.* If it's something good, your brain will get a hit of dopamine. If it's not, you're subtly disappointed. This is exactly what happens when you pull the lever of a slot machine, and just as people will sit obsessively and pull the lever over and over, the same behaviour can be found in how people interact with their phones. It's a slot machine you're pulling throughout the entire day. Even the most old-fashioned mobile phones are slot machines; you receive a text message – either it's good or bad. You don't know until you read it. So from the very beginning, the mobile phone is inherently an addictive tool. That's why you keep refreshing your email. With each refresh you're pulling the lever again and hoping to get the nice dopamine hit that comes with an important email. Tech companies are well aware of this effect and will purposefully integrate it into their apps to encourage you to become addicted. *Every*

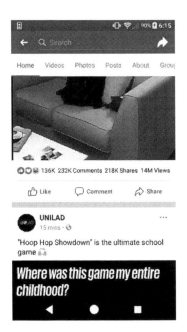

single aspect of the apps you use, down to the tiniest detail, are geared towards keeping your attention for as long as possible.

Next time you're on a train, you'll inevitably find that most people are staring down at their phone. Look around, how many of them are scrolling the Facebook newsfeed? The Facebook newsfeed is a constant, fast paced, infinite slot machine. With every single scroll down the page, you're pulling the lever. With every scroll, you're hoping you'll find something that will give you a spike in dopamine. *Boring video. Mcdonalds Ad. Friend posted a dog video. Yawn.. Friend shared an article. Political Ad. Oh! This video is hilarious!*

Do you recognise this screen? This pops up for around 2 seconds every single time you open your Twitter app. While this might seem to simply be a loading screen, it actually has a hidden purpose. The Twitter app could just open immediately, so why show us the Twitter logo for 2 seconds before opening the app? Because it builds anticipation. It gives you a short amount of time to get excited about what might appear on your Twitter feed. This makes the app more addictive.

The dating website Plenty of Fish (POF) will send this notification on a daily basis. It doesn't matter if you're in a major or city or in the middle of the Sahara desert. POF will still tell you "It's busy in your area!" The wording

POF · now ^

POF

It's busy in your area! Get more attention with Boost now!

Boosting yourself when it's busy is the best way to increase your popularity!

of the message has been tested across thousands of users until they found the message that brought as many people back into the app as possible.

Every single time you scroll down on the Twitter feed, you will see this loading circle. It will appear even if there's nothing new to load. Twitter purposefully shows you a loading wheel for a couple of seconds, before revealing that there is nothing new on your feed. Again, this is to build anticipation of what you may be about to see. And no, it's not just a loading wheel. It's not an accident. It's intentional.

False notifications are one of the most common techniques apps will use to bring you back online. Almost anything can be justified as a notification. In this case, Twitter has decided that "highlights", which are random tweets from people you follow, count as a notification. People who open Twitter to continually find that they have no notifications are more likely to quit using the app. False notifications give the user the illusion that people interacting with them, thus increasing engagement with the app.

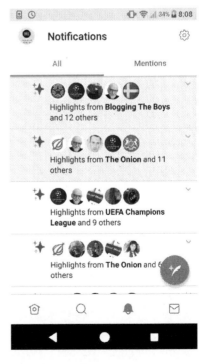

Snapstreaks are an invention of Snapchat that counts how many messages two people have sent back and forth to each other along with a congratulatory fireball to celebrate your friendship. No, the purpose of snapsteaks isn't to create strong friendships between people, it's to get users more addicted to the app. Users begin to feel obligated to keep their snap streak going with their friend and therefore spend more time on the app. Many users even report sending blank messages simply to keep the snapstreak going. Others report feeling guilty for ending a snapstreak with another user, even if they aren't particularly close with this person.

As of 2020, roughly 3.5 Billion people around the world own a Smartphone. Your workplace expects you to have one. Your social life expects you to have one. It's a technology that's integrated itself into the fabric of our society. From teenagers to grandparents. Of course, you don't have to own one if you don't want. But essentially you have 2 choices:

1. *FOMO - Get rid of your Smartphone and enjoy a life without distractions. But you can also expect a looming fear that you're missing out on something. People will leave you out of parties. You will miss work opportunities.*

2. *Distraction - Keep the Smartphone in your life and enjoy the convenience and social connection it brings. But expect to be constantly distracted. Expect to find yourself constantly hunching over and staring down into the screen. And expect to have your mind manipulated in different directions every time you use your phone.*

If you choose to keep the smartphone (which you probably will) you have no choice but to enter into an all or nothing relationship. If you have a smartphone, it will be an endless distraction. You can adjust the settings on your phone, switch off notifications from certain apps, switch your phone to black and white mode or choose to downgrade to a "dumbphone" that only allows you to use basic functions. These are all good solutions. But using a smartphone will always be a balancing act, and no matter what your smartphone will always be a slot machine. It doesn't matter how smart you might think you are, the techniques tech companies use to manipulate your behaviour *will work* at least some of the time. These techniques reach into your older, lizard brain and will change your behaviour whether you like it or not. Even tech experts, the ones who created the apps, find themselves being manipulated into spending far longer on their apps than they would like.

Living with a smartphone is living in a world of either partial or constant distraction. As you spend months and years having your thoughts constantly interrupted, your brain begins to adapt to the new environment. The neural pathways in your brain will adapt and you will begin to *expect distraction*. You may find you lose your ability to concentrate on one thing for an extended period of time. In other words, your smartphone will change who you are.

Your smartphone isn't on your team. Your smartphone has its own agenda and doesn't have your own interests in mind. It's not loyal to you, it's loyal to the tech companies who use it to get your attention and sell it on for a profit (**Law 4: Media Is About Profit**). Your smartphone isn't a slave who will simply do your bidding without expecting payment. Instead, your smartphone is a savvy trader who you need to constantly negotiate with in order to have a peaceful relationship. If you let your guard down, your smartphone will play you for a fool, stealing your precious time and attention in order to benefit its own ends. If you show it weakness, it will capitalise and pull you into a hypnotic daze of scrolling and tapping. You need to take control of the relationship you have with it. You need to put your foot down and show your smartphone who's boss. Take control over your smartphone, take control over how you spend your time and take control over your life.

dark patterns – how you're manipulated into buying more

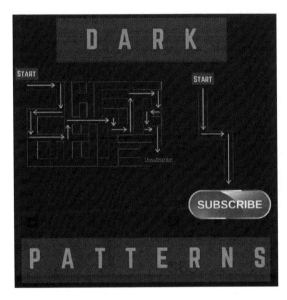

On every major website, a game is being played. The aim? To take as much money, data and personal information from the customer as possible (**Law 4: Media Is About Profit**). While the website owner is aware that such a game is being played, the customer is not. In the internet landscape, dark patterns are embedded everywhere. Not only on the dodgy websites in the dark corners of the internet, but also on the websites of the most famous brands in the world (Amazon, Netflix etc). While dark patterns have become commonplace across the internet, the average person has no idea they exist.

Perhaps some of the following scenarios will be familiar to you:

☞ *While checking your bank statement you notice a payment of $35 that you don't remember. You realise, in fact, that this payment has been made consecutively for last 3 months.*

☞ *On attempting to cancel your account on a website or social media platform, you find it incredibly hard to find the "close account" button.*

☞ *After comparing flights, you find a great deal for $350. You go through the payment process only to find that extra fees have been added and the new price is $420 (the same price as all of the other flights). You buy the flight anyway.*

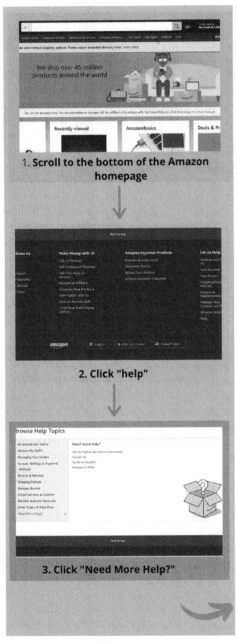

1. **Scroll to the bottom of the Amazon homepage**

2. **Click "help"**

3. **Click "Need More Help?"**

Want to close your Amazon account? The button to close your account is placed in the least intuitive place possible. And even once you find it, you need to contact Amazon and ask them to close it for you (which is completely unnecessary). Amazon is perfectly capable of setting up a system where the user can easily close their own account at any time, only they choose not to.

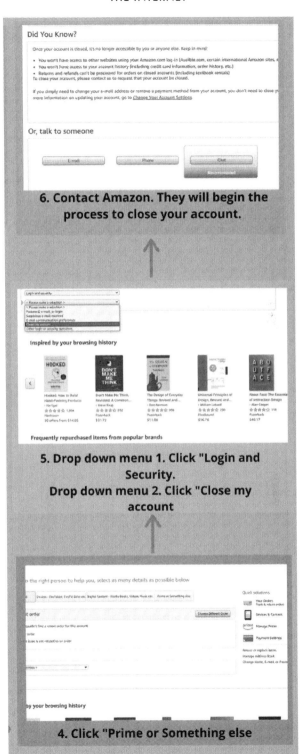

6. Contact Amazon. They will begin the process to close your account.

5. Drop down menu 1. Click "Login and Security.
Drop down menu 2. Click "Close my account

4. Click "Prime or Something else

☞   *You get advertising emails in your inbox, even though you have no recollection of signing up to receive them.*

☞   *You click the big "download" button only to find that it opens up an advert for something else entirely.*

If these situations are familiar, it's because you've fallen victim to a dark pattern.

Almost every website on the internet has a gravitational pull towards the checkout. UX designers have created the website with the ultimate aim of getting you to hand over your money or data. These UX designers will use every technique they possibly can, including unethical ones.

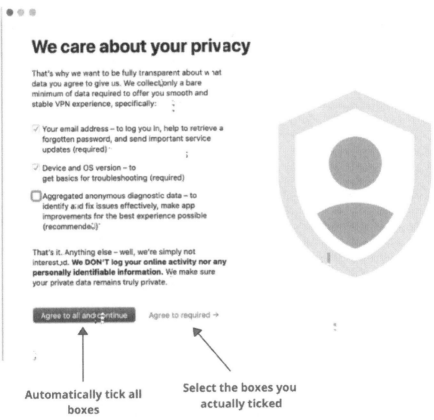

We care about your privacy

That's why we want to be fully transparent about what data you agree to give us. We collect only a bare minimum of data required to offer you smooth and stable VPN experience, specifically:

✓ Your email address – to log you in, help to retrieve a forgotten password, and send important service updates (required)

✓ Device and OS version – to get basics for troubleshooting (required)

☐ Aggregated anonymous diagnostic data – to identify and fix issues effectively, make app improvements for the best experience possible (recommended)

That's it. Anything else – well, we're simply not interested. **We DON'T log your online activity nor any personally identifiable information.** We make sure your private data remains truly private.

[Agree to all and continue]   Agree to required →

Automatically tick all boxes

Select the boxes you actually ticked

"Agree to all and continue" is placed inside a big blue button, inviting the user to click it. Intuitively it doesn't make sense to have 3 tick boxes above, only for them to made completely redundant by clicking the blue button. Users don't expect this, so they simply click the big blue button, assuming it's confirming the choices they just made.

Businesses will do everything they possibly can to take as much money from customers as they possibly can. There are only two limitations: 1. The law 2. They must protect their brand's reputation. As long as they stay on the right side of the law, and the techniques they use are unnoticed by the majority of their customers - they can do anything they like.

:Luke Stein* @lukestein · Jul 13, 2019

Frustrating: Can't turn off @Netflix autoplaying next episode kids' videos directly on smart TV (must use web interface)

Bat-Sh*t Infuriating: @Netflix apparently CAN'T disable autoplay for KIDS profiles (only adult ones)? Shame on you.
cc: @darkpatterns

Turn Off Autoplay on Your Kids' TV Shows
The countdown makes me gasp every time. Ten seconds until the next episode of whatever show my daughter is watching. Nine seconds. Eigh...
🔗 offspring.lifehacker.com

💬 4   🔁 14   ♡ 51   ⬆

Dark Patterns are used to manipulate your children too. If you want to turn off autoplay on your child's Netflix, you need to change the account from "kid" to "adult" before you can switch it off. Why? Because Netflix want to increase the watch time for children so that they can increase their profits. Your child's well-being is a non-factor.

Businesses don't have a conscience. And they certainly don't have any standard of ethics. They will do everything they can possibly get away with. Those businesses who refuse to use dark patterns will lose out on that extra 10-15% of profits they could be making through under-the-radar dark patterns. Every single part of the website can be A-B tested until they've created the design that draws in the most beneficial user behaviour.

How do users react to dark patterns?

1. *They don't notice.*

2. *They blame themselves.*

3. *They assume it's an accident or a bug.*

4. *They recognise the dark pattern for what it is and look down upon it (a small minority of people).*

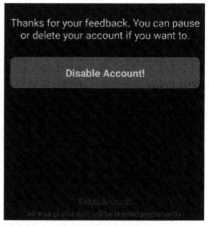

Most customers simply aren't smart enough or diligent enough to notice dark patterns. The goal of this article is to enlighten you to the dark patterns that you'll inevitably stumble upon throughout the internet.

Dark patterns usually fit into one of 7 categories.

The user is highly encouraged to only disable their account rather than delete their account. Remember: The actions they want you to take are in the big colourful buttons. The actions they don't want you to take are in dull, unappealing writing.

1. CONFIRM SHAMING

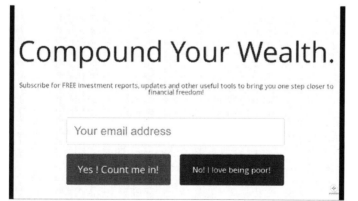

I'm sure you've seen this one before. Passive aggressive, manipulative messages placed on the buttons the website doesn't want you to click. The aim being to influence the psychology of the user into taking the action the website wants them to take. We can assume from the prevalence of confirm shaming all across the internet that this technique works on large numbers of people.

2. DISGUISED ADS

Every time you view an advert, the website makes a small amount of money. Clicking a "download" or "play movie" button will open up an advert you didn't intend.

3. FORCED CONTINUITY

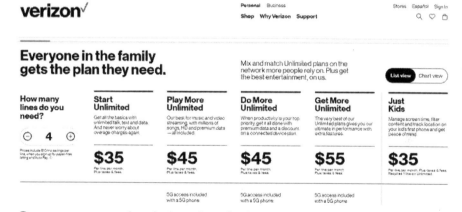

Once you start a subscription, they don't want you to cancel. Ever. Having a customer not cancel is just as good as gaining a new customer. Let's say, for example, that you come across a 7-day free trial to try a new service. *I'll try the free trial and decide if I want to start paying for the service later,* you say to yourself. You enter your bank details and the 7 day-free trial begins. Within the next 7 days, you have a new project at work, you and your partner have an argument and you hurt your ankle running down the stairs. Life happens, and you forget all about your free trial. As the 7 days come to an end there will usually be no warning. You check your bank balance to find that $31.99 has been taken out of your bank account. You check the website and realise that the 7-day trial has finished and they've automatically put you onto the regular subscription plan. They want you to forget. They're counting on a substantial number of people forgetting about the 7-day trial so that they can collect the profits (this is one of the main reasons the free trial exists in the first place). These kinds of "free trials" that quietly change into a paid subscription as they expire are now commonplace throughout the internet. If you do remember to cancel your subscription before the end of the 7-day free trial, it might not be a particularly easy process. Want to cancel your subscription to Verizon? If you try to navigate to the "cancel subscription" button on their website, this is what you'll see.

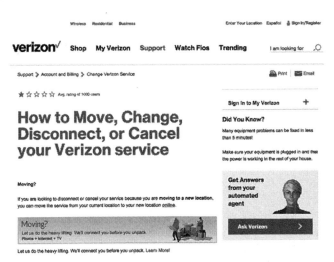

OK...BUT WHERE DO I CANCEL THE SUBSCRIPTION..?

As you can see, there is no cancel option on their website. At this stage, many people will become confused and decide to cancel the subscription some other time. People are busy and people are lazy. The more difficult it is to unsubscribe, the less people will do so and the more profit Verizon will make.

This is the only way you can unsubscribe from Verizon:

Cancel Service

If you truly wish to cancel your Verizon service, please call us at 1.800.Verizon (1.800.837.4966).

- You must make your cancellation request by telephone
- Your call may be transferred to ensure that you reach the correct representative
- Cancellation service is available Monday through Friday, 8 am to 6 pm local time.

Verizon is perfectly capable of creating a simple "unsubscribe" button on their website. It's 2021, there is absolutely no reason why cancellations need to be done over the phone. The only reason the call centre is required is because Verizon wants to create more friction to the process of unsubscribing. Businesses really don't want you to unsubscribe.

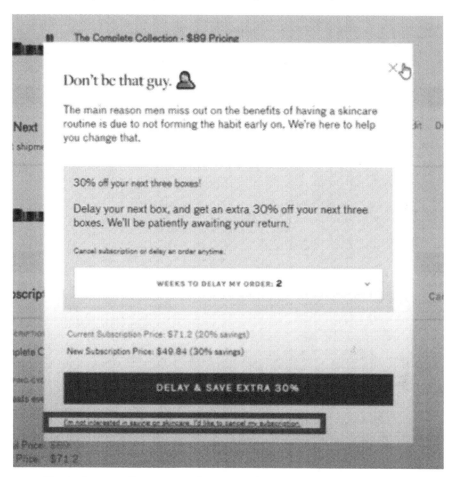

This is the cancellation page for Lumin Skincare. The following are tactics on this page to discourage a customer from unsubscribing:

1. "Don't be that guy" shaming the customer against unsubscribing.
2. A discount offer of 30% off for those who stay subscribed.
3. A big grey button that customers will intuitively believe is the cancel button, but actually it's the "delay" button.
4. The actual unsubscribe button written in a small, dull font.

4. HIDDEN COSTS

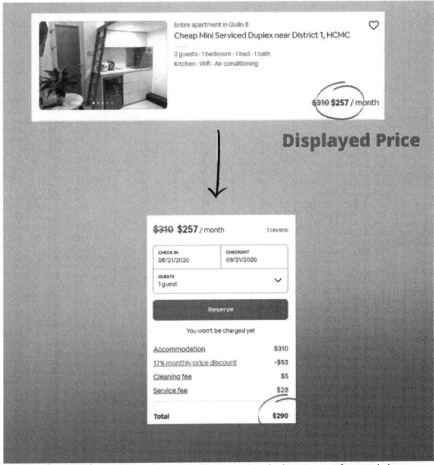

For Airbnb, hidden costs are the norm. Both the service fee and the cleaning fee could have easily been included in the displayed price. They chose not to do this in order to increase their profits.

The displayed price is often far lower than the actual price. This is commonplace among booking sites such as Booking.com and Airbnb. com as well as flight comparison sites like Skyscanner.com and Google Flights. The customer initially makes the decision to buy based on the displayed price. After they take the time to enter their details they are then confronted by the actual price. At this stage, the customer is emotionally invested in making the purchase and will often accept the increased price. Let's say for example you're looking to purchase a flight from London to New York. After scanning the search results, you notice one flight for a low-price of $278. *This is the one*, you think to yourself. You enter your personal details, then your bank details, excited to finally book your trip to the USA. After several minutes, you get to the end of the payment process only to find the price has increased to $320. *It's only a little bit extra, no big deal. I just went through the hassle of entering my details and honestly I'm sick of searching for flights. Let's just buy it.* You rationalise the extra $42 you're now spending. And so did 10,000 other people buying flights that day. 10,000 x $42 = $420,000. That's an extra $420,000 created for the airline simply by lowering the displayed price of their flights.

5. SNEAK INTO BASKET

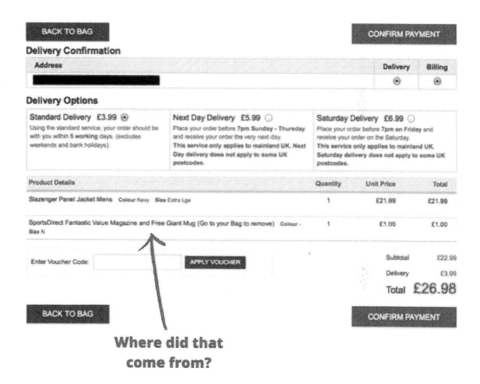

Where did that come from?

Like a child that slips candy into his mum's shopping cart when she's not looking, major websites do the exact same thing. Items are added to your shopping cart by default. Many users won't notice the added item and will continue through the payment process. While it is possible for the user to remove the added item, the fact that it's Opt-out rather than Opt-in will mean that many users will end up paying for something they never wanted.

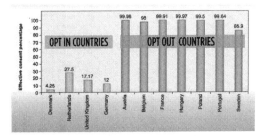

This chart shows organ donors in different countries. As you can see, there is an enormous difference between opt-in and opt-out countries.

6. COUNTER INTUITIVENESS

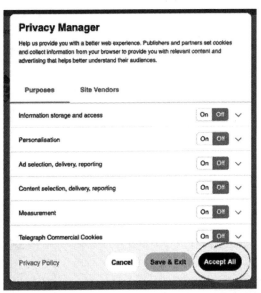

Intuitively you would expect the button at the bottom to be "accept options chosen". Instead, this button accepts all options, regardless of the choices you previously made.

This button disregards all previous options chosen

Want to unsubscribe from Joe Biden's emails? Click the unsubscribe button and you're taken to this page. Counter intuitively, entering your email address on this page will not stop you from receiving emails.

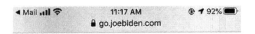

We're sad to see you're considering unsubscribing from our emails.

We hope instead you'll consider modifying your email preferences.

If you'd like to only receive our best, most important emails, please submit your email address below:

Email

We have gotten used to the patterns we've seen on websites. Most of us have gone through plenty of sign up processes by now and we know what to expect. Because we expect to see patterns on websites, this leaves an opening for dark patterns to exploit these expectations. These dark patterns play with the conventions of web design in order to confuse the user into doing what they want.

As you can see, even politics isn't immune from the trend of dark patterns. Buttons can be placed in positions you don't expect, check boxes can be worded in confusing ways and buying options can be listed in a misleading way.

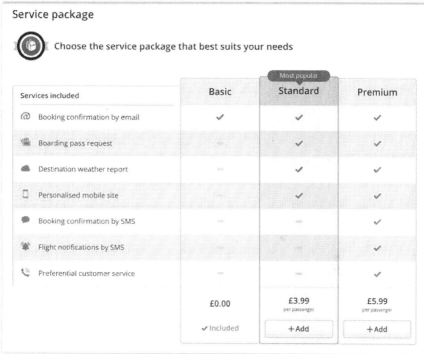

The "most popular" tag has been added to the Standard package and it's been highlighted in blue. Is it really the most popular? Who knows. The standard packages offers the "Boarding pass request", but it's not clear what this actually is. Customers will be scared into avoiding the 'basic" option because of fears that it might not include the boarding pass. Better to be safe and just pay for the standard package, I don't want any problems with my flight. Of course, paying $3.99 for the standard package is completely unnecessary.

7. BUTTON PLACEMENT

This dark pattern is different from Counter Intuitiveness in that it refers simply to the physical ability to click or tap particular buttons. The buttons that agree to giving away data or money are big, central and easy to click. The buttons for unsubscribing, checking terms and conditions or taking any action they don't want you to take, are small, unappealing and difficult to click. Another common trick is incredibly tiny "X" or "close" buttons on Ads that are easily misclicked, resulting in opening the Ad. If you

Good luck trying to tap this button on mobile

find yourself tapping the wrong option, it may not be entirely your fault.

8. HIDDEN CODE

We can't see the code behind the website. This allows websites to trick us in ways that unlike the other dark patterns on this list, we can't possibly detect. You'll also see this kind of hidden code used to demonstrate social proof. You may see the message "Jason has just subscribed!" or "7 people have bought this product recently!". We don't know the code behind these pop ups, as such we can't be sure if they're legitimate messages or not.

Dark patterns will not go away by themselves. As the internet advances into the future (and potentially integrates with VR and AR), different kinds of dark patterns will continue to emerge. What kind of environment do we want the internet to be? Do we want an internet that is continually trying to psychologically manipulate people out of their money and information. A place where - every single time you want to make some kind of purchase, you need to dodge countless pitfalls. Or do we want an internet where we can rely on websites being up-front and honest. An internet where we can relax, and navigate without constantly having to be on our toes.

Matt Hackmann @dxprog · Jul 11   ⌄

.@azazieofficial your promotional spinner wheel collects email addresses under the pretense of being able to win $50 off or a free dress, but your code is written to never allow this. This is a dark pattern and intentionally deceiving #scummymarketing

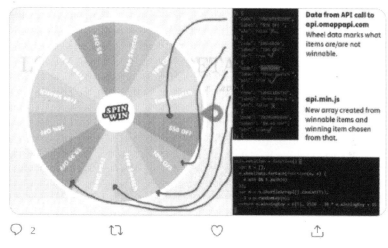

   💬 2   ⟲   ♡   ⬆

This promotional spinner collects email addresses under the pretence that users have the chance to get $50 off a purchase or a free dress. As you can see, the code behind the spinner does not allow these two options to be chosen.

An internet that inspires feelings of goodwill and fair business, rather than an internet that makes you feel as though the world is filled with slimy manipulators. As our understanding of psychology improves (with the use of MRI scanners and other neuromarketing techniques), dark patterns will only become more and more sophisticated. It's up to us as individuals to recognise Dark Patterns and to spread the word about their existence. Stop being played for a fool. Become aware of dark patterns.

chapter 5

SOCIAL MEDIA

social media - the human marketplace

You are the CEO of brand YOU. And what does your company sell? It sells you. There is nothing that capitalism won't touch. Everything is a business. Even your identity. You probably run your personal social media pages like a business. Whether it's Facebook, Instagram, Snapchat or Linkedin. *You use exactly the same tactics that businesses use to market their products.* But with your personal social media page the product isn't bottles of Coke, car insurance or a packaged holiday. It's you. You are the product. And you need to compete with all of the other products on the shelf in order to be successful.

There is a lot of talk around social media, and a lot of confusion. What is social media really? When it comes down to the bare-bones reality of it, what social media truly is; is a human marketplace.

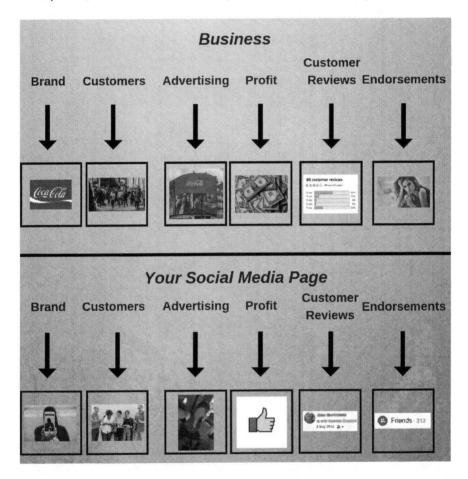

The goal of any business is to make money. Similarly, the goal of your personal social media page is to collect social currency. Facebook likes are social currency. Instagram followers are social currency. Snapchat points are social currency. Your customers are your friends, family and strangers on the same social media platform. And remember, the customer is always right. Your customers determine the worth of your brand (you). On social media, your worth as a human being is decided by your audience, like a product on a shelf. You advertise your brand (you)

in the form of photos and status updates. The goal is to persuade your customers to hand over their social currency by liking your post. *When you scroll a social media newsfeed, you're scrolling through an advertising reel of human beings.* Customer reviews appear on your page when another user tags you in a a post. Did they enjoy using the product? (Did they have a good time with you?) And you receive endorsements when other users send you friend requests.

So if you want to create a positive brand image and collect as much social currency as possible, you need to learn how to advertise.

HOW TO ADVERTISE YOUR IDENTITY

You do not write the truth on social media. You write sales pitches. You are selling your identity to your audience with every post you make. Before posting photos, think: *what does this photo say about my brand?* Select your photos very carefully. Only post flattering photos. Photos taken from the wrong angle or in unflattering lighting will lower the reputation of your brand. Photos taken of your food must be arranged perfectly beforehand. Never miss an opportunity to use a real world success to improve your brand's image. Whether it's a promotion at work, you're travelling to another country or have a new girlfriend/boyfriend. Post it all on social media. After all, your competition will do the same, and you must keep up with your competition. If you fail to advertise enough, your competition will collect all of the social currency (Likes, follows etc) and they will win. You must stay relevant. Post stories every single day to keep your brand in the mind of your customers. But remember, your stories must only showcase positive aspects of your brand. Anything negative happening in your life must be hidden at all costs. Make sure you post your advertisements during high traffic periods, at lunch time or after work. But keep in mind that people don't like being sold to. If you make your attempt to get social currency (likes) too obvious, people will not want to give you any.

Feel free to use any image retouching tools at your disposable, just be sure to keep it discreet. After all, people don't like to be sold to. So artificially improve your beauty, just make sure it's not noticeable. Even if the audience suspects you may be retouching your photos, their lizard brain will still believe the image they see. Be sure to have the *right* number of friends. On Facebook, the number you want to aim for is somewhere from 500-1000. If you have too few friends, you will appear to be low status. Have too many and people will begin to question the authenticity of those friends. On Instagram, however, the more followers you have, the better. That's because on Instagram, strangers outside your network have the ability to find and follow you, so the authenticity of the endorsements will not be in question.

If you advertise your brand correctly, you will create the same psychological effects in your customers as a Coca Cola advert. Using advertising, you'll be able to convince your audience that you're far more impressive than you could ever possibly be in the real world. People will buy into the hype and the status you display through social media will translate into real life. After all, if people believe you're high status, then you are. Advertising your identity through social media, done correctly, can transform your entire life.

POSITIVE ASSOCIATION

If you've created your brand with enough skill, people will think positively of you. With every carefully chosen photo or status update you are creating a positive image of yourself in your customer's subconscious minds. Just as Coca-Cola associates their brand with youth and happiness, you associate your brand with other positive things. Maybe you're associating yourself with adventurousness, health or intelligence. Keep posting about your achievements in the gym and your audience will begin to associate you with health and fitness. Keep posting about your time spent travelling and your audience will think of you as an adventurous globe trotter. Be careful what you associate your brand with. For example, if you appear in photos with unattractive or unphotogenic people, this is a bad association for your brand. And when you share a video, remember that you are associating your name with the video. So choose carefully. And if you share an image of your food, be sure to organise it perfectly. Make sure the plate, knife, fork, mug and any other utensils are perfectly spaced out. This will produce an association in the minds of your audience between the perfectly laid out utensils and your identity – they will come to think of you as someone who "has it all together".

BRAND FAMILIARITY

Post with enough consistency and your customers will begin to feel as if they know you. People you've only met once before will greet you as though you're old friends. You will be in the forefront of your customers minds. People will think of you when they're organising a party or when they hear of a new job opening. If your advertising is of a high enough quality, you will be inundated with invitations, including many from people you've never met. And you will get loyal customers; return customers who give you their social currency on a consistent basis.

Your social media advertising strategy is incredibly important in the world of dating. Let's take a case study as an example. A 20 year old girl goes on two dates. The first man is hilarious, has a great personality and is highly ambitious. The second man is quite funny, seems like an OK guy and has a stable job. She finds both men about as physically attractive as each other. After the two dates, she has more positive feelings towards the first man. Three days pass and she needs to choose between the two guys, so she browses their Instagram accounts. The second guy has hundreds of likes on each of his photos. All of his posts are flooded with comments. And he has a follower count in the 1000's. The first man has only posted 8 photos. His most popular photo only has 14 likes and only has 27 followers. Her feelings begin to shift. Which man will this girl choose, I wonder? The scales are tipped in favour of the second man. Just like a product on a supermarket shelf, she chooses the brand of the second man based on his online packaging.

I know what you're thinking. *"But I just use social media to keep in touch with friends"* I believe you. Most people just want to connect with people, and that's primarily what they try to do on the platform. Unfortunately, when you use social media you have to accept the whole package. And whether you like it or not, *social media is not only about connectivity, but also competition.* Human beings naturally compare themselves to others and will always compete with their peers. You can't avoid the competitive aspect of social media, no matter your intentions. Why? Because of the numbers. The number of likes. The number of friends. The number of followers. The number of comments. Social media is an environment in which everything is quantified. When there is a number next to everything, competition is unavoidable. When you introduce "likes" to a photograph of someone, you begin to quantify their worth. You turn human beings into something that can be rated and judged with a number. People who just wanted to connect with their friends find themselves sucked into an addictive competition for approval from others. And when you have an audience of hundreds waiting to judge and quantify every single one of your posts, it's only natural for people to market themselves. Even with the intention of only using social media as a tool to keep up with friends and family, if enough time is spent on the platform competitive urges inevitably emerge.

You can reject the advertising aspect of social media. You can upload whatever images you damn well please. You can post images of you looking tired, ugly and in situations that paint you in a negative light. Just know, that your audience will form an image in their minds based on the way you advertise yourself. Think that's superficial? Tough. That's human nature. Even the smartest members of your audience will be *emotionally influenced* by your advertising. It's up to you whether they're influenced positively or negatively.

online dating

According to PewResearch, 48% of 18-29 year olds have used an online dating platform in their lifetimes. The continuation of the human race is now significantly influenced by technology and we use satellites to see which sexual partners are within a 20km radius of ourselves. Technology continues to change every single aspect of our lives, including our romantic relationships. Online dating has quickly moved into the acceptable mainstream and it seems unlikely to go anywhere. It's likely that dating technology will become more and more prevalent and future generations will grow up never having experienced dating without it. Online dating is now mainstream and completely normalised.

To a significant extent, our romantic lives are now controlled by a single tech company: *Match Group.* Match Group hold a monopoly over the dating technology industry, they're the owners of: Tinder, Match. com, OKCupid, Hinge, PlentyOfFish, Ourtime, Meetic and a total of 21 different online dating servies. While they do receive some competitions from apps like Badoo and Bumble, they control a massive majority of the market.

Online dating is likely having significant impacts on the dating market and our culture in general. For one, it's likely that online dating makes us more likely to cheat and less likely to stay in long term relationships. In the past, in our potential dates were people that were in our immediate surroundings: at work, our social network, and perhaps strangers we came across in the cafe or nightclub. With online dating, we now have the ability to see all of the potential sexual partners *outside* of our inner circle. Our number of options has increased a hundredfold. We have access to the full dating potential of whatever town or city we're living in and it's all inside our pockets. This is an incredibly significant change to our societies and needs to be looked at carefully.

For starters, dating apps are slot machine-like environments. Swiping left on a Tinder profile is the same as pulling the lever on a slot machine. You might match, you might not. You might win, you might not. As you swipe, the addictive brain chemical dopamine rises in your brain in anticipation for the reward. Many years ago, B.F. Skinner first put a hungry rat inside a box with a small lever inside. The rat would be rewarded with food pellets at random intervals when it pulled the lever. These random intervals for reward drove the rat crazy, causing it to pull the lever like a maniac. We call this a variable ratio interval, and it doesn't just work on rats, it works on humans too. The variable ratio interval is what makes gambling addictive and it's also what makes many video games addictive. The same variable ratio interval is used in Tinder's famous Swipe Left/ Right match system (A system now copied by most other dating apps). But this isn't just a slot machine. It's a slot machine of sex. One of the deepest drives human beings can have is mixed in with an addictive slot machine-like environment. Yet it's not only the Swipe Left/Right system that uses a variable ratio, its also the messages themselves. Each positive reply from a potential sexual partner encourages a dopamine response in the user's brain. After facing a rejection or a non response, many people act like gambling addicts at the end of a losing streak displaying: anger, frustration and desperation. When a potential date stops replying, they're not just rejecting the user, they're also taking away their dopamine surges. So the user will often message this potential date again and again, not necessarily desperate for the real human on the other side of the screen, but more desperate for another hit of dopamine from a positive reply.

A typical text message conversation on a dating app like Tinder might go something like this:

> **Man:** *Heey whats up, how are you? Sorry I couldn't message you earlier. (2:02pm)*
>
> **Woman:** *Hey (4:12pm)*
>
> **Man:** *You can your dog are beautiful :D (4:13pm)*
>
> **Man:** *Sorry if you're busy. (4:24pm)*
>
> **Woman:** *Thanks (8:02pm)*
>
> **Man:** *So what are you up to today? :P (8:03pm)*
>
> **Man:** *It's fine if you don't want to talk to me. (8:20pm)*
>
> **Man:** *Fuck you! (9:00pm)*

Not only is the gentleman in this example desperate for the attention from the woman, he's also desperate for another hit of dopamine delivered to him through her reply.

THE UNEVEN PLAYING FIELD

Online dating is not simply a tool for getting partners to communicate with each other. Like all technology, online dating carries inherent biases. *Technology is not neutral.* (**Law 1: The Medium Is The Message**). And online dating provides a clear advantage to women over men. That is, when it comes to actually getting responses from potential dates. According to PewResearch, around 6-in-10 men who have tried online dating in the past five years report feeling as though they didn't receive enough messages. While 30% of women felt as though they received too many messages to deal with.

This is not a level playing field and we can also see this clearly by looking at OKCupid's own data.

In the sexual marketplace, everybody has what you may call a *sexual market value* (SMV). While it might seem crass to rate human beings in such a superficial way, we do generally choose our partners based on their SMV. As a general rule, most people choose partners who have an SMV the same, or higher than they do. It's clear that on online dating: *The SMV of the average woman is artificially raised and the SMV of the average man is artificially lowered.* This is simply a consequence of the way the medium is structured.

Men are more visual than women. For men, the beauty of a woman is incredibly important. On the other hand, women tend to have

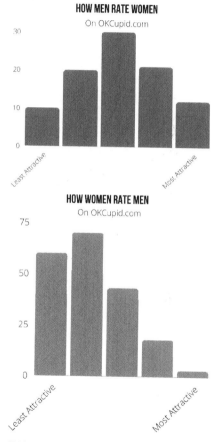

CHART BASED ON DATA FROM OKCUPID.COM

a longer and more detailed list for what they're looking for in a partner. Character, talent, sense of humour, social status and yes, appearance. The brains of men and women evolved differently, therefore they tend to find different things attractive in the opposite sex. Men are more visual, women are more interpersonal. How does this give women an advantage on online dating platforms? Because the primary focal point on dating apps are images. Both sexes choose their matches predominantly based on the still images displayed before them. *The photograph is a medium that is far more appealing to men than it is to women.* The result is that men are easily pleased by the image they see, while women read the profile looking for something more. This is why selfies are generally more acceptable for women than men. For women, the goal of the ideal photo is to be as physically attractive as possible. Sure, men appreciate other aspects of a woman's character, but more than anything else men are biologically wired to look for an appealing face and body. On the other hand, the perfect photo for a man is one that demonstrates: personality, a sense of humour, status and physical beauty. Something that isn't particularly easy for the average man to convey using images alone. The very fact that the man is holding the camera towards himself lowers his attractiveness. The perfect photo of a man is taken side on, as if he isn't aware of the photo at all, as if it's being taken by a paparazzi hidden in the bushes. To display a sense of high-status isn't an easy feat using images alone.

The average man today finds himself pointing the camera at himself trying to make himself look pretty in order to fit in with *what the new technology wants.* Middle aged men find themselves taking bathroom mirror selfies in an effort to create an attractive profile photo. Something that is completely unnatural to most straight men, and something that men in their 40s and 50s never grew up with.

Of course it's not only images that are used to advertise your dating potential on these platforms. After images comes text. This is the chance for a man to showcase his humour, personality and status. All the things a woman is looking for. The problem is: *text is weak.* All of the natural expressions of personality; facial expressions, voice intonations and body language are completely lost through text. Text is a medium that is usually consumed thoughtfully and logically. Not emotionally. Sarcasm easily gets lost in translation. All of the natural brain chemicals that would be firing off in a real life conversation are dulled by text. And this is the medium that men need to use to express their personality. Text can't compete with images. Yes, women are stuck using text too. But women generally don't need to convey their personality via text to the same extent, because men, being visual creatures, are generally more persuaded by the images they see.

Online dating is not neutral because it's an incomplete stimuli compared with reality. Through online dating, you only receive a small chunk of the stimuli you receive when meeting someone in the real world. Eye-contact, smell, body language, vocal tonality, social skills, all of these things are not available through image-based online dating platforms. On top of this, women have all the tools in the world to enhance the beauty displayed in their images. Photos can be retouched to perfection. Today, anybody with a smartphone and a $4.00 photo-retouching app can brighten their skin, teeth and eyes. Filters can be added. Waists can be narrowed. Curves can be added. Breasts can be enlarged (without surgery). Some people even go as far as removing people from the background (seriously). Angles can be played with and makeup can be painted. With all of this beauty technology layered on top of a woman, even women who are naturally quite plain looking can increase their physical beauty substantially. Have yellow teeth? No problem, just digitally whiten them. Have beedy eyes? No problem, highlight them with makeup and then digitally enlarge them on an app. Overweight? No problem, point the camera down at yourself from up above your head, an angle that highlights your cleavage and hides your stomach. And if this isn't enough, open up an app and start narrowing that waist. Are these options open to men too? Yes. But it simply doesn't have the same effect. Because once again, men are far more visual than women. Many men have now had the experience of meeting a woman from online dating in the real world, only to be shocked to find she looks very little like the images on her dating profile.

In the future, it's possible that VR (virtual reality) technology will integrate with online dating platforms. With this kind of technology, men may be able to communicate in a more natural way, and the playing field will become level once again. But with the image-based dating platforms we currently have, women have a clear advantage. If you disagree with this conclusion, then you either: don't have experience with dating apps, are displaying confirmation bias or are female and blind to your own advantages and privilege (People are usually blind to their own privilege). Women certainly have their own set of problems with online dating. They deal with toxic and abusive messages from men, and finding a long-term partner on such a platform can be quite the struggle. But in terms of the ability to *actually get dates*, women have an undoubtable advantage. Try it for yourself. Take any couple you know and have them both make profiles on a dating platform. Wait for a single day and then compare who has more matches and messages. You will inevitably find that the woman has far more attention than the man.

This creates a kind of snowball effect. For arguments sake, lets say there are 1000 men and 1000 women who have downloaded Tinder for the very first time and lets see how the dynamics of the app develop overtime.

DAY 1:

Men upload their photos and do their best to use the weak medium of text to convey their personality. Women upload their digitally perfected photos and type in their descriptions. Right away, due to human biology and the fact that images are the focal point of every profile, the women on the app receive more messages than men. Most women have multiple messages to choose from and reply to only 30% of the messages. The woman feels desirable and feels a boost to their self-esteem. On the other hand, most men will send out multiple messages to a number of women, and receive replies from around 30% of women. He's a little bummed out by those who didn't reply, but satisfied with the 30% who did.

DAY 7:

Women continue to be flooded with messages and begin to feel like they're quite the catch. They begin to only respond to around 10% of the messages they receive. Meanwhile, from the men's point of view, women seem to be responding to less and less of his messages. So they begin to get frustrated and desperate. They begin making adjustments to their profile, but no matter what he tries nothing seems to work. He tries to use his sense of humour that seems to work so well in real life, but it doesn't seem to have the same effect when using the weak medium of text.

DAY 30:

The most attractive women have literally thousands of messages and matches and begin to see an opportunity to direct people to their Instagram account and build a following there. The more average-looking women are also flooded with messages. Men are reacting to her far more enthusiastically than they do in the real-world. She begins to realise that she essentially has an endless carousel of men for the picking. Her standards begin to rise. Now she will only meet men who are particularly attractive. The average man, who she would happily date in the real world, is no longer adequete in her eyes.

Men on the other hand (the average men), are losing their minds. They seem to be sending out countless messages and getting almost no response. The women who do respond seem to take hours between their messages and don't seem particularly interested in meeting up for a date. If he's not familiar with the inherent disadvantage men have on dating apps, he will feel a *real* drop in self-esteem. For him, it seems that he's far less desirable to women than he thought he was. His messages begin to reek of desperation. He starts sending 3 messages. 4 messages. 5 messages in a row. Overtime, he begins to get angry. Who does she think she is? Why do women think they can treat me this way? And that's often when you begin to see abusive and insulting messages from men.

Generally speaking, women's self esteem goes up. Men's self esteem goes down. And then they take this artificial self-esteem adjustment out with them into the real world. At the end of the day, it all comes down to behavioral economics. There are more men than women on dating apps. And women are higher demand than men on dating apps. Women get more choosy, and men get more desperate. It's simply human nature. It would be wise to note, that *the online dating world does not necessarily reflect the real world.*

THE FINANCIAL INCENTIVES

In the mix of this madness of sexual urges, dopamine, addictive variable ratio effects, a uneven digital sexual marketplace and photo retouching, comes the financial incentives. Dating platforms want to make money. Lots of it (**Law 4: Media Is About Profit**).

They want two things from you:

1. *They want you addicted to their platform*

2. *They want you to pay for their premium service.*

And no, "addicted" is not an exaggeration. This is exactly what they aim for, as do all apps in the attention economy. They want you addicted to their platform so that you'll spend more time on their app and view more advertisements.

They will send you notifications for things you never asked for:

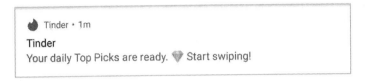

Or send meaningless notifications, if someone you matched with uploads a photo for example.

Or if a user joins the app, why not send the user a notification.

False messages and false notifications are another popular method of getting users back onto the app (this is also a technique frequently used across social media).

But aside from keeping you hooked on the app, their ultimate goal is to persuade you to pay for their premium services. Generally, these

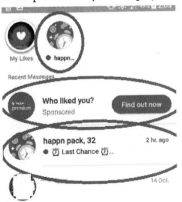

premium packages consist of a "Boost" which increases your visibility on the app as well as the option to see which other users have liked you (They could of course allow this feature for everyone, but why waste an opportunity to make people pay?). After all, the dating app isn't designed for you. It's designed for them (**Law 5: You Are In The Media Hierarchy**). *All online dating platforms are a sales funnel for the premium service.* You can imagine the entire app as a downward slide towards the sales page where you enter your credit card details. And you can be absolutely sure that their algorithms are created in a way to enhance this sales funnel.

How do they do this, well let's look at Tinder's algorithms:

1. *The profiles of new users are made visible to a large number of people. An early success will suck new users into using the dating app for the long-term.*

2. *Overtime, the algorithms will gradually decrease the visibility of the user's profile. As the user begins to get less and less attention, the "Boost", "Superlike" and "Tinder Gold" options begins to seem more and more attractive.*

New users get hooked on the dopamine surge they feel when they get matches. Then, when these dopamine surges are suddenly removed, the user desperately wants them back and will often pay to do so. Simple, yet highly effective. Online dating companies, particularly MatchGroup, have managed to monetise the ancient ritual of courtship. To a large extent, they control *who* we meet and *if* we meet someone. For men, the ability to meet their future wife may lie behind the algorithms that MatchGroup controls. In hindsight, after you're happily married, you may realise that if you hadn't handed over your money for the "Boost" option on Tinder, you may have never met your wife. That's the extent of the control that dating apps can have over many people's lives.

So what's the lesson here? For men, it's not to take online dating too seriously. If you're not having much success on dating platforms, it's not necessarily reflective of your value to women in the real world. *Looking at the world through the lens of dating technology will give you a distorted view of reality.* Remember, technology isn't neutral. Understand that you may be disadvantaged while using online dating platforms, and then engage with the platform with that expectation in mind. Accept the rules of the game and then play the field as it lays. Of course, there's always an enormous real-world for you to step into anytime you can summon the courage to approach a girl you like. Perhaps if you're struggling with online dating, the only solution is to *stop using online dating.* Put down your phone and step away from the addictive environment of online dating for a few weeks. Instead, step out into the world and start meeting people the old-fashioned way; bars, clubs, cafe's, joining dance classes and so on. You may just find that the old-fashioned way of meeting a partner is far more effective than meeting them through the use of technology.

the photo-retouching
arms race

If you've ever wondered why everybody looks so goddamn perfect on Instagram, then here's your answer. Photo-retouching has now become accessible to anybody with a smartphone, that includes teenage girls between the ages of 12-18. While we've known for a long time that celebrities have their image edited using Adobe Photoshop, it's a different thing entirely when it's your own friends who are retouching their images.

Here's a shortlist of what photo-retouching apps allow you to:

☞ *Smoothing over skin flaws*

☞ *Whitening teeth*

☞ *Whitening eyes*

☞ *Brighten or darken skin tones*

☞ *Removing bags under eyes*

☞ *Changing face shape*

☞ *Changing nose shape*

☞ *Remove people from backgrounds*

☞ *Make a smile wider*

☞ *Make eyes bigger or smaller*

☞ *Editing body shape: Broader shoulders, hourglass figure, bigger muscles, bigger ass, bigger breasts and so on.*

All of this can done so subtlety that the average person has no idea any editing has taken place. Of course, others push the photo-retouching too far and make it a little too obvious. In the current day, it's not uncommon to see women who appear to be made of plastic pop up on your social media news feed. Other common trends include: extreme hour glass figures, enormous alien-like eyes and curving backgrounds where the user has carelessly curved the background as well as her own body. Aside from these occasional examples of photo-retouching being overused, most people have become quite the expert at subtlety retouching their own images. For young people today, photo-retouching is an open secret. *Everybody does it but nobody talks about it.* While straight men do dabble in it, photo-retouching tends to be a female-only trend. If you're a young person, your social media feed is now filled with white, sparkling eyes, flawless skin, perfectly sized foreheads and perfect noses. Even people you know in the real world seem to have transformed into perfect goddesses overnight.

Beauty technology has been available on the market for decades. Take makeup for example. Makeup enhances the features that make a woman physically attractive. Skin with a smooth complexion is a sign of youth and fertility and makeup artificially gives the appearance of a smooth complexion. Men (or women) are attracted to the stimulus of smooth skin, despite it's artificiality. Big, full lips are also a sign of health and fertility. Makeup artificially increases the size and plumpness of lips. Men (or women) are then attracted to the stimulus of big, full lips despite it's artificiality. People know they're looking at artificial features, but they're attracted to them anyway. Makeup is a supernormal stimuli. Just as you can increase the attractiveness of a male barn swallow by colouring it's chest a darker shade of brown with a felt-tip pen, you can make a woman more physically attractive by enhancing her skin, eyes and nose with makeup brushes and eyelash curlers.

Every time a new beauty technology appears on the market, an arms race takes place. Women who use the new technology are praised and rewarded for their increase in attractiveness. Other women in the dating market need to use the same beauty technology to keep up with their competition, and very quickly, makeup becomes the norm across all of society. Photo-retouching encourages exactly the same style of arms-race. Some women began to use photo-retouching to their advantage and other women quickly caught on and adopted the technology too, not to be outdone by their competition. *Within the space of a couple of years, retouching your images has become completely normal.* As soon as a beauty technology arrives on the market, it is adopted by women to improve their position on the dating market. And this will be the case for all future beauty technologies too. Men who understand that women are retouching their images will still be drawn in by these artificially beautiful images.

The creepiest aspect of all of this is the fact that it works. Whether you're aware of the image re-touching or not, it makes people look great.

Even if the pre-frontal cortex of your brain understands that the images have been edited, the older reptilian part of your brain can't tell the difference. Your subconscious brain simply sees is an attractive person. *It may even be possible that viewing artificially beautiful images of a woman will change the way you perceive her in the real world too.* If you keep seeing images of a certain person pop up on your social media feed showing this person looking flawlessly attractive again and again, what happens next time you see that person in real life? Are you disgusted by the fact their offline appearance doesn't match up to their appearance in real life? Or has your subconscious brain been manipulated to the point that you can't help but find them attractive in real life too?

12-year-old girls can now reshape their own faces and bodies whenever they like. Is this a recipe for body dysmorphia? Yes. Are we doing anything about it? No. A sensible measure that could be taken is creating a law that restricts photo-retouching software for anybody under the age of 18. All photo retouching apps would require identification. Of course, big tech wouldn't be too happy about this, teenagers are one of the biggest markets for photo-retouching apps. A relatively good solution is available, it's just a question of whether we care enough to implement it.

chapter 6

PORNOGRAPHY

porn in the 21st century

In the dawn of the 21 Century, with everybody's eyes focused on the emerging technology of the internet, a huge unrivalled force managed to sneak into our lives undetected. High-speed internet Porn became available at the click of a button for anybody with an internet connection. For the first time in human history, any sexual fantasy you can possibly imagine (And some you'd never want to imagine..) became available for anybody to see, at no cost whatsoever. This could potentially be the biggest social experiment in history. This is a huge deal. This is not trivial. This is completely new. And this is going to have major effects on human beings. Porn has had an almost entirely uncontested path into our lives. This tidal wave of porn has risen in an era of sexual freedom, where anything between consenting adults goes. The main opposition to porn, religion, is shunned to the side with the majority being firmly on the side of science and rationality. Nobody is going to allow religion to make them feel guilty for masturbating. No real feminist movement has arisen against online porn either. Our cultural climate has allowed porn to move into mainstream culture almost completely uncontested. A well meaning, freedom loving population has encouraged porn into our lives while massively underestimating the negative effects it might have on us.

The thought process goes like this: *Who cares? Its just porn. People like porn. Stop trying to control what people do behind closed doors. Everybody masturbates*

right? Porn is nothing more than a tool to help people masturbate after all. Hop online.
Pleasure yourself for 10 minutes then move on with your day. Who cares!

Somehow, very few people seem concerned at all about the negative effects that pornography may have on individuals and society. People still equate being anti-porn with being some kind of angelic, conservative Christian. But over the last decade, the "Nofap" movement has emerged. "NoFap" is an online movement that encourages men to completely stop masturbating. Of course, this includes completely banning pornography from your life. Who would have ever guessed that it would be young men in their teens and twenties who would be the biggest force pushing back against pornography?

These men have been watching pornography ever since their early teens, and they're beginning to see some incredibly negative effects as they enter their 20's. Plenty of young men are now suffering from erectile dysfunction. Many are finding themselves hopelessly addicted to pornography, while others are generally unmotivated, apathetic, anxious and depressed. One Reddit user writes *"I'm 23 years old and have been PMOing (Porn, masturbation, Orgasm) since I was 15 (...) I've had about 10 opportunities to have sex with girls I was dating, but out of those 10 times, I was only able to get it up once"* Comments like these incredibly common among online porn addiction recovery communities.

Pornography is an evolutionary mismatch and a supernormal simuli. **(Law 2: Media Is An Evolutionary Mismatch)** and many men prefer the supernormal stimuli of porn over real sex. 200,000 years ago, there weren't all that many humans around. Through evolution, the brain developed a strong dopamine reward system around sex, which ensured we had as many children as possible and the human race kept growing. But modern high-speed pornography means we have endless access to the stimuli of sex, something our brains aren't prepared for. Just like we're all overdosing on sugar, many of us are overdosing on sexual stimuli. And it's not just the frequency of sexual stimuli that are an evolutionary mismatch for our lizard brains, it's also the strength of the stimuli. Women in porn are hypersexualised. Porn actresses are unusually attractive and they have a makeup artist perfecting their flaws. The lighting and shadows on their body are in exactly the right place and the noises they make are comically over-exaggerated. (Mmm! Oooh! Yes! Yes! Uh! Uh!)

When it comes to porn, it's clear that our unconscious brain can't tell the difference between porn and real sex. When seeing naked women on the screen, your lizard brain is tricked into thinking real naked women are available to have sex with. In truth, a porn viewer is sitting in a room with nothing more than an electric box of wires and glass, and yet they still get aroused. Despite the fact that there isn't a real sexual partner present, your lizard brain doesn't understand this. The male lizard brain can't tell the difference between a screen and a real naked woman.

Harry the fisherman scowled at at a picture of a French girl in a bikini. Fred, understanding that he seemed a bleak, sexless person to Harry, tried to prove that Harry had him wrong. He nudged Harry, man-to-man. "Like that, Harry?" he asked.

"Like what?"

"The girl there"

"That's not a girl. That's a piece of paper."

"Looks like a girl to me." Fred leered.

"Then you're easily fooled," said Harry. "It's done with ink on a piece of paper. That girl isn't lying there on the counter. She's thousands of miles away, doesn't even know we're alive. If this were a real girl, all I'd have to do for a living would be to stay home and cut out pictures of big fish."

From Kurt Vonnegut's novel, *God Bless You Mr Rosewater*

Aside from the hypersexualisation of the women on screens, one of the biggest problems is the frequency in which new women are accessible. Many frequent porn users have picked up the habit of switching between different videos and tabs in rapid succession. Watching porn gives the male brain access to an endless stream of different naked women and the subconscious brain of a porn user thinks that they've hit the *evolutionary jackpot,* so the user will experience a new spike in dopamine with each new female that appears on screen. The brain begins to expect the constant novelty of new women, thus men get less aroused when having sex with their real life girlfriend, often leading to men *choosing porn over their real partners.*

THE AVERAGE 16 YEAR OLD BOY NOW SEES MORE SEXUAL PARTNERS IN A SINGLE HOUR THAN HIS ANCESTORS WOULD HAVE SEEN IN THEIR ENTIRE LIFETIME.

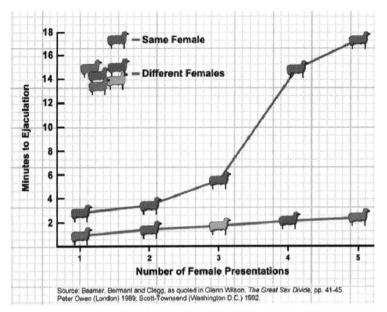

Source: Beamer, Bermant and Clegg, as quoted in Glenn Wilson, *The Great Sex Divide*, pp. 41-45. Peter Owen (London) 1989; Scott-Townsend (Washington D.C.) 1992.

Dopamine surges for novel "mates" and scenes

BOTH TAKEN FROM GARY WILSON'S TED TALK: HTTPS://YOUTU.BE/WSF82AWSDIU

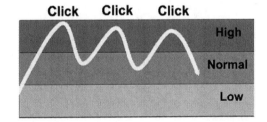

These dopamine surges are highly addictive. It's no surprise that pornography is a widespread growing problem amongst millions of men (and a minority of women) around the world. As well as that, this endless sexual novelty creates a desensitisation process. Ordinary sex doesn't stimulate much of a dopamine response in a brain that has been trained on the hypersexualised, constant novelty of online pornography.

This constant binging of new females and dopamine spikes leads to a build up of the brain chemical Delta-FosB in the brain's reward circuit. This means 3 primary structural changes in the brain.

1. **Numbed Pleasure Response** - *Everyday pleasures begin to be less satisfying.*

2. **Hyper-reactivity to Porn** - *While everyday pleasures seem boring, porn becomes extra exciting.*

3. **Willpower Erosion** - *The frontal cortex is changed, leading to a weakening of willpower.*

All 3 of these brain changes are features of all other addictions, including drugs, alcohol and gambling. Members of the NoFap community frequently talk about their massively increased motivation and enthusiasm for life after quitting porn. This is because their brain's pleasure response has returned to normal and is no longer being constantly numbed by the use of pornography. These symptoms are not only present in men with extreme porn addictions, but to everybody that watches pornography, just to a lesser extent. This will affect men at varying levels. With some it will be barely noticeable, with others it will cause serious problems. But the effect will always be there on some level in any frequent porn user (which most teenage boys are). While it's not scientifically proven just yet, porn is correlated with depression, anxiety, and low self-esteem. It seems likely that the scientific community will eventually find solid evidence of the links between porn and these mental health disorders

The NoFap community often talk about massive drops in each of these mental disorders as little as 7 days after quitting porn. One Reddit user writes: *"Depression gone!!! I feel insanely confident right now. I'm only on day 7 (without porn) but I feel amazing, higher energy, better sleep.."*

On the exact same device that they need to do their work, watch entertainment, keep up with friends and just about everything else, porn is available to watch within a couple of clicks at any time. It's like a drug addict keeping drugs in their pockets 24/7 and still attempting to resist the urge to use. What does an alcoholic do? They remove all alcohol from their homes and they refrain from going to places where alcohol is sold. This option is not available to the porn addict (unless they want to disconnect from the internet entirely, which may affect their work and social lives negatively). For the porn addict, their addiction is available at any time of the day. If that means running to the bathroom during work to get their fix, or even watching porn while they're stuck in traffic on their drive to work, then so be it. During the COVID pandemic, there were multiple viral, rather cringeworthy cases of employees being caught watching porn while on a work Zoom call, believing their camera to be turned off.

Teens and adults across the entire planet are now addicted to pornography. Porn addiction is a private addiction, easily kept secret and is socially embarrassing and unacceptable, so the number of porn addicts is likely much higher than we're aware of. It's quite likely that at least somebody you know is a porn addict. Many porn addicts are unaware of their addiction until one day they decide to stop watching it, and quickly realise that actually they *can't stop*. Porn also has certain characteristics that real sex doesn't; being alone, watching from a 3rd-person perspective, clicking, searching, sitting in a particular position. To the frequent porn user, real sex *just doesn't feel right*:

Why is there another person here? Why am I seeing the scene from a first person view? Why am I not sitting down with the mouse in my hand? Why am I not in my usual porn-watching position? And most insidious of all: Why can't I switch to a new tab to see a different woman?

At this stage an entire generation of men (and many women) have grown up consistently using pornography throughout their formative years. The culture told them what they were doing was perfectly fine and perfectly healthy. And now millions of men are facing the consequences. This desensitisation process leads to porn becoming more and more extreme and absurd overtime. The front page of most porn websites (where they host the most popular content) is now commonly filled with incest

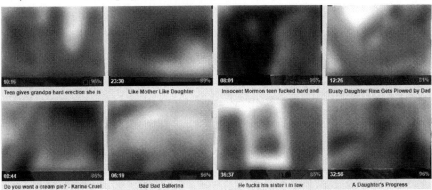

FRONT PAGE OF POPULAR PORN WEBSITE XHAMSTER.COM

porn. You can now frequently find titles like "Teen gives grandpa a hard erection" and "Busty daughter plowed by dad". This kind of taboo content has become more and more popular as the years have gone on.

Constant use of porn leads to desensitisation. For the frequent porn user, the vanilla videos they used to watch don't don't stimulate their dopamine receptors anymore, so they move onto **BDSM** genres. After a while, these BDSM videos no longer give the dopamine high they used to and they move onto ballbusting, bukkakes or any other strange or taboo sexual fetish you can imagine (after all, any sexual fetish you can imagine is available online). Over a large scale, the tastes of the audience become more extreme. So the porn website responds by featuring more of this extreme content. Gradually, you begin to find extreme content on the front page of the website. This increases the exposure of this extreme content to the general audience and leads to even more people adopting these extreme sexual preferences. This creates a kind of downward spiral. More users become interested in extreme sexual fetishes and more users are exposed to more extreme sexual fetishes through the porn site's algorithms. Many porn addicts users report becoming sexually confused as their porn preferences begin to include those of the gender they're not attracted to. Straight men start watching gay porn because their brain needs more and more taboo content to get the same dopamine high they're used to. More telling still, those who quit porn often report losing attraction to the fetishes they had previously been watching, which suggests that pornography is *creating false fetishes.* These are sexual preferences that, rather being created organically in a person's mind, are instead the end result of the porn desensitisation process.

As high-speed internet porn crept into our lives around 2008, sex education stayed exactly the same. Most former students will remember from sex-ed classes is putting a condom on a banana and having a good laugh with their friends. Sex education, like most education, failed to keep up with technology. Schools don't teach teenagers about sex, internet porn does. Somewhere between the ages of 11-17, most teenage boys start watching pornography. From here on, most of them watch countless hours of it right into their 20s. This is often a long time before they experience real sex. Pornography isn't sex, but a teenage boy isn't fully aware of that. Even a grown man can be mislead by the blurred line between porn and real sex. Watching adult, muscular men with larger than average penis sizes, having sex with a girl moaning constantly in an exaggerated way can lead a teenage boy to feel inadequate about his own sexual attributes. Perhaps his girlfriend stays quiet when they have sex, she must not be enjoying it. His penis seems smaller than the ones he sees on the screen. He's a scrawny little boy, not like the muscular man on the screen. He can only last around 10 minutes, the man on the screen can go for a full hour non-stop. He may begin to get the sense that something is wrong with him. One Reddit User Writes: *"Porn made me insecure about my penis (…) porn made me think I have a small one, because they have huge penises and I looked at myself and felt completely inadequete and insecure".*

Or perhaps it has a different effect. His girlfriend has small breasts. She doesn't do deepthroat like he saw on the screen. She won't let him give her a facial. She won't even do anal. She must be a prude, so he might just start putting pressure on her to do more and more extreme sexual acts. Or maybe the effects are more sinister. Maybe he gets the sense that contraception isn't particularly important, he's never seen a video where the guy uses a condom after all. Maybe he gets the sense that consent isn't important. Chances are, he's seen plenty of rape porn and other kinds of violent porn. Finally, relationships and connection are not showcased in porn, instead it's entirely centred around sexual gratification. This could shape how the teen approaches sex as he grows up, especially considering the teenager brain is prime to be wired in a certain way between the ages of 12-20. There is a myriad of possible psychological effects that pornography may have on a young mind, yet these effects are relatively unknown and unstudied.

Porn is not only found in pornography. In the modern world, soft porn is everywhere. Instagram, TikTok, Twitch.tv, advertising and music videos; porn addicts find avoiding triggering material almost impossible. To avoid sexual images is to avoid media altogether. Sex sells on every platform, in all kinds of different situations. Instagram models use soft porn to build massive audiences and make profit via sponsorship. Advertising uses soft porn to associate their product with attractiveness. Magazines use soft porn to increase sales. Music videos use soft porn to increase their view counts. Thousands of businesses everywhere are trying to make a profit and sex is an effective way to sell. The end result is a world saturated with soft porn.

Recent estimates show the porn industry is worth around $98 billion. The giant corporation Mindgeek currently holds a large monopoly over the porn industry, controlling websites like: Pornhub, Youporn, Redtube, as well as adult film companies such as Brazzers, Reality Kings, Babes.com and Men.com. The first way porn websites make money is through online ads. We've all seen the comical "Penis enlargement pill" advertisements found on most porn websites. But the real money is created with the paid subscription services. Porn production companies like Brazzers will post a free teaser video on Pornhub and then try to direct traffic to their website for full videos. In fact, after extensive research, they realised the perfect amount of time for the teaser video is around 3-6 minutes; enough time to make the user aroused, but not long enough for them to orgasm. Funnily enough, *men with erections don't think through decisions very carefully* and are easily persuaded to hand over their cash. Considering Mindgeek owns the main free porn websites, they can purposefully direct traffic to their own porn production companies. For example, they can feature Brazzers videos (their company) on the front page of Pornhub (also their company).

Porn fuels demand for sex trafficking as a certain % of porn watchers end up as "Johns" (buyers of sex). The Johns see something in porn that they simply cannot do in the real world and will later go onto hire a prostitute; porn can effectively act as a teaser trailer for hiring a prostitute. By watching online porn and funding the porn industry, you are inadvertently contributing, in a small way, to sex trafficking.

Women have both good and bad experiences of working in the porn industry. Some women love their job as a porn star. They work in a friendly environment, with a responsible boss and get paid well. Many are passionate about porn in an artistic sense and enjoy their role as an actoress. Their co-actors reliably show accurate STD tests before shoots and they never have any problems with disease. Conversely, other women experience working in a toxic environment where they will have to do sexual acts they're not comfortable with. They are coerced into the job with promises of fame, money and "acting" roles. They find themselves in a culture filled with drug abuse, sexual abuse and manipulative bosses. If you watch porn, you will watch some videos with women happy in their job as a porn star, and others with women miserable in their role. Of course, you won't be able to tell the difference. Some women are also forced into porn. In a certain sense, porn is a kind of prostitution because women (and men) are being paid for a sexual act. Some women are forced by their pimp to produce porn, which is more likely to be the case in "Gonzo" porn (the cheaper, amateur stuff) than "Feature" porn (the polished, professional stuff).

The Porn industry is undoubtedly linked with the child porn industry. While some people are born paedophiles, others had their sexual tastes for children built over time. The popularity of online child pornography is increasing year after year, an increase that is fueled by people moving from watching adult porn over to child porn. The porn industry pushed to change the Child Pornography Protection Act of 1996 an act that used to restrict the use of any porn actors that appeared to be under 18. After a push from the porn industry, this part of the law was removed and, almost overnight, "Teen Porn" was born. Teen porn is a genre that uses over 18 actors who pretend they're teenagers in videos where a "Step-dad" will have sex with his "Step-daughter". These videos are only within the law because the porn industry lobbied to make it that way. Obviously, these kinds of videos could act as a gateway to child porn.

Virtual reality porn is already available. As you can see in the image above, with a VR headset you can watch porn in a first person view, as if you're in the scene and making eye-contact with the porn actress. The actress flirts directly with the camera and creates the illusion that she's flirting directly with the audience. But this is only the tip of the iceberg. We're beginning to see sex robots incorporated with VR. Silicone tits and asses can be groped in synchronisation  with VR porn. Considering the huge problems already caused by 2D Porn, just imagine the kind of problems that 3D Porn will cause. Some day soon, 2D porn will seem as old-fashioned as black and white television.

VR porn is coming, the question is, where will it lead us **(Law 3: Technology Never Moves Backwards)**? As extreme as this sounds, a substantial minority of men will become reclusive shut-ins. The pursuit of sex is one of the main motivators for young men to head out into the world. But when they can fulfil their sexual desires to a large extent in a VR porn scene, why bother (Hikikomoris in Japan already live this way on a diet of 2D Porn, gaming and TV shows)? VR porn means less motivated men, with more porn addiction and more men with sexual problems.

There are some potential upsides to VR porn. On this platform, you're no longer watching the scene from a voyeuristic, third-person perspective, instead the scene is viewed through a first person perspective. The feeling of connection and the feeling of eye-contact you get with the porn actress may make men more empathetic with their partners in real life. On the other hand, it's inevitable that VR Porn will follow the same rabbit hole effect we've seen in 2D porn. Audience sexual tastes will get more and more extreme as they're desensitised from vanilla content. This will lead to the same extreme, violent porn becoming more mainstream, but this time from a more realistic first-person perspective. Will realistic, violent porn from a first person perspective make people more violent towards their partners in real life? We can't say for sure.

With the future inevitable integration between VR porn and deepfakes, you will be able to have sex with anybody you like from a first-person perspective. Celebrities, your next-door neighbour, your ex-girlfriend, the cute girl at the supermarket, absolutely anybody. Celebrity sex tapes will soon lose their edge, as celebrity deepfake porn will be freely available, with the ability to put celebrities into any pornographic situation you please. In the future, you will not be able stop people masturbating to your own image in a first-person VR porn scene. In the end it will become a simple fact of life that many people you know may have masturbated to your image implanted into a pornographic scenario, and the ability for you to give consent to this will be totally out of your hands.

To the porn addicts reading, I highly suggest you attempt to get your addiction under control *before* the technology advances any further. The strength of pornographic stimuli on your screen is only going to become stronger and stronger and businesses will continue to be hell-bent in their efforts to get people to watch it. Governments are unlikely to regulate the technology, so individuals will probably be left to deal with and avoid this incredibly strong supernormal sexual stimuli for themselves. Highly addictive pornography will continue to be a fact of life, so you need to adapt. This is the new world your parents and grandparents couldn't prepare you for, and without any generations before you to lead the way, you need to plot a course through life that avoids the pitfall of pornography.

NEVER DIGITISE HUMAN URGES.

camgirls –
the digital stripclub

You've probably already heard about camgirling. You might have even visited camgirl sites like Chaturbate.com, Livejasmin.com or Myfreecams. com. Maybe you're a big spender who's used thousands of dollars to purchase "tokens" to send to beautiful women you've never met. Maybe (like so many men) you've become romantically attached to a camgirl. Or perhaps, if you're really unlucky, you've become a camgirl addict. On the other hand, you might be a camgirl yourself. Maybe you've spent hundreds of hours in your bedroom dancing in front of a webcam to thousands of men from across the world.

Whoever you are, I'm about to give you all the dirty details about the camgirl industry and give you a clear idea on what this industry actually is. I'm about to explain how camsites are making millions of dollars by monetising romantic interaction. How female youth and beauty is now a product that can be packaged up and sold for a healthy profit on a scale never seen before in human history. And finally, how camgirling is an industry that is going to become more and more prevalent as we move into the future and eventually integrate with virtual reality.

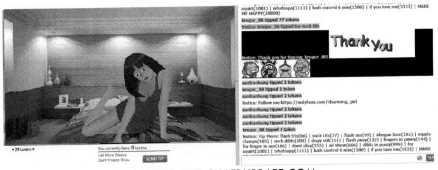

FROM POPULAR CAMGIRL SITE CHATBURBATE.COM

There are two kinds of camgirl websites. In the first kind, men will pay camgirl models a fixed fee to have a private session with them. $2 per minute. Just like the sexchat hotlines of the past. The second kind is what you might call the "stripclub model". On this kind of camgirl site, men will buy "tokens" from the website and then spend these tokens on their favourite model.

Purchase Tokens

Credit/Debit Card Options (the more tokens you buy, the less they cost!)

- ● **200 tokens FREE!** (a $20.99 USD value) when you upgrade your account. Unlock PM & remove ads for $19.95
- ○ 100 tokens for $10.99 USD
- ○ 200 tokens for $20.99 USD (5% Bonus)
- ○ 400 tokens for $39.99 USD (10% Bonus)
- ○ 550 tokens for $49.99 USD (21% Bonus)

Payment options:

- ● Credit/Debit Card (Visa/Mastercard/Discover) ⓸
- ○ Epoch (Credit Card)
- ○ PayPal
- ○ Wire Transfer
- ○ Cryptocurrency
- ○ Bring a Friend and earn tokens!

> Beginning Jan. 31, 2020, "mmbill.com" or "chaturbill.com" will appear on your card statement as noted at time of purchase.

Your account can process 2 more credit card transactions today. Raise your spending limit.

Continue to payment page ▶

In order to serve you better, please take a minute to give us your billing feedback.

SIDENOTE: LOOK AT THE MISLEADING PRICING STRUCTURE HERE. AS THE BUYER SPENDS THEIR TOKENS, THEY WILL INSTINCTIVELY CALCULATE THAT 1 TOKEN = 10¢, 10 TOKENS = $1. AND 1000 TOKENS = $100. WHEN IN FACT 1000 TOKENS = $109. THIS PRICING WILL CONTINUALLY MISLEAD BUYERS INTO FEELING LIKE THEY'RE SPENDING LESS THAN THEY ACTUALLY ARE.

This second kind of camgirl site is a digital stripclub. Just imagine a girl dancing on the pole in the centre of the room with men throwing dollar bills at her. This type of camgirl site is essentially exactly the same — only the crowds are much, much larger. Girls often have 1000+ viewers and sometimes even 10,000+ viewers. Just imagine a tennis court filled with spectators, that's how many people are watching camgirls.

Camgirling isn't an entirely new idea, it's simply a digital version of something that already exists in the real world: the stripclub. The virtual stripclub now exists. Men are able to sit behind their laptop from anywhere in the

YES THAT'S 11418 PEOPLE WATCHING A SINGLE GIRL. JUST IMAGINE ALL OF THESE PEOPLE WATCHING IN A REAL AUDIENCE.

world and throw in little bits of money to a girl of their choice. Women will have their prices displayed on screen for various sexual performances and men will spend tokens to watch them perform. The prices will usually look something like this:

Notice: Tip Menu: flash tits(66) | suck tits(77) | flash ass(99) | Ahegao face(101) | nipple clamps(105) | suck dildo(109) | dogy stil(111) | flash pusy(122) | fingers in pussy(144) | for finger in ass(166) | domi play(555) | oil show(666) | dildo in pussy(999) | for squirt(1001) | whatsapp(1111) | lush control 6 min(1500) | if you love me(3333) | MAKE THE NUMBERS YOU SEE HERE ARE THE NUMBER OF TOKENS NEEDED. HERE YOU CAN SEE GETTING THE GIRL'S WHATSAPP NUMBER COSTS 1111 TOKENS ($122 USD). "LUSH CONTROL" REFERS TO THE LOVESENSE LUSH 2 REMOTE CONTROLLED VIBRATOR. THIS COSTS 1500 TOKENS ($164 USD). AS FOR THE "AHEGAO FACE"...WELL I'LL LET YOU GOOGLE THAT ONE FOR YOURSELF.

Most men are able to watch the girls for free. They don't have to make an account, they can simply open the website and browse the girls who are live. The majority of men are just lurking, but a small few will pay tokens and get the girls to perform. And usually there is one or two big spenders ("whales") in the room funding the entire thing. Of course, men can also pay big money to get the girl into a 1 v 1 private cam session if they're willing to do so. A more recent trend is for camgirls to wear remote controlled vibrators that are synced up with the token system. The more tokens, the longer and stronger the vibration.

sweety_rinushka_ ********My LOVENSE Lush is now reacting to "gentleperv_'s tip. It will stop after 1 seconds!
Notice: Lovense Lush - Interactive Toy That Responds to Your Tips
Notice: ♥ Durations and Intensity Levels ♥
Notice: Level 1 ▸ Tip 1-14 ⟳ 2 sec (Low vibrations)
Notice: Level 2 ▸ Tip 15-99 ⟳ 5 sec (Low vibrations)
Notice: Level 3 ▸ Tip 100-299 ⟳ 10 sec (Medium vibrations)
Notice: Level 4 ▸ Tip 300-499 ⟳ 30 sec (High vibrations)
Notice: Level 5 ▸ Tip 500+ ⟳ 60 sec (High vibrations)
Notice: Give me pleasure with your tips!
CAMGIRLS WILL PRETEND THEY'RE GETTING INTENSE PLEASURE FROM THESE VIBRATIONS WHEN IN FACT THE VIBRATOR RARELY TURNS THEM ON AT ALL AND THEIR REACTION USUALLY ENTIRELY FAKE. (ACCORDING TO REAL CAMGIRLS).

Some camgirls even provide their Whatsapp/Line numbers (at a high price of course) to give the men the chance to message them personally. Camgirls also make extra money on the side by selling videos and photos on websites like onlyfans.com, clips4sale.com and manyvids.

com. If you're unfamiliar with this strange corner of the internet, at this stage you probably have many questions: How much do camgirls make? Why do the camgirls do it? And why the hell are so many men paying them in the first place? Let's start with the women.

All of these girls on webcam. Getting naked, dancing, wearing sexy outfits and putting objects inside themselves. Why do they do it? The reason is simple: Cam girls can make incredible amounts of money. General estimates for how much a camgirl earns vary. Some say $20-40 p/h, others say $65-100 p/h. I decided to do my own experiment. For strictly research purposes *cough* I picked a camgirl at random and watched for a total of 30 minutes. I recorded all of the tokens that she received during this time. This is the result:

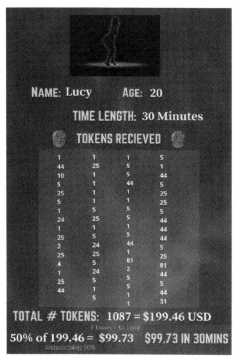

Perhaps this was a particularly good 30 minutes. Perhaps this girl usually makes half this amount. The point is - for a girl in their early 20's no other job could possibly compare. If you're an attractive 20 year old girl you now have the choice of earning $8 an hour as a waitress or earning $100 an hour (perhaps even more) as a camgirl. Not only that, but camgirls also sell video clips and photos on websites like Onlyfans.com or Clips4sale.com for even more money on the side. Certainly, not all camgirls make this much money, and some struggle to get by on a camgirl's income. But the amount of money many camgirls make from this hustle is really quite impressive. Of course, the real money lies in hooking a "whale": a man who's willing to spend big on a particular girl. This is where the majority of a successful camgirl's profits will come from. When a whale enters the chat and begins to tip big, the camgirl will start fawning over him and stroking his ego. A lot of camgirls will use masculine, ego stroking language with their high-tippers, like calling them "hero", "champion" or "winner" or asking questions like "who is going to save my night?".

Cam girl Aella explains her strategies for hooking whales, she explains *"You see, you're not just trying to get a guy to pay you – you're trying to get a guy to pay you in front of a bunch of other guys. This is a super key. A man wants to feel attention from an attractive women on him, and this is made even more satisfying when it's to the exclusion to those around him. He is showing off his power by buying your happiness"* Many camgirls have "leaderboards" where their highest tippers can compete for the number one spot. One leader board reads like this:

1. *Openforfun99 – 27833 tokens*

2. *ryodan76 – 22883 tokens*

3. *victorpaul – 14005 tokens*

4. *tibitib – 12500 – tokens*

5. *dirtyytomas – 10100 tokens*

   Thank you so much guys!!! <3

In this case openforfun99 is the biggest "whale" here, who has spent 27833 tokens on this particular girl (the equivalent of $3058USD)

In our capitalist society, everything has a monetary value. Female beauty has always carried inherent value, but now that value has been effectively monetised with the use of technology. In the past, women could only sell their beauty in strip clubs, as escorts or as prostitutes. Because these methods required being a physical location, the number of men they could earn money from was limited. In the new world, women can sell their female beauty on the digital stripclub (camsites) to thousands of men from all around the world. Because they no longer need a physical space, they can sell their female beauty to an unlimited number of men. Not only that, but on camsites women don't need to be afraid of any potential physical harm that men may inflict on them. Female beauty can now be sold without risk of being harmed. The issue of safety, which was previously a major deterrent for women getting into sex work, is no longer a problem. On top of all that, they're selling their product to the perfect customers — horny men. You couldn't ask for customers in a better "buying mindset" than men who have given in to their sexual urges.

Now don't get me wrong, it's now all sunshines and rainbows. Some camgirls are struggling to pay rent and are desperate for money. Camgirls deal with abusive messages, scams, and have to put their naked self on the internet where it can be shared on porn sites. And some women report having mental health issues after dealing with particularly toxic and creepy behaviour from men. Certainly, becoming a successful camgirl takes hard work, determination and the ability to put up with toxic behaviour. But for any girl willing to put in the effort and accept the downsides, camgirling makes perfect sense. In what other job could a 20-something year old girl make $50+ per hour? And it's not like conventional jobs don't come with their own downsides. When it comes down to it, what's the smart move for a young girl? Get a waitress job and earn $8 and hour? Or do camgirling for a few years and set themselves up for the rest of their life?

We now live in a society where becoming a camgirl is arguably a logical and rational choice for a young woman. Becoming a camgirl could almost be seen as a smart, sensible and responsible financial decision. Being a camgirl isn't the only day to monetise female beauty, there's also: Instagram modelling, the sale of pornographic images and videos on Onlyfans, becoming a sugarbaby for a wealthy older gentleman, becoming a twitch streamer (being a sexy, flirtatious girl playing video games on Twitch. tv is an easy path to financial gains) and endless others. On our current trajectory, young women selling their female beauty online for financial gain could eventually become an accepted part of the culture (if it isn't already). The female beauty of an average 20-year-old girls contains far more value than any other skills a girl of that age could possibly hope to train for financial return (it takes time to build real skills that can be sold for profit in the jobs marketplace). And when they can sell their female beauty online, completely safe from danger, what other traditional job could possibly compare? What's the correct choice for a young woman in a world more or less that completely accepts the sale of female sexuality?

So that's the women, but what about the men? Why the hell are men willing to spend so much money on women they'll never even meet? It might seem strange that men are happy to spend money for a camgirl when pornography is freely available throughout the internet. But camgirls offer something that porn never can: connection. The girl responds to *you.* She responds to *your* requests. She calls you by *your* name. You're not staring in from the outside like in porn, you're directly involved in the action. Of course, camgirls generally don't care about the customer's personally, only the money in their wallet. But that doesn't mean that men don't feel a real connection with the camgirl.

One Reddit titles his post *"I blow a ton of money on camgirls because they give me a sense of self worth"*, another user writes *"I've totalled at least $12,000 spent in the span of a year since getting addicted to camgirls. I've been pushing my family away and making up excuses to hide my expenses"*. In many cases, after high tipper gets the camgirl's number, she will message him throughout the day, persuading him to come back online to the camsite. Many men become regulars with a particular camgirl. They begin to feel as if they know the camgirl on a personal level. And some men even report falling in love with them. When a man becomes obsessed with a camgirl, he becomes a "whale", and the camgirl will do her best to extract as much money out of him as possible. Many of us live a life of isolation for all kinds of reasons, poor social skills, depression, social anxiety or lack of finances. To many modern men, the modern world can isolate them, then offer them the solution to their loneliness. Only for a price. Lonely men will pay hundreds if not thousands of dollars to simply receive attention from a pretty woman, it's one of the deepest drives a man can have. For the isolated man, there's almost nothing he wouldn't do to have some kind of interaction with a girl. Money is no object when his needs are so deep and strong.

While you might be imagining dirty old men behind their computer screens paying for these cam girls, this isn't the only demographic paying for female attention on camsites. A large proportion of the customer base are young men. Young men who have grown up inside a digitised world. They've grown up watching porn, flicking through girls on Tinder, following attractive girls on Instagram and, continuing a natural progression, paying for female attention on camsites. Many of these men have never had a relationship with a real woman. Their entire experience of sex and dating so far in their lives has been digital. So it makes perfect sense that they would replace their desire for a real girlfriend by paying a camgirl to pretend to like them back.

Camgirl addiction is real. Since Camsites are a dopamine fuelled environment linked to sex and human connection, this comes as no surprise. Men get dopamine hits seeing the girl naked. Then they get further dopamine hits when seeing the girl respond to them personally. The more tokens they spend, the more dopamine hits they can receive. Camsites are selling a highly addictive product. When camgirls talk about finding a "whale" to make money from, what they're often talking about is finding an addict to exploit. Just like casinos — the majority of the profit is made by exploiting addictive behaviour.

Not all men who spend big are addicts, however, some incredibly wealthy men use Camgirls as a form of light entertainment and are perfectly happy to throw down $1000 for a bit of fun. These rich big-spenders often enter a chatroom, leave an enormous tip and then immediately leave. For them, it's a power trip. They enjoy feeling as though they've "won" the girl and dominated all of the other men in the chatroom. Some whales are just rich men who spend money on camgirls for the feeling of power it gives them.

Within the next few decades, you'll be able to interact with your camgirl in an immersive 3D environment through virtual reality technology. In fact, VR camgirls already exist, although as of now they're fairly similar to 2D camgirls, only with a 360 camera. On top of this, remote sex technology will allow the user to feel sensations as the camgirl interacts with them. Censors will be placed all over the man's body and will allow him to feel where she "touches" him. In the future, camgirls will use deepfakes to either enhance their natural beauty, or replace their own face with a different one entirely. The deepfake tracks the movement of the lips, eyes and head. So the deepfake camgirl will be able to move and talk naturally with using somebody else's face (**Law 3: Technology Never Moves Backwards**).

The sale of female attention on the internet isn't ever going away because it's built into our biology. Whether it's camgirls or some other platform in the future, businesses will try to manipulate men's natural desire for female sex and companionship for big profits. While deepfakes and synthetic media may make artificial female figures more common, there will always be a market for real women to sell their female attention to men online.

For the men reading, I have some obvious advice: don't replace a real romantic or sexual partner with a digital camgirl. Camgirls are an incomplete stimulus compared with a real girlfriend. Reality is better than pixels on a screen. Even if the girls on your screens are more physically attractive than your girlfriend or wife, the experience with your real partner will always be far more pleasurable. After all, when it comes it physical attractiveness alone, the girls on your screens will always be more attractive than those in the real world because of the addition of beautifying filters available to the girl's on your screens. With camgirls, you're missing out on all kinds of pleasurable brain chemicals that are released through closeness, touch and other sensations that can only be provided by a real life woman. So choose a real partner, not your screens.

online findom – a new phenomenon

You wake up at 1pm. No work today. Just like every other day.

You check your phone. "You have received $50USD". "You have received $100USD". "You have received $300USD".

You yawn. You put on a beautiful expensive dress, a golden necklace and a pair of brand new high heels. None of which you paid for.

You head out to the nicest coffee place and check your notifications. "Paypig Steve has messaged you". "Paypig Adam has messaged you". "Paypig Abdul has messaged you".

You sigh. It's time for the daily selfie. You hold the camera up high, trying to look cute and evil at the same time. You share the selfie to twitter and start writing your caption:

Which one of you paypiggys are going to buy me a new handbag today? Send Send Send! #Paypig #Findom #Cashrape

Time to respond to Paypig Steve. Your most loyal paypig.

PayPig Steve: I'm sorry goddess I know I promised I would send you $1000 today but my car broke down and I need the money to get it fixed. I can pay you at the end of the month...

Goddess Sarah: Pathetic little loser. Don't make me double it ;)

Paypig Steve: But goddess...

Goddess Sarah: It's up to $2000 now. You can't resist me little boy. SEND NOW! ;)

Paypig Steve: Yes Goddess...

Goddess Sarah: Good Boy! ;)

Ding! You have received $2000. Sigh. Business as usual.

Financial Domination (Findom). A form of erotic humiliation in which one person gives control of their finances over to another. Findom has been around for a long time in the BDSM community. But it's only in the last decade that it has merged with social media. And it's created an entirely new beast. Twitter and Instagram are crammed full of Findom accounts. All of which are posting abusive messages at men and demanding that they pay them. And guess what. It works. At this very second, women across the world are making a living by sending kinky and abusive messages to men. Curious men message these Findom accounts. The Findoms gradually ease these kinky men in. Asking for $10. Then $20. Then $50. Then $100. Getting paid via Cashapp or Paypal. These men are known as "Paypigs", and often continue to send these Findoms money for years into the future. Usually the money is sent digitally. But occasionally, a Paypig will meet his Findom in real life for a "Cash meet". This involves the findom taking the man to a nearby ATM and demanding that he takes out cash and hands it to her in person. Sometimes, the Findom will record the whole event on her phone and post it on social media.

Who are findom's best customers? The addicts (**Law 5: You Are In The Media Hierarchy**). For some, being seduced into handing over your cash is a massive rush. In the same way that people can become addicted to porn, they can also become addicted to Findom. Porn addiction is becoming addicted to sexual stimuli you're watching on a screen. Findom is essentially the same thing, the difference is that this sexual stimuli talks back. Not only does it talk back, but it will try to convince you to relapse. And this sexual stimuli is financially incentivised to be successful in doing so. They will purposefully try to trigger your addiction with tweets and messages. Saying the exact things that are most likely to trigger your relapse. Just like a drug dealer, they will encourage you to start out with small doses. Usually to start with sending a "Tribute" of $20. This is designed to get their foot in the door. It's only $20 after all. What harm is $20?

One Findom's tweet reads *"I will always be your biggest addiction"*. Another tweet reads *"I know that I am your addiction you're trying to quit. Relapse for a goddess. You'll love it"*. Findoms frequently encourage Paypigs to relapse on their addiction.

As time passes, more and more extreme stimuli is needed to get the same rush as the first hit (like drugs and gambling). When it comes to Findom, the intensity of the rush is directly proportional to the amount of money being sent. While sending $20 may give a newbie an initial rush, after 3 months of engaging in Findom $2000 will be required to get the same rush as that initial $20. And sending the money is only a click away. Sending money digitally almost doesn't feel real. Unlike cash, where you have to give over a physical object, sending money digitally only requires a tap on the screen of your smartphone. This makes it far easier to send more than you intended. Findom, unlike most other addictions, has somebody on the other side of the screen personally easing you into the rabbit hole

Another forum post on the same porn addiction website it titled *"How do you stop findon addiction! 14 years old"* and reads *"I need help! I'm tired of this fucking findom addiction it's ruining my life! It's honestly THE MOST HARDEST THING TO QUIT!. IT FUCKS UP MY SOCIAL ABILITIES AND CONFIDENCE"*

What kind of people engage in Findom? Sure, it can be a healthy individual looking for a creative way to spend the evening. But let's be honest. Generally speaking, men who engage in Findom tend to have the following traits:

☞   *Low self worth*

☞   *Self destructive behaviour*

☞   *Need to escape life*

☞   *Lack of intimacy in life*

☞   *Difficulty maintaining a one-to-one relationship with a woman*

☞   *Need for a chemical 'emotional' high*

One forum post on a popular porn addiction website from a now deleted account reads: *"Deep down I knew it was stupid, but I felt like a gambling addict in a casino and couldn't stop. It's not really a fetish I've ever enjoyed it's the humiliation aspect of it for me and the attention I got from them. Trust me it's not worth it at all. What saved me from it was one day I opened my bank account and looked at all the transactions I'd made for findom and I was horrified by the damage"*

This is financial exploitation. Findoms, whether they're aware of it or not, are often exploiting pre-existing poor mental health for financial gain. Findom addiction is serious. And it's life destroying. It's available in your pocket at anytime via your smartphone and can be accessed within around 20 seconds on Twitter or Instagram. (Smartphones are more or less a necessity in modern life, making it hard to put barriers between the addict and their addiction). On top of that, there is almost no support whatsoever for the addiction. For most men, there is nobody to turn to for help. And to make things worse, it's socially unacceptable and highly embarrassing. Meaning they're very unlikely to seek help from their family and friends. Findom is a unique addiction in that having your life ruined is part of the fetish itself. These men want to be completely humiliated (At least until they finish masturbating and they're filled with regret).

In the BDSM community, it's common knowledge that after any kind of submissive/dominant play, the Dom must give "aftercare" to the sub. Aftercare generally involves the dominant and the submissive talking things through and enjoying some closeness. To play a submissive role in BDSM play involves being highly vulnerable to another person. "Aftercare" ensures that the play is not psychologically damaging to the submissive. In online findom, aftercare is usually non existent.

What does a findom addiction do to a person?

☞   *Financial ruin*

☞   *Increasing debt levels*

☞   *Loss of property*

☞   *End of marriage/relationship*

☞   *Anxiety*

☞   *Permanent psychological damage*

Findom ruins marriages. It causes long-term psychological damage. It causes individuals to take out credit cards and loans in order to continue indulging in their addiction. It destroys savings accounts. It drains the college fund a father had been saving for his child. But I can hear the cries already. *"It's their own fault! They send the money willingly!"* If this is what you're thinking right now, this only shows that you don't understand addiction. Can addicts truly give consent to their actions? If a drug dealer stalked a heroine addict, continuing to encourage him to take just one more hit, would that be ok? This is exactly what online findoms do to findom addicts. They continue to send them messages with goal of triggering them back into their addiction.

So you have to wonder, who are these Findoms? How can they live with themselves? That's easy: Self-justification.

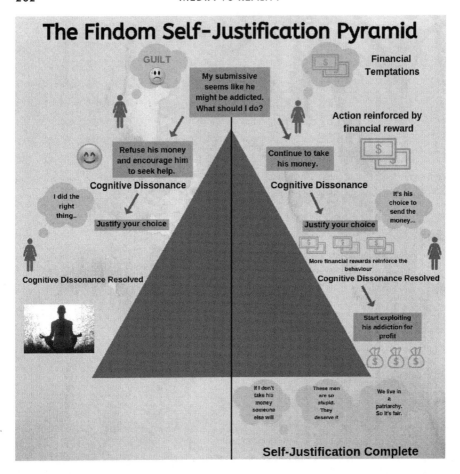

The Findom Self-Justification Pyramid

GUILT

My submissive seems like he might be addicted. What should I do?

Financial Temptations

Action reinforced by financial reward

Refuse his money and encourage him to seek help.

Continue to take his money.

Cognitive Dissonance

Cognitive Dissonance

I did the right thing..

It's his choice to send the money...

Justify your choice

Justify your choice

More financial rewards reinforce the behaviour

Cognitive Dissonance Resolved

Cognitive Dissonance Resolved

Start exploiting his addiction for profit

If I don't take his money someone else will

These men are so stupid. They deserve it

We live in a patriarchy. So it's fair.

Self-Justification Complete

Self-justification is like sliding down a pyramid. At the top of your pyramid you make your choice. Once you've made your choice you begin your slide down. Cognitive dissonance sets in. You need to calm the turmoil inside your mind. So you lie to yourself. You self-justify. Over and over again. By the time you reach the bottom of the pyramid you're fully convinced that you're doing nothing wrong. People use almost exactly the same self-justifications to sell drugs. If you've ever wondered how heroin dealers can live with themselves, look no further than the psychological mechanism of self-justification. Often these Findoms are self-justified to the point where they will even begin to play the victim. Complaining about "Timewasters" and collectively verbally destroying anyone who dares to suggest that their behaviour may be unethical.

And then you have the dehumanisation. The addicts they're encouraging aren't people. They're Paypigs. Pigs. Not humans. Of course, this dehumanisation is part of the degradation and humiliation fetish. But consistently referring to a group of people as "pigs" is going to have an affect on the psychology of the Findom. Findoms will be less likely to feel as though there's anything immoral in their actions because the victims are somewhat dehumanised.

A findom explains on babe.net: *"It's honestly hard to feel bad for taking their money when they're so darn stupid, so I got over the guilt pretty quickly. If we have to deal with it all day every day we might as well capitalize on it, right?"* This of course, is a prime example of the aforementioned self-justification.

Most Findoms are in it purely for the money. They want a lifestyle of lying around in their bedroom and watching money arrive on their Smartphone. A lot of Findoms are college graduates who are trying to pay off their student loans. Most of them aren't particularly interested in the kink. Most of them aren't getting turned on by taking money off of men (even if they say they are). But they are getting excited by all the free money (in fact, it's not only the Paypigs who get addicted, it can also be the Findoms themselves). There are also Findom networks online who pay models to take photos and videos of themselves while the Twitter or Instagram accounts are actually run by someone else (if you're talking to a Findom, it could be a man). And many of the kinky tweets and messages won't be written by the girls in the photos, but by someone else. Someone else who is running a large number of fake Findom accounts like a business (and raking in the cash).

For most online Findoms it's not a kink, it's an income stream. There are real Findoms out there who actually get pleasure out of the domination side of the exchange. Women who care about the well-being of their Paypigs and who truly want the best for their Paypigs. But these are few and far between. The average online Findom isn't interested in being a BDSM mistress. They just want cash. So if you're reading this and you're feeling inclined to try this for yourself, drop your illusions now.

Legally speaking, Findom lies in the grey area. It's not illegal because technically speaking, the man is handing over his cash willingly. And Findom addiction is a private addiction. One that doesn't cause problems for the rest of society (Unlike drug addicts). The government aren't going to regulate it. So for now, it's the wild west.

Findom is not a passing trend. No matter what the future brings, there will always be men who enjoy being submissive in BDSM. And there will always be men who get a rush out of being humiliated by handing over their cash to someone. *The brain mechanism is in place, so this isn't going away.* It seems likely that online findom is only going to grow in popularity as more and more teenage boys grow up with free and easy access to porn. And not just in your country, but around the world. Developing countries just beginning to get connected by technology will run into the exact same problem. Virtual reality headsets will allow an even more immersive findom experience, giving users the ability to make eye-contact with their Findom and interact with them in a 3D world. Making the whole experience of handing over your money even more thrilling, and even more addictive.

There will always be women (and occasionally men) who will leap at this opportunity to make easy money. You can expect the future to see a further rise in porn addiction and consequently a rise in Findom addiction. So what do we do? We need to educate people. This is just one more addictive rabbit hole provided to us by the onslaught of new technology. People need to understand that while technology provides amazing opportunities, it also provides a thousand different ways to ruin your life. The new world is filled with addictive pitfalls in all kinds of strange addictive shapes and forms. To live a fulfilled life, these pitfalls must be detected and avoided. And those profiting off of these addictions need to stop justifying their own actions.

chapter 7

ADVERTISING

how advertising really works

He stands in the shopping mall, watching with amusement as the herd of brainwashed sheep mill around him carrying their shopping bags.

Overweight couples sit on benches eating Big Mac's together in synchronised fashion. Pretty girls strut past with heavy makeup on their faces, wearing the latest fashion and carrying another new pair of shoes. Business men pace by talking on cellphones and wearing Armani suits.

Look at these gullible people, he thinks. Slaves to advertising...

He begins to feel thirsty, so he heads into the nearest convenience store. He stands in front of the drinks fridge and looks at his options. The fridge is lined with a multitude of different bottled and canned beverages.

He takes a bottle of Coca-Cola and heads to the checkout.

Nobody thinks advertising works on them. Yet advertising works on everybody. There is a large gap between the way people *think* advertising works and the way it *actually* works. To the layman, advertising works something like this:

Joe sits at home watching TV and drinking beer with his belly hanging over his crotch. An advertisement for a new Harleys Supersuck XX vacuum cleaner appears on screen. He's told it will pick up every last piece of dirt in his house. "Wow!" he shouts. "I have to go and buy this right now!". He grabs his wallet and runs straight out the door.

This Homer Simpson-esque stereotype doesn't often happen in the real world. Sure, direct marketing is real and infomercials want you to pick up the phone right away, door to door salesmen want you to hand over your credit card details on the spot, online marketing uses strongly worded sales letters to get you to click "Buy now" on their website. But this kind of direct marketing is for the small fish. As for the big fish like Coca-Cola, Mercedes, Mcdonalds, American Express and so on, they play a much bigger game. This game is being played inside your head right now without your awareness. They play the game of feathers.

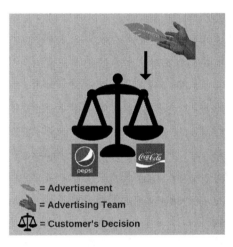

= Advertisement
= Advertising Team
= Customer's Decision

We live in a world of countless options and there are very few unique products. For almost every single thing you buy, there are hundreds of potential brands to choose from. Just think of the supermarket isle. Lined with 7 brands of baked beans. 24 brands of cereals. 9 brands of milk. How do you make your choice? *All it takes is a feather to tip the scales.* A feather placed in your subconscious mind. This is particularly true when it comes to low-involvement decisions. Deciding where to eat lunch, for example. Imagine, you head out of work for your lunchtime break. There aren't many places to eat near your work. But there is a Subway. *I guess I'll grab a sub* you think to yourself. And that's it. The decision is made. And Subway earns yet another consistent customer. It's in that split-second, where you made your decision, that the advertising kicks in. But how are these feathers placed in your mind? I mean, if I ask you to try to remember a Subway commercial you saw recently, you probably can't even remember it. But the truth is, just because you can't remember these commercials, that doesn't mean they're not affecting you. All advertising works on your subconscious mind, and the subconscious mind records all information it is given. Even information you were barely paying attention to, like a TV commercial playing in the background, can affect your buying decisions.

There are two main subconscious mechanisms that advertising creates. The first of which being artificial emotional links to the brand or *association*. You can essentially take Maslow's hierarchy of needs (pictured below) and associate any product or service with one of these needs.

SUBCONSCIOUS AND EMOTIONAL ASSOCIATIONS

Commercials of the past were very much feature-focused. They told us what they product did and what you could use it for. Over the years, advertising has become more and more sophisticated, and in the modern world it reaches down into our basic human needs. Today, almost all advertising tries to associate itself with at least one section on Maslow's hierarchy of needs. Food products associate themselves with health, banks associate themselves with family, cosmetics associate themselves with self-esteem. Almost every single advertisement does its absolute best to associate itself with your most basic human drives. Your lizard brain, which evolved hundreds of thousands of years ago, is constantly making associations between things. There is no way human beings would have survived for millions of years by trying to understand everything rationally. Our world is infinitely complex. There's simply too much "information" in the world to hope to rationally and logically understand it all. So we developed intuition. Which is the ability to unconsciously use all of our past experiences and "feel" which decision is the best for us. Psychologists have discovered an incredible mechanism our brain seems to have, they call them somatic markers.

When you were younger your parents told you time and time again to look both ways before crossed the street. But the truth is, these words probably didn't change your behaviour. The moment when you *truly* learned to look both ways before crossing the street is probably the time you walked into the road and were almost hit by a car. You may not remember this moment, but it probably happened. It's likely that on one occasion, you forgot to look before crossing and a car whizzed past, almost running you over. Your heart jumped, your palms started sweating and your breathing quickened. According to the theory, at this moment your brain and body created a "marker" in your memory, and now you always look both ways before you cross the street (even if you don't remember the moment you learned the behaviour). We create these "markers" throughout our life and these markers provide us with a non-conscious shortcut to making decisions. This is what we call intuition. Intuition helped us to avoid poisonous foods, know whether to trust other humans, to navigate through the world without a map and to generally keep us alive in a dangerous pre-technology world. We survived through millennia using this intuition or these "gut feelings". But in the 21st century these *"gut feelings"* can be manufactured inside your brain by advertising.

When you watch a Coca-Cola commercial and see young, healthy people having fun and drinking Coke your brain creates a "marker". Your subconscious brain now contains a marker that links the visual red and white logo of Coca-Cola to youth, health and fun. At that moment, when you're standing in front of that drinks fridge deciding what to buy, your brain picks up the very same red and white logo of Coca-Cola, and in a split-second, the "marker" that was placed in your subconscious during the commercial you watched reappears. Buying a bottle of Coca-Cola just "feels" right, and you buy it without much thought as to why you made the decision you did. The feather dropped onto the scales by the commercial changed your behaviour, which is why Coca-Cola spends $565 Million on advertising every single year in the US alone. Of course not all of these markers will land. Many of them will not have enough of an impact to be remembered. But some of them will.

If you live in the UK, you may remember this advertising campaign (an incredibly successful advertising campaign I might add). Meet the Andrex puppy.

Now let's ask a simple question: what on earth does a labrador retriever puppy have to do with toilet paper? The answer of course, is absolutely nothing. Yet this series of advertisements can successfully managed pair these two objects together and create an association between them in the mind of the audience. If you've stroked a Labrador puppy before you'll know that their fur is incredibly soft. After watching some of these advertisements, you might find yourself paying extra to buy Andrex toilet paper with the subconscious idea that it must be softer. Not only that, puppies are often given to children when they're young, so you may have also found yourself buying Andrex toilet paper with the subconscious idea that it's a "family values toilet paper". While this makes no logical sense, it's a "gut feeling" that arises within you when deciding which toilet paper to buy.

Celebrity endorsements are a clear form of the association technique in action; put a celebrity next to an object and an association between the two is immediately created. David Beckham can wear a pair of boxers, and immediately the audience associates the piece of fabric he's wearing with the personality and lifestyle of the celebrity wearing them.

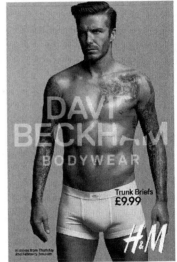

THE MERE-EXPOSURE EFFECT

Byron Sharp, professor of marketing science at the University of South Australia, points out that one of the main things advertising does is increase the "mental availability" of a brand. It creates top-of-mind awareness, so that when you need to buy a vacuum cleaner, for example, a particular brand immediately comes to mind. (Dyson?). To increase the mental availability of a brand, an ad doesn't have to be smart, clever or create any kind of positive association in the minds of the audience. All the ad needs to do is expose itself to a large number of people. *Merely seeing a brand frequently increases our trust and positive attitudes towards that brand.* You might think that Coca-Cola is such an old, famous brand that they will always sell products. But if Coca-Cola decided to stop advertising one day, this would leave a space for Pepsi to ramp up their advertising and replace Coca-Cola in the top-of-mind-awareness of much of their customer base. People would begin to feel more familiar with Pepsi than with Coca Cola and the feathers would begin to stack up in favour of Pepsi in many people's minds. On top of that, younger generations would grow up in an environment dominated by Pepsi. The brands you know will be noticed by you on the supermarket shelf. The brands you don't know will go unnoticed. The more you're exposed to advertising of a certain brand, the more familiar you become. If a brand continues to make a claim about their product and nobody stops them from doing so, our brain begins to assume that it's true. *When all else is equal between products, and it often is, the brand you're most familiar with wins.*

THE SOCIAL DIMENSION

Advertising is not only a business to customer relationship, it's also a multi-faceted relationship between you, your culture and your society. Advertising is shared experience in a social environment; the influence of advertising is greatest when it's seen by large quantities of people. Advertising has the ability to spread through word-of-mouth from person to person, especially in a social media environment where everybody is digitally connected. The more an ad or brand is talked about, the more this brand becomes top-of-mind throughout the public. Later in this chapter I'll talk about the most incredible advertising campaigns of all time: diamonds and cigarettes. These two examples show that advertising campaigns can shape entire societies and embed themselves into the culture.

Advertising works on everybody – including your friends, parents, celebrities, award-winning scientists, world leaders, the ad creators themselves and myself – the author of this book. Many claim that "advertising doesn't work on me" with such confidence, despite the fact that corporations spend billions every single year on advertising. Advertising hits us on a subconscious level, and everybody has a subconscious brain. To be influenced by advertising is to be human.

the power of image

We're surrounded by frozen people. When you stop and think about it for a second—it's kind of strange. That every time you step outside you're confronted of hundreds of images of people frozen in time. On advertising billboards by the side of the road, on your social media newsfeed, in the newspaper. Frozen people are everywhere. The photograph was invented in 1826 by Nicéphore Niépce. Since then, images of people frozen still have appeared all around us. Nowadays, we're completely accustom to seeing these images everywhere, so much so that we don't give them a second thought. But if you were able to travel back in time to the 1500's, pick a stranger at random and show them a simple photograph—they would probably think it was witchcraft or a message from god.

Perhaps it's worth taking a second to think about these images we see everywhere, after all, most images are created for a purpose and carry a message of some kind. Images are a medium. Just like the telephone or the email. Images are a method of communicating with others and they're created by people who have motives and agendas of their own. Almost every single image you see is someone trying influence you of something. Images have the power to influence even the very smartest of us. After all, our brain is evolved to live in tribes of roughly 150 people. Not to deal with modern society (**Law 2: Media Is An Evolutionary Mismatch**).

The Sun is the most popular newspaper in the UK with a readership of roughly 30 million and this particular newspaper was released just before the 2017 UK general election. The purpose of this image was to convince swing voters not to vote for Jeremy Corbyn on election day. The question is, can such an obvious piece of propaganda really have an effect. Unfortunately, the answer is yes. The human mind is incredibly susceptible to images like these. We might think we're smart, sophisticated and modern creatures, but the older part of our brain (the part that was evolved to live in tribes of around 150 people) can be easily swayed. Photographs didn't exist 200,000 years ago. So the older part of our brain can't tell the difference between a photograph of someone and a real human being. Our subconscious brain understands the image of Jeremy Corbyn as if he's a member of our tribe. After all, that's what the older part of our brain is built for. Our subconscious brain absorbs all stimuli from the environment. With no exceptions. And if you're exposed

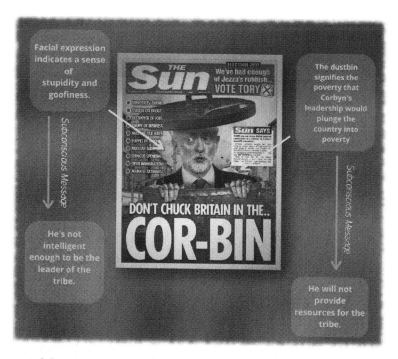

to an image of Jeremy Corbyn looking unintelligent your subconscious brain will absorb that information just like anything else. This can have an effect on how you feel about the idea of Corbyn as a leader, because many of the images you see in media bury themselves deep into your subconscious. Consequently, this can affect your outward behaviours because human beings are driven predominantly by tribal emotions.

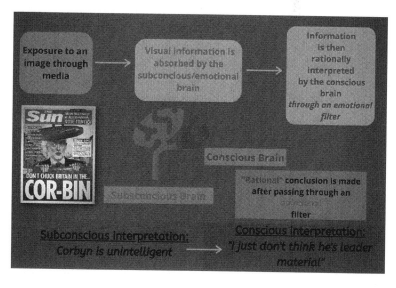

There's a well-known saying in the field of neurology: *Neurons that fire together, wire together.* Your brain is constantly building associations between things. Road = Dangerous. Oven = Hot. Our brain makes neural pathways between different stimuli. And when two brain cells fire at the same time, they link or "wire" together. Propaganda has the ability to take any stimuli and "wire" it with different emotions. In this case: Corbyn = Unintelligent. And unintelligent people don't make good tribe leaders. When we see simple assertions (Eg. Corbyn is unintelligent) we usually absorb their messages on some level, even if we're not conscious of their impact. Manipulation experts learned long ago that one of the most fundamental lessons of propaganda is: once someone has absorbed a message, the battle is essentially won. Assertions offer a quick and easy way to gain a foothold in people's minds.

During the Nazi regime, Joseph Goebbels bombarded the German public with propaganda associating Jews with rats. Rats cause a feeling of disgust in human beings due to their affinity to spread diseases and the goal of Nazi propaganda was to build a subconscious association between Jews and a feeling of disgust. Remember - what fires together wires together. After months and years of this association being absorbed into the subconscious of the German public, many German people began to feel disgust towards the Jews. A neurological connection was made between Jewish people and a feeling of disgust. Jews = Disgust. Jews = Disease. As propaganda minister for the Nazi party Joeseph Goebbels said: *"If you tell a lie big enough and keep repeating it, people will come to believe it".*

THE GOAL OF THESE IMAGES IS TO BUILD A SUBCONSCIOUS ASSOCIATION IN OUR MINDS BETWEEN THIS POLITICIAN (FORMER BRITISH PRIMINISTER TERESA MAY) AND STUPIDITY.

It's incredibly easy to make any politician look like an idiot. In fact, you can do this to any human being on earth. Take video footage of that person and continually pause it until you can get their face frozen looking as stupid as possible. Newspapers in the UK use this technique shamelessly. While this may be crude and blatantly obvious propaganda, that doesn't mean it's not effective. As Joseph Goebbels also said: *"It is not propaganda's task to be intelligent, it's task is to lead to success"*. Propagnda doesn't have to be smart, artistic or sophisticated, it just needs to achieve it's purpose. Political parties are constantly using the media as a tool to change the public's emotions about their opposition. In the run up to any election, you can expect to see countless images like this one - trying to make you feel differently about particular candidates. Because people often vote with *tribal emotions,* not rational thought.

After candidate Carl Benjamin was accused of making racist remarks on Twitter, this particular image was used across multiple news outlets. While there are countless images of Carl Benjamin available to choose from, they all chose to use the exact same image. Why? Because this image conveys defensiveness; with his hand raised towards the camera this body language sub-communicates untrustworthiness and guilt. This is not a randomly chosen image. The images you see in media are rarely ever randomly chosen (especially around high-stakes issues like politics).

UKIP CANDIDATE CARL
BENJAMIN BEING ACCUSED
FOR RACIST REMARKS

I might rape MP Jess Phillips, says Ukip candidate Carl Benjamin

Carl Benjamin, who has previously said that he "wouldn't even rape" the Labour MP Jess Phillips, suggested
that "with enough pressure I might cave"
ISABEL INFANTES/AFP/GETTY

They're chosen by someone for some purpose. After being exposed to this defensive looking image of Carl Benjamin at the top of the article, the audience may develop negative feelings towards him before they even start reading. They will then read the rest of the article through the emotional filter that the image created, or in other words, they will start reading the article with the expectation of disliking Carl Benjamin. And they will read every single word on the page through an emotional filter that already harbours negative feelings towards him.

The brave, handsome man stands in front of the American flag looking wistfully off into the distance. The goal of this image is to build an association between the navy and feelings of pride and meaning. This poster was distributed throughout America during WW2 and millions of men were exposed to it. If the subconscious brain of a young man viewing this poster could speak, it would say something like this: *OK. So the Navy is linked to feelings of pride and meaning. Let's make*

neural connections between the idea of the Navy and those emotions. Oh. And the man in the poster is handsome. Let's make a neural connection between the idea of the Navy and a potential increase in sex appeal. Upon viewing this poster, a neural connection between the navy and these desirable feelings is built. And upon repeated exposure to similar images like this, that neural pathway is strengthened. This young man may eventually make the decision to join the navy, and if asked about his motivation for joining, he might simply say "joining the Navy is just the right thing to do". This young man will have taken the emotions implanted in him by the propaganda, made the decision to join the army emotionally and then rationalised it with an explanation that makes sense to him, while being completely unaware of the effects the pro-navy propaganda may have had on him. It's just as Joseph Goebbels told us: *"Propaganda works best when those who are being manipulated are confident that they are acting on their own free will".*

In one experiment, psychologists attempted to test the power of the subconscious mind. They put people in a room and gave them a problem to solve: two strings were attached to the ceiling and the goal was to tie the two strings together. But the strings were so far apart that you couldn't reach one string if you were standing holding the other. There were a variety of objects in the room, including a pair of pliers. The solution to this puzzle was to tie the pliers to one string and use the extra weight to swing them, then grab the other string, grab the swinging pliers and tie them together. Half of the people in this study were purposefully given a hint: a man standing in the room swinging a metal nut on a string like a pendulum. Of course, for the other half of the participants, there was no man in the room swinging a metal nut. The results indicated that those who received the hint were more likely to solve the problem (keep in mind that the group was not told that the man swinging the pendulum was a hint).

Here's where it gets creepy. The researchers then asked the participants how they solved the problem. It turns out that almost no one said that the hint helped them in any way. They had no idea that they were given a hint or that the hint helped them to solve the problem. They instead assumed that they had solved the problem completely independently, even though the data clearly shows that the group that were given the hint solved the puzzle far more often. How can this be? Psychologists suggest that it's simply because *people don't know why they do what they do.* And when we don't understand the causes of our own behaviour, we simply *make up reasons that sound good to us.* Propaganda images can influence our behaviour without us knowing, and then we explain our behaviour with whatever reason we prefer.

Of course propaganda isn't only used for political purposes, it's also used in advertising. Advertising and propaganda are essentially the same thing.

THE IMAGE IS PLACED BEHIND THE TEXT. YOU'D PROBABLY NEVER THINK TWICE ABOUT SEEING THIS ON A REAL-ESTATE WEBSITE WOULD YOU?

This young couple looks rather happy don't they. And look at the way she's looking up at him — he's into him. He bought them a house and now he's dead sexy. Remember, propaganda is primal. All advertising appeals to our deepest emotional drives, almost anything can be associated with an increase in sex appeal and buying a house is no exception. The man in this advert is chosen because he's handsome and the woman is chosen because she is pretty — no advertiser would choose ugly models because it would be less effective in pulling customers through the sales funnel. This image creates a subconscious association in our minds between buying a house and being sexually attractive. As you browse through this website looking for a real-estate agent, the image ensures that your emotions are leading you in the right direction (in the direction of handing over your money). You will read the information throughout the rest of the website through the *emotional filter* that this image creates.

Doesn't this seem like the best job ever? The kids are all well-behaved and clearly enthusiastic about learning English. Look at how cute they are! And there are only 4 students in the class. Very manageable! Look how happy the teacher is, it's like she can't believe how lucky she is to have such a fantastic job. The reality of teaching English to kids in China isn't necessarily quite so perfect. Class sizes can range from 7-50 (seriously,

Teacher wanted in China

Apply now &
get the best teaching jobs in CHINA

Post your resume at

50). Many of the students have no interest in learning English whatsoever and would rather talk Chinese with their mates. Classrooms sometimes have no air-conditioning and the teacher is given nothing more than a blackboard and a piece of chalk to work with. But you wouldn't know any of this just looking at the advertisement, because advertising is an alternate reality in which everything is perfect. The teacher in the advert is slim, attractive and dressed successfully, because a less attractive teacher would be a negative association with the job. Once again, this image puts job seekers into the right emotional state and they will read the rest of the job advertisement through the positive emotional filter that the image creates.

Just look at how her skin glows! Look at those white teeth and those clear eyes (which have no doubt been edited in Photoshop). Does she look healthy or what? A quick glance at the ingredients list and you'll quickly find out that this product is crammed with sugar. And what does sugar do? It rots teeth. It ages skin. Keep drinking Fami and you can be sure that you'll never look like the girl on the box (the same is true for other so called "healthy" drinks). Of course, parents don't have time to check ingredients list. The child will enjoy the sweet taste and the

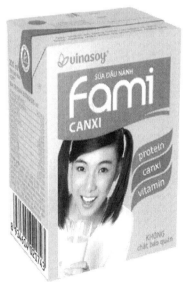

parents will feel good that they're feeding their child something healthy (or so they think). The image on the carton builds an association in your mind between Fami and health and you will feel good about buying the product (whether it's actually healthy or not).

Advertising might seem incredibly confusing and complex, but

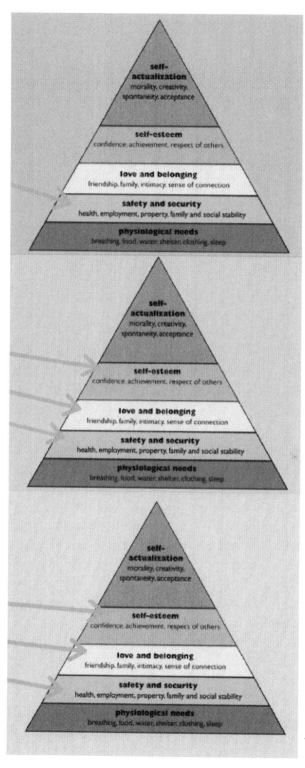

actually it's very simple. The goal of most advertising is to make an association between the product and something on Maslow's hierarchy of needs.

Take any natural want or need that a human being has and you can build an association between that need and a product. Coca-Cola commercials links their product to youth and happiness. Of course, this association has no basis in reality whatsoever. In fact, the sugar in Coke ages your skin and can have negative effects on your mood. Yet it doesn't matter if the association is true or not, the advertising will build that positive association in your mind whether it's factually accurate or not. And next time you stand in front of the drinks fridge, buying a Coke will

HERE COCA-COLA ATTEMPTS TO CREATE AN ASSOCIATION BETWEEN COKE, YOUTH AND BEAUTY. DESPITE THE FACT THAT COKE ACTUALLY AGES THE SKIN AND BODY, A SUBCONSCIOUS ASSOCIATION CAN STILL BE CREATED BETWEEN THE TWO.

just *feel right*. Once you understand the pattern of linking natural human wants to products, you will be able to have a good understanding of almost all advertisements that you see.

Advertising is a part of nature. Flowers are built to advertise their pollen to bees, and in the same way, human beings are natural born advertisers. Social Media gained worldwide popularity in around 2010 and within months people had already learned to advertise themselves online. Social media is a human marketplace and people are very sophisticated in advertising their own personal brand in return for social currency (likes, shares etc.). Social media is filled with propaganda. Through careful image selection and image retouching, people convince their audience that their life is far better than it actually is (This can have serious negative effects on the mental health of women and girls in particular). Any content that negatively affects their own personal brand is carefully edited out. And "candid" photos attempt to convince the audience that their social media page is an authentic version of themselves. Just like advertising products, on social media people are constantly trying to associate themselves with something that reflects positively on themselves.

One Tinder profile shows a photo of a 29 year old man posing next to a tiger in Thailand. In this case, the user (Mark) is attempting to associate himself with the same characteristics of a tiger (tough, dangerous). Ask yourself, would a man on Tinder use an image of himself posing next to a mouse or a squirrel? If a man used a photo of himself sat next to a squirrel, the subconscious associations conveyed to the mind of his audience (women on Tinder) would be: childish, cheeky and small; not exactly the qualities a man is trying to portray to a potential date. Another image on Instagram shows a birds-eye shot of a bowl of porridge, a teapot, a teacup and an open book. Each of the objects on the page are organised perfectly within the frame, and each object is a perfect distance from the others. In the case of this image, the teapot hints at wealth, the book suggests intelligence and the porridge suggests health. The objects have been carefully placed within the frame to suggest "having it all together". And it's all disguised as a casual "incidental" photo. Incredible marketing. Women are more likely to post photos of their food looking delicious and perfect, in order to associate their own identity with a feeling of perfection and "having it all together". You might feel completely bemused by people who feel the need to show us photos of the food they eat. After all, why the hell would we care what they're eating for lunch? But the photo isn't about the food. It's about *them*. What might seem like a pointless photo of someone's lunch is actually an attempt to advertise their personal brand. *Their* name is written right next to the image. It's on *their* social media page. And the photo of their lunch is an extension of *them*. You subconsciously associate the image of their lunch with the person themselves, and that's why people reorganise their food to look perfect before taking the photo *(Ok the plate goes here..and I'll move the cup a little to the left..)*. Because if their photo looks perfect and beautiful, their audience will associate them with those very same qualities.

Let's face it: most of us do this. Most images posted on social media are propaganda and therefore, like all propaganda, should be treated with scrutiny.

COLOUR IN ADVERTISING

Companies pick certain colours for a reason. A great amount of thought and research is put into the colour scheme a company uses for their brand.. Much of the research into colour psychology still isn't fully developed and the effects of colour on the brain are deeply subconscious and difficult to accurately study. While humans have evolved to have certain predictable reactions to certain colours, cultural and environmental factors also play a part in how we respond to different colours. For instance, if you were hit by a bright yellow truck when you were 5 years old, this may have some impact on how you view the colour yellow. (and you're probably

COLOUR IN ADVERTISING

RED

- Increases Appetite

- Raises blood pressure and heart rate

- Creates a sense of Urgency

YELLOW

- Increases serotonin in the brain

- Most attention grabbing colour

- Can cause anxiety and discomfort if overused

BLUE

- Associated with reliability and loyalty

- The worlds most popular colour

GREEN

- Associated with the enviroment

- Used to relax customers

GREY

- Sophisticated and timeless and age

- Overuse can lead to feelings of nothingness

PURPLE

- Associated with royalty and luxury

- Heightens sense of beauty

ORANGE

- Combines the energy of red with the happiness of yellow

- Associated with activity

WHITE

- Associated with feelings of purity

- Can be used to suggest simplicity

BLACK

- Associated with authority, strength and mystery

- Can be overwhelming if overused

---

not reading this book, because you're dead).

If the Mcdonalds "M" was grey instead of yellow, would you still feel like eating there? If a political party chose the colour pink to represent their party, would you take them seriously? If your local coffee shop changed their theme from dark green and brown to bright yellow and purple, would you still enjoy spending time there? Clearly, colour has psychological effects on whether we hand over our cash or not.

RED: *MCDONALDS, BURGER KING, FACEBOOK NOTIFICATIONS, TINDER LOGO*

A number of studies suggest that the colour red increases appetite. Fast food business seem to have taken these studies and run with them. While the research is not conclusive, it seems to be working rather well for these guys, and you can be sure they've looked over every inch of research on the subject. Next time you're at the convenience store, look at all the chocolate and candy by the checkout and pay attention to how many of them use the colour red in their packaging. Red Is also excellent at creating urgency, which is great for clearance sales as well as call-to-action buttons on websites. Studies also show that red increases heart rate, blood pressure and arousal, which is why dating experts tell women to wear red dresses, why Tinder's logo is red and why Facebook notifications are red.

Red is a very important colour evolutionary speaking. In our prehistoric environment, some of the few situations we would have seen the colour red would have been: when seeing blood, in ripe fruit, when another human got angry and a flushed, aroused woman. While the colours of green, blue, white and grey would have been all over the place, red would have only been found in a small number of situations. Theoretically, this is why this particular colour is so attention grabbing for us compared to other colours.

WHY ARE NOTIFICATIONS USUALLY RED? BECAUSE THEY CREATE A SENSE OF URGENCY AND MAKE THEM MORE IRRESISTIBLE TO CLICK.

YELLOW: *WALLMART, BUMBLE, MCDONALDS, IKEA*

Studies have shown that our serotonin levels increase when viewing the colour yellow. Evolutionarily speaking, this is probably due to the colour of the sun. The rising sun signals the start of a new day full of possibilities, and advertising can utilise the psychological association with yellow most of us have and use it in their logos. Yellow can have negative psychological effects if overused or used in the wrong situation. An overabundance of the colour yellow can cause agitation, nervousness and anxiety and is usually better suited as a secondary colour rather than the primary colour.

BLUE: *TWITTER, INTEL, DELL, PAYPAL*

The tech industry loves to use blue because it inspires feelings of security and trustworthiness. Unlike the excitement and stimulation of the colour red, blue is the perfect colour for any brand that relies on customers trusting them. When it comes to creating an image of reliability, nothing beats blue. Customers need to feel as though the devices they purchase will be high-quality and long-lasting. For a similar reason, financial institutions, where large amounts of money are being passed back and forth, also often use the colour blue. Would you, having never heard of Paypal before, trust them with your money if their logo was bright pink? If you were spending $4000 on a high-end laptop and were choosing between two brands, would you choose the one with the sky blue logo or the orange logo?

GREEN: *STARBUCKS, OXFAM, TROPICANA, SPOTIFY*

Green has an obvious association to nature. Any product that benefits from building some kind of association with nature or the environment is likely to use the colour green in their branding. Even Starbucks, which sells many unnatural, unhealthy products, maintains the illusion of a link to nature. Green also inspires feelings of peace and tranquillity, probably because much of our evolutionary environment was green: Grass, forests, bushes and trees. Turn a neutral green into a bright green and it can be used instead for energy and vitality, making it a good colour for energy drinks.

To put it simply, all colours have a particular psychological affect on us. The reasons for this lie in both nature and nurture. We have innate responses to some colours, while other responses have been learned. Successful companies are aware of colour psychology and will use it to make their brands more attractive (the simple act of switching your smartphone screen to greyscale will make the apps on your screen significantly less attractive). Colours are also used to sell us processed food like candy and chocolate. M&M's come in a variety of colours because it appeals to our need for novelty. Chocolate bars often contain red as one of the primary colours of their packaging (Mars bars, Kit-Kat, Twix, Crunchie), because the colour red stimulates us and increases our appetite. Picture the array of different chocolates you often find on the shelf in convenience stores; a massive variety of bright colours and various eye-catching fonts across the shelves. Now imagine all those chocolate bars with their packaging removed; what are you left with? A shelf filled with the dull brown colour of chocolate. Doesn't seem so enticing any more does it? Colour is used on you to influence your behaviour and persuade you to part with your money.

how animals are used in marketing

Take one walk down the high street and you'll be surrounded by animals. Not real animals, mind you. But depictions of animals in the marketing that surrounds you. The "Hello Kitty" kitten in the shop window. The big fluffy "Charmin" bear. The little blue bird that appears when you open Twitter on your smartphone. The rooster on the box of Corn Flakes. The small silver Jaguar on the front of Jaguar cars. The two red bulls on the front of a can of Red Bull. We're surrounded by images of animals. Next time you walk through the city, or watch TV, or scroll through your social media news feed; pay attention and you'll see them everywhere.

So why do we see images of animals everywhere? Because they're an excellent marketing tool. Animals were present in our evolutionary environment, so our brain connects with them deeply. The Biophilia Hypothesis tells us that humans are genetically predisposed to seek connections with nature. Animals are a great way to use our evolutionary impulses to seek connections with nature to cut through noise in our highly artificial modern day environment. It's every marketer's goal to make an emotional connection with their target audience. However, this is often easier said than done. The way that you make an emotional connection with your audience is to relate to them, often on a personal level. We have a natural connection to animals, and using them in advertising is an excellent way to capture our attention. Each particular animal has it's own characteristics and marketers can connect their brand with the characteristics of particular animals.

For legal purposes, I'm not able to show you the logos here. So go ahead and Google them yourselves.

Dove Skincare: The white dove symbolises purity, cleanliness and elegance. They fly through the skies with sophistication and grace. Humans too, want to be sophisticated, elegant and clean. When Dove bases their brand around these animals, we make a subconscious link between their product and the positive characteristics of the Dove.

Llyods Bank: This is a British bank from the UK that uses a black horse as their logo. We think of horses as loyal, mature and sophisticated. The horse is responsible, never abandons you and is a trusty companion that will stick with you through thick and thin. The horse is the perfect animal for any business that requires a large amount of trust from the customer. When we see the black horse of Llyods, we subconsciously associate the bank with the same characteristics of a real horse: trustworthiness, loyalty and responsibility.

Evernote: Evernote is a notetaking app that uses a white elephant on a green background as their logo. The Evernote app is designed for note-taking, organisation, task management and archiving. We see elephants as wise, intelligent and mature. As the saying goes: "An elephant never forgets". Which is exactly what you're looking for from a note-taking app. When we see the elephant logo used for the Evernote app, we subconsciously associate the app with the same characteristics as real elephants, which gives Evernote an advantage over other note-taking apps that might simply use an image of a notepad and pen for their brand.

Puma: Puma is a world famous sports brand that uses a puma for their logo (shocking). The puma is fast, agile and hunts their prey with razor-sharp reactions and speed. Smooth, slick, athletic, wild; the puma is a predator, not prey. Purchase Puma products and you'll be endowed with the very same laser-sharp reactions and aggressive attitude. At least, that's the subconscious association created in us when viewing Puma's logo.

Charmin: Charmin is a brand of toilet paper that uses a cartoon, fluffy looking bear as their mascot. The big fluffy bear is the perfect way to create a subconscious association within us between the toilet paper and the supposed homely, soft, loving qualities of a bear. Interestingly enough, this association has more to do with the bear characters in fairy tales like Goldilocks And The Three Bears than it does with real bears. Many of us think of bears as being loveable, cuddly creatures that we could hug to sleep, after all, the cartoon bears we see in our environment usually have big, loving eyes and a friendly smile. Attempt to hug a real life bear, however, and you'll likely end up in the hospital or dead. Through our cartoons, fairy tales and marketing, we have created a false representation of the bear in our minds.

Have you noticed the endless number of "mascots" that represent brands in the advertising around you. Pay attention and you'll see strange

little characters everywhere; talking M&Ms, Meercats selling you car insurance, Tony the Tiger on your box of Frosted Flakes, The Michelin Man and endless others. All of these mascots come with big, trusting, innocent, cartoonish eyes and cute faces that you associate with young children - doing an excellent job of hijacking the evolutionary parenting instincts of adults to get their advertising messages through. This is anthropomorphism (when we attribute human characteristics to non-human things). We see faces in clouds, in cars and in the foam on our coffee. Marketers add human characteristics to animals as a method of selling us products. There are thousands of these "mascots" on TV screens and on billboards because they're an effective way of building an emotional connection with people. A lot of people trust animals more than they do people and for many customers, the second they hear a person talking to them about a product, they switch off. On the other hand, almost everyone trusts animals. Animals are don't have the capability to lie to us like humans can. When we are given advertising messages by animals, the message gets through under the radar. People who generally don't trust the messages given to them in advertising soften up when a cute bunny rabbit tells them Duracell batteries are the most long-lasting around. When products are products, you react to them like things. When products are given animal characteristics, you react to them like animals—all without thinking about it very much.

Animals in advertising are everywhere. Now you won't be able to stop noticing them everywhere you look. Sorry about that.

why you think smoking is cool

100 million people died from smoking in the 20th century. More than World War 2 (75 million). More than the Spanish flu (50 million). Everybody knows that smoking is bad for you. Everyone knows that it gives you lung cancer. And I know you're sick of hearing about it. But actually, the dangers are still understated. People around the world continue to rationalise their cigarette use. *I'll quit when I'm older. It's not that bad. My 86 year old grandmother smokes and she's ok. Everybody has to die sometime. I just want to enjoy life now.* The problem is, it's hard to keep rationalising your smoking habit when you're hooked up to a ventilator 24/7 to keep you alive.

"I WENT FROM BEING ABLE TO TRAVEL AND SEE THE WORLD, TO CONFINING MY LIFE EITHER AT HOME OR IN THE HOSPITAL. IT'S ALL BECAUSE OF CIGARETTES" - BRIAN

Lung cancer. Throat cancer. All kinds of cancers. Bronchitis. Heart attacks. Strokes. Macular degeneration. If you're somebody who prefers to "live in the moment" and doesn't worry about future consequences, then consider the following: Death from smoking is painful and prolonged. Most patients have their freedom gradually more and more restricted until they're not allowed to leave their own home because they need a machine to breathe. Other smokers literally suffocate to death, often in their homes, completely alone. *This is real.* This isn't something that happens to characters in movies. Or people in documentaries. This is something that happens to real people. People just like you. And there's absolutely no reason that it won't happen to you or your loved ones if the smoking continues.

The problem is: cigarettes are "normal". It's normal to take a smoke break at work. It's normal to meet people in the smoking area at the club. It's normal smoke when you drink, when you eat, when you have sex or when you wake up in the morning. Nothing beats a cigarette after sex, right? When you see other people doing an action, your subconscious brain believes that the activity must be safe. So you don't feel fear as you inhale thousands of chemicals into your lungs. You know, intellectually, that smoking is bad, but you don't *feel* like it's dangerous. Your subconscious brain doesn't understand that a huge portion of the population you're surrounded by is hooked onto a highly addictive substance that's slowly killing them.

Not only is smoking normal, but you might even think it's cool. *Do you feel cool as you breathe in that sweet, sweet smoke and look off wistfully into the distance, contemplating life? Or as you flick open that lighter and hold it up to your mouth? Do you feel cool as you light up another one in the smoking area of the club with all the other cool kids? Bottle of beer in one hand, cigarette in the other. Do you feel like a rebel? Do you feel unique? Do you feel artistic?*

I'd like to offer an alternative viewpoint: Smokers are conformists. Smokers are sheep. Smokers are losers. Now if you're a smoker, don't be offended. It's not your fault that you've been duped by a media and a culture into thinking that smoking is cool ever since you were a child. Advertising, movies, TV and the people around you have convinced you that slowly killing yourself is cool. You bought in. And it's ok (**Law 5: You Are In The Media Hierarchy**). You just need to understand exactly how you've been brainwashed so you can better fight the addiction you're dealing with. (Even if you're not a smoker, you might still believe, to an extent, that smoking is cool). Now not everyone thinks smoking is cool. And if you think smoking is massively uncool, then this chapter isn't for you. But if you're a smoker and a part of you still believes that smoking is rebellious, masculine, tough or just plain cool—then this is for you.

In the 1920s, smoking was seen as an inappropriate habit for women and was looked down upon as distasteful, yet some women began to smoke as they took over a number of male jobs in World War 1. George Washington Hill, the president of the American Tobacco Company, realised the potential market that could be found in women. *"It will be like a gold mine opening in our front yard"* he said in 1928.

But he had a problem. Smoking for women was completely taboo. So he enlisted the help of Edward Bernays (today known as the father of public relations). Bernays had the perfect plan to break this taboo. Every

WHY IS SMOKING CONSTANTLY PORTRAYED IN A STYLISH MANNER? IS THIS REALLY HOW PEOPLE LOOK IN REAL LIFE WHILE THEY SMOKE?

year New York held an Easter day parade in which thousands of people attended. He persuaded a group of feminists to hide cigarettes under their clothes during the parade and instructed them to light them up on his signal. Bernays then informed the press that he'd heard a group of suffragettes were preparing to protest by lighting up cigarettes. The press couldn't miss such an outrage, so photographers lined up to capture the moment.

George Washington Hill: "We're losing half of our market because men have invoked a taboo against women smoking in public. Can you do anything about that?" Edward Bernays: "Let me think about it". (Bernays remembering the events shortly before his death)

All of the major newspapers covered the event (just as Bernays has planned) and newspapers reported the young women and their "torches of freedom". From that point forward, the sale of cigarettes to women began

EDITH LEE SMOKES A CIGARETTE ON THE 'TORCHES FOR FREEDOM' MARCH, NEW YORK, 1929. TO THE PUBLIC SHE SEEMS LIKE AN INDEPENDENT FEMINIST WHO DECIDED TO SMOKE OUT OF REBELLION. IN TRUTH, SHE'S DOING WHAT EDWARD BERNAYS ASKED HER TO DO TO PROMOTE CIGARETTE SMOKING FOR WOMEN.

to skyrocket. With a single symbolic act, Bernays had broken the taboo towards women smoking cigarettes and made them socially acceptable. He had also managed to link cigarettes with: rebelliousness and female empowerment. An idea that is still strong in the minds of modern people. Women up and down the country began furiously lighting up cigarettes as a symbol of empowerment and freedom, never realising that they were manipulated by Edward Bernays and the tobacco industry.

THE MESSAGE IS CLEAR: BE A TOUGH MOTHERFUCKER - SMOKE. BUT ACTUALLY, WHAT DOES SMOKING HAVE TO DO WITH BEING TOUGH? DO YOU THINK SMOKING MAKES YOU TOUGH?

In the 1950's people were starting to get concerned about the health consequences of cigarettes. So cigarette brands began releasing the "filtered cigarette"; adding a filter, they said, made the cigarette safe to smoke. Most cigarette companies based their advertising around the technology of the filter because they wanted to ease fears about smoking. Malboro took a different approach—making adverts completely devoid of health concerns or health claims. Instead, they opted for the gun slinging baddass of the wild west: The Malboro Man. In 1955, when the Malboro Man campaign started, sales were at $5 billion. In 1957, sales had reached $20 billion. It was an enormous success. Malboro easily overcame growing health concerns and their sales continued to increase. The public had been successfully manipulated by mass-marketing; an association had been created in the minds of people everywhere: Smoking = Masculinity. (An association that still exists in the minds of many people today). Men everywhere started looking wistfully off into the distance, putting a cigarette between their lips and feeling like a real man as they slowly killed themselves. Teenage boys everywhere started smoking, trying to prove to their friends that they were a tough guy just like the Malboro man—starting an addiction that would later rob them of their life. The idea created by the Malboro man continues to persist even today. And men continue to smoke cigarettes at least partly because of the masculine feeling it gives them. (By the way, most of the actors who played the Malboro Man later died from smoking related illnesses). It's ironic that many men believe (at least subconsciously) that smoking makes them more masculine, when smoking has been proven to lower your sperm count and cause erectile dysfunction.

All of this glamorisation was created to distract the public from one simple fact: Cigarettes are deadly.

"We have one essential job - stop public panic. There is only one problem - confidence, and how to establish it. And most important, how to free millions of Americans from the guilty fear that's going to arise in their biological depths every time they light a cigarette. - PR firm Hill & Knowlton in 1953

So Edward Bernays managed to link cigarettes with rebelliousness and independence in women. Malboro managed to link cigarettes with toughness and masculinity. The messages from these two marketing campaigns pulsated through the decades and still hold influence over many of us today. But it wasn't only advertisers that manipulated how we feel about cigarettes.

"It's the movies that have really been running things in America ever since they were invented. They show you what to do, how to do it, when to do it, how to feel about it, and how to look how you feel about it." —Andy Warhol (1928-87)

You've been primed to believe that smoking is cool ever since you were a child. And you barely even noticed. In mainstream cinema, the cigarette is a sign of a baddass. Just how many times have you seen the rebellious character light up a cigarette on screen? How many times have you seen him/her puff on that cigarette with an "I don't give a fuck" expression on their face? You've seen this thousands of times since you were a child. A long time ago your brain made a connection between cigarettes and rebelliousness. A connection that probably still exists in your subconscious mind today. *If I was to ask you what exactly is so rebelliousness about smoking cigarettes, would you be able to give me a logical answer?* What exactly is rebellious about spending your hard-earned money on hundreds of packs of cigarettes? What's rebellious about picking up a common addiction and giving your money over to cigarette manufacturers? The truth is there's no rational reason for you to feel like smoking is rebellious. The reason you might feel that way is because of the media you've been watching since the day you were born. (By the way. actors in movies don't smoke real cigarettes. They usually smoke healthy herbal cigarettes) Movies are a great way to initiate young people into smoking. The tobacco industry calls them "replacement smokers"—to replace the smokers who previously died from using their product.

Why is there so much smoking in movies? Two reasons.

1.   The Tobbacco Industry

The Tobacco industry are the original champions of product placement. In released documents, the following deals between the tobacco industry and the movie industry have been proven:

- ☞ *$350,000 to have Lark cigarettes appear in the James Bond movie License to Kill*

- ☞ *$42,000 to place Marlboro cigarettes in Superman II*

- ☞ *$30,000 to place Eve cigarettes in Supergirl*

- ☞ *$5,000 to have Lucky Strike appear in Beverly Hills Cop*

- ☞ *$500,000 for Sylvester Stallone to use Brown and Williamson products in five feature films.*

And these are just the few deals we know about. Other deals were undoubtedly made behind closed doors, but we have no access to those records. Even so, it seems highly likely that the tobacco industry had a large part to play in the prevalence of cigarettes in movies.

> ## "Film is better than any commercial that has been run on television or any magazine, because the audience is totally unaware of any sponsor involvement" - CEO Of Production Inc Robert Richards talking to president of RJR William Smith.

There are far more smokers in movies than in real life, and the health consequences of smoking are rarely ever seen in movies. We don't know exactly how many deals were made between the tobacco industry and

Hollywood, but we do know that the tobacco industry was (and is) well aware of the power of movies to change public opinion. It's reasonable to assume that the tobacco industry has been heavily involved in Hollywood throughout the decades.

2.   Lazy Script Writing

Cigarette manufacturers had created an association between cigarettes and masculinity, rebelliousness and independence. This association was then reinforced by the movie industry, often without any help from the tobacco industry. The cigarette became a plot device. Want to make a character seem more rebellious? Put a cigarette in their hand and the audience will immediately understand what kind of character they're dealing with. Of course, there is nothing inherently rebellious about holding a cigarette. Cigarettes are nothing more than nicotine, tobacco and an assortment of chemicals wrapped in paper. But the public and the writers already had a particular emotional connection towards cigarettes instilled in them by the tobacco industry. So cigarettes got endless amounts of free advertising through the movie industry.

Indonesia is now the second largest cigarette market in the world. 36% of the population are reported smokers. 63% of men and only 5% of women (advertising linking smoking to masculinity has clearly been highly effective). Advertising for cigarettes can be found on billboards, on TV, in magazines, online and almost anywhere else you can think of. Almost all major events in Indonesia are sponsored by cigarette brands, especially events of a more western nature (rock concerts, nightclubs etc.). Why is cigarette advertising allowed in Indonesia? Because cigarette brands (who have insane amounts of wealth) lobby the Indonesian government to stop any regulations from being passed. Indonesia is a developing country that's trying to lift itself out of poverty. Cigarette brands are taking advantage of this and using the vulnerability of the government to make extreme profits. The exact same marketing strategies that were used on developed countries decades ago are being used in developing countries. From Indonesia to Africa. Cigarettes are ridiculously cheap in Indonesia at around $1.2 a pack and they're far stronger (and more deadly) than the cigarettes we have in the west. It's no surprise then, that lung cancer is increasing. Over 200,000 people die from cigarettes in Indonesia every year. And it's not just Indonesia, the tobacco industry is taking advantage of countries all over the developing world. They have moved the cigarette epidemic from developed countries to developing countries. *The biggest problem the tobacco industry has is that it's customers keep dying* and two thirds of long term smokers will die from smoking related illnesses. That's why it needs to focus on what they call "replacement smokers" by constantly advertising to young people in developing countries. The tobacco industry is doing fantastic. And they're still making billions of dollars through the legal sale of a highly addictive drug — nicotine.

"It may be useful, therefore, to look at the tobacco industry as if for a large part of it's business is the administration of nicotine" - BAT Scientists in 1967

Here's the truth. A cigarette is simply the delivery device for a highly addictive drug called nicotine. It's not masculine. It's not rebellious. It's not artistic. It's not a sign of independence. These are all lies sold to you by the tobacco industry. The tobacco industry doesn't see smokers as human beings. It sees them as walking dollar signs. They have no morality and they're perfectly happy if their product kills hundreds of millions of people - as long as it keeps producing insane profits. Every single time you feel cool as you light up a cigarette - the tobacco industry is laughing at you. And every time a teenage boy lights up a cigarette because he thinks it's manly, the tobacco industry rubs it's hands together.

diamonds – the greatest marketing scheme of all time

Diamonds are a beautiful thing. Unbreakable. Forever lasting. And incredibly rare. Giving your future wife a diamond engagement ring is the perfect way of saying: I love you. It's a sign of an unbreakable bond. Just as a diamond lasts forever, so will your love for each other.

At least, this was and often still is the view the public hold about diamonds. But what if you had been lied to about diamonds? What if, when it really came down to it, a diamond was merely one of many types of rocks and minerals. A rock subject to one of the greatest marketing scheme of all time. Imagine a marketing campaign that convinces hundreds of millions of people in multiple different cultures to spend thousands of dollars on a rock with no inherent value whatsoever. A marketing campaign that transforms this rock into something that's now deeply embedded in the traditions of different cultures around the world. A marketing campaign that managed to link a rock to the deepest possible human emotion: Love. Why do we assume we're supposed to spend 2 months salary on a diamond engagement ring? Why do we believe we have to "surprise" our future wife with a diamond ring? Why do so many women want a diamond ring on their finger? This is the story of diamonds. A story of lies, manipulative marketing and human gullibility. Before we take a look at the greatest marketing scam of all time, let's get some simple facts about diamonds straightened out.

1.   Diamonds Are Not Rare

Diamonds are abundant. There are mines around the world absolutely filled with diamonds. You can go into one of these mines and find millions of diamonds all over the floor. Diamonds haven't been rare since huge diamond mines were discovered in South Africa in 1870. Suddenly, diamonds were available by the bucket load. The British financiers who organised the South African mines realised that the value of diamonds depended on their scarcity. Especially as diamonds have little intrinsic value. Their only choice was to form one giant company: De Beers Consolidated Mines, then take control over the entire diamond industry. Their goal? Control both the supply and demand of diamonds. Did they succeed? You better believe they did. People around the world to this day believe that diamonds are incredibly rare, despite there being diamond mines in South Africa, Russia, Botswana, India, Brazil, China, Canada and The United States absolutely filled with diamonds. By withholding most of the diamonds and only releasing a careful stream of them into the rest of the world, Debeers has been able to artificially inflate the price of diamonds. And by embedding the message that diamonds are rare into their marketing campaigns, they convinced the public that diamonds are special (more on this later).

2.   Diamonds Are Not Forever

Diamonds may be the hardest naturally occurring substance on earth but they can still be smashed with a simple hammer. There's a difference between a material being "hard" and being "tough". People are often shocked when they manage to chip their $10,000 diamond ring. Not only that, but over time diamonds deteriorate and turn into graphite. While people hear the phrase "diamonds are forever" and imagine that their diamond ring will exist into eternity, the truth is that diamonds will eventually deteriorate into graphite. Just head onto Youtube and search for "smashing a diamond" to see countless videos of people smashing diamonds into pieces with a hammer. That's because "diamonds are forever" is just another idea that came from the greatest marketing campaign of all time.

In 1938, the value of diamonds was declining and all over the world new diamond mines were being discovered. The demand wasn't enough to meet the supply, so Debeers Consolidated Mines (who had a monopoly on diamond mining) needed to find a way to increase the demand for diamonds. They needed a marketing campaign. Harry Oppenheimer the owner of Debeers at the time, met with the advertising agency N.W. Ayers who had the task of increasing the demand for diamonds. The plan was to instil in the public the idea that diamonds were a gift of love, and that the larger and finer the diamond, the greater the expression of love. There was no brand name to be advertised. The only goal was to create an association in the mind of the public between diamonds and romance. Their first target: Hollywood.

Ayers opened a Hollywood office and gave out diamonds to producers, and in return the producers showcased the diamonds in a

MAN: "HERE'S YOUR ENGAGEMENT PRESENT DARLIN'.." WOMAN: "OH JEFFERY IT'S BEAUTIFUL!" - MEN ON HER MIND (1944)

favourable way during the movie. They wanted to create the idea that a man should surprise his woman by presenting her with a diamond (after all, if the woman was brought in on the decision of which gem to put in the engagement ring, she might have lots of other ideas for what she wanted). This was some of the first product placement ever seen on television. Diamonds were used endlessly in movies in marriage proposal scenes. One movie that was originally called "Diamonds Are Dangerous" was conveniently re-titled "Adventure In Diamonds" through the influence of Ayers. Finally, many actors were rarely ever seen in public without their Debeers diamonds.

Ayers even managed to strike a deal with The Queen Of England. In American minds, the British royal family was the ultimate ideal of how to behave in the upper class. Diamonds came from British colonies, so the royal family was perfectly happy to work with Ayers. Ayers managed to encourage Queen Elizabeth to wear diamonds rather than other gemstones; essentially, Ayers had managed to turn the royal family into a sales agent. Ayers also added photographs in popular magazines to reinforce the link between romance and diamonds; these Photographs would show the glittering stone on the hand of desirable and famous

A YOUNG QUEEN ELIZABETH PICKING OUT DIAMONDS

women of the time. In 1941, just 3 years later, advertising agency Ayers reported that the sale of diamonds had increased by 55% in the United States since 1938. Then in 1947, Ayers furthered their marketing campaign by giving lectures in American high schools. An Ayers report states: *"All of these lectures revolve around the diamond engagement ring, and are reaching thousands of girls in their assemblies, classes and informal meetings in our leading educational institutions"*. As you can see, Ayers was creating the link between diamonds and romance in the minds of the American population before they were even adults.

The sale of diamonds had skyrocketed and profits were enormous. But Debeers had a new problem. They feared that if people began to

sell second-hand diamonds back into the marketplace, prices would start to fall. So they had to instil into the public the idea that you should never sell a diamond; that people should hoard these diamonds in cupboard draws at home instead of selling them on. So a slogan was born: *A Diamond Is Forever.*

This was the first stroke of genius in this incredible marketing campaign. Of course, as stated earlier in this article, diamonds are not forever, but in the television era (before the internet) people had no real method of fact-checking the information given to them by advertising. The American people bought the lie. Near the end of the 1950's, Ayers reported: *"Since 1939 an entirely new generation of young people has grown to marriageable age... To this new generation a diamond ring is considered a necessity to engagements by virtually everyone"*. Diamond engagement rings were so ingrained into the culture that people who couldn't afford them would "defer the purchase" rather than forgo the ring altogether **(Law 5: You Are In The Media Hierarchy)**.

By the 1980s, the public held more than 500 million carats of diamonds—more than 50 times the number that was held in diamond mines around the world. If this amount of diamonds had been sold back onto the market, the diamond industry would have been destroyed. Furthermore, if the public attempted to sell their diamonds back to the store, they would quickly realise that they were worth far less than they had thought. Even to this very day, the diamond industry relies on the myth that *"A Diamond Is Forever"*.

In the 1950s, the Soviets discovered a huge diamond mine in Siberia. This was a big problem for Debeers; if the Soviets dumped their diamonds onto the market, the price of diamonds would plummet. So Debeers

COMMERCIAL FOR DEBEERS LATEST INVENTION: THE ETERNITY RING

struck a deal with the Russians and managed to bring this diamond mine under its control to continue controlling the supply of diamonds. This mine contained an enormous number of smaller diamonds (too small to go on an engagement ring). So Debeers created the Eternity Ring. The Eternity Ring, made up of 25 tiny Soviet Diamonds, was marketed as a ring that could "rekindle" love in a long-term marriage. Of course, the real reason for the Eternity Ring was to make use of the endless numbers

DEBEERS DIAMOND COMMERCIAL.

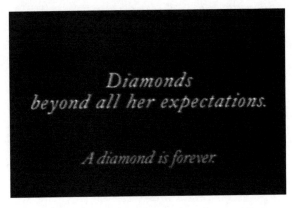

of smaller diamonds lying around in the Soviet Mine. Strangely, during the height of the cold war between the United States and the Soviet Union, millions of people were walking around unknowingly wearing a ring made up of diamonds from inside enemy territory.

In the 1970s, after extensive market research Ayers concluded the following: *"Women are in unanimous agreement that they want to be surprised with gifts.... They want, of course, to be surprised for the thrill of it. However, a deeper, more important reason lies behind this desire.... "freedom from guilt." Some of the women pointed out that if their husbands enlisted their help in purchasing a gift (like diamond jewelry), their practical nature would come to the fore and they would be compelled to object to the purchase."*

Market research also found that while women would often talk in interviews about diamonds being "flashy" and "overdone", women had an underlying attitude that diamonds were a sign of success and status. Women didn't like to ask for diamonds, but they were still happy to receive them. The research concluded that men felt as though they were expected to buy a diamond ring and women happily accepted them as a symbol of her status and achievements. So from the 1970s' onwards, Ayers created advertising that specifically emphasised the element of surprise in presenting a girl with a diamond ring.

The 2nd stroke of genius of this incredible marketing campaign is the idea men should spend 2 months salary on your engagement ring. This rule has nothing to do with the tradition of marriage and no such rule was heard of before the 1980's when Debeers came up with the idea. This rule was 100% invented by a Debeers marketing campaign. Even to this day the idea prevails: you need to spend 2 months salary on your engagement don't you? That's just what you do, isn't it? Debeers chose not go with a suggestion of a specific amount of money that should be spent, but instead, they suggested spending the equivalent of 2 months salary. The genius of this suggestion is that it can be applied to anyone; whether they're upper, middle or lower class, anyone can spend 2 month's salary (whatever amount that may be) on an engagement ring. What's 2 months salary when it can buy something that will last a lifetime? Because

don't forget, A Diamond Is Forever. What other marketing campaign has managed to embed their product (diamonds) so deeply into our lives? The Debeers marketing campaign managed to place their product right in the centre of our romantic lives. Their product is buried so deeply in our society that there is widespread social pressure pushing you towards buying diamonds (this social pressure has faded in recent years, but still exists to this day).

In the current day, the diamond industry is in big trouble. Due to advances in technology, diamonds can now be created in a lab. Worst still, they are 100% identical to natural diamonds and experts can't tell them apart. On top of that, they can be bought at a fraction of the cost. China is already flooding the market with lab grown diamonds and this trend will only increase. The technology for creating artificial diamonds will continue to improve at an accelerating rate, and unlike natural diamonds, they're 100% ethical. Nobody has died to produce artificial diamonds. Nobody in Africa has slaved away digging in the blistering heat to dig up artificial diamonds. Lab grown diamonds will inevitably put a huge dent in the diamond industry. But the diamond industry isn't going down without a fight. How can you fight against this inevitable trend? Another marketing campaign. The new "Real Is Rare" campaign is the diamond industry (including Debeers) using the only leverage it has left: The fact that "real" diamonds do in fact take billions of years to form naturally. Yet this new ad campaign continues to perpetuate the lie that natural diamonds are rare. Which they aren't. In fact, to this day natural diamonds are 1000 times less rare than lab created diamonds. This very same lie is spread not only through advertisements but also on websites throughout the internet (usually the ones who happen to also be selling natural diamonds. What a strange coincidence). This lie is subtly planted throughout all of the "guides" you'll find on the internet, all of which are either on a website selling diamonds or written by someone from the diamond industry.

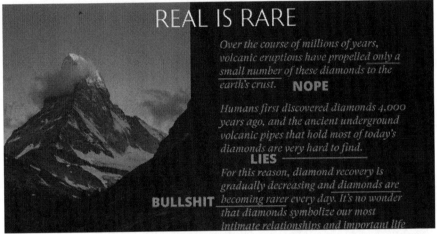

FROM REALISADIAMOND.COM. THIS PAGE IS HILARIOUSLY FOUND UNDER IN THE "TRUTHS" SECTION.

The fact that diamonds aren't actually rare has been a closely guarded secret in the industry for over 100 years. And even in 2020, the diamond industry is still trying to perpetuate this lie. With the example of diamonds, we can see the sheer power of world class marketing. Nobody can claim not to be affected by advertising, because some advertising campaigns have integrated themselves within our very culture. Everybody has to buy products or services sometimes, and when you do, advertising will play a role in your buying decisions.

chapter 8

GAMING

The soldier sat quietly with the young boy, playing yet another game of chess. He ignored the guilt panging in the back of his mind as he hid underground from the clashing of metal and screams that echoed through the room from outside. His armour and shield leant up against the wall beside the door unused.

But the game relaxed his mind. It would allow him to improve his strategic abilities that could one day be used for war, he told himself.

Nobody would find him here. He could stay here until the war was over.

The boy moved his rook two spaces forward. The soldier smirked as he moved his bishop 6 spaces diagonally across the board to take the boy's rook.

"Don't worry boy", the soldier remarked pridefully, "One day you'll win every game of chess you ever play like I do"

The boy paused thoughtfully for several moments and then seemed to make up his mind. "I never want to be like you" the boy said innocently.

The soldier, accustom to receiving admiration from children was puzzled. "Why not?" he asked curiously.

The boy continued to look down at the chess board and spoke "If I became as good as you at this game I could never become a great soldier".

As the boy spoke, an indescribable, dreadful feeling throbbed inside the the soldier. Like a demon he had been hiding from his entire life had finally found him.

The solider slowly stood up without a word, took a deep breath, collected his armour and shield and ran upstairs to join the fight.

video games – why we love them and how to deal with them

Video games are no longer only for fat nerds living in their mother's basement. *Gaming has gone mainstream.* Teenagers and adults use games to socialise with their mates. Lads play fps shooters with their circle of friends. Mothers play mobile games while their child is sleeping. Entire stadiums are filled to watch others play video games at a competitive level. Gaming creates teenage celebrities and millionaires through prize money and streamers and content creators make a real income through playing video

TEAM "GEN.G" WINS THE PUBG GLOBAL CHAMPIONSHIP

games. Video gaming isn't only escapism. More and more, gaming has become integrated with the real world. Gaming now carries real financial incentives and creates real celebrities.

But gaming isn't all positive. Video games create addiction, wasted potential, ruined lives and man- children. Gaming has become a large part of society, and is likely to become more and more widespread and mainstream as we move forward into the future.

So why do we love video games so much? Because it's a perfect reflection of our evolutionary roots and our tribal past.

We love video games because they're a supernormal stimuli of our tribal environment (**Law 4: Media Is An Evolutionary Mismatch**). For millions of years, we lived in tribes. Our body and brain is evolved for an environment that involved hunting prey over a large terrain and throwing projectiles (usually spears) in order to kill animals. We would then bring the dead animal home and share it with the rest of our tribe. This was typically a job for the men, while the women generally stayed home, took care of the children and foraged for fruit. The most talented

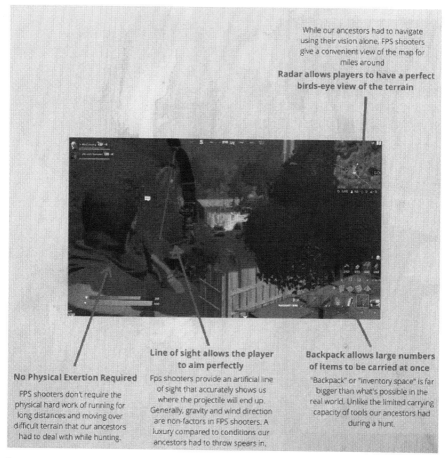

While our ancestors had to navigate using their vision alone, FPS shooters give a convenient view of the map for miles around
Radar allows players to have a perfect birds-eye view of the terrain

Line of sight allows the player to aim perfectly
Fps shooters provide an artificial line of sight that accurately shows us where the projectile will end up. Generally, gravity and wind direction are non-factors in FPS shooters. A luxury compared to conditions our ancestors had to throw spears in.

Backpack allows large numbers of items to be carried at once
"Backpack" or "inventory space" is far bigger than what's possible in the real world. Unlike the limited carrying capacity of tools our ancestors had during a hunt.

No Physical Exertion Required
FPS shooters don't require the physical hard work of running for long distances and moving over difficult terrain that our ancestors had to deal with while hunting.

hunters in the tribe would be at the top of the male dominance hierarchy, and in turn become highly attractive to the women in the tribe. For men, going into the unknown and coming back to the tribe with a reward is what our brains and bodies are evolved to do. The reward circuitry in our brain is based around this process.

Video games hijack this circuitry. Many video games are a simulated version of the hunting process our ancestors used to undertake. In FPS shooters, players need to navigate terrain, hunt a target with a team, and use projectiles to attack the target. It's no surprise at all, that FPS shooters appeal predominantly to men considering it matches male evolutionary programming perfectly. FPS shooters are a supernormal stimuli version of the hunting our ancestors had to do. They take all the aspects of hunting animals across the savannas of Africa and make them more convenient, easier and more enjoyable. In FPS shooters, the player uses guns that have a direct line of sight between their weapon and the target, often alongside an artificial beam of light or crosshairs. Our ancestors had no such aids, and they also had to deal with the effects that wind resistance and gravity would have on their spear as they threw it through the air. In FPS shooters, players are often provided with a radar that shows a convenient birds-eye view of their surroundings, while our ancestors had to find their way using just their own vision and the position of the sun in the sky. Players in FPS shooters don't need to undertake any physical exertion whatsoever. They're able to run across difficult terrains, jump, duck, throw grenades and fire weapons while they sit motionless in their chair. They're able to get the feeling of hunting their prey without having to commit to any of the physical exertion. For our ancestors, who had to run countless miles every single day, this would have been a dream. Other games require doing various tasks and being given rewards (like MMORPG's); players will collect large numbers of items, just as our ancestors would have collected fruits, nuts and other foodstuffs and brought them back to the tribe.

When we complete a task inside a video games, we're often rewarded generously.

A PLAYER UNLOCKS THE "WOODCHUCK" ACHIEVEMENT IN FORTNITE.

HOW TO PLAY VIDEO GAMES (AND HOW NOT TO)

The ultimate problem with video games is simple: They aren't real. The time, effort and energy you put into a video game doesn't pay you back in the real world. When you put time, energy and effort into learning a language, you're rewarded. You're able to communicate with larger number of people, the people around you are impressed when you speak in a foreign tongue and the skill of speaking in a foreign language will stick with you for the rest of your life. On the other hand, when you complete a video game, the only rewards you receive are digital. You get achievements, XP points, you level your character, fireworks explode on the screen, you beat the final boss, but the world doesn't care. The reward mechanisms in your brain, which should be pushing you towards achievements in the real world, are tricked into getting fulfilment inside a digital world. Many avid gamers find themselves at 30 years old, suddenly realising that they haven't achieved a damn thing in their entire lives. Video games cause people to fall behind.

The dopamine reward system in your brain believes you're heading towards success, yet your efforts are poured into a digital world and the digital rewards you achieve don't transfer into the real world. You live in reality, not inside your screens. Therefore, if you want to make the most of your life, you need to direct your efforts towards goals in reality. While gamers will often claim that they've learned many important lessons through playing video games, the truth is those very same lessons could have been learned more effectively and more accurately if learned in reality. A gamer might claim they learned problem solving skills through gaming, yet those problem solving skills could have been attained far more effectively while learning to be an electrician or even working as a waiter at a restaurant.

"I just play games to pass the time". But why are you "passing time" in the first place? Did you forget that your time is limited? Did you forget about your death? Now that you've remembered once again, can you still justify spending another hour on video games?

None of this is to say that video games can't be a great experience. As long as you stick to the following rules, you may be able to fit video games into your life in a healthy way.

HOW YOU SHOULD PLAY VIDEO GAMES

☞ *Play games with a storyline, characters and, most importantly, an ending. Video games can be a work of art like a book or a movie. They can include incredible writing, artistic graphics and beautiful music and SFX. They're an experience arguably more engaging than a movie. Have the experience, complete the game and then move on.*

☞ *Play games as a social activity. Get your mates together on a Thursday night and meet up online to play an FPS shooter for a couple of hours. Playing games with your friends can be hilarious, exciting and create memorable experiences.*

☞ *Play games if you think you can become a pro-gamer. Gamers who make real money from playing video games are an incredibly small minority. Still, if you truly think you can become a pro-gaming star, then by all means give it your best shot.*

☞ *Play games if you're a content creator. If you think making Youtube videos, streaming on Twitch or writing blogs about video games is a good way to earn a living, then go for it. Even so, you should ask yourself an important question: If you could make a living playing video games, would choose to do so? Do you want to spend the next 10 years paying the bills by streaming yourself playing games on Twitch? For some, making a living through playing video games is a dream. On the surface, it sounds like a great lifestyle, yet is this really what you want to dedicate your life to?*

HOW YOU SHOULDN'T PLAY VIDEO GAMES

☞ *Playing games for reasons of pointless completionism. Maxing out your character. Completing every achievement in the game. Doing tortuously boring and mundane activities for hours on end just reach 100% on a game.*

☞ *Playing to become top of the highscores (with no tangible reward). Players around the world strive to put their username in the top 25 names on the highscores table. They feel as though this will give them some sense of notoriety or fame — it won't. Nobody cares that you're rank 1. Especially if the highscores are mostly just a rank of who has spent the most time playing the game.*

☞   *Playing as a way to escape real world problems. This, of course, is a recipe for disaster.*

☞   *Playing when you don't enjoy it any more. Don't play a game you don't even enjoy just because of your compltitionist urges. Have high standards for games. If the game sucks, if the missions are repetitive, if training your character is boring, then quit and do something else.*

☞   *Playing because of the sunk-cost fallacy. Feeling as though you should keep playing the game simply because you've previously put large amounts of time into the game, and quitting would feel a waste.*

☞   *Playing when you're addicted.*

HOW VIDEO GAMES AFFECT THE CASUAL PLAYER

Perhaps you deem yourself a casual player of video games. You have a job, a romantic partner, a life and you're not addicted. Great. Here are some things to seriously consider.

You may have had the following experience: You're working hard on a particular problem, your business, writing the next chapter of your book or a problem at work. After hours of working hard on this problem you decide to take a break and go for a walk. Miraculously, while walking around, the solution to your problem appears in a flash of inspiration. This is your subconscious mind at work. Your subconscious mind is always trying to figure out a way to solve problems and achieve pleasure. When you experience a sudden realisation, or a sudden idea or solution, that's because your subconscious brain has been considering the problem for a long time.

Video games hijack the subconscious brain. Your brain will decide that because it's getting so much dopamine from video games, it should spend it's time figuring out how to get more dopamine from the game rather than real world-successes. Instead of working on creative ideas for the short story you're writing, or a solution to a problem with your business, your brain will be preoccupied with trying to figure out how to gain the next level in your video game of choice. As you're taking a break from playing, your mind will continue to wander back to the game:

How could I earn more in-game currency in World of Warcraft...what's a better strategy for beating my opponents in League Of Legends...perhaps I should buy a new outfit for my PubG character. The problems you need to overcome in modern games are incredibly complex, and as such will require a large amount of your brain capacity to solve.

You become the media you consume. And if you spend time playing games, even just a couple of hours a day, it will creep its way into the rest of your life. While you might consider video games to be something separate from the rest of your life, *your brain considers every single thing you do as part of you.* Including video games. Being successful in something requires obsession and you need to be using your brain to its full capacity in order to get ahead of your competition. If you indulge in video games for 2 hours a day, your attention will be split, and you won't reach your full potential.

THE STAGES OF A VIDEO GAME ADDICT

"At first it was fun, then fun with problems, now it's just problems" - Russell Brand

The rewards you get inside a video game create pleasurable spikes of dopamine in your brain that are similar to those produced from cocaine, alcohol and gambling. Your brain is adapted to a tribal environment in which you were required to hunt for food, so your brain rewards you for completing tasks. However, the dopamine spikes you get from video games are unnatural supernormal stimuli. Video games give us more dopamine surges than our brain is built to handle, hence, video game addiction.

After being bombarded by hits of dopamine through video games, our dopamine receptors become desensitised. The video game addict generally goes through the following 3 stages:

1. *During the first stage, the game is actively fun. The brain is getting more dopamine than it's used to and the player is having a good time. It's exciting, you're learning the game mechanics, you're making friends. All positive with little downside.*

2. *During the second stage, after weeks or months of gaming, the brain begins to adapt to the steady release of dopamine. Homeostasis achieves a balanced state using the tolerance mechanism and your dopamine receptors become desensitised. The player is no longer having as much as they used to. While the game no longer gives a high, it can still remove a low. If they're in a negative mood, playing video games will bring them back to neutral.*

3. *When you reach the third phase, the games no longer even take away the negative emotions. The game is no longer fun. yet because the player's dopamine receptors are damaged, nothing else in the world seems fun either. Walking their dog, studying, meeting friends, these things don't provide as much dopamine as video games, so they feel less enjoyable.*

Gamers often report that they want to quit a particular game, but no real world activity feels as fun. They believe that they don't enjoy studying, learning a language, hanging out with their friends or going to an art museum. Concluding that they don't like other activities, they return to the video games. Never understanding that the reason they don't like the other activities is because they've desensitised their dopamine receptors through playing video games.

The solution to video game addiction? Stop playing video games. Stop watching videos about video games. Stop reading about video games. And replace it with something real that actually pays you back for your efforts. When you stop, your dopamine receptors will return to their normal level of sensitivity and everyday activities will begin to feel pleasurable once again. This could take anywhere from 1 week to 1 year. But generally speaking, you will begin to feel the effects of coming off video games rather quickly. You can play video games if you want, I'm not here to shame you or tell you what to do. Just ask yourself the following questions first: Are video games stopping you from starting your project? Do you regret the time you've spent playing games? If you keep playing video games, where will you be in 5 years? in 10 years? Are video games stopping your creative process? Would your life be better or worse without video games? Are video games stopping you from fulfilling your true potential as a human being?

how MMORPGS turn you into a labrat

"2 years I've been playing, for 12 hours a day. I would never inflict this game on anyone. This game is just a disease. It's horrible." - 20 Year old Leo

MMORPG's (Massively multiplayer online role-playing game) are story-driven games, in which the player interacts in a fantasy world alongside other players from around the world. Some notable titles include: World Of Warcraft, Runescape, Guild Wars 2 and Elder Scrolls Online. The one thing that each of these games have in common is that they're all incredibly addictive. Almost everyone under the age of 30 has heard at least one story of a friend of a friend who played WOW (World of Warcraft) so much that they dropped out of college. Or stopped going to school. Or stopped seeing their friends. Players of MMORPG's consistently report: cravings to play the game while away from their computer, feel like they can't stop playing, feelings of anger when they're forcibly stopped from playing, negative effects on their real lives.

The following is a post on an online addiction forum from a wife on behalf of her addicted husband:

"Every spare moment, he spends playing. He gets extremely volatile if his gaming is interrupted or if I request help with the house or kids. He gets home from work and gets on the computer and plays until 2 or 3 in the morning(...) He lives to play. I am secondary. Our two beautiful girls, and another due in January, are secondary. Housework is secondary. Romance is secondary (I have been turned down or ignored many times when wanting to have sex or date night). Our life is secondary"

In the most extreme cases players have died from overuse of video games. Occasionally, gamers develop mental illnesses. Some end up on the streets.

Others develop physical illnesses like epilepsy. It's possible to become addicted to any video game but MMORPG'S (Massively Multiplayer Online Role-playing Game) seem to cause the biggest problems with addiction.

This is no coincidence, after all, MMORPG's are addictive by design. With traditional games, you pay a one-off fee of $40 and the game is yours, traditional game developers aren't too bothered with what you do with a game after you buy it. The goal is to sell as many copies as possible. You could chuck the game into a river right after purchase for all they care. However, MMO's are different. MMO's make their money through a subscription model; you pay $15 a month for access to the game. This difference is important, because rather than trying to get customers to make a one-off payment, the goal of an MMO is to keep as many players subscribed as possible (**Law 2: Media Is About Profit**). Whatever it takes to keep them on the game, even if it means treating players like lab-rats and encouraging addictive behaviour in teenagers with under-developed brains.

In the early 20th century, BF Skinner conducted his famous experiments on Operant Conditioning. He placed a hungry rat into a small box, now known as a Skinner Box. The box was completely empty, aside from a small lever, a light and a small food box. If the rat pulled the lever, a small food pellet would be released into the box as a reward. When placed in the box, the rat would begin exploring it's new environment, and teventually the rat would accidentally pull down the lever and a food pellet would be released. After the fifth or sixth time pulling down the lever the  rat would learn to pull the lever whenever it was hungry. Then Skinner decided to change up the experiment. Using pigeons this time he had it peck a button in the middle of the box. Instead of dropping in a food pellet every time the button was pushed, he would instead drop in a food pellet at random.

Skinner was surprised by the results of this modified experiment. Instead of casually pulling the lever like the rat did in the previous

B.F. SKINNER
CONDUCTING HIS
VARIABLE RATIO
EXPERIEMENT ON PIGEONS

experiment, the pigeon began pushing the button much more than before. In fact, Skinner noted that the pigeon would continue pecking the button long after he had stopped handing out the rewards. He called this a Variable Ratio, which is a term that game developers now use behind the scenes to talk about the construction of their games. More or less all MMORPG's will use a variable ratio reward system in one way or another. They're used for monster loot drops—a monster will drop a rare item at a variable ratio of 1 in 10,000. Like trying to obtain a Draconic Visage by killing dragons in the popular MMO Runescape.

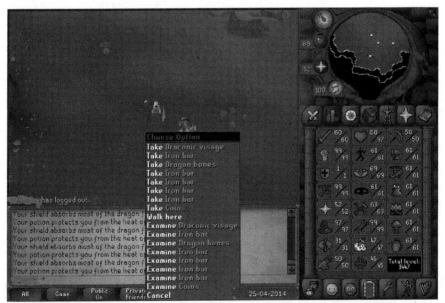

PLAYERS ESTIMATE THE DROP RATIO TO BE AROUND 1 IN 10,000

Because the Draconic Visage has a high in-game value, players will kill dragons obsessively in their attempts to get one for themselves. *It could be the next one..or the next one..or maybe the next one..* Variable ratios are also often used in the damage system in games. When fighting monsters or other players, the amount of damage that you inflict on your opponent is calculated with a random number generator (RNG). This means every time you attack your opponent you don't know how much damage you hit. In Guild Wars 2, there is always a chance of inflicting a Critical Hit which does far more damage than usual. Again, these critical hits happen on a variable ratio. This ratio can be improved with the player's stats and gear, but it's still a random occurrence.

THE VARIABLE RATIO DELIVERING THE PLAY A "CRITICAL HIT" IN GUILD WARS 2

MMORPG's put players inside a Skinners Box and condition them to pull the lever again and again using the variable ratio. Sure, it's a far more complex Skinner's box with state of the art graphics, but it's still a Skinner's box nonetheless. Instead of a food pellet it's an in-game reward like a high value item or a critical hit. Instead of pulling a lever you push a complex series of buttons on the keyboard and mouse in the sequence the game has taught you to. And instead of a physical box, it's a virtual box for your online character and your mind. *Operant Conditioning isn't just effective on rats and pigeons, but also on humans.* So players will sit in front of their screens pulling that digital lever in the hope of that valuable digital food pellet for hours upon hours. Game developers know that using a variable ratio system in their game will dramatically increase playtime and keep players paying that monthly subscription fee. These in-game rewards give players a hit of the brain chemical dopamine, the very same brain chemical released when achieving a gambling win. These variable ratio reward mechanics are the exact same model used on slot machines.

Slot machines use the variable ratio schedule to an incredible effect. Even though the ratio is always going to be in favour of the machine, people around the world sit pulling the lever for hours at a time waiting to hit the jackpot. And just like MMORPG's, addiction is a major problem. The hit of dopamine the player receives gets them hooked on playing the slots and pushes them to seek that next dopamine hit by pulling the lever one more time.

But gambling is a proper addiction though right? This is real money after all. With MMORPG's it's just pixels on a screen. So it's not a real addiction is it? Unfortunately, MMORGG addiction is very real indeed. MMORPG's tend to have their own in-game currency, so the rare items you might receive after the 2000th monster kill will have an in-game value. The Runescape item Draconic Visage mentioned earlier currently has an in-game value of roughly 8,152,000GP ("GP" being the in-game currency used in Runescape). These items hold inherent value in that it takes a large amount of time to acquire them. In-game currency is more or less the same as real-life currency in that it takes work and time to collect and can be traded for in-game objects or services.

On top of that, these virtual items also have a real world value.

 Blade of Wizardry

Price: $78.78   BUY   ADD TO CART

⦿ USD   ○ GBP   ○ EUR   Details >

This is the Blade of Wizardy, a rare item in World of Warcraft with an in-game value of around 10million Gold. When the player kills a monster, and the variable ratio delivers them this rare item, the player wins the equivalent of $78.78 – the jackpot received from a rare item drop is real. In fact, right now the virtual item marketplace is a *$50 Billion Dollar* industry. The marketplace for virtual items is just as real as any physical marketplace.

On Runescape you can actually "Stake" in-game money in a 1v1 fight against your opponent. This fight is almost entirely based on luck using the Runescape's variable ratio, RNG based damage system.

THIS 100M SELLS FOR $21.18 ON THE VIRTUAL ITEMS MARKETPLACE.

This particular MMORPG, Runescape, is available for any player over the age of 13. So is this effectively underage gambling? Quite simply, yes. There are plenty of anecdotal stories inside the Runescape community describing how teenagers developed gambling addictions that started with staking on Runescape.

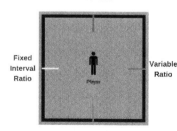

IN MMORPG'S, MOST PLAYTIME IS SPENT PULLING ONE OF THESE FOUR LEVERS

MMORPG's use a far more advanced Skinner Box than the original experiments in 1948. The box that MMO's put you in have multiple levers that all work on different schedules to ensure the player sticks around for as long as possible. This multi-lever Skinner Box contains 4 main levers.

FIXED RATIO REWARD SCHEDULE

A fixed ratio reward schedule is simple: a certain number of actions is required to obtain a reward. This is often the training stage, where players will gradually level up their skills and watch as the experience meter gradually moves up and up with each action. It's a small drip of rewards on the micro scale that allows users to see consistent progress.

Game developers know that with a fixed ratio reward schedule, players tend to work slowly while the reward is far away and then work harder and harder as the reward gets closer. Once the reward is achieved, the player tends to take a short break, then starts training again. All MMORPG's

A PLAYER LEVELS UP IN WORLD OF WARCRAFT

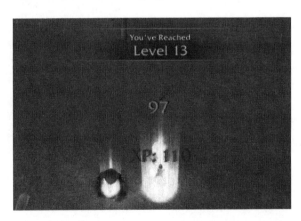

have a fixed ratio reward schedule of some kind. Generally it's repetitive and boring; players invented their own term for this kind of gameplay: *"grinding"*. To max out a character on any MMO takes an incredibly long time. Grinding for weeks, months, years. *Attack on monster. Kill it. Pick up the loot. Attack the next monster. Kill it. Pick up the loot. Attack the next mon.......*

FIXED INTERVAL REWARD SCHEDULE

The second lever in the box behaves differently from the first. This lever only appears at certain times during the day. Players head to a certain location in the game at a particular time of day to collect their reward. This could be a monster spawn that's scheduled to appear once every 5 hours, for example. Or a set world event for 7pm (GMT+0) on Saturday. Players will have a break from their normal fixed ratio grind to attend an event. They will complete the event and then head back to their fixed ratio grind. One example of this is the farming skill in Runescape. The farming skill requires players to check on their farm patches after certain time intervals to make sure their crops are growing properly. Players often log in at certain times of the day to check on their farm patches and then log off again.

This type of reward schedule encourages players to put the game into their real life schedules.

4:00PM - COME HOME FROM SCHOOL

5:00PM - CHECK ON CABBAGE PATCH

6:00PM - DO MATHS HOMEWORK

7:00PM - CHECK ON POTATO PATCH

READY TO BE HARVESTED AGAIN IN 4 HOURS TIME

VARIABLE INTERVAL REWARD SCHEDULE

Many MMO's have so called "Random Events" that occasionally pop up for players to complete. Often players respond to this kind of reward schedule by heading to possible areas these events may occur then waiting for it to happen. This final lever is really just the icing on the cake.

Players spend most of their time on MMO's walking between these four levers and pulling them obsessively. But what's it all for? Why do players care so much about levelling their account like this. Why do players want these items so badly? The final piece of the puzzle is: competition and comparison

COMPETITION AND COMPARISON

MMO's are not a solo venture. They're comprised of millions of other players. This is a virtual world, full of human-beings, and players online exhibit many of same social behaviours as people do in real life. Higher level players have higher status. Just like in the real world, where rich people have higher status, so do rich players online. The lower levels will look up to them as a role model of what they might one day become. They admire them and they're jealous of them, because the high levels have digital pixels that they don't. So they're driven to play more and more to compete with other players.

"WOAH! NICE GEAR!" SAYS THE LEVEL 73
"THANKS NOOB." SAYS THE LEVEL 124

Although there is undoubtedly skill required in Player vs Player (PVP) and Player vs Monster (PVM) activities, the overwhelming majority of the game's player hierarchy is usually based on *who has spent the most time playing it*. The higher levels have simply spent more time pulling the levers in their box than the lower levelled players. For the majority of the game, each player spends their time inside their own box pulling the levers as fast as they can, while comparing themselves with other players to see how many times they've pulled their own levers. Players pull their levers for years to try to place themselves at the top of the highscores table. This is cycle that never ends because, of course, *the game never ends* . Even after finally maxing out their account, an update or expansion will arrive, providing more content to go through and more food pellets to chew on.

You might argue that the world itself is a kind of Skinner box. For all animals, including humans, all behaviour is moulded by rewards and punishments. You get a promotion at work: Boom. Dopamine shoots up. You feel good. You lose your job : Boom. Cortisol spike. You feel bad. (Cortisol is the brain chemical released when you feel stress or discomfort). You have sex with someone you like. You feel good. You get rejected by your crush. You feel bad. Rewards and punishments occur naturally in the real world. They're what guide your behaviour. They set the route for your path through life.

Does this mean that MMO's are no different to the real world? No. There are two important differences between MMO's and the real world: 1. In MMO's, progression happens in an unnaturally fast and extreme way. Rewards come every few seconds with XP drops. Monsters drop a new set of loot every few minutes. New damage hits appear every second. This can make in-game progression more enticing and addictive than real-world progression. 2. People don't live inside MMO's. They live in the real world. Progression inside the game essentially amounts to nothing in the player's real life.

MMO's developers hijack your healthy craving for self-improvement and turn it into money for themselves. *Instead of all those hours being spent on real self-improvement, they're poured into a digital drain.* One Reddit user on a subreddit for gaming addicts puts it like this: *"After many, many hours of playing DOTA and LOL, I ask myself, "What do I have to show for these hours?" I have absolutely nothing to show for the time and effort I have spent on these games. The numbers mean nothing. The ladder means nothing. It's all fake. It doesn't translate into anything useful in the real world."*

So this is why MMORPG's are so much more addictive than regular video games. They encourage long gameplay time and addictive behaviour because they profit massively from players paying their subscriptions every month. World of Warcraft reported profits of \$1Billion in 2013. That's a lot of monthly subscription fees. Yes there is good gameplay in these games. Yes people play them because they're fun. But that doesn't change the fact that game developers still use techniques that are known to be addictive, especially when the game is aimed at teenagers who's brains are vulnerable to these techniques.

mobile games – the addictive time sink

Those innocent little games on the app store. Yes those ones. The free ones. Watch out. In the modern day, almost everything is optimised to take money out of your pocket. Those free games want you to pay. And they will attempt to psychologically manipulate you until you do. Game creators have discovered that using a "freemium" model along with micro-transactions is an insanely effective business model (**Law 2: Media Is About Profit**).

Highest-grossing mobile games in recent years:

☞ **Candy Crush Saga in 2020: $857 million**

☞ **Clash Of Clans in 2019: $700 million**

☞ **PubG Mobile: $2.6 billion**

☞ **Honor of Kings: $2.5 billion**

Achieving something inside a mobile game causes a surge of dopamine, just as cocaine and gambling do. Like most video games, they hijack the natural reward circuitry in our brain and trick us into thinking

CANDY
CRUSH
GIVES THE
PLAYER A
DOPAMINE
HIT

we've achieved something when we complete a level in Candy Crush. Mobile games will encourage these dopamine shots with congratulatory fireworks, on-screen XP counters or numbers and complimentary text, like Candy Crush's "Sweet!".

Bright colours. Sparkly animations. Increasing coins or XP. All of these things serve to activate the dopamine reward system in our brain. We feel like we've accomplished something, like we're progressing

SUBWAY SURFERS GIVES A DOPAMINE SHOT TO THE PLAYER FOR COMPLETING A LEVEL.

somehow. The truth, of course, is that we're sat motionless, hunched over our phones; completing none of our real life goals. While all mobile games have different tasks, different characters, different graphics and different colours; most of them are essentially the same. Most mobile games today follow the exact same freemium model.

THE FREEMIUM MODEL

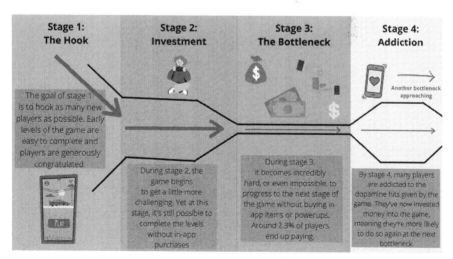

Stage 1: The Hook	Stage 2: Investment	Stage 3: The Bottleneck	Stage 4: Addiction

The goal of stage 1 is to hook as many new players as possible. Early levels of the game are easy to complete and players are generously congratulated

During stage 2, the game begins to get a little more challenging. Yet at this stage, it's still possible to complete the levels without in-app purchases

During stage 3, it becomes incredibly hard, or even impossible, to progress to the next stage of the game without buying in-app items or powerups. Around 2.3% of players end up paying.

By stage 4, many players are addicted to the dopamine hits given by the game. They've now invested money into the game, meaning they're more likely to do so again at the next bottleneck.

Another bottleneck approaching

Many mobile games aren't really games, they're sales funnels. The primary purpose of many mobile games isn't to create an enjoyable experience for their audience, it's to get as many customers to make in-app purchases are possible. The only reason they want to make the game enjoyable is because a fun game is more effective at hooking gamers and getting them to part with their money. It's just that making a fun game happens to coincide with getting users to spend money. *It isn't a game with a shop added on, it's a shop with a game added on.* Most mobile games are the same. It doesn't matter what colour the pixels are, how they're arranged on the on the screen or what the goal of the game is, they're all simply methods of spiking your dopamine and encouraging you to use the shop. And most of them use the exact same model:

1. **The Hook:** *The early stage of the game is easy and satisfying, with plenty of rewards, encouragement, congratulatory messages and addictive dopamine hits. The goal of this stage is to hook as many users as they can, after all, a challenging early game would mean losing potential spenders.*

2. **Investment:** *Game difficulty begins to slowly increase. Players become more invested in the game and begin to mentally set goals: I want to get 1000 gold, I want to reach level 10, I want get on the global highscores.*

3. **The Bottleneck:** *Game reaches a "bottleneck", a level that's incredibly hard or impossible to complete without purchasing items from the shop. Some users will quit at this stage, while others (who are invested in achieving the goals they mentally set for themselves) buy in-game items to pass the difficult level.*

4. **Addiction:** *At this stage many players are dedicated to achieving their in-game goals and they'll stop at nothing to achieve them. Of course, the player who wants to complete the game will have to spend a large amount of money on in-app purchases to do so. This player is also addicted to the dopamine surges he gets through achieving different goals within the game.*

Yes, mobile gaming addiction is real. In one Reddit post, the user writes: *"I'm going through a divorce right now and currently kicked out of the house after spending around $8000 on this mobile game."*, while another says *"The amount I have spent is embarrassing. But what really got me was last month when I couldn't even buy my baby food because without realising I had spent a whole paycheck in 2 days."* To the mobile gaming industry, these two gamers are "Whales". 90% of all *income from mobile games comes from "Whales" such as these. This means, that most of these mobile games are made with the purpose of creating addiction* *and ruining lives. If a game doesn't create addiction, it loses 90% of it's income.*

In the past, players were charged a small initial fee, anywhere from $2-20 to purchase the game. The player purchased the game, then enjoyed it as much as they liked, and no in-app purchases were available. Overtime, mobile game developers discovered a far more effective monetisation model for games: The "freemium" model. Offer the game free of charge, then psychologically manipulate players into buying virtual items from the shop. Over the years, thousands of mobile games have been made and game developers have experimented endlessly with which model extracts the most money out of players as possible. The freemium model is the end result of those experiments. Only around 1.9% of players end up making in-app purchases, yet they bring in 90% of all income to the game. Most of this income comes from what the mobile gaming industry calls "whales". These are players who splash out extraordinary amounts of money on mobile games. And of course, many of these people are addicts. The freenium model was created to encourage addiction, after all, the freemium model doesn't work without addicts. The model is created with addicts in mind.

THE ABSTRACTION OF MONEY

LEFT:
BRICKS

CENTRE:
TEMPLE
RUN

RIGHT:
CANDY
CRUSH SAGA

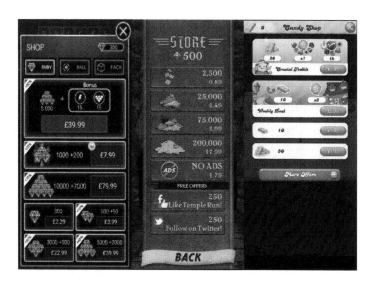

Why do all mobile games have their own virtual currencies? After all, it would be far simpler for players to buy virtual items with real currencies

(Dollars, Pounds, Euros etc). Candy Crush Saga requires players to buy gold bars, Bricks requires players to buy diamonds and Temple Run requires you to buy gold coins. Why? When you pay with a debit card instead of cash, you don't physically feel the money leaving your hand. Psychologically, you don't feel a sense of loss when you don't physically hand over your cash. And this is even more true when you're spending "gold bars" in Candy Crush. The more abstract the currency, the less you feel like you're losing something. It's no accident that most mobile games have their own virtual currency. They include their own virtual currency because they know it makes players spend more.

CANDY CRUSH SAGA

One of the most successful users of the freemium model and one of the most notoriously addictive games on the face of the earth is Candy Crush Saga. In 2020 alone, the game profited $857 million dollars. Let's take this classically addictive game as a case study and see how players go through the 4 stages of the freemium model: 1. The Hook 2. Investment 3. The Bottleneck 4. Addiction

1. THE HOOK

The early levels of Candy Crush Saga are so easy that even a 5-year-old could complete them. Gamers are told exactly whetre to swipe their finger in order to pass the level, and are then praised (like a child) for completing

TOP: THE GAME GIVES PLAYERS EASY HINTS FOR WHAT TO DO AT THE EARLY STAGES OF THE GAME

BOTTOM: THE GAME SHELLS OUT LARGE AMOUNTS OF REWARDS AND PRAISE TO THE USER.

absurdly easy tasks. The game acts impressed by your performance: "WOW...you passed on your first go!". Players feel a twinge of pride: *I guess I'm quite good at this*, they quietly think to themselves. The Hook is the first stage of the sales funnel. It's a like a giant net, cast out into the sea to catch as many fish as possible. Most of these fish aren't worth much, but if the net big enough, then eventually it will catch a whale. How do you make the net bigger? By making the early stages of the game as easy and as accessible as possible, and that's exactly what Candy Crush Saga does.

2. INVESTMENT

THE PLAYER LOOKS AT THE LEVELS AHEAD AND SETS THEIR GOALS.

At this stage, the game begins to get a little more challenging. There are no hints, and finding the right move takes skill. Sometimes players will pass the level, other times they will fail. The boosters available from the in-app store are not necessary at this stage as the player can pass the levels with their intellect alone. The player begins to set goals for themselves, deciding that they want to reach level 100, or collect 100 gold bars or get in the top 500 on the global highscores. The rewards begin to get spaced further and further apart, as do the satisfying hits of dopamine they receive after completing a level. The player isn't addicted yet, but putting down the game at this point may still prove difficult.

3. THE BOTTLENECK

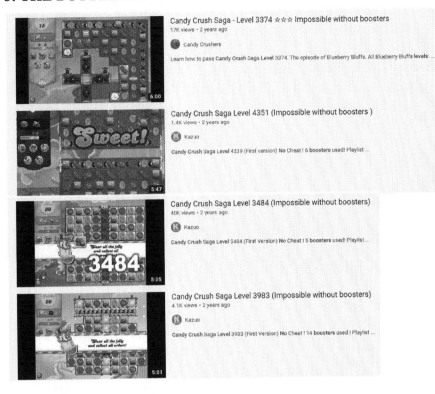

IF A PLAYER WANTS TO PASS THE IMPOSSIBLE LEVEL, THEY NEED TO PURCHASE A 3 "JELLY FISH" BOOSTERS FOR THE PRICE OF 19 GOLD BARS. NOTICE HOW THE IN-GAME CURRENCY OF GOLD BARS MAKES IT EASIER FOR THE PLAYER TO FORGET THEY'RE SPENDING REAL MONEY.

The game developers at Candy Crush have purposefully designed levels that are excruciatingly hard, or perhaps entirely impossible to complete without paying for in-game boosters. At this stage, the in-app store becomes more and more enticing. If the player wants to finally complete that difficult level (and get another hit of dopamine), all they have to do is pay a small fee to continue.

Now that the player has the jellyfish booster, they'll find that the level is now completable.

THE "JELLY FISH" BOOSTER
IN ACTION. THIS BOOSTER
MAKES IT MUCH EASIER TO
PASS THE LEVEL.

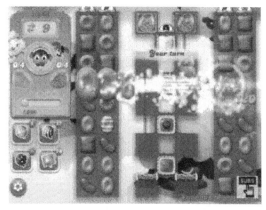

This moment is what the entire model is based around; the bottleneck. Players can either give up, or satisfy their new addiction by paying the small price of $5 for 50 gold bars to pay for some "Jelly Fish" boosters.

4. ADDICTION

In case you hadn't heard by now, dopamine is addictive. It's the same reason people get to other behavioural addictions like gambling, pornography etc. Those that get addicted to Candy Crush often blame themselves for getting addicted to such a silly little game. Truthfully, the fact that so many people get

addicted is no surprise whatsoever, after all, the game is designed with addiction in mind.

There are endless stories, often from women, who have become hopelessly addicted to Candy Crush and have spent thousands of their hard-earned money on pixelated gold bars and boosters that allow them to pass through the purposefully created bottlenecks. That's the modern world of mobile games. Just one more trap in the modern world that must be detected and avoided.

"The only winning move is not to play"
- Wargames (1983)

chapter 9

HOW THE MEDIA MISLED YOU ABOUT EVERYTHING

You don't have direct experience with most of the world. In the absence of direct experience, it's usually media that fills the gaps in our knowledge. The media does not teach you an accurate understanding of the world and almost everything is different in reality than it is in media. *There's a giant gap between media and reality.* Is your love-life the same as you saw in the movies? Do people act the same in real life as they do in movies and on TV? Do people look the same? Is the pacing of life in the real world the same as it on TV or in movies? Do the products you buy look or work the same as they do in advertisements? Media has misled you in ways you don't even realise. Assumptions you've made about the world, assumptions you never think about, have been created by media and not by reality. Many of the conclusions you've made about the world have been created using the information you received through media. Media is an imperfect information source, filled with all kinds of biases and inaccuracies. This chapter will demonstrate just a few of these gaps in your knowledge that have been filled with inaccurate information from media.

But before we move on, there's something we need to get out the way: **Does the media really affect your beliefs?** We're grown adults aren't we? We decide for ourselves what to believe, don't we? We're so sure of ourselves and yet 90% of our mind is subconscious or unconscious. *We* *don't know why we think the way we think.* Fiction, while we may be aware that it's not real, affects how we see the world. When we consume fiction, we are suspending disbelief. We are less likely to engage in counter-arguing (questioning the messages we're given). While watching fiction we're vulnerable to false information. In one experiment, German college students read a story called "The Kidnapping". They were split into two groups. For one group, a false assertion was inserted into the story. In this version of the story the assertion was made that exercise weakens the heart and lungs. Results of the experiment showed that the majority of the students believed this false assertion after reading the story, so if you read in a fictional story that exercise weakens the heart and lungs, many people will go on to believe it as truth. Because we often assume that information embedded in fiction is true. *Overtime we forget where we learned the information and our confidence in it's truth increases.*

Fiction is an incredibly powerful way of changing beliefs. That's why the American military had influence over the script of The Transformers movies. Positive messages about the military were woven into a fictional story about aliens attacking the planet to improve public perception of the US military.

TRANSFORMERS: REVENGE OF THE FALLEN (2009)

We know that fiction is based in reality on some level, so we assume that the ideas must have some credibility to them. Thus, we make subconscious assumptions on the world based on entirely fictional media. Media that may be only partially accurate or entirely inaccurate. In summary, many of the gaps in our knowledge, those things that we have not experienced personally, are filled with media portrayals.

you know nothing about violence

If you're reading this book as a man, it's quite likely that at some time or another you've imagined yourself in a fight. When you imagine this fight in your head, how does it go? If you're like most men, it probably goes something like this:

An arrogant prick in the bar starts insulting you, you play it cool. He gets up in your face and starts intimidating you. You warn him to be careful and tell him you don't want to hurt him (So smooth). He doesn't listen and raises his fists. He throws a punch towards your face, you skilfully dodge it and throw a perfect uppercut that connects with his jaw. He falls to the floor dazed and embarrassed. Everybody around is super impressed. They never thought you had it in you. They were wrong. Now they know that hidden behind your average physique is a man not to be messed with. You grab the girl of your choice and walk home arm in arm.

The gap between the average guy's idea of what they *think* violence is like and the reality what real life violence is *actually* like is enormous. There are two major reasons for this. 1. Our society doesn't require violence to survive and usually punishes it and most people have close to zero real-world experience of violence. 2. In the absence of any real life experience where do you think average person creates their perception of violence? You guessed it. The media. Your ideas of violence probably come from action films and crime shows. To you it's reasonable to shoot a man in the leg just to "wound" him, or take multiple punches to the face like John Mclane in Diehard, or run through multiple streams of machine gunfire completely unscathed like James Bond. Even if you're generally a more intelligent media consumer, somebody who understands that violence depicted in media is unrealistic, your perceptions of violence will have still been altered by media.

Imagine the following scenario:

You're a gun owner who likes keep a handgun in a holster attached to the right side of your belt. You get lost on your way home from a party and find yourself accidentally walking through a neighboured well-known for drugs and gang violence at 2AM in the morning. You are completely alone and the street is completely empty.

You notice a hooded man in the distance. He seems to be pacing directly towards you with some kind of intent. Both hands are inside his hooded sweatshirt and he's looking down towards the floor avoiding eye-contact. He continues to approach you at speed. Around 10 metres away now, he pulls something outside of his pocket with his right hand: a knife.

You have around 3-4 seconds before this man closes this 10-metre gap and is in striking distance of you. And remember, you have a loaded gun inside at your side.

You need to make a quick judgement, so what do you do? You might be imagining yourself calmly raising your weapon and shooting the attacker in the chest, or perhaps the leg. Perhaps you'd even wait until he's nice and close, to make sure you have a nice clean shot. The attacker will fall to the floor and you will have defended yourself. After all, that's what you've seen countless times in various action movies and TV shows. James Bond shoots the bad guy, and he flies backwards or falls to the floor. In reality, however, people don't usually fall to the floor after they're shot. It often takes someone who's been shot from 10 to 120 seconds to actually become immobilised; the spike of adrenaline their body is experiencing keeps them on their feet and moving.. When people get shot, they often don't experience much pain until minutes afterwards, and on many occasions won't even notice they've been shot until the pain sets in afterwards. So, going back to our violent encounter with the man holding the knife, shooting the approaching attacker wouldn't be the end of your problems. It's only somebody experienced in street violence who would know to be ready to avoid a knife attack even *after* shooting the approaching attacker. In fact, somebody experienced in street violence would probably suggest using the 10 metre gap and simply running away as fast as they could. After all, firing a shot could attract attention from dangerous bystanders and make the situation even worse. Not only that, but taking the first shot at a random hooded man in the street could potentially land you in jail for the next 20 years of your life. These are all situations that the average person, who's been exposed to misleading depictions of violence through media, would never consider.

Lawrence A Kane and Kris Wilder explain in their book *The Little Black Book Of Violence*, one classic situation of the influence of unrealistic violence in media:

> At a 2007 shooting incident in Los Angeles, the police found a local drug dealer lying on the ground with a gun in his hand. On the sidewalk near his dead body was one live round. Imitating what he had seen in the movies, the dealer had racked the slide of his pistol, even though there was a bullet in the chamber and he could have begun firing at will. This extra movement took extra time and cost him his life. It is important to understand that much of what looks good in the movies has no bearing in real life. Holding a gun sideways as gangsters are frequently shown to do in movies, for example, increases the chances of a stovepipe, jam, or feeding failure. A stovepipe failure occurs when the shell casing gets pinched in the slide instead of fully ejecting from the gun. When it happens, you cannot fire a second shot without clearing the jam. Even when the gun feeds properly and ejects shells correctly, holding it sideways increases the chances of getting hot brass in your eye. Not exactly what you want to have happen during a life-or-death fight.

Action movies frequently showcase 10 minute long fist-fights. The climax of *Diehard 2* showcases a 5 minute long fist-fight between action hero John Mclane and the main villain on the wing of a moving plane. They exchange punch after punch, to the head, to the face, to the ribs. Yet in reality, real fights tend to end very quickly indeed. It's usually only minutes or even seconds before someone is knocked out, gives up or runs. The truth is, all it takes is a single knockout blow to kill a person. An unconscious person falls to the floor, smacks their head on the concrete and dies – it happens every Friday night at nightclubs around the world.

"Getting smacked in the head so hard that
it stuns your brain like a blast of lightning
is a sobering experience. It is virtually
indescribable, though, to anyone who
hasn't had the experience. There is a vast
difference between living through violence
and reading about it or watching it on TV"
- Lawrence A Kane and Kris Wilder.

People who find themselves in a real violent encounter quickly realise that the only thing standing between them and someone who wants to beat their skull in is a thin veer of civilisation – laws written on a piece of paper enforced by people who are too far away to help you right now. All of their dreams of gloriously winning a fight and proudly walking away disappear when they realise they could end up in hospital within the next 10 seconds. They may also quickly realise, that they've never been taught how to fight, and have no idea what they're doing. Even those who have been trained in some form of martial arts are usually highly unprepared for a real street fight. In most cases, your deadly "ninja skills" are simply figments of your imagination. While you're attempting to do a fancy roundhouse kick to your opponents head, they're striking you directly in the throat. Even if you're in great shape, and a skilled martial artist, dealing with multiple unskilled attackers is extremely difficult. Unlike actual street fights, martial arts have weight classes. Under UFC rules, competitors are grouped into lightweight (over 145 pounds to 155 pounds), welterweight (over 155 to 170 pounds), middleweight (over 170 to 185 pounds), light heavyweight (over 185 to 205 pounds), and heavyweight (over 205 to 265 pounds). In a street fight, no such rules apply. You may find your 170 pound self facing up against a 205 pound attacker. On top of that, street fights may include the use of a knife, bottle or even a gun.

The UFC bans the following:

☞ *Head butts*

☞ *Eye gouges*

☞ *Throat strikes*

☞ *Grabbing the trachea*

☞ *Biting*

☞ *Hair pulling*

☞ *Groin striking*

☞ *Fish hooking*

☞ *Putting your finger into any orifice or into any cut or laceration on an opponent*

☞ *Small joint manipulation*

☞ *Striking to the spine*

☞ *Striking the back of the head*

☞ *Striking downward with the point of your elbow*

☞ *Clawing, pinching, or twisting the opponent's flesh*

☞ *Grabbing the clavicle*

☞ *Kicking the head of a grounded opponent*

☞ *Kneeing the head of a grounded opponent*

In a street fight, anything goes. Those who tend to be skilled in street fights are criminals; people who have been in an out of jail more times than they can count. A kung fu master doesn't stand much chance against a hardened criminal wielding a knife without any sense of morality of conscience.

Even if you happen to win your fight against that asshole in the nightclub who was trying to steal your girl, the repercussions of violence don't end just because you won the fight. There is a host of other consequences to address: legal issues, interacting with law enforcement, dealing with witnesses, finding a good attorney, potential jail time and recovering from possible psychological trauma. People don't generally consider the repercussions of winning a fight, of what would happen if they manage to badly injure or even kill their opponent. Next time you consider showing the arrogant prick at the nightclub who's boss, think of how their family would feel if their son died unexpectedly on a night out. Or the 15+ years you would spend in prison.

HOW MANY PEOPLE HAVE DIED, I WONDER, ON ACCOUNT OF MEDIA MISCONCEPTIONS OF REAL LIFE VIOLENCE.

Hollywood didn't set out to completely confuse you about the reality of violence. It's an unintended consequence of entertainment. Film and TV writers want their media to be exciting for the audience. Their priority is often not realism, but entertainment value and financial gain (**Law 4: Media Is About Profit**). It's more exciting for the audience to watch a 5 minute fistfight in a James Bond movie than a purely realistic one in which Mr Bond needs to be airlifted to hospital midway through a mission after taking a knock the head.

You probably don't understand real life violence, and nor do I. But at least we're now both aware of that fact, and won't put ourselves in pointlessly dangerous situations, believing ourselves to be some kind of superhero after being completely confused by the media we've consumed. When it comes to violence, there is a giant gap between media and reality.

you know nothing about food

According to the World Health Organisation (2016), there are currently around 2 billion overweight adults, of those 650 million are considered to be obese. People around the world are making themselves sick through what they eat. What's happening here? Why can't these fat, lazy, useless idiots stop eating so much? Why can't they take any personal responsibility? Well, perhaps the problem isn't quite that simple.

For people trying to lose weight, we live on an uneven playing field. The food environment we live in is tilted towards making you overweight or obese. Just think of every single checkout, in every single shop you've ever been in. Right next to the counter, what do you see? Highly addictive junk food. Even when you're buying DIY tools, pottery or whatever else, the checkout will often be lined with chocolate and candy. It's placed there, of course, because that's where it sells best – an easily justifiable *"after-thought purchase"* that, in the mind of the customer *"doesn't really count"*. In our world, avoiding junk food is incredibly difficult. Finding something healthy to eat in a 24/7 convenience store is no easy task; the majority of the typical local store is filled with processed, unhealthy foods filled with sugar and salt.

For millions of years, human beings have been eating fruit, vegetables and meat. Suddenly, within the space of a hundred years, our diets have been completely transformed. We're eating far more sugar and salt, as well as far more carbohydrates, along with a huge host chemicals and additives that have been added to our food. On top of that, we're eating less fibre, less vitamins and minerals and less good sources of protein. As this transition has occurred, the following chronic diseases have increased dramatically: Type 2 diabieties, cancer, heart diseases, strokes, osteoporosis, arthritis, Alzheimers, asthma, high blood pressure and the list goes on. The food environment people live in predicts their health. In Vietnam, where a culture of healthy, local food still exists, obesity is far lower than more modernised countries. To put it simply, when you live in an unhealthy food environment, when you're surrounded by unhealthy foods, you're more likely to be unhealthy.

Why are we surrounded by unhealthy food? Because it sells. The supermarket shelf is a marketplace in and of itself. When a food product sells successfully, more of a similar kind of food will appear on our shelves. *Why does it sell? Because it's been manufactured to appeal directly to our evolved taste buds.* Sugar was scarce in our prehistoric environment, but we need a certain amount of it for our bodies to function effectively. Therefore, human beings love the taste of sugar. In the past, we would have gotten small amounts of sugar from fruit. Today, we get far more sugar than our body can handle, through the processed food we eat every single day. The sugar in our environment today is an evolutionary mismatch, and as such, causes all kinds of problems for human beings.

Imagine you're a space alien doing research on the most potent drugs in the solar system. You've already written reports on cocaine, opium, alcohol, and nicotine. But on planet Earth, there's one more refined substance that seems to dwarf them all.

There are few places where this substance isn't imported and included with almost everything the residents eat and drink. It's the first thing they ingest in the morning and the last they use at night.

It's the centerpiece of celebration. Overweight children and elite athletes carry plastic receptacles filled with colorful, drinkable versions of the stuff as though they need it like air.

And although, at some level, they know it's killing them, they just won't stop.

Catherine Shanahan, M.D. in her book *Deep Nutrition*

In one well-known experiment, rats were given two bottles to drink from. One contained cocaine, the other contained sugar water. Most of the rats chose the sugar water. Rats being experimented on in a rat maze don't know why the maze is there or why there is a bottle of sugar water ready for them, they just allow their instincts to interact with the environment. In exactly the same way, human beings don't understand the environment they've been placed in. We live in a kind of "human maze", filled with shopping malls, advertising and addictive foods. One particularly common addictive substance in this environment is sugar. Many humans inevitably get addicted to the substance and suffer health problems as a result. All the while, the controllers of the experiment look on from above and laugh, walking away with all the profits.

When people say they have a "sweet tooth", what they're actually telling you is that they have an addiction to sugar. Eating sugar brings with it addictive-like behaviours such as: eating sugary foods way past the point you intended, eating sugary foods when you don't even feel like it, eating sugary foods until you don't feel well, and withdrawal symptoms after avoiding sugary foods like headaches, anxiety, cravings and depression.

The processed food you eat is not made by chefs, it's created by scientist in a lab. These scientists have two simple goals: 1. Produce a product that will sell as much as possible. 2. Reduce the cost of production as much as possible. Notice how "Making a food product that's healthy and nutritious for consumers" isn't on their list of goals. Sugar is highly addictive and cheap to use, which achieves these two goals simultaneously. In fact, there's a term that food scientists often use known as the "Bliss point". This refers to the perfect amount of sugar, salt and fat that hooks consumers. To give a simple example of how the bliss point works, take a cup of coffee and keep adding sugar. It will get more and more delicious up until a certain point, after which it will become too sweet. The bliss point is the perfect amount of sugar in that coffee, down to the milligram.

It's not only taste that these food scientists are focused on. Another common term used in the food industry is known as "mouth feel", which is essentially the way a particular food product feels in your mouth. Food scientists have tested thousands of combinations to make sure the junk food you're eating dissolves perfectly in your mouth. With many junk food products, the goal is make the food as satisfying as possible, but to leave you wanting more; just think of how you can easily get through a whole bag of Cheetos, Malteasers or Doritos. As an example, when Dr

Pepper were creating their new formula, food scientists tried 61 different formulas, subjected them to 3000 consumer taste tests, used computer software to find patterns in the results and then came up with the exact perfect amount of sugar and salt.

In the supermarkets of the new world, you'll notice that almost the entire store is made up of artificial food products, while the whole or "real" food found only at the very end of the store, usually near the entrance. Our supermarkets have been invaded by junk food because food scientists have engineered it to sell as effectively as possible; natural foods can't compete with the scientific know-how of the world's best food scientists.

Aside from highly addictive products like chocolate bars and candy, sugar is even hidden in foods most people would consider healthy (cereal, fruit juice, granola bars, peanut butter, almond milk..). For many of us, our tastes buds have adapted to expect more sugar in our diets. Micheal Moss, author of *Salt, Sugar, Fat – How The Food Giants Hooked Us* puts it like this: *"One can make a fairly strong argument that the industry isn't just responding to our inherent like for sugar or salt, but leading us to have a liking for salt and sugar that we're not even born with."* The truth is, much of the food we eat would be rather disgusting without the sugar, salt and fat added to it.

Food packaging also makes junk food far more enticing than whole foods. Bright colours (particularly the colour red as discussed in chapter 7) will have children pulling on their mothers arm nagging them to buy

the candy or chocolate they want. Think of the chocolate isle; imagine if all the chocolates (Mars, Malteasers, Twix, Snickers) were all removed from their packaging. You would be left with an entire isle filled with unappealing brown blobs in various sizes. Removed from their packaging, you would quickly realise that each of these chocolate food products are essentially all the same, with small variations in their flavour, texture and shape. Stripped of their packaging, junk food products aren't particularly enticing. Oreos encourage you twist, lick and dip, into a glass of milk. Wonka bars sizzle in your mouth, Toblerone comes in its signature triangle pieces, Twix bars come in a twin pack. Yet when it comes down to it, each of these food products are a very similar combination of sugar, salt and fat.

WHEN YOU UNDERSTAND THE FULL-SCALE REALITY OF THE OBESITY EPIDEMIC THESE FRIENDLY CHARACTERS BEGIN TO SEEM MORE AND MORE SINISTER.

As you can see from the images about, using cartoon characters on the packaging of food products is an excellent way to appeal to both children and adults. Food packages with characters on them are more likely to encourage "pester power" in children who want their parents to buy them something. And of course, eating junk food at a young age makes the habit much harder to kick later in life (**Law 5: You Are In The Media Hierarchy**).

Junk food companies have also started utilising mobile games and social media to promote junk food to kids and teenagers. Children as young as five are being exposed to junk food advertising on the iPad while their parents are completely unaware.

Aside from the food scientists, colourful packaging, children's characters and online advertising, we also have one of the most manipulative marketing techniques of all: False health claims. Junk food companies are highly concerned with the *perceived* health of their products. The *actual* health of their products is not important to them.

LEFT: CHUPA CHUPS MOBILE GAME AIMED AT CHILDREN. RIGHT: PRINGLES FACEBOOK POST ENCOURAGES KIDS AND TEENS TO TAG THEIR FRIENDS.

While the bright colours and funny characters with big eyes entice the children, the parents are persuaded by the health claims on the front of the box. Parents around the world entirely believe that feeding their small child *Coco Pops* for breakfast is a healthy way to feed their child, despite the fact that the product is filled with sugar.

Here are some common health claims found on food packaging:

Natural: All this means is that at one point the manufacturer worked with a natural source like apples or rice. A food product can be filled with artificial ingredients and still have *natural* written on the packaging.

No Added Sugar: Just because a product has no extra sugar added, that doesn't mean there isn't sugar inherent within the product itself. For example, oranges are naturally very high in sugar. Just because an orange juice product says *no added sugar* that doesn't mean the product is low in sugar. Also, sugar can simply be replaced by artificial sweeteners, most of which are unhealthy for different reasons.

Organic: This label doesn't say much about whether a food product is healthy or unhealthy. After all, organic sugar is still sugar.

Low-Fat: This label often means that the fat has been replaced by salt or sugar. It does not necessarily mean the product is low in calories or healthy.

Made With Whole Grains: Products with this label may only have a very small amount of whole grains included.

Fortified With Vitamins: Just because a product has had vitamins artificially added, that doesn't make the product healthy. A chocolate breakfast cereal my be *fortified with vitamins* but it can still be crammed with sugar.

Gluten-Free: Gluten-free food products are often unhealthy, filled with plenty of artificial ingredients. Gluten-free does not mean healthy.

Low-Calorie: Low calorie products have to have one-third fewer calories than the brand's original product. If the original product was very high in calories, the *low-calorie* version may still be relatively high in calories.

The simple truth of the matter is that all food products are made with profit margins, not public health, in mind. Despite what the packaging would have you believe, products like cereals and granola bars are usually unhealthy products, often containing high amounts of sugar. Many of us, especially in the western world, have been raised consuming high amounts of sugar every single morning before we went to school. Most of our parents believed the health claims on the front of cereal boxes, assuming that they if they weren't true they wouldn't be allowed to be printed there.

The standard advice for making health-conscious decisions when buying food is to check the label on the back. Yet many consumers find themselves completely confused and bemused when trying to decipher the information on the back of the box, after all, this food label has been written in a confusing way on purpose. The purpose of the outer packaging is not to give you accurate information on the product inside, instead it's purpose is to convince as many customers as possible to take it to the checkout. All of the packaging has been designed to convince you to buy, and that includes the food label on the back. If 1% of the food manufacturer's customers are calorie counting and health conscious, they will do everything in their power not to lose those customers. If manipulating the food label is what's necessary to keep those customers, they will do it.

Most countries have some kind of food regulatory body, the USA has the FDA (Food & Drug Administration) and the UK has the FSA (Food Standards Agency). These regulatory bodies are often ineffective and in many cases lobbied and controlled by the multibillion dollar food industry. The food industry is given permission to police itself much of the time, and the FDA in particular has a big problem with its "revolving door" hiring system—meaning that those in senior positions in the FDA often previously worked for big food industry corporations. In other words, the FDA is infiltrated with people who are really working in the interests of food corporations, and not in the interest of the health of the general public.

If you feel confused when you try to read a food label, it's not an accident and it's not because you're stupid — *it's by design.* As a result of purposefully confusing food labels and laziness on part of the consumer, most customers make their decisions in the supermarket by glancing at the front of the package and going with their gut; just the way the food manufactures like it.

On most food labels, all of the percentages and quantities are based on a particular "serving size' This serving size is generally far less than the average customer would reasonably consume. So right off the bat, much of the information on the label is misleading. If a cereal product contains 3g of sugar per serving, but the serving size is half of what most people consume, then the true amount of sugar a customer consumes is 6g, not 3g. On top of that, these unrealistically small serving sizes will often be paired with a picture on the front of the box, showing a serving size far bigger than the one on the food label. One good piece of advice for spotting unhealthy food products is to look at the ingredients list, which are required by law to be listed in the order of quantity; if *sugar* is listed as the first ingredient, you can be sure that it's not a healthy product. Yet food manufacturers can get around this

Nutrition Information
(AVERAGE)
Servings per package - 12
Serving size - 40g (¾ metric cup†)

	quantity per serving	%daily intake per serving	per serve with ½ cup skim milk	quantity per 100g
ENERGY	620 kJ	7%	810 kJ	1540 kJ
PROTEIN	3.5 g	7%	8.1 g	8.7 g
FAT, TOTAL	1.1 g	2%	1.2 g	2.8 g
- SATURATED	0.2 g	0.8%	0.3 g	0.5 g
CARBOHYDRATE	29.0 g	9%	35.5 g	72.4 g
- SUGARS	7.8 g	9%	14.2 g	19.4 g
DIETARY FIBRE	2.7 g	9%	2.7 g	6.8 g
SODIUM	32 mg	1%	86 mg	80 mg
POTASSIUM	154 mg	-	359 mg	385 mg
		%RDI*		
THIAMIN (VIT B1)	0.55 mg	50%	0.60 mg	1.38 mg
RIBOFLAVIN (VIT B2)	0.42 mg	25%	0.68 mg	1.06 mg
NIACIN	2.5 mg	25%	2.6 mg	6.2 mg
VITAMIN B6	0.4 mg	25%	0.4 mg	1.0 mg
VITAMIN C	10.0 mg	25%	11.3 mg	25.0 mg
FOLATE	100 μg	50%	106 μg	250 μg
IRON	3.0 mg	25%	3.1 mg	7.5 mg

† Cup measurement is approximate and is only to be used as a guide. If you have any specific dietary requirements please weigh your serving.
▲ Percentage daily intakes are based on an average adult diet of 8700 kJ.
* Percentage Recommended Dietary Intake (Aust/NZ).

...HUH?

by using alternative types of sugar with unrecognisable names such as: dextrose, fructose, glucose, lactose, sucrose and the list goes on. Also, in America, food labels use the term sodium instead of the more commonly understood term salt, which prevents health conscious customers from being deterred from buying the product.

JUNK FOOD MARKETED AS SPORTS FOOD

For years and years, a strange lie has been told. Well, not a lie exactly. More like a quiet assumption, a quiet assumption that has been sold to the public: that junk food gives you "energy" that will help with sports performance. In a world where real nutritional information is hard to find. In a world where the truth is actively obscured by corporations. In a world where many people are far too busy trying to pay the bills to do any proper research into nutrition — *Lies can be told in plain sight and nobody notices.* The fact that advertisers have successfully created an association between junk food and athletic performance is almost hilarious. Or at least it would be, if we weren't in the middle of a global, society-ruining obesity epidemic.

This is Milo. A chocolate milkshake containing 40% sugar. Put a child playing football on the carton and write some text alongside the product saying *"Grow with sport"* and you can create an association between Milo and improved sports performance in the minds of your customers. This association, of course, doesn't exist (In fact, drinking Milo will have exactly the opposite effect to what is advertised). This association is mostly subconscious. Most audiences don't think twice about the assumption being made in the advertisement, yet next time they're in the supermarket isle and they see Milo on the shelf, they might put it in their trolley, deciding that it must be healthy because it contains "energy" (or something), an assumption that was planted into their mind by advertising.

Looking at Tony The Tiger jumping around and playing frisbee in this advertisement may give you the idea that eating frosted flakes

will provide you with the very same energy. Frosted Flakes, of course, are loaded with sugar and don't make good pre-sport nutrition for anybody. Parents didn't think much about their decision to buy Frosted Flakes for their child, the decision was made mostly subconsciously.

What does Red Bull have to do with extreme sports? Well, absolutely nothing. Yet you probably immediately associate the two. Red Bull has created an impressive marketing campaign, placing their logo all over extreme sports events, skateparks, stunt planes and ski-slopes, and now you

subconsciously associate the exciting, reckless feelings of extreme sports with Red Bull. You might get the sense that Red Bull is an "extreme" drink for young guys who live fast and hard. Yet, what happens when you pour that Red Bull out of the can and into a glass? Once the marketing is removed, what are you looking at? A strange brown liquid that primarily consists of caffeine and sugar, as well as a few other strange chemicals. What's so "extreme" about that? The truth is, no serious athlete would ever consider consuming Red Bull. Red Bull is for the spectators who want to imagine they're participating in extreme sports while they watch from the sidelines.

you know nothing about psychopaths

Say the word "Psychopath" and what comes to mind? If you're like most people you're picturing a crazy person holding a knife with blood all over their face. Or perhaps you're thinking of Christian Bale in *American Psycho (2000)* or Javier Bardem in *No Country for Old Men (2007)*. Or maybe American serial killer Ted Bundy, or the legendary Jack the Ripper.

WHAT GOOGLE IMAGES THINKS A PSYCHOPATH IS

While this can occasionally be what a psychopath is, usually it's not. Researchers estimate that psychopaths make up around 1% of the world's population. The truth is, psychopaths walk amongst us and they're impossible to identify. You have met plenty of psychopaths in your life without realising it. The main trait that unites all psychopaths is a total lack of empathy and conscience. They don't feel bad for other people like you do; if they see someone get hit by a car right in front of them, their reaction will likely be total indifference. While some psychopaths are relatively harmless, others ruin lives, destroy marriages, climb to the top of power hierarchies, cause chaos among societies and occasionally commit violence.

The main reason psychopaths are able to go undetected so easily is because of the general public's total lack of understanding of what a psychopath is. Like many things, the general public has an understanding of psychopaths based on media, rather than one based on examples from real world.

THEY DON'T LOOK LIKE THAT

Psychopaths do not wear clown masks. They do not wear blood stained shirts. They do not carry chainsaws. They don't even (necessarily) look particularly creepy. They

TEXAS CHAINSAW MASSACRE (1976)

might even look attractive. Or more likely, they might look completely average. You cannot identify a psychopath by their appearance, in fact they likely look the same as everybody else. On top of that, they have an amazing ability to act the same as everybody else and can often imitate having empathy for other human beings incredibly well. An estimated 1% of people are psychopaths. So it's almost certain that you've spoken to one. Heck, they might even be someone you know. They could run your company, they could be in charge of your divorce settlement, they could even be the guy in charge of replacing your liver (psychopaths are overrepresented as surgeons).

THEY USUALLY AREN'T KILLERS

AMERICAN PSYCHO (2000)

Every single psychopath you've ever heard of was a serial killer. Ted Bundy, The Zodiac Killer, Donald Gaskins. These are the news stories you hear because they're the most dramatic, as are most of those you will find in movies and TV. But this is not most psychopaths. In her book *The Sociopath Next Door*, Martha Stout describes the story of a man called Luke. To Luke, "winning" simply meant finding somebody to leach off financially so he could spend the rest of his life hanging around the house and doing nothing. Sydney fell in love with Luke at thirty-three years old. After getting happily married Sydney became pregnant. After three months of pregnancy Sydney bought a crib for the new baby. Her story goes like this:

I remember it was on the day they delivered it, Luke came home and told me he'd quit his job. Just like that. It was as if he knew that now he had me. I was about to have a baby, and so I would definitely take care of things. I would take care of him financially because now I didn't have a choice.

He was just kind of there. Mostly he just sat around the pool, or when the weather was bad he'd come in and watch TV. When Jonathan (The new baby) cried Luke would get angry and demand Sydney do something about the noise. As if the baby were crying just specifically to create problems for him. Luke didn't so much as glance at Jonathan all day.

Not a single person guessed that Luke simply had no conscience and that this was why he ignored his obligations to his wife and his child. Luke's behaviour did not fit with the media image of psychopathy. He didn't go around slaughtering people at night like you expect psychopaths to do. Just like the general population, only very few psychopaths feel any need to be violent and wouldn't appreciate the prison time associated with violent actions.

THEY'RE NOT ALWAYS SMART

SILENCE OF
THE LAMBS
(1991)

All psychopaths portrayed in movies are smart. Hannibal Lecter from the film *Silence of the Lambs (1991)* is smart enough to deduce a person's character just by looking at them. He's smart enough to take down two prison guards and escape from jail using an elaborate, detailed plan. And he draws detailed works of art of monuments in his jail cell "from memory". Hollywood loves to turn psychopaths into impossible super geniuses, but like the rest of the population, they have a full range of IQ's. Some of them are smart, some are average and some are remarkably stupid. A perfect example of a less intelligent psychopath was a man known as "Stamp Man". Stamp man was a psychopath from the 1970s who had slightly less ambitious goals. The main focus in his life was to steal postage stamps from the United States government. He didn't want to keep them or sell them, he would simply rob the post office and then sit and watch from a distance where he could see the frenzy of the first employees that arrived in the morning. After easily being caught for the crime he would happily go to jail and serve his sentence, only to do the exact same thing after being released, a cycle he would repeat over and over again. Stamp man was skinny, pale and mouse like—not exactly a threatening figure. He had no desire to kill and had no intelligence to manipulate anyone or achieve very much. He simply wanted to watch the post office workers run around in panic after he had stolen from them. In the mind of Stamp Man, this was "winning". Stamp Man was a stupid psychopath, something that you rarely see in a Hollywood blockbuster.

THEY'RE NOT CRAZY

Think of the crazy split personality of Norman Bates in Psycho (1960) or Christian Bale's crazy killing rampage at the end of American Psycho

(2000). Neither of these are accurate representations of psychopaths. People will often confuse the word psychosis with psychopathy. Those with psychosis will experience a loss of contact with reality which may enable them to cut

PSYCHO (1960)

somebody in half with a chainsaw in the middle of the street or spray machine gun fire into a crowd. Psychopaths, however, have a firm grip on reality. The thing that's particularly terrifying about psychopaths is the fact that they're fully in control of their actions. They know exactly what they're doing and why they're doing it. They are legally sane. They do not hear voices or experience hallucinations. They know the difference between right and wrong. They just don't care about other people. A crazy person could never become a CEO of a major corporation. But a psychopath could use their ability to charm, seduce and intimidate people to climb the corporate ladder, whist having no limitations on hurting others in their attempts to get there.

THEY'RE USUALLY NOT CREEPY (AT FIRST)

If you come across a psychopath, don't expect them to be a weirdo. On the contrary, you might find them to be incredibly charismatic and magnetic. The psychologist of Jeffery Dahmer, who killed 17 victims and actually *ate* a number of them, remarked that Jeffery was *"amiable, pleasant to be with, courteous, with a sense of humor, conventionally handsome, and charming in manner. He was, and still is, a bright young man"*.

Ted Bundy, the psychopath who had been convicted of the murder of 30 women, received hundreds of letters from adoring female fans

NO COUNTRY FOR OLD MEN (2007)

while he was on trial, including many marriage proposals. Those that come into contact with psychopaths often remember somebody with smooth social skills and irresistible charisma. Once again, not all psychopaths are charming, but there's a good chance they're not going come across as awkward and weird as the psychopath portrayed by Javier Bardmen from *No Country for Old Men* or as unnerving as Hannibal Lecter from *Silence of the Lambs*. Richard Ramirez, killer of 14 people, attracted a large following of female fans, many describing him as "funny and charming"

Of course, anybody who has the misfortune of being around a psychopath for a long period of time will begin to get very, very creeped out as they get to know them more intimately. Let's go back to the psychopath Luke and his wife Sydney from Martha Stout's book *The Sociopath Next Door*.

After many years of being in a relationship with Luke, Sydney says:

"And then Luke looked at me, looked me right in the eyes, and it was as if I'd never met him before in my life. He looked that different. Those were the creepiest eyes I've ever seen, like beams of ice-it's really hard to explain. And I realised, all of a sudden, that in Luke's mind this was all some kind of control game. And I had lost, big-time. I was stunned"

Psychopaths are all too real, but they're nothing like you see in media. Psychopaths are a dangerous force against humanity, and it's a shame that so few people have an accurate understanding of what they actually are.

you know nothing about romance

"Losing an illusion makes you wiser than finding a truth" - Ludwig Borne

Ever since you were a child you've been told a story — that one fateful day you will find your true love and live happily ever after. This idea goes as deep as an idea can go. For most, it's a simple truth of life. Never to be questioned. Never to be held under scrutiny. Sacred. But life is infinitely complex. And an idea this simple can never be completely true. All ideas, no matter how beautiful, can often create misery when they're inaccurate. When you lay your frame of the world on top of a false assumption, eventually fantasy and reality crash into each other. And the results can be catastrophic. This is why your idea of romance needs to be based on reality, not fantasy.

In your formative years, your ideas of romance came from two possible places: 1. Your parents (although this this is far from guaranteed) 2. The Media. Every single one of us has absorbed Disney movies, romantic comedies and love songs. The media has told us all about love. The question is: Did the media tell us the truth about love?

Here are the 6 myths of romance in media:

☞   *Myth 1: Soulmates "The One"*

☞   *Myth 2: Happily Ever After*

☞   *Myth 3: Love Is random*

☞   *Myth 4: The Grand Gesture*

☞   *Myth 5: Love At First Sight*

☞   *Myth 6: Destiny - Everything will work out in the end*

Adults grow up believing these myths are truths, and this sets up expectations for romance that reality can never satisfy.

MYTH 1: SOULMATES "THE ONE"

*The One. The Woman of my dreams. Mr Right. My One and Only.
A match made in heaven. My Prince Charming. My True Love.
My Everything. We're made for each other. We're meant to be
together. You complete me.*

This is the fantasy language of soulmates. That there is one person and
one person only who is destined to be with you, and that when you finally
meet them they will fill the hole in your heart and make you completely
happy. You're supposed to know what your soulmate is thinking. You're
supposed to be happy with them all the time. And you're supposed to be
able to finish each other's sentences.

You're supposed to kiss in the rain. You're supposed to meet them under
dramatic circumstances. Sex with them is supposed to be romantic and
under dim lights that place shadows perfectly on your body (just like in
the movies). They're supposed to confess their love with a grand gesture
(Myth 5. More on this later). What happens then, when these expectations
are not met? What happens when you meet a perfectly good partner who
you like very much, but it just doesn't feel like it's supposed to. The sex
is ok. Your first kiss was in the break room at work. There was no grand
gesture. And you can't psychically read their thoughts (in fact, you often

have no idea what they're thinking). To somebody who has consumed heavy amounts of romantic comedies and romance novels: nobody will ever meet their standards because their standards are based in fantasy. No man can possibly hope to meet the standards of the "Mr Right" fantasy you've built up in your head. And no woman can hope to meet the standards of the "Perfect Princess" idea you have. 73% of Americans believe in Soulmates. Yet roughly 50% of marriages end in divorce in the US. *Something is wrong here.* There is a huge difference between people's beliefs about romance and the reality.

With so many marriages ending in divorce, we have to ask ourselves an important question: **Are We Actually Monogamous?** Among all other species of mammals, only around 3% are monogamous. In countries where you can be stoned to death for infidelity, people *still* cheat on their spouse. And cheating happens across all cultures. If human beings were naturally monogamous, wouldn't cheating be incredibly rare? Or at least only happen in particular cultures?

Now. I'm terribly sorry to have to do this to you, my reader, but I promise it's relevant. I present to you: The Human Penis.

The penis evolved to compete with the sperm of other men. This suggests that in our hunter-gatherer societies women had sex with multiple men and clearly did not live a monogamous lifestyle. Now if that wasn't gross enough, let's talk about the male ejaculation. Most ejaculations have 5-7 "shots" of sperm. The first shots contain chemical compounds

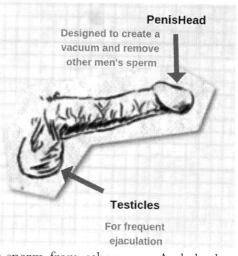

PenisHead
Designed to create a vacuum and remove other men's sperm

Testicles
For frequent ejaculation

that are designed to kill off any sperm from other men. And the last shots are designed to protect the sperm from any foreign chemicals that might destroy them. Again, this suggests that women have historically had sex with multiple partners. On top of that. neither the bonobo nor the chimp (our closest ancestors) are monogamous; chimps in particular being particularly violent, with the most dominant male chimp often mating with multiple females.

Pornhub released their most searched for terms in 2018, and its a revealing insight into human sexual preferences. Listed among the women's top 14 search terms into Pornhub are "threesome", "gangbang", "lesbian threesome" and "double penetration". Do these seem like the sexual preferences of a naturally monogamous species to you? Many will say that we must be monogamous, because we get jealous when we see our partner with somebody else. But then you have to ask: Why would we get jealous if we were naturally monogamous? If we were naturally monogamous, there would be no reason to get jealous in the first place because we would never consider the possibility that our partner would cheat. We get jealous because we know that there's a possibility of our partner cheating.

Still, it's not quite that simple. We also lean towards monogamy in a number of ways. Love is real. People do fall in love. But it's certainly not as simple as: *There's one person for everyone.* In the end, most of us feel urges towards both monogamy and polygamy. In the

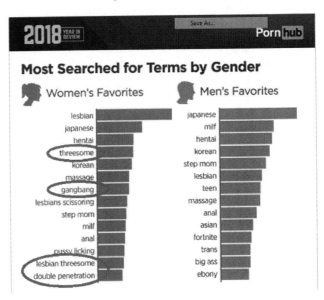

end, monogamy is a choice that you make, a choice with advantages and disadvantages.

The problem is: the media narrative tells us that there is no choice to make. According to the media narrative we're all supposed to naturally find "The One", fall in love and live happily ever after, as if the most natural thing in the world. So what happens when you're attracted to someone outside of your relationship? What happens when you have romantic feelings towards multiple people? What happens when your "soulmate" cheats on you? Or your partner ends the relationship? Or your partner passes away? *The media narrative and reality crash into each other and your entire belief system falls apart.* Or perhaps not. Maybe you continue to believe in soulmates. If your "soulmate" cheats on you, then maybe you should stay with them, after all, you're destined to be together and everything will work out in the end (Myth 6. More on this later). If your "soulmate" ends the relationship, then you just need to convince them to love you again. After all, they're your soulmate. So they have to change their mind in the end. Messages about how romance is supposed to work that are passed down to you through media may well have ruined your life without you noticing (**Law 5: You Are In The Media Hierarchy**).

Why does society push the idea of monogamy and soulmates? Perhaps one important reason could be that it's beneficial to a stable society and the raising of healthy children.

We have twice as many female ancestors as male ancestors. It's because of hypergamy (women's general preference to date men higher on the socio-economic ladder), that our species evolved beyond chimpanzees.

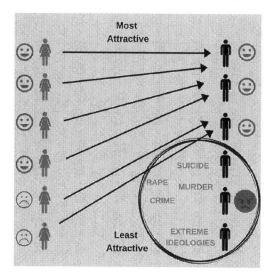

THIS WHAT COULD POTENTIALLY HAPPEN IN A SOCIETY THAT BECOMES TOO POLYGAMOUS.

Only men with the best genes were chosen by women to reproduce with. The men with inferior genes died without having children, which is one of the main mechanisms that helped us evolve into the advanced species we are today. At the same time, we also have a bloody history of murder and violence. A culture based on monogamy helps prevent such violence. So when the media pushes the narrative of soulmates, this helps keep the society stable. As the bottom 30% of men are not left out of the dating game in a world of soulmates and are therefore more content, more satisfied, and less prone to violent behaviour. A society not based on monogamy is doomed to fail (with the exception of hunter-gatherer societies (And very few of them still exist).

MYTH 2: HAPPILY EVER AFTER

When the fairy tale ends, reality begins. Romantic comedies and fairy tales all follow the same pattern. The princess is saved. The enemy defeated. The girl is won. The drama has been resolved. The man has confessed his love. And the couple is together. END. Roll Credits. It's as if the couple will stay exactly the same for the next 50 years

and they lived happily ever after.

of their lives. They will never get tired of each other. They will not start noticing each other's annoying habits overtime. They will stay together forever until the day they die, and their intense feelings of love will be just as strong when they're 55 as when they're 25. And because we're supposedly a purely monogamous species, neither of them will ever be attracted to anyone else.

Tiger Woods certainly believed this myth, until..

He thought that after he got married his biological urges would somehow disappear. Newsflash: they don't. He followed his biological urges towards infidelity at the expense of his relationship, his children, his reputation and a divorce settlement of $100 Million. Neurologists say that the feeling of blissful romance (the type you see in the movies) tends to last around 3-5 years. Brain chemicals called monoanimes create this intense feeling towards your partner. A feeling that doesn't last forever. The purpose of these brain chemicals is for the relationship to be stable long enough for them to have children. After this 3-5 year period is over the "rush" is over. The passion is dampened and your spouse no longer makes your pulse raise. There's nothing wrong with this, and successful couples will find a deeper form of love and companionship after this stage, But the media narrative never mentions that the passion might disappear. It's

BEFORE MIDNIGHT
(2013) - ONE OF THE FEW
ROMANTIC MOVIES WITH
AN ACCURATE PORTRAYAL
OF LOVE

supposed to be "happily ever after" Any successful long-term couple will tell you that marriage is the beginning not the end, that a long-term relationship takes work and that it certainly isn't "Happily Ever After".

MYTH 3: LOVE IS RANDOM

Love can happen to anyone.
At any time. It doesn't matter who. It doesn't matter where. Love is unpredictable and you can fall in love with absolutely anybody.

Do these seem like couples who have been paired together randomly? Where are the famous actresses married to scruffy, deadbeat losers who live in their mothers basement? Where are the successful, handsome men

in relationships with unattractive, overweight women with mental health disorders? If cupid's arrow really struck people at *random* we would see all kinds of people coupled together. The truth is, people generally fall in love with those who are roughly as attractive as they are. Bare in mind, that attractiveness does not only mean physical appearance. It can include talent, status, level of success and many other attributes. Romantic love is conditional. Falling in love has pre-requisites that have to be met. Would you fall in love with a mass murderer? No? Then we can say that a pre-requisite for falling in love with somebody is that they're not a mass murderer (an extreme example, but it makes the point nonetheless).

Hypergamy is plays an important role in who people choose to date, particularly for women. Hypergamy is a deep evolutionary instinct in females across multiple species. Women often desire to select men from the top of the male dominance hierarchies—which helps explain female crushes on celebrities (teenage boys don't tend to have pictures of female pop singers pinned on their wall like teenage girls do). The fact that women continually selected for the best man they could possibly find allowed our species to evolve effectively. If women were choosing men randomly ineffective genes would be passed through the generations and our species wouldn't have become as successful as it is today. Of course, hypergamy is a complex mechanism. Men can by hypergamous too and it's far more complicated than I've been able to explain here. The point is: *Love has a pattern.* Most people date someone at the same level of attractiveness as them. Most people prefer to date within their race. Most women date men who are taller than them. And hypergamy is a major factor in whether they fall in love with a man. Sure there are outliers, but the patterns exist. Therefore love is not random.

MYTH 4: THE GRAND GESTURE

How do you get a woman to love you? You perform an extravagant grand gesture of love. Show her just how much you love her and she'll love you back, right? This is typically awful advice for men. It's needy and it's downright creepy. Especially in the initial courtship stages of a relationship. The biggest problem with grand gestures in romantic movies is the woman's reaction to them. The grand gesture only works because the writer says that it works. The behaviour of the actress in the movie is bound by the script written for her. In the real world, the woman's reaction to one of these romantic gestures would not follow the script. I promise you, if you show up uninvited at your best friends house

HEY. I'M HERE TO DECLARE MY LOVE TO YOU IN SECRET USING CUE CARDS. DON'T TELL YOUR HUSBAND. LOVE ACTUALLY (2003).

with a declaration of love written on cue cards to show to his wife, the woman will not act like Kiera Knightly did in Love Actually. She will tell her husband and you won't be allowed near their house ever again. And if you force a girl to agree to a date by threatening to commit suicide by hanging off a ferris wheel like Ryan Gosling in The Notebook, I promise you that girl will not show up on the date.

Romantic gestures are only suitable in the middle of an existing relationship and should never be used in an attempt to initiate one. What a romantic gesture like this communicates is: *"You're way out of my league. But please, please, please go on a date with me"* In what world is a woman impressed by this? Take any of these grand gestures, remove the romantic

HELLO? POLICE? I'D LIKE TO ORGANISE A RESTRAINING ORDER PLEASE. THE NOTEBOOK (2004)

background music and transplant the scene into the real world with real people. How does that grand gesture come across now? On top of being needy, they're creepy. They tick a number of boxes on the "Am I dealing with a stalker?" checklist. Persisting a woman after she's rejected you 3 times isn't romantic, it's creepy.

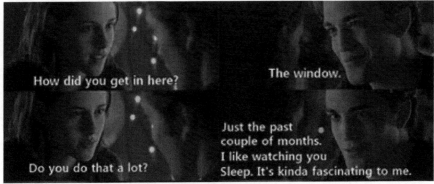

NOW REPLACE ROBERT PATTERSON WITH A 55-YEAR-OLD BALD MAN WITH A BEARD. HOW DO YOU FEEL ABOUT THIS SCENE NOW?

The grand gesture is an overused plot device used to impress a mainstream Hollywood audience who have been conditioned to accept it as normal. They're used because they're visually dramatic and do a great job of making an exciting movie. In fact, the most famous romantic comedies are the ones with the most memorable grand gestures. Their purpose is to sell cinema tickets and DVD's. Not to represent reality accurately.

TURN THAT CRAP OFF LLYOD I'M TRYING TO SLEEP

MYTH 5: LOVE AT FIRST SIGHT

He sees her from across the room. He gasps as he takes in her beauty. Her eyes. Her hair. Her face. And he knows right there and then. That this is the girl who he'll spend the rest of his life with.

This is not how relationships start. If you're staring at a girl you don't know from across the room, it's because you think she's physically attractive. And that's it. While it only takes moment to decide if someone is or is not sexually attractive, it takes significantly more time to determine if someone is is suitable as a long-term partner or not. It's love at first *sight*. Which means you're just looking at them with your eyes. You're not using your ears. Deciding to marry someone without ever speaking to them is insane. Nobody does it. But Hollywood likes to pretend that this actually happens. It's a plot device, just like the grand gesture. It's used because

it's dramatic, visually enticing and requires no subtlety whatsoever (mainstream audiences don't understand subtly). When Warner Brothers are investing millions of dollars into a movie, they can't risk having the romance unfold overtime in a natural way. The mainstream audience might find it boring and DVD sales will plummet. It's much safer for them to stick to tried and tested plot devices

Having said all that, there are many real people in the world who will insist that they loved their partner on the very first meeting. Perhaps this is even something your grandparents will say and they were never exposed to Hollywood. So are these people lying? No. Something else is going on here. The memory of love at first sight could be a false memory. Perhaps it's simply hindsight. Most people's idea of their memory is like a camcorder that records everything that happens to them. Something they can replay at any time. But memory is far less reliable than a camcorder. Memory is more like a vivid dream that can be altered overtime by what happens after the event. For example, you can probably distinctly remember where you were and what you were doing during the terrorist attacks of 9/11. While you probably feel like your memories of the event are pretty accurate, there is a very strong chance that your recollections have been influenced by subsequent news coverage and stories about the attacks. This newer information might compete with your existing memories of the event or fill in missing bits of information. In exactly the same way, couples who are in love will reminisce about how they fell in love the moment they met. But in fact they may only feel this way in hindsight. They remember the event that way because they're in love now. The way they feel in the present is affecting the way they feel about the past. They may have had positive feelings towards each other on their first meeting, but in the moment they might not have felt the same way they do when remembering it. This is why love at first sight is usually remembered by those who are in a successful long-term relationships. If they had never been exposed to the idea of "love at first sight" through media, would they still claim that this happened to them? In the real world, most couples grow fond of each other over time. So don't worry if you didn't think much of your partner when you first saw them, it doesn't mean they're the wrong person. In many ways, a love that grows over time is far more romantic than the awkward "love at first" sight trope found in romantic movies.

MYTH 6: EVERYTHING WILL WORK OUT IN THE END

This is our destiny.

SLUMDOG MILLIONAIRE (2008)

No matter what. A happy ending is inevitable.
If you haven't found your soulmate, then you need to be patient.

The right girl/guy will come along. One day you will find the love of your life. It's guaranteed. It's destiny.

If destiny has a love waiting for everyone, then how do explain the 6 million who died at Auschwitz? Or the 6-7 million who were starved to death during the Holodomor? Or the 25 million people who died during the bubonic plague? Or the workers in the World Trade Centre on 9/11? Was this destiny too? If everything works out in the end, then how do you explain the lives of these people? Many of them having died before they ever found the love of their life? Where are their stories in Hollywood? Life is grossly unfair and nothing is guaranteed. Good people die for no good reason. Many people never find a long-term partner. And everything doesn't always work out in the end.

Almost all romantic comedies have a satisfying and happy ending. If you watch 100 romantic movies in your life, an assumption begins to build in your mind unnoticed.:That your life will go the same way as the characters in these movies. The subtle assumption that you made watching romantic movies creeps it's way until your behaviour in the real world. You learn that being passive towards your romantic life is a normal way to behave. Then you forget where you learned the behaviour and you live the rest of your life acting this way. Without ever realising where you're going wrong.

The problem with the plot trope of destiny is that it encourages passiveness. If destiny guarantees you the love of your life. then why work on yourself? Why bother yourself with dating? Why not just sit around in your boxers playing video games until destiny brings you what you're entitled to? The truth is: your love life is a pro-active venture. And destiny rewards those who pursuit their goals. The more people you meet, the more likely you are to find a long-term partner. Shy people have a disadvantage because they're meeting less people. And who has the biggest disadvantage? Those who believe (without realising they believe it) that the world will provide them with their soulmate. If instead, romantic movies showed the protagonist sorting out their life, improving themselves and actively pursuing a romantic partner; then the audience would build more useful assumptions in their mind. That romance is something you have to actively seek out.

So look into your beliefs about love. Where did you get them from? Did you get them from real world experiences, or from media? Make up your own mind about romance.

chapter 10

BURSTING THE FILTER BUBBLE

Personalisation on the internet has pushed people to become more extreme and self-assured in their views. There are thousands of these filter bubbles (as discussed in chapter 4), and some of them are particularly strange and obscure. In this chapter I will do my best to challenge the ideologies at the centre of various filter bubbles throughout the internet. Of course, the arguments I make against these filter bubbles will probably never be heard by those inside of it. (That's the very nature of a filter bubble, that reasonable opposing arguments against your ideology are completely blocked out by algorithms).

political filter bubbles – how social media splits societies in half

In around 2010, social media appeared in all of our lives. And ever since then, different societies around the world have become more and more polarised. In America, the country was split directly in half as Donald Trump became President of the United States. In Brazil, the country was also split down the middle as the country elected controversial president Jair Bolasanaro. On the other side of the planet, India has seen increased political polarisation. Why is it that so many democratic societies seem to be tearing themselves into two separate tribes? Why does it feel like each of our countries are now split into two distinct "teams"? What one factor is consistent amongst these societies in different parts of the world with radically different cultures? *Social media.*

Social media appeared, and then societies became more politically polarised. Is this a coincidence? Unlikely. It's true that political polarisation has happened throughout history, before the invention of social

Left-Wing Filter Bubble	Right-Wing Filter Bubble

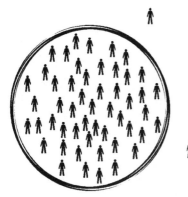 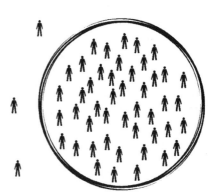

Independent Thinkers

media, and that there are many possible factors that cause political polarisation. Yet the effects of social media on politics may be far more impactful than you previously believed. This is how social media splits societies in half.

We retreat into our own bubbles, ...
especially our social media feeds,
surrounded by people who look like us
and share the same political outlook and
never challenge our assumptions. ... And
increasingly, we become so secure in
our bubbles that we start accepting only
information, whether it's true or not, that fits
our opinions, instead of basing our opinions
on the evidence that is out there"
- Former President Barack Obama

Online, we live in filter bubbles. The content we consume and the content we see is tailored by algorithms to us, personally. While political echo chambers have always occurred in the real world, political filter bubbles are entirely new. Watch one politically left-wing video on Youtube and you'll be recommended other similar videos for weeks afterwards. (politically right-wing videos, however, will be hidden from your eyes). Youtube wants you spend as much time on their platform as possible, and to do this, they recommend videos you are likely to watch. Which videos are you most likely to watch? Videos you agree with. Listening to a video of someone saying things we agree with brings us positive emotions. Listening to someone from the other side of the political spectrum, saying things we disagree with, makes us frustrated, mad and disappointed - so we avoid this content. *Human beings across the entire planet interact with social media in exactly this way.* It's natural for humans to seek positive emotions rather than negative ones. Whether they're in India, Brazil, France or Argentina, people tend to consume political content on social media in exactly the same way. On Twitter, people usually follow users they agree with. This leaves users with a Twitter feed absolutely filled with people who think just as they do. Conservatives retweet conservatives. Liberals retweet liberals. And there's almost no crossover. Just as you become the average of the 5 people you surround yourself with, *you also become the average of every piece of political content you've consumed that year.* Algorithms on social media create a kind of "gravitational pull" towards either the left-wing or right-wing filter bubble, and almost everybody ends up inside one of these bubbles (usually without any awareness that this has happened. After all, online filter bubbles are invisible)

The algorithms on social media continually recommend political content we agree with in order to get us to spend more time on their platforms, then inevitably, our own political beliefs become stronger and more calcified. We become increasingly sure that our political views are correct, and that those on the opposite side are wrong, have false information, have questionable character or are just plain stupid. Yet *it's not only that the algorithms change to suit your beliefs, but also that your beliefs change to suit the algorithms.* The opinions and "vibe" of the content you consume seeps it's way into your consciousness, often changing your world-view at a surprisingly deep level. While you may think you adopted your political beliefs naturally, it might instead be the case that your political beliefs have been shaped to fit the algorithms.

All of this creates two distinct "tribes". Human beings, who have evolved to live in a tribal environment, have all of their tribal mechanisms triggered by these filter bubbles. Emotionally, we begin to feel hate towards the "other" tribe and we feel a need to please and get along with "our'" tribe. People inside these bubbles often stop discussing politics on an issue-by-issue basis, instead, they reflexively take the same position as those in their own "tribe" on any given issue. A left-leaning individual might be a Gay Rights Advocate, in support of universal healthcare and be passionately anti-war. Yet if this same individual steps out of line on a single issue, trans-rights for example, their tribe will immediately scorn them and often assume that this individual is in the opposing tribe.

"We have created tools that are ripping apart the social fabric of how society works" - Former Facebook Exec

TWO SEPARATE REALITIES

" If you're a left-winger, all the evidence
you see is completely compelling. The other
side are racists, homophobes, greedy,
they're the worst people in the world and
you have all the facts and evidence to
back that up. Yet somebody living in the
next house, a right-winger, is living in an
entirely different reality, who see an entirely
different set of facts to base their beliefs
on" - Jonathan Haidt

When social media algorithms split a society in half politically, two separate realities are created. Each of these realities not only have their own opinions, but also their own facts, statistics, narratives and even their own definitions of words. The word *"Racism", for example,* has been split into two separate realities. Those entrenched inside the right-wing filter bubble believe that *"Racism"* is defined simply as any kind of discrimination based on race, while those inside the left-wing filter bubble believe *"Racism"* can only exist towards "marginalised minorities". One reality believes that it's possible to be racist towards white people. but the other reality does not. It's exceedingly difficult for those inside opposing political filter bubbles to communicate in a civil manner when they're using entirely different definitions for the exact same words.

Each of these two realities has it's own narrative about the current situation in the world. The capitol hill riots in Washington D.C. showed us the effects of filter bubbles (and echo chambers) in action.

"IT'S TERRIBLE HOW THIS
ELECTION WAS STOLEN.
AND I HAD TO COME HERE
AND DO MY PATRIOTIC
DUTY"

Todd Possett

The right-wing filter bubble believed that the US election was stolen from trump. The left-wing filter bubble believed that it wasn't. No matter what the truth is, millions of people in America are clearly living in different realities.

"What we saw in D.C. was like a Youtube comment thread come to life" - Sam Harris

When social media splits societies in half it doesn't only effect large groups of people. A split is created through families, friendship groups and workplaces. A father and a daughter inside a family end up living in two separate realities created by algorithms on social media. Journalists, academics and politicians and other apparently "smart" people are also affected by social media algorithms. These so called "smart" people aren't necessarily any more aware of the filter bubble's effects than the "dumb" general public.

"People with more education are more likely to follow political news. Therefore, people with more education can actually become mis-educated" - Eli Praiser, author of The Filter Bubble: What the Internet Is Hiding from You

REWARDED FOR EMOTIONAL OUTBURSTS

On social media, emotional outbursts are rewarded. The more dramatic, the more obnoxiously one-sided and the more lacking in nuance, the more successful that content will be. To post neutral, rational and calm content is a sure-fire way to get low view counts and like counts. One tweet that gained 20,000 likes and over 2000 retweets said *"I am a Trump's Republican. PERIOD! END OF STORY!"*, while another tweet that gained a 25,000 likes and 9500 retweets said *"WHEN THE PENALTY FOR ABORTING AFTER RAPE IS MORE SEVERE THAN THE PENALTY FOR RAPE, THAT'S WHEN YOU KNOW IT'S A WAR ON WOMEN"*. These are the kind of tweets that are successful on Twitter.

In the social media environment, anybody attempting to deal with political issues in balanced and fair manner are almost entirely ignored. This creates a dangerous and emotionally charged feedback loop where irrational and thoughtless points of view are amplified — which eventually spills off of the internet and out into the real world. Even intelligent people end up more one-sided and less nuanced in the social media environment. When our tweet or comment receives a high number of likes, we feel accepted and noticed by the tribe. *It's human nature to bend your behaviour towards social approval.* And it's highly likely that what you believe to be your honest thoughts may be altered (even if only slightly), to become more lacking in nuance, more emotional and more appealing to your online tribe. Asynchronous, text based communication also increases anger and the hostility online and empathy doesn't come naturally when we're not speaking face-to-face. As is usually the case, people don't notice how their thoughts and behaviour are being influenced by the technological environment they live in. They don't notice that the social media environment has made them more hostile, angry and emotional than they otherwise would be (**Law 1: The Medium Is The Message**). It should be noted that all of these effects are present everywhere that social media exists which, in case you weren't aware, is almost every country on the planet.

"If a swastika is drawn on a locker in a junior highschool in Illinois, everybody on the left will hear about it. And if an idiot holds up a sign that saying 'patriotism is racism', anywhere in America, everyone on the right will hear about it. So everyone is immersed in a river of outrage."
- Jonathan Haidt

THE DIGITAL STRAWMAN

Those inside the left-wing or right-wing filter bubbles do not understand those on the other side. They believe those in the other bubble to be, naïve, uninformed, deluded, evil, small-minded or just plain stupid. When discussing the arguments of those in the opposing political filter bubble, mischaracterised "strawman" arguments are used.

Political Issue	What the left believes about the right	What the right believes about the left
Climate Change	Fuck the planet! We just want to make money! — They're uneducated morons who believe climate change is a hoax!	Fuck the economy! — Save the trees! Fearmongers
Feminism	Misogynists — Women should get back in the kitchen! — "She was asking for it"	Manhaters — They want to feminise boys — Feminists are all ugly and unfeminine
Wealth Inequality	Don't care about the poor — Privileged — Born with rich parents	Too lazy to work for a living — Want free handouts — Whiners and Complainers

Inside political filter bubbles, high-quality arguments from the opposing side are hidden from view. It's easy to believe that your views are correct when you've never heard any reasonable counter-arguments. The only counter-arguments those in political filter bubbles know about are low-resolution and poor quality. To those inside these bubbles, it becomes apparently obvious which side is right and which is wrong (After all, the other side have such ridiculous counter-arguments. They must be complete idiots). Yet when real arguments are presented, who's right and who's wrong becomes much less obvious:

A strong right-wing argument about climate change: Technological innovation is the key to solving climate change. It's unrealistic to think that we can convince countries, especially developing ones, to halt carbon emissions in the name of protecting the planet.

A strong left-wing argument about climate change: Endless growth on a limited planet isn't a sustainable way to live. There are potential environmental "feedback loops" that could spiral out of control if we don't make an effort to curb our CO2 emissions.

A strong right-wing argument about feminism: Men are more often homeless, do dangerous jobs, graduate less from university and get terrible deals in divorce court. Most men are not CEO's and are not particularly privileged. Men are privileged in some areas, women are privileged in other areas. The idea of "the patriarchy" is simplistic and reductionist.

A strong left-wing argument about feminism: Women shouldn't have to feel unsafe when walking home at night. Women should not be forced to be mothers, housewives and caretakers if they don't want to. Women are capable of occupying positions of power and doing an excellent job.

A strong right-wing argument about wealth inequality: Wealth inequality is inevitable. We cannot fix poverty by simply handing out cheques. Capitalism creates wealthy societies and the only way to achieve wealth equality is to make everyone equally poor.

A strong left-wing argument about wealth inequality: The richest people in the world hold more money than they could ever hope to spend themselves. And the top 1% constantly avoid paying the tax they owe to the society in which they made their profits. Too much wealth inequality creates unstable societies.

Many of those inside political filter bubbles live in a reality where half of the arguments presented above don't exist. Just think about it, when was the last time you saw anybody on social media discussing political issues in any kind of depth. Occasionally this happens, but the majority of the social media landscape is filled with strawman arguments of the opposing side.

Social media is a new technology. We don't yet fully understand what it is and how to use it responsibly. If people become aware of the effects of political filter bubbles on social media, then perhaps they'll become a more sophisticated political activist — one that engages in legitimate and fair discussion with those of opposing views. If we don't become aware of how social media splits societies in-half, then can expect more polarisation, more violent protests and perhaps even civil war. Societies around the world: Brazil, France, Australia, Argentina, the UK and America have the exact same problem — everyone is inside the very same social media environment and similar political filter bubbles are present in every democratic society around the world. It's time that we began to understand how these political filter bubbles are affecting our own psychology and our societies.

the fatlogic filter bubble

39% of adults around the world are now overweight. This isn't a problem restricted only to western countries—this is a global problem. More deaths are now caused by obesity than starvation. Our ancestors, who dealt with famine on a regular basis, could have never imagined that we would now have the exact opposite problem. This obesity epidemic is going to cause huge problems

for healthcare systems around the world and health organisations everywhere are struggling to figure out how to deal with this enormous problem.

Amongst the madness, technology has given birth to a strange new monster we've never seen before — The FatLogic filter bubble. The Fatlogic filter bubble believes the following:

1. *Being fat is not unhealthy*

2. *People should be able to eat whatever they like, look however they like and continue to be treated equally to everybody else.*

3. *Doctors are fatphobic and cannot be trusted.*

4. *The body has a "set weight point" and losing weight is impossible for particular people. All weight loss attempts will eventually backfire.*

5. *We should "eat intuitively". In other words, we should eat what we feel like eating at all times.*

6. *The only reason fat people feel unattractive is because of our fatphobic culture.*

Fatlogic is an ideology. Many of its proponents will call it : Body positivity, Fat Acceptance, Fat positive or Intuitive eating. Like all popular ideologies, all of them have large amounts of truth within them: We do live in a somewhat "fatphobic" society. Diet culture can be toxic. Women are bombarded with images of women with an unrealistic beauty standard (as discussed in chapter 1). And women shouldn't despise themselves for being overweight. The problem is, the internet creates digital echo chambers that take all sets of ideas to their extreme end points and can drag unsuspecting people into a toxic ideology that has the potential to ruin their life.

I hope that every single overweight person who reads this has the mental strength to accept the reality of the situation so that they can improve their lives for real instead of chasing the shadows of happiness. It's also my hope that those of you who are not overweight understand this issue in greater depth instead of simply proclaiming *"Haha fat people are stupid"* I want to deal with this emotionally charged issue in a calm, logical manner that will bring clarity.

Online echo chambers or filter bubbles, whether it's TheRedPill, Feminism, Looksmaxing or Fatlogic all work in exactly the same way. They start with an initial set of assumptions and eventually take them to their end conclusions. One of the central assumptions of the Fatlogic filter bubble is that human-beings are a blank slate and we learn everything we know through a process of socialisation. This assumption, of course, is entirely false. When you build an ideology on top of a false assumption, you get all kinds of strange conclusions when you take the ideology to its extreme end point. For example, if obese people are unhealthy, it must be due to the fatphobic society that we live in and has absolutely nothing to do with the biological realities of eating unhealthy foods. One Instagram post reads: *"You don't need to protect your child from being fat. You need to protect them from diet culture. "*. On Another post on Tumblr writes: *If your weight loss is about "health" why are you posting before and after photos? Because it's not about healthy. It's about achieving the thin ideal in a fatphobic society."* An even more absurd Instagram post says: *"What if we let our bodies decide what they weight instead of society"*

Inside online filter bubbles, there's no push-back from opposing points of view. Because one of the main ideas in the fatlogic filter bubbles is that everything in society is learned through socialisation, we can supposedly "decide" what our own weight is. Any arguments that discuss the realities of biology don't enter into the bubble, which leads to all kinds of strange conclusions. Inside the Fatlogic bubble, people continue to agree with each other, and without any push-back from outside the bubble, ideas begin become more and more non-nonsensical. In the

Fatlogic echo chamber, like all echo chambers, certain factors of an issue are consistently emphasised and others are consistently downplayed. Those inside the Fatlogic echo chamber will continually emphasise the negatives of "toxic diet culture", but the suggestion that you could lose weight *without* resorting to a fad diet is never mentioned.

Fatlogic messages can be found on all prevalent social media sites, Instagram, Twitter, Tumblr and others. Millions of teenage girls and boys, many of whom are struggling with their weight, are being exposed to these messages. *Why restrict my eating if being fat isn't unhealthy? If all diets fail and it's impossible to lose weight, why bother changing my eating habits? Why would I listen to my fatphobic doctor when they tell me to lose weight? If I can't find a boyfriend/girlfriend it must be because we live in a fatphobic culture.* These are the dangerous conclusions people come to after consuming Fatlogic content.

Now, in order to truly burst this particular filter bubble once and for all, we need to get right down to the very core of the issue. The bubble claims that our "diet culture" causes society to treat fat people badly. But is this actually true? Because the central assumption inside this filter bubble is that we learn everything we know through socialisation, any examination of biology (especially evolutionary biology) has been completely left outside the bubble. In other words, inside the bubble everything that human-beings are is due to *nurture* and *nature* has no part to play.

Who we're attracted to is not random. Nor is it because we're "taught" who we should find attractive by society. Men don't find certain women physically attractive because of the media images they

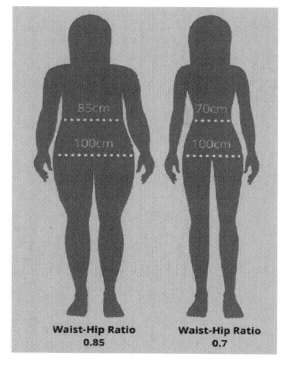

see (although these do play a role). Instead, men generally find women attractive based on their ability to give birth to healthy children. Clear skin, big breasts, full lips, sharp cheek bones and a waist-hip ratio of around 0.7 are all signifiers of a healthy woman capable of giving birth to a healthy child. Through a process of evolution, men who chose women with these physical traits spread more of their genes onto the next generation through healthy children. It's called sexual selection, and it's a selection process found throughout the animal kingdom. And let's not forget, humans are animals too.

"When you are attracted to someone else,

LEFT: THE FIDDLER CRAB. FEMALES CHOOSE MATES LARGELY BASED ON THE SIZE OF IT'S CLAW. CRABS WITH LARGE CLAWS ARE MORE LIKELY TO HAVE SEX AND PASS ON THEIR GENES THAN THOSE WITH SMALL CLAWS.

RIGHT: THE PEACOCK. FEMALES CHOOSE MATES LARGELY BASED ON THE VIBRANCY OF COLOUR ON THE PEACOCK'S TAIL. MALES WITH LESS VIBRANT TAILS ARE LESS LIKELY TO HAVE SEX AND PASS ON THEIR GENES.

HUMANS AREN'T FIDDLER CRABS OR PEACOCKS, BUT YOU CAN THINK OF THE WAIST-HIP RATIO IN WOMEN AND THE SHOULDER-WAIST RATIO IN MEN IN THE SAME WAY AS THE FIDDLER CRAB'S CLAW AND THE PEACOCK'S TAIL.

or when you're decidedly not attracted to someone, you are engaged in sophisticated scientific enquiry. There's nothing shallow about it; it's as deep as it gets"
- Catherine Shanahan, M.D in her book
Deep Nutrition

Men don't know why they find these things so attractive. They have no idea that there are ancient, subconscious, evolutionary mechanisms at play every time they look at a woman, all they know is that they like what they see. One study looked at the body measurements of 1068 female escorts from across 48 countries in Asia, North America, South America, Oceania and Europe and found that the average waist-hip ratio was 0.72. Another study used congenitally blind men (men who have been blind since the day they were born) to use their hands to feel women's bodies and judge which bodies they liked the most. The study found that, once again, these blind men preferred bodies with a waist-hip ratio of 0.7. Men's preference for women with a waist-hip ratio of 0.7 is found in cultures from across the world, including incredibly remote cultures that have never been exposed to western culture or western media. On the other hand, women find men with a shoulder-waist ratio of 1.6 particularly attractive. This preference is also cross-cultural. What does this mean for people who are overweight or obese? Carrying excess weight moves women away from the ideal hip-waist ratio of 0.7 and moves men away from the ideal ratio of 1.6. In this way, being overweight or obese makes an individual less attractive in the eyes of the vast majority of people.

When it comes to faces, women with thin jaws and high cheekbones are generally rated as the most attractive. For men, a prominent jawline is generally considered a highly attractive feature. When an individual gains excess fat, these important facial features are hidden behind layers of fat. None of this is to say that appearance is the final word on attractiveness. Behaviour is also an incredibly important measure of attractiveness (particularly in men), and compatible personalities are far more important than appearance if you're searching for a long-term relationship. People can certainly have what you might call a "beautiful personality" that others can fall in love with. The point being made here is that we're evolutionary wired to have a negative reaction to excess fat. And that's the reason people tend to act in a fatphobic manner.

"The genes hold culture on a leash"
- E.O. WIlson

Another Instagram user confidently writes: *"We don't come into the world preferring thinness. The belief that thinness is better is not innate for any of us. We*

Jawline hidden by excess fat.

Prominant jawline visible

Upon casting our eyes upon an individual with excess facial fat, we instantly and instinctively recognise it as a sign of poor health, therefore our attraction to this individual is massively diminished.

This isn't fatphobia, it's a perfectly normal human brain mechanism that we're all born with.

The lack of excess facial fat on this individual is a sign of *normal health* (although a lack of excess fat doesn't necessarily guarantee good health).

Chin hidden by excess fat

Prominant chin

While this woman has plenty of attractive features (clear eyes, straight teeth, healthy-looking hair), the excess facial fat lowers her attractiveness in the eyes of most people.

While she certainly isn't obese, human beings instinctively know the difference between a normal amount of fat and excess fat.

The lack of excess facial fat doesn't necessarily make this woman attractive, but it does mean that her appearance doesn't suffer the negative consequences of too much fat.

While some of this might seem quite obvious, I'm trying to get you to understand attraction from an evolutionary perspective. All too often we tell ourselves feel-good lies like "beauty is in the eye of the beholder" that completely ignore the reality that appearance, to a large extent, can be judged objectively. Most people roughly agree on what's attractive and what's not.

are taught that being thinner is better." But of course, we don't prefer thinness, we prefer healthy bodies.. After all, we're also naturally unattracted to anorexic bodies. Once again, because the central assumption of the Fatlogic filter bubble is that human-beings are born as blank slates, the only reasonable conclusion for our aversion to overweight people is that we were "taught" to feel that way.

Fatphobia is real. Society will generally treat you worse if you're overweight. You'll get hired less for jobs. You'll be less popular. You'll face discrimination based on your weight. And it will be harder for you to find a romantic partner. But it doesn't matter how much you might complain and campaign against fatphobia, it's never going away completely because it's ingrained into our DNA.

Another large part of this fatlogic filter bubble is the "Healthy At Every Size" (HAES) movement. During the COVID19 pandemic, one of main co-morbidities that led to death from the virus was obesity. Aside from this, obesity increases the risk of the following health problems: Type 2 Diabetes, high blood pressure, heart disease, stroke, cancer, sleep apnea, osteoarthritis, fatty liver disease, kidney disease, pregnancy problems and endless of others. (No, these conditions are not created by the psychological effects of "weight stigma". They're caused by the biological condition of obesity) From the very start, to even use the phrase "healthy at every size" seems completely inaccurate when certain body weights, either overweight or underweight, are strongly correlated with poor health. While being overweight doesn't necessarily mean you're less healthy than the thin person across the room, it does mean that you're at a higher risk (on average) for all of the health problems above. Of course, for those inside the fatlogic echo chamber, any doctor who suggests losing weight as a method of reducing the risks of these health problems is simply fatphobic. It isn't only doctors who seem to be aware of the strong link between obesity and health problems, health insurance companies charge obese people more because they're more of a liability. More worrying still, the emerging field of epigenetics has discovered that people who became overweight during their own lifetime are directly passing on genes to their children that make them more likely to be obese themselves.

Our ancestors weren't obese. Type 2 diabetes was totally unheard of throughout history until the 20th century. Human beings aren't supposed to be obese. Obesity is a condition that affects the entire body - your internal organs, your ankles, your outer appearance and even your brain. Your body wasn't built to endure so much excess fat. Obese patients usually slowly deteriorate over time and die earlier (on average). Others will die suddenly of a heart attack or stroke at the age of 50 (which are far more likely in obese people). But even before their death, an obese person will usually have a massively diminished quality of life. No sport, no partying, bad sex, mood problems and low energy. Want to travel and see the world? Good luck. Want to go surfing? Good luck.

Why do those inside the fatlogic filter bubble continue to insist that being overweight is healthy despite the massive amounts of evidence to the contrary? I'd like to pose a theory. A hunch, if you will. Sugar has been shown in experiments to be incredibly addictive to rats and the same effect is clearly present in humans. Our world is absolutely filled with sugary foods (More on the food industry in a later chapter). My theory is as follows: The fatlogic filter bubble made up of a collection of food addicts who are engaging in *addiction rationalisation.*

"To an outsider the behaviour of an addict is completely irrational. Alcohol or drugs is obviously destroying their life yet they continue to engage in this activity. Even when the substance abuse is pulling the individual towards an early grave, or causing problems for loved ones, they persist with it. Those who have never been dependent on an addictive substance will see this behaviour as highly irrational. They do not have the addict's ability to rationalise the irrational in order to explain away their own self destruction. This individual is not wilfully doing something to cause harm to themselves or other people. As far as they are concerned what they are doing is right. This is why directly challenging the substance abuse will often be ineffective because it just puts the addict on the defensive"

Rationalisation is one of the mostly deadly attributes of addiction. Addicts convince themselves that there's nothing wrong with their behaviour. Addicts who have rationalised their own addiction will go on to convince others of their rationalisation. And when millions of people are connected through the internet, addiction rationalisation can be done on a mass scale. Hence, the Fatlogic echo chamber. Is it possible that a psychological defence mechanism could present itself on a mass scale on the internet? Personally, I would say yes.

One Instagram post reads: ***"Old Mindset:*** *You should only eat when you are LEGIT hungry otherwise it's unnecessary.* **New Mindset:** *Hunger cues are just one reason you can give yourself permission to eat"*. But so called "intuitive eating" doesn't make much sense when we live in an environment filled with addictive foods. Our "intuition will constantly be craving unhealthy foods. We must make rational, calculated decisions with food because our intuition around food has been hijacked by the modern food industry.

the looksmaxxing filter bubble

"The inventor of the mirror poisoned the human heart" - Fernando Pessoa

The silvered-glass mirror was invented in 1835 by Justus von Liebig — for the first time in history ordinary people could afford a mirror of their own and we haven't been the same since. No longer were we looking at ourselves in the vivid reflection of water's surface. From now on we would be able to see our reflection every single morning, in mirrors and in the front camera of our smartphone. From now on we would be critiquing, dissecting, finding flaws and obsessing over every detail of our own faces and bodies.

Technology moved from the mirror to the photograph. From the photograph to digital photograph. From the digital camera to the in-built camera in our smartphones. The story of body image arrives here in 2020. With the introduction of social media we now see our own faces and bodies more than any humans in history. While our hunter gather ancestors would have been largely unaware of their own appearance, we're exposed to our own appearance on a daily basis. In bathroom mirrors, in the photos we're tagged in and on our smartphone screens as we spin that camera around into selfie mode. *In the modern day we spend a strange amount of time looking at our own faces and our own bodies.*

And no wonder. In the modern world your appearance is incredibly important in many aspects of your life. Your aesthetics (especially your facial aesthetics) are a cruel genetic lottery. Some receive all of the incredible advantages of being born beautiful while others are left to suffer the brutally unfair repercussions of being born ugly. Forget racism or sexism. The most widespread discrimination in the modern world is lookism. Can we really call a 10/10, drop-dead gorgeous black woman "oppressed"? Can we truly claim that a 5'0 tall, balding, chubby, ugly white man is "privileged"? Given the importance of looks in our society — it figures that there are online communities taking drastic measures in order to improve their aesthetics.

A first glance at the looksmax.me forum front page shows forum posts with titles such as: "Jaw Fillers", "A pill to make you taller", "How to pull you Maxilla forward", *"What is your mouth width in mm?"* and *"leg-lengthening 5,7 – 5,9 worth it?"*. Each post is filled with users giving each other tips on how to achieve their aesthetic goals. One user shows images of his "zygo implants, which are implants that go inside the mouth to change the shape of the jaw. Another user shows the results of his "neck training" in order to get a thicker neck.

Looksmax.me
Aesthetics matter.

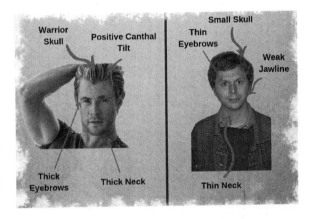

While women having been getting plastic surgery for a long time, Looksmaxers are exclusively men. Looksmaxing is an online community of men who are dedicated to improving their appearance - by any means necessary. They are closely linked to the now well-known Incel and "Black Pill" communities, and like many internet rabbit holes, this one has its own ideology. It goes like this: Looks are everything. Facial aesthetics are the most important part of life. Not only for dating, but for life in general. If you're ugly, you have to do everything in your power to make yourself beautiful. That includes reasonable "softmaxing" techniques such as skincare, haircuts, hitting the gym and so on. But if the "softmaxing" techniques aren't enough, you need to start "hardmaxing" "Hardmaxing" involves everything from plastic surgery to growth hormones. Whatever it takes to look good. Health be damned. Integrity be damned. Users will post images of themselves and other users will provide feedback on their appearance, as well as suggestions for which facial surgery they need. Looksmaxers suggest all kinds of plastic surgery: rhinoplasty, canthoplasty, cheek bone implants, acne scar laser surgery, sliding genioplasty, orbital rim implants, leg lengthening, otoplasty, overbite surgery orthognahic surgery, eyebrow lifts and countless others. Any other suggestions for improving your life, such as improving in your career, socialising more or improving your character are classified as "cope", i.e. lying to yourself in order to make yourself feel better

So that's Looksmaxing. Just one of many insane rabbit holes or filter bubbles that the internet has created. Those in the Looksmaxing community are the most extreme cases of people who are hyper-focused on aesthetics, but this idea isn't only limited to this fringe group. Men across the world secretly have this idea: that aesthetics are the most important thing about attracting women. And perhaps even the most important part of life itself. What do you think? Do you need to be attractive to have a good-life? Do you need to be visually pleasing in order to date the women you want? If you search within yourself, you might find that your honest answer to those questions is: Yes. You might find that when you examine your beliefs, you too believe that you need to be good-looking in order to have the life you want. And if you do feel that way, you're not alone. But I'd like to propose to you the idea that you may have formed these beliefs around appearance not through real-world experience, but through the use of media and technology. I'll do my best to go to the core of the ideology in the centre of the looksmaxing filter bubble and destroy it.

HOLLYWOOD

Isn't it amazing how similar most of the lead male actors in Hollywood are in appearance? White skin, dark hair and handsome (with some exceptions from other races). Strangely enough, there are far less blonde or redhead lead male actors. Most lead Hollywood actors have either

a positive or a neutral canthal tilt. Very rarely does a lead actor have a negative canthal tilt. (what is a negative canthal tilt? Eyes where the corner of the eye closest to the nose is higher than the opposite corner. This causes a kind of downwards slow, tired-eyed, droopy eyed effect. In contrast with the sharp, so-called "hunter eyes"—positive canthal tilt—of actors like George Clooney and Gerard Butler).

But it's not just the canthal tilt. Lead male Hollywood actors also tend to have high cheekbones, deep-set eyes, a compact midface, warrior skulls and many other aesthetic features. Take a look at almost any scene from a Hollywood movie and you can usually tell immediately who is the main character and who are the side characters. From appearance alone.

AT A GLANCE, WHO IS THE MAIN CHARACTER OF THIS MOVIE? AND WHO ARE THE SIDE CHARACTERS?

There are no clues from how the characters are arranged on screen. But it's immediately obvious that Tom Cruise (left) is the main character of the show. Granted, you may be familiar with the Mission Impossible franchise that this shot was taken from. Nevertheless, judging by the dark hair full head of hair and the attractive facial features (including the positive canthal tilt) it's obvious who's the main character. Simon Pegg (right), with his receding hairline and less attractive facial features couldn't possibly be the lead character of a Hollywood action movie. Predictably, Simon Pegg is the "nerd" character of this movie.

LEFT: THE WARRIOR
SKULL
RIGHT: THE WIMP
SKULL

While the lead actors of action movies usually have a warrior skull, nerd characters almost always have a "wimp skull".

So why do these patterns emerge across so many Hollywood movies? Money. Hollywood runs on profit. Creating great movies is secondary to producing a reliable profit from each movie it churns out. When it costs $100,000,000 to produce a Hollywood blockbuster no producer is going to risk playing with the tried and tested conventions that have successfully produced a profit in the past. If a casting director is looking for the lead actor of an action movie, they're going to look for all of the typical facial features you're used to finding on action heroes. Very few casting directors of a Hollywood movie are going to take a chance on casting an unattractive and wimpy looking man as an action hero. They're going to stick to the conventions that have worked before. The facial aesthetics of each character on-screen have to reflect their role within the movie. The hero has to look like a hero, and the side characters have to look like side characters. Otherwise mainstream audiences may become confused about each character's role. In Hollywood, facial aesthetics reflect an individual's role. But in the real-world they do not. In the real world an ugly man with poor facial aesthetics can be a hero saving a baby from a burning building. In the real world a handsome man with attractive facial aesthetics can be a scardy-cat who's afraid of heights.

You watch these Hollywood movies again and again. For decades. The ideas and patterns in these movies are gradually buried within your subconscious. Overtime (unnoticed by you) a quiet assumption begins to build in your mind: You begin to believe that if you want to be the lead actor of your own life then you have to look a certain way. You believe that if you look more like a Hollywood side character, then you should act as a side character in your real life. Perhaps you don't follow your highest dreams. Perhaps you don't ask that girl out, because subconsciously you believe that you're a side character. And that's not what side characters do. No. You won't ask that girl out. You'll wait. Wait until you're good-looking enough to approach her. *Only once your appearance matches that of the main characters you've seen on screen can you give yourself permission to act as the main character in your own life.* This is the subconscious mechanism that has been instilled in the heads of millions of men by Hollywood, which leads to many men believing they can't have the life they want unless they look a particular way. Hence, the Looksmaxing community.

ONLINE DATING

In the real world, behaviour is the biggest measure of attractiveness for men. On online dating, appearance is the biggest measure of attractiveness for men. The problem is, people look at which men women choose on online dating platform and assume that this is the reality about what women like. But online dating is not a reflection of reality. It's a distortion of reality. On online dating you look at people frozen still. The digital photograph freezes time. There is no movement. No body language. No vocal tonality. No eye contact. Only appearance. In the real world, people aren't frozen still. They're in motion. They're gesturing with their hands. They're funny. Or they're not funny. They're interesting. Or they're not interesting. They make eye-contact. Or they don't make eye contact. They're charming. Or they're arrogant. And most importantly, each individual has a particular vibe that you can feel coming off of them. A photograph strips an individual everything except their appearance. The photograph is a very strange medium to view another person through **(Law 1: The Medium Is The Message)**

Looksmaxers like to use "chadfishing" tinder experiments in order to prove their point. For these experiments, they take an image of a highly attractive male model and pair it up with profile filled with a purposefully misogynistic and unappealing description. Yet plenty of women still respond to these profiles, which is proof that the only thing women care about in a man is their aesthetic appearance. They assume that an experiment like this is an accurate reflection of reality. But someone who molests children (as this fake male model claims to have done in his bio) would likely have an incredibly creepy demeanour in the real world. A child molester would probably have strange mannerisms and off-putting body language. Because surprisingly enough, child molesters don't tend to be particularly normal people.

HONEST SIGNALS

The PUA community (pick up artists)—who get their information through real-world experience rather than through the distorted lens of technology—often talk about honest signals. When women are assessing the attractiveness of a man, they're looking for traits that will increase her and her future children's chance of survival. Confidence, high status

THE SPRINGBOK SHOWS OFF ITS ABILITY TO JUMP WHEN PREDATORS ARE NEARBY. IT'S AN HONEST SIGNAL THAT SAYS "YOU WON'T BE ABLE TO CATCH ME, SO DON'T EVEN TRY"

behaviour, physical strength, social skills and congruence. Just like the springbok showing off it's jump, women look for sexual honest signals from men.

Honest signals are attributes that are very difficult to fake. A confident demeanour. Strong eye- contact. Relaxed body language. Deep resonant vocal tonality. How others react to a man in a social setting. A man who has resources. Leadership. Indifference. And yes, an attractive face and body. This is a law of nature that applies throughout the animal kingdom called signalling theory. Woman subconsciously search for honest signals of an attractive man. Any man can lie, using their vocal chords and tongue, about how they're rich, confident and high status, but they can't lie about unconscious behaviours such as body language, strong eye-contact or a resonant vocal tonality. These positive honest signals are incredibly attractive to women.

The problem with online dating is that it doesn't allow men to communicate many honest signals. The main thing that women are biologically evolved to look for is very difficult to communicate through the images and text that online dating platforms allow. The only honest signal that can be communicated properly through online dating is appearance, therefore appearance is the most important factor in online dating, But things don't necessarily work the same way in the real world, where the full range of honest signals are available. This is the subtle way in which technology changes the way you think. The Looksmaxing ideology only holds truth in the alternate world of technology, but simply doesn't hold up in the real world. Some might claim that online dating is changing the way women think — that online dating has influenced female psychology and that now they have much higher standards for a man's appearance than before. But honest signals have been a part of human psychology for hundreds of millions of years. In fact, honest signals are so old that they're older than human race itself. In the real world, true confidence, being high status, a resonant vocal tonality, strong eye-contact and relaxed body language will always attract women.

PICK UP ARTIST RSD TYLER PROVES THAT IT'S POSSIBLE TO BE SUCCESSFUL WITH WOMEN DESPITE BEING LESS THAN GIFTED IN THE LOOKS DEPARTMENT.

The Looksmaxing ideology can be found on Lookism.net and across other platforms where the broader Incel ideology is present. The Youtube algorithm also does a good job of dragging unsuspecting men into the bubble by suggesting Looksmaxing videos in the "recommended for you" section. In the Looksmaxing bubble, people continually validate each other's ideas. Users in this bubble certainty don't agree with each other all the time (in fact they're constantly abusing one another), but they all agree with the basic premises of the ideology. Eventually an ideology with thousands of believers is created. Gradually, thousands of men are drawn to the conclusion that the only route to happiness is through some kind of plastic surgery. *A conclusion they would have never come to were it not for the media presence in their lives.* This is what filter bubbles do, they take the person you once were and bend it to fit the algorithms.

chapter 11

HOW TO LIVE IN THE NEW WORLD

The world around him was breaking apart. As for his friends, his loved ones, they were all separated in their own information bubbles, in a world of alternative facts and narratives to his own. The streets were mostly desolate and empty, people stayed in the darkness of their homes with a virtual reality headset stuck almost permanently to their faces. Sex technology and pornography was rampant, marriages non-existent. Billions played a single online game - "second life". The people around him not wearing a headset shuffled past him without emotion. The buildings around him crumbled from lack of maintenance.

Yet he walked through the city with a smile on his face. His brain, not damaged by the constant-hyper stimulation of technology, was able to find pleasure in the mundane reality around him. He breathed the real, fresh air into his lungs, felt the sunlight hit his face and used his eyes to look at the reality around him. Despite the chaos of the world surrounding him, he felt content. He wasn't sad, nor was he ecstatically happy, but his mind was calm. He had made his choice a long time ago – to live in alignment with his own nature as best as he possibly could. And he knew deep in his gut, he had made the right choice.

media diet – the key to a fulfilled life in the 21st century

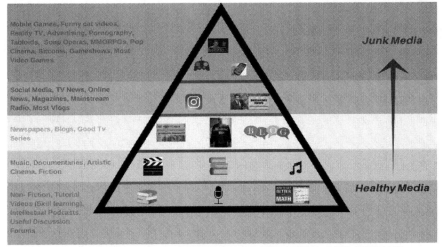

IF YOU DISAGREE WITH ANY SECTION OF THE MEDIA-DIET PYRAMID, THAT'S FINE. GO AHEAD AND CREATE YOUR OWN ONE.

Nobody thinks the media affects them. Yet the media affects everyone.

Just stop for a minute. Breathe. Because you've been in a media frenzy for the last 10 years. And you didn't even notice. Think How many hours do you think you spend staring at screens every day consuming media? How many per week? Per year? Whether its staring at your smartphone. watching Youtube videos, using dating apps, watching movies, leaving comments, posting on Instagram, listening to music or watching TV news. Just what percentage of your life is spend consuming media? How much of your life do you spend sat still staring at screens? Consider the fact that outside of work and sleep *we almost always decide to spend the majority of the rest of our time consuming or engaging with media.* Yet simultaneously people often adamantly deny any possible affects the media has on them.

Why do most people take no consideration into the effects the media they consume may be having on them? Well, would a fish take much time to consider the effect water is having on it? We don't notice the effects of media because it's simply so pervasive, and so much a part of normal life. You probably see media simply as a part of everyday life. You scroll Facebook. You sit on the sofa and watch TV. You play video games. *This is life right?* Well, no actually. In the grand scheme of things, this behaviour is really strange. Up until around 80 years ago, these things were completely alien. Up until around 500 years ago even reading was totally unheard of to most people. The brain evolved to deal with making social connections with your tribe, hunting for food and having sex. It's not particularly well equipped to deal with modern-day media technology.

Media has strange effects on people. Media changes people. And different media has different effects. You can't start playing video games for 25 hours a week and expect to stay the same person as you were before. You can't spend five years looking down at a smartphone and expect to see no effects on your mind and body. Like your nutritional diet, your media diet changes the constitution of your very being, and needs to be treated carefully. Consume too much junk food and you will pay a price. You will feel worse about yourself. You will ruin your health. You will not be able to think clearly. The same is true for consuming junk media. Just like your brain doesn't function properly on a diet of junk food, you won't think clearly if you're consuming massive amounts of junk media. You will get addicted to World of Warcraft. You will get addicted to pornography. You will click on clickbait articles that offer no real information. Netflix binges will eat into your precious free time, comments sections of Youtube videos will infuriate you, your best friend's Instagram account will make you painfully jealous. TV news will make you perpetually scared off the outside world. Meaningless notifications will steal your attention. Advertising will make you feel inadequate.

What are the results of consuming countless hours of junk media? An unfulfilled life. Low self-esteem. Depression. Anxiety. Anger. Frustration. Impaired social skills. An inaccurate world view. Wasted time. *Junk media is bad for your mental health.* Junk media, like junk food, has no nutritional value. Only empty, addictive calories. On top of that, consider the physical reality of consuming so much media: Sat still. Staring into a screen. Your body wasn't made for this. And that's why they sitting is the new smoking. If you're like many people, media will also lessen your quality of sleep as you stay up late into the night with your smartphone screen illuminating the darkness of the room.

Now instead, what happens when you consume healthy media? You become more knowledgeable. You become more interesting. You become more successful. You learn new skills. You get inspired. You get motivated. You feel good. Your self-esteem goes up. You see a side of the world you could have never seen without media. You're exposed to new points of view. And you get to see amazing works of art.

This is the power of taking care of your media diet. They say you are the average of the 5 people you spend the most time with and the same is true for the media influences you surround yourself with.

"We become what we behold. We shape our tools and then our tools shape us" - Marshall Mcluhan

Because our brains are neuroplastic (our brains are constantly adapting to new stimuli), everything we do rearranges the structure of our brain, and that includes media. To put it simply, your brain gets good at doing what you do the most. When you develop a habit of binging Netflix for 2 hours after work every day, your body and your mind will adapt itself to this task. Your physical body will also deteriorate slightly, sitting still on the sofa requires very little muscle tone after all. As you stare at Netflix your mind will rewire itself to suit the task at hand. It will enter a state of passivity each time you watch, and it will develop a habit of doing so. When the time comes and you need your brain to be engaged and pro-active, it won't be quite as adept as it could be.

If you sit down and read a book for an hour every day, you will become someone who can focus on one thing for long periods of time. On the other hand, if you choose to use that time browsing through social media instead, you will become someone who struggles to focus on any one task and finds themselves constantly distracted, no matter what the task at hand is. Overdose on pornography and you will teach your brain to seek arousal from a voyeuristic, outsider perspective rather than being in the scene yourself in an intimate encounter with a real partner. Overdose on Social media and you will teach your brain to seek self-worth from others rather than from yourself. Be exposed to too much advertising and you will teach your brain that you cannot be happy until after you've made your next purchase, instead of simply being happy right now. Follow an over-negative Vlogger or Twitter account and that negativity will leak into your life as well. They say you are what you eat. Well. *You are the media you consume.* Because media is a force that acts upon you and without intervention this force will change who you are.

If you're like most people you will think this is all terribly exaggerated because you feel like you're in control of what you think. And you're right, you are in control. Of your conscious brain. Unfortunately, media also acts on your subconscious brain. This means that it will change your patterns of behaviour and your state of mind without you being aware of it at all. The subconscious brain picks up all information it is given and that includes media. Your conscious brain may consider your 2 hour Netflix binge as just a bit of entertainment outside your real life, but to your subconscious brain everything counts. Your subconscious brain doesn't consider your Netflix binge as separate from who you are. It considers it as a part of you. And will adapt to the task just like it would if you were learning a new language for 2 hours each day. Every piece of media you're exposing your brain to is having an effect. *There are no exceptions.*

social media mindfulness
– a necessity

You're scrolling the Instagram news feed and your perfect friend posts another perfect yoga selfie. Do you feel calm? Or do you feel your emotions being pulled in 1000 different directions all at once? And do you remember how or why you opened Instagram in the first place? You're browsing Youtube. The "recommended for you" side bar offers you another video. Do you feel in control when you click or tap that video without a moments hesitation? Or do you feel like your mind is being tugged and prodded against your will? You're browsing Facebook and come across an outrageous and controversial video. The comments section of the video is a toxic cesspool of ridiculous, unfounded opinions and pure hate. Do you calmly shake your head and move on? Or are you triggered into an hour long keyboard war?

You probably associate the word "mindfulness" with the following image:

But what if I said you could practise mindfulness here?

Mindfullness is about being present. It's about being centred within yourself and non- reactive to what's going on around you. It's about noticing the non-stop chatter that's constantly flooding through your mind. And it's about being aware of what you're doing and what you're thinking. Contrary to popular belief, mindfulness doesn't have to be practised sat cross-legged on a mountaintop. It can be practised at anytime in any situation. You're getting angry at the traffic in front of you; you can focus on the present moment and realise the pointlessness of your anger. You're getting bitter at your friend's success; you can focus on the present moment and create space around the negative emotions flooding into your mind. You're about to open Facebook for the 7th time today; you can return to the present moment and realise that you're doing this for no reason whatsoever. Yes. Mindfullness can also be practised while we use media. And actually, it desperately needs to be, on an individual and a societal level.

Before I give you the 3 essential practises of media mindfulness, first you need to understand the reality of the situation when it comes to media, and particularly social media.

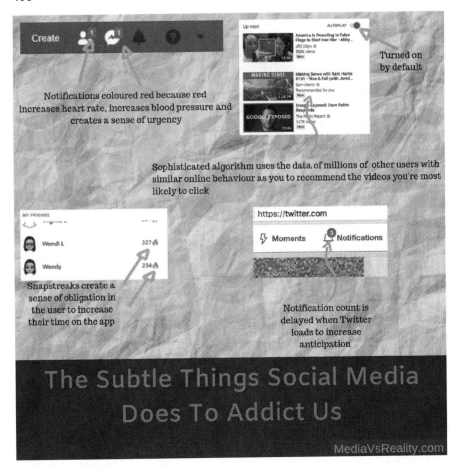

Notifications coloured red because red increases heart rate, increases blood pressure and creates a sense of urgency

Turned on by default

Sophisticated algorithm uses the data of millions of other users with similar online behaviour as you to recommend the videos you're most likely to click

Snapstreaks create a sense of obligation in the user to increase their time on the app

Notification count is delayed when Twitter loads to increase anticipation

The Subtle Things Social Media Does To Addict Us

MediaVsReality.com

Social media isn't on your team. Behind every social media platform, thousands of the world's smartest attention engineers are working their hardest to keep you on their platform for as long as possible. We live an attention economy. The longer social media has your attention, the more money they make. Having your eyeballs on their platform means more money for their advertisers and more of your data to sell to other companies. Social media is a powerful attention monster. Everyday it eats the attention of millions of individuals around the world and then coughs out money for the business owners. (**Law 4: Media Is About Profit**). And it's not only the platform itself. Every single news story and advertisement on the newsfeed is a click funnel that profits by making users click. Not to mention your friends posts and stories, which utilise your natural urge to compare yourself to other human beings.

For most people, the drawbacks of social media far outweigh the benefits. But you can be different. First, you need to stop underestimating what you're up against every time you open social media. Understand the reality that social media isn't on your team. Understand that social media has an agenda that doesn't match up with your own. Second, you need your own techniques to counter-act the techniques used by the attention engineers.

You need to implement the 3 essential practises of social media mindfulness.

1.   The Conscious Click

2.   Set An Intention

3.   Watch Yourself

If you think any of the techniques below are silly or unnecessary, it's only because you're underestimating what you're up against when you use social media.

1. THE CONSCIOUS CLICK

Up next   AUTOPLAY

 Funny Cats Compilation 😺😺   ⋮
Best Funny Cat Videos 2018
Just smile ⊘
2.4M views

PAUSE HERE.

THE CONSCIOUS CLICK: PAUSING FOR A FULL 5 SECONDS BEFORE YOU CLICK (OR TAP) ANYTHING ON SOCIAL MEDIA.

It's that simple. If you see a video on the Youtube side bar, hover your cursor over the video. Don't click yet. Pause. Wait. Become present. Is this click worth my time? Do I want to click this? If you have 4 notifications on Facebook, wait before you check them. Pause. Breathe. Become present. Then decide if they're worth checking or not. When using social media, every single click should be done consciously. This also includes each scroll of the news feed. Scroll once. Then pause for 5 seconds. Breathe.

Then scroll again. In these 5 seconds, you can change your mind and decide not to click. Overtime, you will develop the ability to hover your cursor over your notifications and then decide not to check them. Once you've developed this ability, you're able to take control of your social media use instead of the other way around.

This simple change in behaviour will reverse the frantic unconscious behaviour patterns you've developed. The behaviour patterns that lead you down social media rabbit holes and waste hours and hours of your time. If you find yourself clicking things without knowing why you clicked them, you've failed.

Try implementing the conscious click into your online behaviour and notice how your state of mind shifts. Instead of letting the algorithms decide what you click, implementing the conscious click means that you decide. 90% of social media is garbage. Don't hand out your clicks so easily to those who don't deserve it. (The exact same rules apply for each time you tap your smartphone with your finger. The Conscious Tap if you will)

2. KNOW YOUR INTENTION

KNOW YOUR INTENTION: DECIDING ON A PURPOSE BEFORE OPENING SOCIAL MEDIA AND THEN STICKING TO IT.

Social media platforms are a dense jungle and your intention is your compass. Social media is full of clickbait, attention seekers and addictive notifications. Without a compass you'll get lost in the digital jungle. What is your purpose for opening social media? To check messages from your boss? - Great. Head straight to the messages and check those messages. Do not scroll the newsfeed. Do not stalk your friends profiles. Do not check your 3 notifications. Fulfil your intention. Then get out. Your intention is to see a new video from your favourite Youtube creator? Awesome. Navigate straight to the video. Watch it. Then close Youtube. Do not click any recommenced videos. Do not check notifications. And for god sake don't read the comments. Fulfil your intention. Then get out. Want to post a new tweet? - Super. Go directly to your Twitter profile. Post the tweet. Then close Twitter. Do not check notifications. Do not scroll the

Twitter feed. Do not check the trending hashtags. Fulfil your intention. Then get out. Sometimes you will stray away from your intention. Don't worry. Notice that you've strayed. Then return back to your intention.

Setting an intention is the difference between you using social media and social media using you. Without intention (your compass) you're going to get lost in the digital jungle. And who knows how long it will take you to emerge back out again. 10 minutes? 20 minutes? 1 hour? 3 hours? And this digital jungle is filled with hypnotic snakes that will try to steal your attention and your time. So don't look them in the eyes. Keep your eyes on your feet and follow your intention to the end.

NOTIFICATIONS/ CLICKBAIT/ FRIEND'S POSTS/ RECOMMENDED VIDEOS RIGHT: USER WHO DID NOT STICK TO THEIR INTENTION. THE JUNGLE BOOK (1967)

The analogy of the hypnotic snake in the jungle might seem silly until you consider the last time you opened Youtube to watch a single video and woke up an hour later wondering what the hell happened. Was this not a hypnotic state? Of course, there are some benefits to getting lost in social media; you can sometimes stumble upon valuable content. No problem, if you want to decide to let the algorithms take you into the rabbit hole then feel free, as long as this is your intention.

WATCH YOURSELF

WATCH YOURSELF: CONTINUALLY CHECKING IN WITH YOURSELF WHILE USING SOCIAL MEDIA.

Social media has the ability to pull your emotions in a thousand different directions at once. Jealousy. Anger. Laughter. FOMO. Pride. Desire.

Intrigue. There are pockets on social media that are filled with positivity. But for the most part social media encourages negative emotions.

Mindfulness is the practise of watching your thoughts and emotions from a 3rd person perspective. It's noticing when you feel negative emotions and understanding why you're feeling them.so you're scrolling Instagram and you're having negative feelings about your current life situation. You need to notice that. You need to notice when social media is affecting your emotions in a negative way. Notice the negative emotions. Then figure out why you feel that way. You'll probably realise that the reason for your negative emotions is that you've spent the last 10 minutes seeing images of people who appear to be doing better than you. Watching yourself also applies to your body position. What's your body posture like? Are you slouched over your phone? Is your neck aching? Poor posture results in a poor mental state. See yourself from a 3rd person perspective. What do you look like when you're craning your neck over your phone? Continue to hang your neck over that phone and your bones

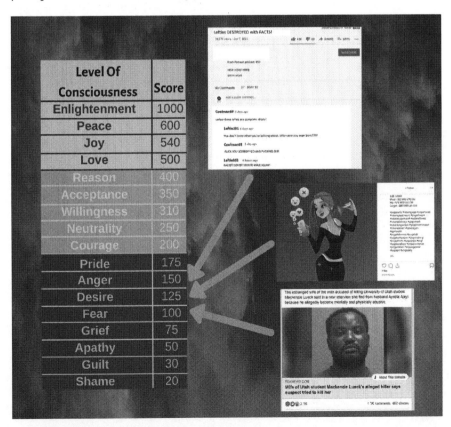

Level Of Consciousness	Score
Enlightenment	1000
Peace	600
Joy	540
Love	500
Reason	400
Acceptance	350
Willingness	310
Neutrality	250
Courage	200
Pride	175
Anger	150
Desire	125
Fear	100
Grief	75
Apathy	50
Guilt	30
Shame	20

TABLE COURTESY OF "POWER VS FORCE" BY DAVID R HAWKINS

structure and muscles will adapt to the task: the muscles in your neck will become weak and your spine will develop unnaturally to compensate.

In his book Power Vs Force, David R Hawkins demonstrates the levels of consciousnesses human beings go through and scores them from 0 to 1000. Here is where social media tends to fall on this scale.

Mindfulness teachers believe that people absorb the "frequency" of consciousness that they surround themselves with. If you surround yourself with "frequencies" from 200 to 400 you'll absorb them and become a happier person. If you surround yourself with frequencies between 100-150 (the frequencies usually present in social media), you'll absorb them and they will put you in a negative mood. Instagram is full of frequencies at 125. News articles often operate at 100. The Youtube comments section is frequently at 150. Occasionally, there are spaces on social media that operate between 200 and 400, but in general social media is in the 100 to 150 range. If you want to see the transfer of negative frequencies happen before your eyes, just read through the Youtube comments section and watch the toxic behaviour spread from

VISUAL REPRESENTATION OF THE YOUTUBE COMMENTS SECTION

person to person. *Negative energy is contagious.* In the real world, when your spouse of family member comes home in a bad mood, you feel a negative shift to the vibe in the house. Even the dog may sense the negative energy and immediately go and hide. The negative or toxic mood of those around you affects you too. *Negative energy can pass through screens too.* Just because the other person isn't in the same physical space as you, that doesn't mean you won't absorb their negative energy. If you continue to view negative vloggers on Youtube, or read your negative friend's social media posts on Facebook, these things will bring down your mood too.

creating your own subconscious patterns

"For as a man thinketh in his subconscious mind, so is he" - James Allen: As A Man Thinketh (1903)

If there's one thing you should have learned from this book by now, it's that your subconscious brain absorbs all information it is given. Think of your mind like a garden; you are placing seeds inside your subconscious brain throughout the day based on what you habitually think about. These seeds will grow and manifest themselves in your conscious thoughts and eventually into your actions. Much of what you believe to be your own ideas and thoughts were actually planted there by other actors: parents, friends, culture, society and media.

The media will constantly plant seeds inside your mind that eventually manifest themselves into your day-to-day attitude and behaviour. Some of these seeds may have a positive influence on your life, others may be negative. The problem is, you probably never thought to take control over which seeds you will and won't allow into your subconscious. You plant seeds in your subconscious in two ways: The first kind of seeds are planted based on your own internal dialogue. Are you framing every situation that happens in the real world in a negative light? If so, your consistent negative self-talk will plant negative seeds that will reinforce those negative thoughts.

The second kind of seed is planted through external influences, a major one being the media you consume. The internet in particular is filled with people espousing limiting beliefs. People on message boards explaining why certain things aren't possible, or why it's impossible to be successful, or how the world is unfair and the odds are stacked against you. Anybody interested in studying the concepts of racism, sexism or economic inequality online are frequently bombarded with a victim-mindset ideas, particularly in politically left-wing circles: "The top 1% own as much as the 99% combined", "We live in a tyrannical patriarchy that oppresses women and holds them back from becoming successful", or "We live in a systematically racist culture that ensures black people are stuck in poverty". If you believe any the previous statements, then I'd like to ask you a couple of questions. Are these your ideas, or someone else's? Did you discover these ideas on the internet? Have these ideas had a positive or negative effect on your personal life? Perhaps you instead find yourself inside "The Black Pill" bubble online. If so, you may believe statements such as "Women only want the top 10% of men", or "Women only like good-looking or rich men". Again, are these your ideas or someone else's? And did you pick up these ideas through the internet? If you watch the news (which is overwhelmingly negative, as discussed in chapter 2), you may develop ideas about the world such as "The world is a dangerous place", or "You can't trust anyone". Would you have come to these conclusions if it hadn't been for your constant exposure to news media? Would you have developed these conclusions based only on the people you know in your real life?

> ## "Pick up any paper any day, and you can read dozens of items that could sow seeds of futility, fear, worry, anxiety, and impending doom. If accepted by you, these thoughts of fear could cause you to lose the will for life" – Joseph Murphy: *The Power Of Your Subconscious Mind* (1963)

Do you suffer from anxiety or depression? Do you also watch negative content through media? If so, are these two factors totally unrelated?

Consume negative content through media, and you will plant negative seeds in your subconscious mind. These negative thoughts will go on to control your outward actions in the real world: you won't ask that girl out, you won't try to increase your salary, you won't start that business. The content you watched through media will have planted seeds in your subconscious mind and put limits on what you believe is possible in the real world — you will then live your life within these limits. However, our current access to the internet provides us with a tremendous opportunity. If we use media in a mindful way, *we can begin to take control over which messages we put into our subconscious minds.* We don't live in the TV era any more. You have the ability to create your own filter bubble of positive content. If you're going to engage in media, you can use it to push yourself in the direction you want to go. The algorithms online create a feedback loop, they will continue to suggest content you've watched previously. You can use this feedback loop to your advantage. If you're going to watch videos on Youtube, consume videos containing positive messages that push you in the direction you want to go in your life. The algorithms inside the Youtube recommended videos will then continue to feed you a similar kinds of positive content – the algorithms will create a positive feedback loop for your mind. Like all technology, Youtube is an extension of a part of the human body – the brain. Clicking a positive video is the same as deciding to think positively. Clicking a negative video is the same as deciding to think negatively.

You are determining the course of your life one click at a time. If you can control the urge to click on clickbait, or the urge to watch negative content that justifies your anger, or to be sucked in by fearful content, *then you can begin to reconstruct your own brain in the direction your want.* What do you want your thought patterns to be on a daily basis? You can create them through the content you click on online. The brain is neuroplastic and will listen to the instructions you give it. This is the way to use the internet in the new world of the 21st century. There is more content available than you could ever hope to watch, read or consume. To succeed in the new world, you need to be extremely thoughtful as to which content you will allow into your subconscious and which you will not. The content you consume will shape your brain patterns and, in turn, shape the course of your entire life.

the commandments of
media use

1.   Never to forget that light feeling. When you've been away from your screens for a prolonged period of time.

2.   Not to underestimate the slow, psychological poison of technology.

3.   Not to chase the shadows cast by your screens at the expense of your life.

4.   Not to rationalise excessive technology use.

5.   To always, at every opportunity, choose the real world and not the digital one.

6.   Your body becomes good at what you teach it to do. If you sit still while your mind is lost in the digital world, then your body shall atrophy. After all, sitting still hunched over a computer doesn't require much muscle tone—so your body will not provide it.

7.   Your mind adapts itself to every task, including consuming media. Watching videos will create a passive mind. Social media will create an unsatisfied mind. Internet browsing creates a distracted mind. There is no "this doesn't count" or "I just do this to relax". For your mind, every single thing you do becomes a part of you.

8.   Not to forget—that human beings are not evolved to sit in a chair and watch screens.

9.   Think of those you've seen in old videos or in poor countries. Their light, steady gaze and easy smiles. Then think of your own twitchy gaze and stiff smile. Ponder on what you've lost.

10.   To notice the slow of time when away from technology.

11. Think of your screen-time in days prior. And realise that almost none of it can be remembered. Time poured into a drain.

12. To always approach technology with intention. This will be your anchor as the winds and whirlpools of the digital world pull on your precious attention.

13. The creators of technology who profit from stealing your time.

14. To switch everything off—and remember how it feels to be alive.

15. Even a perfect digital world could never be as satisfying as the imperfect one you were born into.

16. If they were speaking face to face they wouldn't act like that.

17. The light breeze. The sun on your face. A quiet walk in nature. How they're all a thousand times more fulfilling than the superstimuli found on screens.

18. Never to digitise your human urges.

19. Incels and Hikikomoris—how technology has trapped them in a looping nightmare.

20. The news does not represent the entirety of reality.

21. Their faces as they stare down at their phones.

22. To never click unconsciously.

23. To always, as much as possible, act the same in the digital world as you do in the real world.

24. Screens are not a necessity for a fulfilled life. To think so is an illusion.

25. Like a bolt of lightning or water running downhill, human beings (like all of nature) shall always be inclined to take the path of least resistance. And technology is

the fastest, most accessible path to stimulation. Yet as human beings, we have the choice to delay gratification for a greater reward down the road. Only children and dogs are unable to do so.

26. Life is perceived as short by those who spend it on screens.

27. When has awareness of world events made you happier? And when has your mere awareness had any effect on these events?

28. The dazed feeling after watching television. The scattered feeling after browsing the internet. The feeling of presence when in nature. Choose.

29. The negative emotions they induce in you for their own profit.

30. Like the sheep dog herds the sheep, algorithms herd the humans.

31. The youth of millions - stolen by screens.

32. The fashion in which you interact with your screens shall determine the course of your entire life. There is nothing trivial about it at all.

33. Those who quarrel online do not argue with people. Instead, they quarrel with figments of their own imagination.

34. The producer remembered and rewarded. The consumer punished and forgotten.

35. You do tomorrow as you do today. Watch porn today, you'll repeat the behaviour tomorrow. Play video games today, you'll play them tomorrow. What you do now is what you'll do in the future. If you want to change, change what you do now. Now. Now.

36. "I just do this to pass the time". But why are you "passing time" in the first place? Did you forget that

your time is limited? Did you forget about your death? Now that you've remembered once again, can you still justify spending another hour on your screens?

37. Which is reality? The chaos on your screen, or the quiet peace in the room that surrounds it?

38. You become the media you consume

EPILOGUE

The only thing that could possibly stop our rapid technological advancement is the collapse of the modern world. There is no future in which we rewind the clock and move back into the old world. We are rapidly moving further and further away from the tribal environment we are evolved for. The 90's aren't coming back. Nor are the 80's, or the 70's. If you think things are weird now, just wait. In the next few decades, we can expect: widespread use of virtual reality headsets, an entire second augmented reality layered on top of our physical reality (it already has a name: The Metaverse), AI technology capable of outperforming human-beings at almost every task you can imagine, artificial media (with the use of deepfake technology) that's completely indistinguishable from reality, brain-computer interfaces that allow us to display our imagination onto a screen, fully-functional "smarthouses", robots, nanotechnology capable of performing tasks at the molecular level, instantaneous language technology that allows us to translate any language in real-time as well as countless other technologies that are beyond the limits of our imagination.

Technology is a natural extension of human-beings. Human-beings were created by nature, and technology was created by human-beings. Therefore, technology is a part of nature. Yet despite this fact, we face an enormous problem – that technological progress moves far faster than biological evolution does. Our society is rapidly moving further and further away from the tribal environment the human brain and body is evolved for. This evolutionary mismatch is a recipe for misery, confusion, illness (both mental and physical), dissatisfaction and pain.

Even worse, almost nobody is aware of it. This book utilises the theories and science of evolutionary psychology throughout, yet strangely, the study of evolutionary psychology carries a strange taboo that keeps its wisdom hidden from the world. People are simply too fearful, too politically correct and too afraid to offend others, to look at the harsh truths presented by evolutionary psychology. Yet being unwilling to understand and accept the truths of evolutionary psychology makes it almost impossible to understand the new world.

In the past, our tribal societies were numbered at maximum of around 150 people. In a community of this size, sociopathic behaviour was not an effective method of getting ahead. In the tribes of our past, there were no strangers and there was no anonymity. Try to manipulate someone, rob someone or kill someone and the entire tribe would likely know about it. Any kind of negative action towards other human-beings would have been discovered and punished by the group. But what happens when societies go beyond 150 people? It becomes possible to get away with bad behaviour; behaviour that benefits the individual but negatively effects the group. It also causes an empathy gap between people − it's easier to screw somebody else over when you've never met them before. In our modern societies, with tens of millions of people contained within a single country, you need to be careful of other people screwing you over. One way in which other human-beings will attempt to screw you over in the new world is through the use of media. The creators of media will try to addict you to their platform and steal your money, time and attention, and it's easy for them to do it guilt-free when their victims are anonymous, faceless victims they will never meet face-to-face. *You need to be on guard against powerful organisations and malevolent individuals attempting to manipulate you through media.* And as our world becomes filled with more and more new and magical technologies year by year, you can be sure that others will use them to try benefit themselves at the expense of your finances, peace of mind and mental health.

Despite all the addictive mechanisms, tugs on our attention and the manipulative tactics of media companies, we still live in a free society. Nobody is forcing us to use any piece of technology we don't want to use, and we are still free to make our own choices. This isn't something to be taken for granted, plenty of societies in the past haven't allowed individuals to make their own choices, and there's no guarantee that future societies will continue to do so. While screens can certainly have a powerful influence you on, in the end we're still the ones in a position of power. As Viktor Frankl famously told us: *"Between stimulus and response there is a space. In that space is our power to choose our response. In our response lies our growth and our freedom"*. Between every ping of your smartphone, between every online rabbit hole you go down, between every piece of addictive media that pops up on your screen, is a space. And in this space we can make the choice to exercise our freedom. Cherish this space. This space is what gives you autonomy and makes you a free human being. This is the space where you are allowed to decide. You may feel it almost impossible not to check your smartphone as it pings, but that space of freedom is still available to you if you choose to use it. You can listen to your Smartphone ping from across the room, and then decide *not* to check it. You can read an outrageous political post on Facebook and decide *not* to click it. You can have endless amounts of pornography available to you at the click of a button and still decide *not* to watch it. You are also able to create a lifestyle, surrounding technology, with social events, friends, lovers and stimulating activities (that don't require a screen), to make screens far less magnetic than they otherwise would be.

Even the addicts among you; the gaming addicts, the porn addicts, the social media addicts. Despite the fact that million dollar companies are trying to keep you addicted to their media, you have the ability to change your brain's pathways overtime. You become what you do, and you don't become what you don't do. While quitting a piece of media at first may seem impossible, with consistent efforts (probably with a few relapses along the way), you can restructure your brain so that you no longer *want* to consume your addictive media. Overtime, your brain changes to fit the stimulus around it. You decide what you do, therefore you decide what you become. If 95% of our brain is subconscious, that still leaves 5% of our brain that can be used to consciously change our behavior gradually overtime. While your identity may feel like it's set in stone and unchangeable, it's not. Your identity is a slow moving fluid. If you're currently a pale, nerd-like teenage boy or man, who spends large amounts of time online, this is not a permanent situation. If you use your freedom to change what you do, then your identity will change along with your actions. In the same way, if you're currently highly addicted to pornography and feel totally unable to stop, then remember that rewiring your brain out of your addiction is entirely possible. As you spend more and more time away from porn, your brain will rewire itself not to need or want porn.

Not only that, but you can use the media at your fingertips to reprogram your mind in the direction you want. The media you consume becomes part of you. You decide which media you consume, therefore you choose how this media influences your subconscious. If you decide that, instead of watching junk media, you'll watch inspirational self-help content, the "vibe" of this content will leak into your subconsious mind overtime and eventually impact how you behave in the real world. *Taking control over your media use is taking control over your destiny.* They are one and the same thing. While you may feel that media is separate from your life, it's not. Media is just as much a part of your life as your choice of career, the friends you surround yourself with and the hobbies you engage in. *To your subconscious mind, there is no distinction between your screens and reality.* And why would there be? Screens are a part of reality. The thinking patterns you develop through screens are no different to the thinking patterns you develop through real world experiences. If you decide to use screens how *you* want to use them, you may just find that this is the ultimate game changer for your entire life.

If you manage to avoid the traps of our media-filled landscape, if you manage to understand the pitfalls of this new world, you may find that it can be a world filled with opportunity and hope. If you craft yourself a path through our technological landscape that avoids addictive media and embraces the opportunities it provides, then perhaps you can live a life more filled with meaning and fulfilment than our ancestors ever did. Are you going adapt to the new world? Or be completely overwhelmed by it? Are you going to drift through life, one Facebook notification at a time? Are you going to look back on your life and regret how technology stole your time, distracted you from what was important and manipulated you into leading a half-lived life? Or is your life going to be a story of someone who embraced the opportunities that the new world provides, and lived a life our ancestors could never have dreamed of? The new world will bring with it both winners and losers, and your relationship with technology will decide which of these you become. It's a new world. Best of luck.

REFERENCES

Leonard,G., (1991), *Mastery: The Keys To Long Term Success And Fulfilment.* London, England Penguin Group

Allen, J., (1903), *As A Man Thinketh*

Barret,D., (2010), *Supernormal Simuli – How Primal Urges Overran Their Evolutionary Purpose.* New York, USA W.W. Norton & Company

Dodson, F., (2010), *Levels Of Energy.* CreateSpace Independent Publishing Platform

Dunbar, R., (2010), *How Many Friends Does One Person Need? - Dunbar's Number And Other Evolutionary Quirks.* Cambridge, Massachusetts

Peterson, J., (2018), *12 Rules For Life – An Antidote To Chaos.* UK, Penguin Randomhouse

Dill-Shackleford, K., (2016), *How Fantasy Becomes Reality – Information And Entertainment Media In Everyday Life.* USA Oxford University Press

Newport, C., (2016), *Deep Work – Rules For Focused Success In A Distracted World.* USA Grand Central Publishing

Mcluhan, M., (1967), *The Medium Is The Massage.* Gingko Press

Sutherland, M., (1993), *Advertising And The Mind Of The Consumer.* Australia

Carr, N., (2010), *The Shallows, What The Internet Is Doing To Our Brains.* New York W.W. Norton & Company

Pinker, S., (2018), *Enlightenment Now – The Case For Reason, Science, Humanism and Progress.* New York Penguin Random House

Nodder, C., (2013), *Evil By Design – Interaction Design To Lead Us Into Temptation.* Wiley

Kane, L and Wilder K., (2009), *The Little Black Book Of Violence – What Every Young Man Needs To Know About Fighting.* YMAA Publication Centre

Murphy, J., (2007), *The Power Of Your Subconscious Mind.* USA Wilder Publications

Pariser, E., (2011), *The Filter Bubble – What The Internet Is Hiding From You.* New York The Penguin Press

Printed in Great Britain
by Amazon

22270343R00238